Victorian America

Victorian America

A Family Record from the Heartland

MARGARET BAKER GRAHAM

TRUMAN STATE UNIVERSITY PRESS

Published by Truman State University Press, Kirksville, Missouri 63501
tsup.truman.edu

Library of Congress Cataloging-in-Publication Data

Graham, Margaret Baker, 1951–
    Victorian America : a family record from the heartland / Margaret Baker Graham.
        p. cm.
    ISBN 1-931112-21-5 (pbk. : alk. paper)
    1. Machette family. 2. Machette family—Archives. 3. Fulton (Mo.)—Biography. 4. Fulton
(Mo.)—Social life and customs—19th century. 5. Fulton (Mo.)—Social life and customs—19th
century—Sources. 6. United States—Social life and customs—1865–1918—Sources. 7. Middle
class—United States—Social life and customs—19th century—Sources. 8. Whites—United
States—Social life and customs—19th century—Sources. I. Title.
    F474.F85 G73 2003
    977.8'335—dc21

                                                                                    2002014104

Cover design: Teresa Wheeler

Scripture quotations are taken from the King James Version, unless otherwise noted.

Printed by: Thomson-Shore, Dexter, Michigan

Type is set in Centaur and Vivante

This book is dedicated to
Mary Virginia Baker
and Sam, Scott, and Matt.

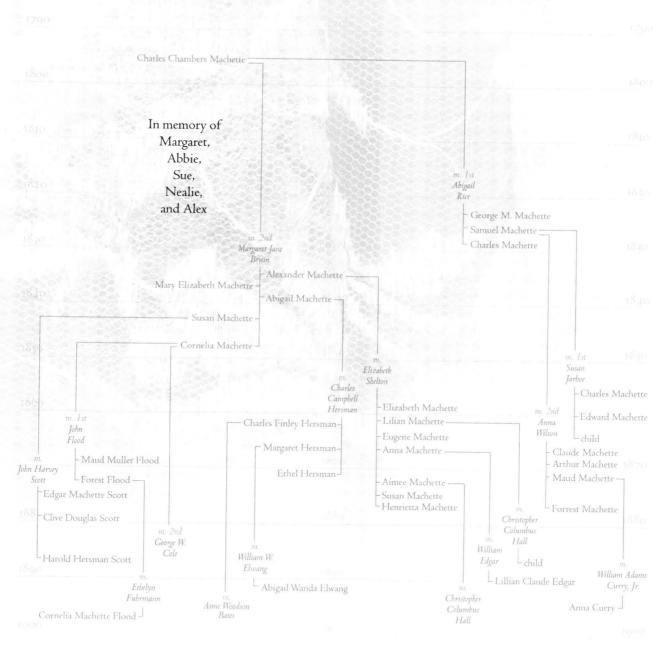

In memory of
Margaret,
Abbie,
Sue,
Nealie,
and Alex

Charles Chambers Machette

m. 1st
Abigail
Rice

George M. Machette
Samuel Machette
Charles Machette

m. 2nd
Margaret Jane
Bruin

Alexander Machette
Mary Elizabeth Machette
Abigail Machette
Susan Machette
Cornelia Machette

m.
Elizabeth
Shelton

m. 1st
Susan
Jarboe

Charles Machette

m. 2nd
Anna
Wilson

Edward Machette

child

Claude Machette
Arthur Machette
Maud Machette

m.
Charles
Campbell
Hersman

Elizabeth Machette
Lilian Machette
Eugene Machette
Anna Machette

Charles Finley Hersman
Margaret Hersman
Ethel Hersman

Aimee Machette
Susan Machette
Henrietta Machette

Forrest Machette

m. 1st
John
Flood

m.
John Harvey
Scott

Maud Muller Flood
Forest Flood

Edgar Machette Scott
Clive Douglas Scott

Harold Hersman Scott

m. 2nd
George W.
Cole

m.
William W.
Elwang

Abigail Wanda Elwang

m.
Christopher
Columbus
Hall

m.
William
Edgar

child

Lillian Claude Edgar

m.
Christopher
Columbus
Hall

m.
William Adams
Curry, Jr.

Anna Curry

m.
Ethelyn
Fuhrmann

Cornelia Machette Flood

m.
Anne Woodson
Bates

1790
1800
1810
1820
1830
1840
1850
1860
1870
1880
1890
1900

Contents

Acknowledgments

I am indebted to many people for helping me to put together this collection. Primary thanks go to my mother, Mary Virginia Baker; my aunts, Sue Gould and Shirley Payne; my uncle, Harold Scott, Jr.; and my cousins, Sue Peek and Lallie Scott; for sharing freely their portion of the letters and documents. A special debt also goes to Ruth Buckland and Janet Weir Scott. Ruth Buckland, niece of Mary Buckland and Will Dobyns, was raised by the Dobyns after her parents' death. Although she was in her nineties when I located her, and physically frail, she was able to provide me with a wealth of information about her family, information I doubt I could have gotten any other way. Janet Weir Scott, a Machette descendant, has compiled an extensive geneal-ogy of the Machettes, making my research on the family much easier to complete. The staffs at the Callaway County Recorder's office and at the Parks Library at Iowa State University were particularly helpful. I also thank the administrators at Iowa State Uni-versity for granting me a sabbatical to work on this book. I am grateful to Paula Pres-ley, Nancy Rediger, and Judy Sharp of Truman State University Press for their creative work on this book.

References to books and journals are included in the bibliography, but below are the names of people from across the country who have helped me complete this project.

Ovid H. Bell, Gene Cannon, Doris Davis, Donald Gordon, Mary Belle Grant, John Cannon Harris, Mary Lois Harris, H. Edgar Hill, Susan Grant Krumm, E. Jeffrey Richards, Ann Stinson.

Descendants of people mentioned in the letters

Paul G. Anderson, Washington University School of Medicine Archives, Becker
   Medical Library, Archives and Rare Books Division
Carolyn Branch, Fulton Public Library
William B. Bynum, Presbyterian Historical Society, Montreat, North Carolina
William S. Coker, author of works on Peter Bryan Bruin
Cecil Culverhouse, Fulton Presbyterian Church
Lt. Col. Jim Delaney, Kemper Military School
Mary Ellen Embree, Madison, Missouri
Michelle Evans, Clarksville-Montgomery County Public Library, Tennessee
Debbie Flood, genealogist, Utah
Howard Gallimore, Southern Baptist Historical Commission
Sharon Hasekamp, Powell Memorial Library, Troy, Missouri
Cathy Haymart, City Clerk's office, Fulton, Missouri
Ara Kaye, State Historical Society of Missouri, Columbia
Elizabeth Gates Kesler, Rhodes College
Patrick Kirby, Westminster College
Kathleen Kurosman, Vassar College

Archivists, educators, government officials, historians, and librarians

Nancy Maddox, Fulton Public Library
Mark McWeeney, Lindenwood College
Marjorie Miller, Montgomery County Historical Society
Lorna Mitchell, Westminster College
Nancy O'Neill, Santa Monica Public Library, California
William E. Parrish, historian, Mississippi
Carolyn Reese, Albuquerque/Bernalillo County Public Library System
Cecy Rice, Moberly, Missouri
Nancy Riggs, Pleasant Hill, Missouri
Lucile Wiley Ring, author of *Breaking the Barrier: The St. Louis Legacy of Women in Law*
Kenneth Ross, Presbyterian Historical Society, Philadelphia, Pennsylvania
Lucille Shelton, St. Charles County Historical Society
John Simon, Southern Illinois University
Ida Sorci, American Osteopathic Association
C. Vaughn Stanley, Washington and Lee University
Susan Sullivan, Presbyterian Historical Society, Philadelphia, Pennsylvania
Anke Voss-Hubbard, Lafayette College
Carol Wilkins, St. Charles County Historical Society
Charles Yrigoyen, General Commission on Archives and History, The United Methodist Church

Staff at Iowa State University   Rebekah Bovenmyer, Lucinda Carter, Billie Green, Autumn Hare, Doug Hurt, Christie Pope, Amanda Sanders, Deanna Stumbo.

Friends and family   Jack Boyd, Will Boyd, Jim Gilchrist, Joni Gilchrist, Sue Gray, Willie Jones, Barbara Baker Lacewell, Carol Leininger, Neville Graham Rapp, Elizabeth Saltzman, Kate Saltzman, Richard Saltzman, Pauline Scott.

Introduction

1860–1902

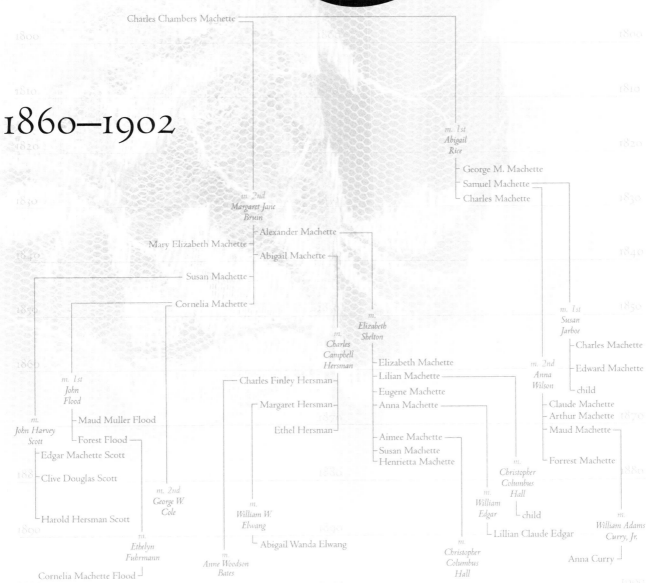

Charles Chambers Machette

m. 1st
Abigail
Rice

— George M. Machette
— Samuel Machette
— Charles Machette

m. 2nd
Margaret Jane
Bruin

— Alexander Machette

Mary Elizabeth Machette

— Abigail Machette

— Susan Machette

— Cornelia Machette

m.
Elizabeth
Shelton

m.
Charles
Campbell
Hersman

m. 1st
Susan
Jarboe

— Charles Machette

m. 2nd
Anna
Wilson

— Edward Machette

— child

— Claude Machette
— Arthur Machette
— Maud Machette

— Elizabeth Machette
— Lilian Machette
— Eugene Machette
— Anna Machette

Charles Finley Hersman

Margaret Hersman

Ethel Hersman

— Aimee Machette
— Susan Machette
— Henrietta Machette

m.
Christopher
Columbus
Hall

— Forrest Machette

m. 1st
John
Flood

m.
William
Edgar

— child

m.
William Adams
Curry, Jr.

— Maud Muller Flood

m.
John Harvey
Scott

— Forest Flood

— Lillian Claude Edgar

Anna Curry

— Edgar Machette Scott

— Clive Douglas Scott

m. 2nd
George W.
Cole

m.
William W.
Elwang

m.
Christopher
Columbus
Hall

— Harold Hersman Scott

m.
Ethelyn
Fuhrmann

— Abigail Wanda Elwang

m.
Anne Woodson
Bates

Cornelia Machette Flood

At one level, the Victorian age—with its hoopskirts and bustles, its washtubs and fire-heated flatirons, its calling cards and mourning cards—seems utterly foreign to the twenty-first century. [1] Yet at another level, something about this time period remains compelling. The portrait of a family sitting together after dinner in the parlor or study—playing the piano, acting out a play, reading aloud to one another— represents a sentimental vision of home life many today cherish but seem unable to attain. To some extent, we cannot escape the middle-class consciousness of Victorian America.

This collection, which includes mostly letters but also journal entries, narratives, Bible records, receipts, newspaper clippings, recipes, and photographs, documents the lives of one family in the heartland of Victorian America. By including the correspondence and documents of multiple members of the Machette family, as well as letters of their friends and acquaintances, the collection offers not only a portrait of one family but also a domestic history of white, middle-class, middle America in a time that is both near and far from the middle-class culture of today.

In 1834, when she was scarcely seventeen, Margaret Bruin, who would become matriarch of the family, married Charles Machette (pronounced mə–shet'), a widower with two sons. Charles, a merchant originally from New Jersey, had arrived at St. Charles, located on the Missouri River, between the time that Lewis and Clark set off from there in 1804 to explore the Louisiana Purchase and St. Charles was made the first capital of Missouri in 1820. [2] As part of the Missouri Compromise, Missouri entered the union as a slave state, and Charles Machette owned slaves in St. Charles. [3] Margaret

---

1. Queen Victoria reigned in England from 1837 to 1901, but historians may mark the Victorian age in the United States differently, sometimes earlier as well as later than her reign. Fixing a firm date for Victorian sensibility in America is impossible, but central events in defining Victorianism include the opening of the United States railroads in the 1820s and 1830s, the Transcendentalist movement of the 1830s and 1840s, and the publication in 1851 of the novel emblematic of Victorian sentimentalism, *Uncle Tom's Cabin.* The death knell of the Victorian age seems to have occurred by the 1910s when the automobile, the electric home, the *Titanic,* and the First World War represented what is called the modern age. The Ford Model T was introduced in 1908, transforming society just as dramatically as trains had decades earlier. Electricity in the home in turn transformed both domestic work and entertainment. Thomas Schlereth, *Victorian America: Transformations in Everyday Life, 1876–1915* (New York: Harper-Perennial, 1991), 164, writes, "By 1915, the electric home symbolized the middle-class home." The sinking of the "unsinkable" *Titanic* in 1912 gave the lie to the notion that technology could defeat nature. The First World War, despite Allied optimism at its beginning in 1914, would not be "the war to end all wars."

2. In 1821 Missouri became a state, and the capital was moved to Jefferson City.

3. Native Americans and blacks were slaves in the early years of the state. Indian slavery was outlawed

and Charles Machette had five children—Alexander, Mary Elizabeth, Abigail, Susan, and Cornelia. Charles died in 1851. Two years later, according to a receipt, Margaret Machette sold "Real Estate and Slaves" belonging to her husband's estate. Her oldest daughter, Mary Elizabeth, died of diphtheria in 1854, and around that time the Machettes left St. Charles, eventually settling in Fulton (Callaway County), Missouri, less than twenty-four hours away by stage.[4] Although Margaret Machette and her children had assets from her husband's estate, she brought additional income into the family by running a boarding house for students attending Westminster College. This volume begins in 1860, a few years after Margaret Machette settled in Fulton to run the boarding house; it ends in 1902, the year she died.

Attesting to the importance that both religion and education played in the lives of the people in this collection, one of the male correspondents was a Presbyterian minister and professor of Greek, another was a Baptist minister, and a third was a professor of mathematics. Margaret Machette's daughter Sue was a teacher before her marriage, and her only son, Alexander, ran a school for a short while. Family members were either devout Presbyterians or Baptists, and their letters are full of the details of their religion: reading the Bible, going to church regularly, attending revivals, and disagreeing about doctrine. The Machettes represent a larger Christian movement as membership in United States churches rapidly increased from more than 7 percent of the population in 1800, to almost 25 percent in 1860, and to more than 40 percent by 1910.[5] During the mid-nineteenth century, Protestant consciousness was, in effect, domesticated as strict Calvinism gave way to a gentler, more hopeful notion of religion.[6] The letter-writers in this collection, consequently, wrote fervently and confidently of the joyous reunion they would have with loved ones after death.

Much of the middle-class impulse to build educational institutions came out of the Protestant belief that a good education was required to understand the Bible. Private education in Missouri grew rapidly in the nineteenth century, although many private colleges did not last long. By 1870, the number of private colleges in Missouri stood at thirty-seven.[7] Colleges in Fulton, where Margaret Machette had settled, included Westminster College and the Fulton Female Seminary, both founded by the Presbyterian church in the 1850s. The female seminary closed during the Civil War, and in 1873 the Presbyterian church established the Fulton Synodical Female College to take its place. A third college, the Female Orphan School, was founded in 1890 by the Disciples of Christ church; it would later become William Woods College.

Margaret Machette's son and three sons-in-law attended Westminster College, and at least one of her daughters attended Fulton Female Seminary. Margaret Machette also sent her daughters away to school, even when she was facing economic difficulties at home, and she hired men who were teaching at Westminster to give her youngest

---

in 1834 and, as Perry McCandless, *A History of Missouri*, vol. 2: *1820 to 1860* (Columbia: University of Missouri Press, 1972), 52, writes, by the mid-1830s "the native peoples would be pushed from the state."

4. The Westminster College catalog for 1853–54 states that the stage between Fulton and St. Louis took "about twenty-four hours." St. Charles is just west of St. Louis, on the opposite side of the Missouri River.

5. Harvey Green, *The Light of the Home: An Intimate View of the Lives of Women in Victorian America* (New York: Pantheon, 1983), 173.

6. James J. Farrell, *Inventing the American Way of Death, 1830–1920* (Philadelphia: Temple University Press, 1980), 42.

7. *The Statistics of the Population of the United States . . . from the Original Returns of the Ninth Census (June 1, 1870)* (Washington, D.C.: Government Printing Office, 1872), table 13.

daughter lessons in algebra, grammar, astronomy, and Latin. Margaret Machette's son, Alexander, also supported the notion of educating daughters. When he was too poor to send one of his daughters away to school, he used a school catalog to fashion a curriculum for her at home.

Public schools took hold more slowly in Missouri than Christian institutions, and from the letters it appears that none of Margaret Machette's grandchildren, although well educated, attended public schools. The University of Missouri at Columbia was established by the 1839 Geyer Act, and it graduated its first students in 1843. The first public high school in Missouri was established in 1852–1853 in St. Louis, but it was not until after the Civil War that the local public school system began in earnest.[8]

In addition to religion and education, the letter writers exhibit a strong interest in their community and the home life of their neighbors and friends. On a certain level, a commitment to community was an extension of a commitment to religion and family. That is, often the friends and neighbors they wrote about were members of their church or an extended family that included distant cousins and relatives of relatives.

The letters themselves—written to wives and husbands, children and grandchildren, parents and grandparents, cousins and in-laws—attest to these people's devotion to family. Familial relationships were cherished partly because of the precariousness of life. The letter writers wrote about women who died in childbirth; children who died from diphtheria, whooping cough, measles, and scarlet fever; and people who died from cholera and tuberculosis. When she died, Margaret Machette had outlived two of her five children and eight of her fifteen grandchildren. However, more was involved in the Victorian idealization of the home than simply the threat of death at a young age. Colleen McDannell in her book on Christian domesticity argues that in sentimentalizing home life, middle-class Americans in the nineteenth century were able to create a "domestic religion," which permitted "the more abstract traditional symbols [of denominational religion] to assume a real presence in everyday life." Social historian Margaret Marsh, in turn, links domestic sentimentality to the effects of capitalism: "The model woman was a wife and devoted mother whose principal responsibility was to create a domestic environment that offered an alternative to the conflict and competition of the marketplace economy. In her home, a spiritual and emotional oasis, she succored her husband and nurtured her children."[9]

Literature of the day not only sentimentalized the role of mother, it also glorified domesticity in general. For example, Catharine Beecher and Harriet Beecher Stowe's guide for homemaking, *The American Woman's Home*, attempted to recast cooking and cleaning, as well as child rearing, as "the most sacred" of earthly duties.[10] From the Machette materials, it appears that Margaret Machette's daughters, Abigail and Cornelia, sentimentalized the raising of children, and Sue joined her sisters in sentimentalizing children who had died; however, their descriptions of domestic chores in the Machette collection are decidedly unsentimental. The women wrote of putting butter in pickle, preserving apples, making sausage, weaving fabric, and making carpets, as well as sewing dresses, underdrawers, and linen pants. Sometimes they wrote with satisfaction

8. McCandless, *History of Missouri*, 2:194. Lawrence O. Christensen and Gary R. Kremer, *A History of Missouri*, vol. 4: *1875 to 1919* (Columbia: University of Missouri Press, 1997), 53.

9. Colleen McDannell, *The Christian Home in Victorian America, 1840–1900* (Bloomington: Indiana University Press, 1986), 151. Margaret Marsh, *Suburban Lives* (New Brunswick, N.J.: Rutgers University Press, 1990), 8.

10. Catharine E. Beecher and Harriet Beecher Stowe, *The American Woman's Home, or Principles of Domesti[c] Science* (New York: J.B. Ford, 1869), 221.

about a garment or a meal they had made, but expressing satisfaction was not the same as romanticizing domestic work. The women also expressed their exasperation over walls that still did not look right after whitewashing, of stoves that did not function, and of such coughing or shaking that they could not do their chores properly. Most often they wrote matter-of-factly of their work around the home as something that simply needed to be done and should be done well.

Perhaps the Machette women did not sentimentalize the domestic chores because they embraced another Victorian value, that of duty or the expectation that lives should be useful. This concept of secular duty came out of the belief system of the Presbyterian church and similar denominations. In the January 28, 1875, issue of the *New York Observer*, which Sue's family subscribed to, an article on the virtue of diligence stated, "In the Christian life, diligence consists in firmly and constantly doing all known duty, and in suffering all God's known will. It is full of vigor and energy; it's jealous of all intrusions upon its attention." A. Dakin, in his book on Calvinism, states that in connecting work with religious value, "we have the exalting of daily work...."[11] Exalting, however, meant patience, steadfastness, and humility—not sentimentality.

The women and men in these letters valued work and expected it to be a constant part of their lives. On a piece of brown wrapping paper, Sue Machette Scott wrote:

> It is a pet fancy of mine to rake into the old family stories, collecting reminiscences from the few relatives who remain—perhaps getting hold of a few letters now and then and then again a picture, an old shadowy daguerreotype. Shall not I select a fragment here and there from these good and useful lives and prevent their altogether into oblivion?

Whether these words were hers or her rendering of someone else's is unclear; nonetheless, the sentiment captures the value of sifting through the ephemera of generations past. More important, they identify a key concept in middle-class Victorian society: to live "good and useful lives." When Margaret Machette was a landlady, her letters were full of her own labor and economy in running a business and home. When she no longer operated a rooming house, but lived with one of her daughters, she wrote, "I believe I spend more idle time now than I ever did in my life. I feel bad to think of it." The desire to become wealthy through work was never written about in these letters, and in fact, in one letter by Finley Hersman, Margaret Machette's grandson, he explicitly rejected the notion of working for wealth. Sue's husband, Harvey, never retired, and in 1934 earned a spot in *Ripley's Believe It or Not* for teaching at Westminster College for sixty-five years.[12]

At the same time that the middle class in Victorian America was committed to values still revered today, there was also a complacency, even arrogance, in the belief that they could control or create order in everything, from turning the American wilderness into farms, towns, and cities, to standardizing time, to using science to prolong life and romantic sensibility to domesticate death.[13] There was also, of course, the stunning, almost casual, ability of many whites to accept the institution of slavery prior to the Civil War and to replace it after the war with enforced segregation.

---

11. A. Dakin, *Calvinism* (Port Washington, N.Y.: Kennikat, 1972), 222.

12. *St. Louis Post-Dispatch* (July 18, 1934).

13. "Domesticating" death is a term used by Farrell, *Inventing the American Way of Death*, 34, as well as Ann Douglas, *The Feminization of American Culture* (New York: Alfred A. Knopf, 1977), 200.

Theodrick Boulware, Daniel D. Ford, B.P. Evans, Joseph Flood, Jeptha Harrison, Frederick Kemper, George Law, William W. Robertson, Daniel Tucker, William W. Tuttle, William Van Doren, Samuel Watson, Henry Wright, and Ann Young, people who were mentioned in the letters and who were ministers, professors, merchants, lawyers, county officials, and farmers, are listed on the 1860 census as slave owners. Only three other counties in Missouri had more slaves than Callaway County.[14]

The Machettes owned slaves when they lived in St. Charles, but apparently not when they lived in Fulton; nonetheless, they continued to participate in the institution of slavery. A receipt from Rufus Abbot, the father of friends of the Machette daughters, indicates that Margaret Machette hired a "negro boy" to work three days. She also hired Andrew, likely one of the slaves of Henry Wright. At the same time that Margaret Machette participated in the institution of slavery, the letters also indicate her willingness to circumvent the law in order to help a black man. When Andrew wanted to avoid conscription in the Union army, Margaret made him calico shirts to take with him on his escape westward.[15] It is difficult to know if Andrew was a slave when he left Missouri, but certainly Margaret Machette was breaking the law by aiding his escape from the army. Thus, both her complicity in slavery and her action to help Andrew reveal the unresolved contradictions that existed for many whites in their treatment of blacks.

Segregation, already established by custom, was inscribed by law in the 1875 Missouri Constitution, the same constitution that mandated local public school systems. Article XI, section 3, of the 1875 Constitution stated, "Separate free public schools shall be established for the education of children of African descent." In 1879, Lincoln Institute, which had been founded after the Civil War by members of the 62nd U.S. Colored Infantry for freed slaves, became part of the state university system and was set aside for the high education of blacks. Ten years later in 1889, writes David Thelen in his history of Missouri, "the legislature enacted custom by formally prohibiting blacks from attending white public schools. The state segregated colleges and institutions for the blind, deaf, consumptive, and feeble-minded."[16] Blacks, who in an 1847 amendment to the Missouri Constitution could not be taught to read or write, could now be educated at public expense but only in separate—and typically unequal—institutions.[17]

At the same time that religion, education, community, family, and work were valorized, those values also were being rewritten and redefined. While duty or work was valued for its own sake, John D. Rockefeller, Andrew Carnegie, J.P. Morgan, and other practitioners of social Darwinism were amassing great wealth. The Reverend Theodore Cuyler, an influential Presbyterian minister of the nineteenth century and quoted in one letter in the collection, wrote in his autobiography: "They [ministers at the turn of the century] are surrounded with an atmosphere of intense materialism.

---

14. *Population Schedules of the Eighth Census of the United States, 1860. Missouri Slave Schedules* (Washington, D.C.: National Archives, 1967).

15. General Orders No. 135, issued in November 1863, six months before Andrew left Missouri, required "All able bodied colored men, whether free or slaves" in Missouri to join the federal army. *The War of the Rebellion: A Compilation of the Official Records of the Union and Confederate Armies*, series 3 (Washington, D.C.: Government Printing Office, 1900), 3:1034.

16. David Thelen, *Paths of Resistance: Tradition and Dignity in Industrializing Missouri* (New York: Oxford University Press, 1986), 139.

17. William E. Parrish, *A History of Missouri*, vol. 3: *1860 to 1875* (Columbia: University of Missouri Press, 1973), 145.

The ambition for the 'seen things' increasingly blinds men to the 'things that are unseen and eternal.' Wealth and worldliness unspiritualize thousands of professed Christians."[18]

Another factor in change was the railroad, which allowed for the rapid development of a society of small towns and farms and fostered the growth of capitalism and urbanization. Lawrence Christensen and Gary Kremer comment on the effect the railroad had to Missourians: "No single force changed the lives of Missourians more during the last half of the nineteenth century than did the railroads. The railroads changed people's notions of space. The isolation that Missourians had felt in their overwhelmingly rural state began to lessen in the generation after the Civil War." "The railroads," they continue, "and the entrance into a national market that they encouraged and facilitated, dramatically changed the Missouri economy."[19] Margaret Marsh describes the effect of urbanization in the United States: "More ominous for those who believe that agrarianism and democracy were synonyms, urban centers had proliferated.... As for the lowly 10,000 figure that had marked the largest cities in 1820, more than a hundred cities had surpassed it by 1860, and city life was no longer confined to the eastern seaboard."[20] By 1900, thirty-eight cities in the country had populations of 100,000 or more, numbered among them St. Louis, Kansas City, and St. Joseph.[21]

Even the lives of those who, like Margaret Machette and her daughter Sue, remained in small towns were being transformed by technology. A sense of localism and place was eroded by improved transportation, which made people increasingly mobile. Margaret Machette herself took advantage of the railroad, frequently leaving Fulton to visit relatives in other parts of Missouri, as well as Tennessee and Colorado. Furthermore, as Ann Douglas comments, increased technology and improved transportation were responsible for "the shifting status of the matron of the house from producer to consumer."[22] Although Sue continued to grow fruit and vegetables for her family, this movement from producer to consumer can be seen in her 1899 journal in which she mentioned selling her milk cow.

The American culture, despite the rise of church membership, was also becoming increasingly secular. In fact, both William McLoughlin and George Marsden in their books on religion in America have argued that the turning away from strict Calvinism was a response to technological advances and economic growth. McLoughlin writes that "science was giving man new control over his environment, new control over disease and pain, a new sense that he was master of his own fate because he could master Nature instead of being enslaved to it. Men became less willing to accept the mysteries of the Bible and less submissive to the unfathomable will of God, because they found less need to be submissive to the world in which they lived."[23] Marsden observes that "one of the first dictates of Common Sense philosophy was that individuals were moral agents capable of free choice. These premises—which were essential to the economic, political, and religious individualism so widespread in America—were at odds

18. Theodore L. Cuyler, *Recollections of a Long Life* (New York: Baker & Taylor, 1902), 80.

19. Christensen and Kremer, *History of Missouri*, 4:28–29, 51.

20. Marsh, *Suburban Lives*, 1.

21. U.S. Bureau of the Census, *Twelfth Census of the United States Taken in the Year 1900. Population, Part 1* (Washington, D.C., 1901), table XXII.

22. Douglas, *Feminization of American Culture*, 49.

23. William G. McLoughlin, *The Meaning of Henry Ward Beecher: An Essay on the Shifting Values of Mid-Victorian America, 1840–1870* (New York: Alfred A. Knopf, 1970), 35.

with traditional views of determinism and depravity."[24] With an emphasis on the beneficence of God and an accompanying de-emphasis on the innate depravity of humanity, religious practice became less central to the lives of many middle-class Americans at the same time that church membership increased.

To a certain extent, the lessening role of organized religion cannot be seen in the Machette collection, even in the correspondence written in the first decade of the 1900s and later. There were, after all, two ministers in the family. The family wrote of going to church regularly and serving in various church roles. Nonetheless, there are hints that a part of the Machette family was affected by the secularization of society. Occasionally, they would write that they did not go to church because they did not want their clothes to be rained on or they just did not feel like attending. Perhaps more significantly, they participated in secular entertainment that became part of society and competed with both the Victorian notion of duty and earlier notions of religion. One of Margaret Machette's grandsons, Forest Flood, became a stage actor in the last decades of the nineteenth century. Although some of the family apparently did not approve of his occupation, his mother was extremely proud of his profession. In the letters written after 1902, members of the family wrote enthusiastically of the Chautauqua movement, which brought lectures, skits, and recitals to towns across the country. The collection that ends at 1902 includes comments on religious periodicals, such as the *New York Observer* and the *St. Louis Presbyterian*; after 1902, the family wrote about *Scribner's*, *Harper's*, and *Time*.[25]

Novels, which rose in popularity in the nineteenth century, can also be seen as emblematic of the secularization of society. The Reverend Theodore Cuyler, for example, wrote about the influence of novels at the turn of the century: "The increasing rage for novel reading betokens both a famine in the intellect, and a serious peril to the mental and spiritual life."[26] At least some of the Machettes were part of the society that greatly enjoyed reading fiction. In 1864, one of Margaret Machette's daughters, Cornelia, wrote about how much she was looking forward to reading *Thaddeus of Warsaw*, a popular novel of the day, and how disappointed she was when her brother-in-law began reading aloud *Great Truths of the Bible* instead. As Cornelia's sister Sue became more a consumer and less a producer of domestic goods, she had more time to read widely, and it is evident from her letters written after 1902 that she derived far more pleasure from the books of Thomas Hardy, Ivan Turgenev, Leo Tolstoy, and Jane Austen than from domestic chores.[27]

The letters, finally, also reveal some of the constraints white women endured in the late nineteenth century. In the first chapter, for example, there is the small story of Louise Atwood, a friend of the Machettes, who vainly hoped to marry her sister's widower. Her plight speaks to the private tragedies unmarried women suffered in their middle-class society. The expectation that women belong in the domestic sphere also explains the decision Margaret Machette made when she found herself a widow. She needed a livelihood, but in her society a married woman or widow who had to work

24. George M. Marsden, *Fundamentalism and American Culture: The Shaping of Twentieth-Century Evangelicalism, 1870–1925* (New York: Oxford University Press, 1980), 16.

25. Although a religious paper, the *New York Observer* had a regular column in 1876, which recommended selections from *Harper's*, *Scribner's*, and other popular magazines. Margaret Machette subscribed to *Harper's* but did not refer to it in the extant letters.

26. Cuyler, *Recollections of a Long Life*, 282.

27. As has often been pointed out, white women of the middle and upper classes also gained time by hiring other women, frequently recent immigrants or blacks, to do domestic chores.

could best retain her middle-class status by working within her home.[28] Becoming a landlady was an obvious choice. Unfortunately, being a landlady to college students was a precarious occupation during the Civil War when economic hardships brought many Missourians to bankruptcy and when the armies depleted most of the student population of Westminster College.

Although Margaret Machette's life represents a time when middle-class women were associated with the home, it would be a mistake to perceive of the public and domestic spaces of life as wholly separate from one another. The Civil War intruded in her life, raising her taxes and widowing one of her many visitors, her niece and namesake, Margaret Bruin Rice. Church and school, two public arenas, were very much a part of Margaret Machette's life as she entertained and socialized with religious leaders and college officials.

A gentle erosion of domesticity can be seen in the family letters written after Margaret Machette's death in 1902. As noted, her daughter Sue read widely. Sue also took an avid interest in political and social events beyond Fulton, and she voted in 1920, the first time women in the United States could vote in a national election. Anne Bates Hersman, who married one of Margaret Machette's grandsons in 1894, became an attorney specializing in criminology after her husband's death. But this collection, ending as it does in 1902 with the death of Margaret Machette, does not tell that story. This volume is, rather, the story of a way of life when white, middle-class women stayed at home.

The Collection

The letters in the volume are part of a larger collection of more than three thousand letters, which extend from 1823 to the death of Susan Machette Scott in 1937. The collection was begun by Margaret Machette, who saved letters and documents that she and her husband had received. A few letters written to the family of her daughter, Cornelia Machette Flood, survived when Cornelia's husband contracted tuberculosis. In the Floods' haste to leave Fulton for better climate in the West, they left behind many of their possessions. Cornelia's mother shipped them their belongings, evidently retaining the correspondence they left behind. When Margaret Machette died in the home of her daughter, Sue inherited her mother's and Cornelia's letters and added them to her own extensive collection of letters that she had saved over the years. Sue's husband, Harvey Scott, also saved letters from his family. Both Sue and Harvey kept journals and scrapbooks as well. When Sue, a widow, died in the home of her son, Clive then inherited the letters and other ephemera and added them to his own extensive collection. When Clive died in 1965, his nieces and nephews inherited his property. Packing up the estate, they found the documents and saved most of them. The largest part of them went to Mary Virginia Baker, because she lived in Fulton and it seemed the convenient thing to do. The rest went to her brothers and sisters. Some letters have been lost over the years; still, a remarkably complete collection exists. I offered to edit the letters because of my interest in nineteenth-century American literature, narrative practice, and women's studies. All the descendants have graciously lent their portion of the collection for this volume.

Most of the letters were written to or by Susan Machette Scott. Although she once mentioned destroying some old letters when she was cleaning, she kept letters that the writers asked her to burn. Sue never mentioned the possibility that her family's letters

---

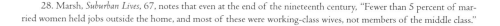

28. Marsh, *Suburban Lives*, 67, notes that even at the end of the nineteenth century, "Fewer than 5 percent of married women held jobs outside the home, and most of these were working-class wives, not members of the middle class."

might someday be published, but at some level she must have been aware of their potential. In her letters written after 1902, she frequently mentioned collections of letters that she enjoyed reading—those of Jane Austen, William Cromwell, Mary W. Montagu, Robert Louis Stevenson, and William Thackeray. She expected her sons to write her every week, and she encouraged her son Clive to use a diary form of letter writing.

In addition to the letters, the family saved photographs, scrapbooks, journals, receipts, recipes, newspaper clippings, jottings on pieces of scrap paper, and Bible passages. Although this domestic history is told primarily through the letters, some of this ephemera is included because of the way it changes and adds to the narrative of these people's lives revealed in the correspondence. For example, clippings that Susan Machette Scott saved show that she was attracted to sentimental poetry and evidently used it to find comfort after a death of a loved one.

A primary issue in editing this volume was to make the texts easily readable. Margaret Machette, while she had a graceful penmanship, seldom used punctuation or capitalization, making her letters difficult to follow.[29] Her daughter Cornelia was a poor speller and did not use much paragraphing; in fact, in the 1860s, she would fill up a page and then turn the sheet of paper on its side and fill up the page again (see caption, p. 32). To improve readability, conventional spelling, punctuation, and paragraphing are used except in letters written by children where all their errors are preserved. During the nineteenth century, the family's last name evolved from "Machet," to "Machett," and finally to "Machette." This volume uses the spelling "Machette" throughout.

Brackets are used to improve meaning or to add words that were accidentally omitted. Ellipses indicate deleted text—typically general statements on the weather, acknowledgments of letters received, closings, and random comments about people or events that did not figure in the major story lines. Many of the letters did not include at the top of the page the place where the letter was written, but that information has been added to help orient the reader. The dates provided for the letters are those supplied by the writers. A few times the writer obviously misdated a letter (e.g., November 31); these have been silently corrected.

This family record is as much about the Machettes' community and church as about their family. Although the constraints of space force me to omit a number of references to friends and acquaintances, I spent six years researching names by visiting and writing archives across the country; talking to descendants of the people in the letters and looking at their family records; examining county, state, and federal records; and tramping through cemeteries searching for names and dates. One thing I discovered was the elusiveness of facts: Was a person born in this year or that year? Was a person's name spelled this way or that way? Where possible, I use the dates and spelling on tombstones or death certificates although I realize that errors could exist on them as well as in newspapers or census figures. More important than dates and spelling is the information I discovered about these people, information that often extends beyond that given in the family record.

Cousins, even first cousins, married each other, and siblings from one family married siblings from another family. For example, Margaret Machette's son Alex married Lizzie Shelton, while Margaret's niece, Jane Dutton, married Lizzie's brother Jake. Sue and Abbie Machette married men who were first cousins to each other. Footnotes are used to delineate relationships and how people in a community were part of each

---

29. Margaret's father, Timothy Bruin, a constable in St. Charles, was literate, but her mother, Margaret Galbraith Bruin, was not. Margaret Machette might have been among the first generation of women in her family to be literate.

other's lives for decades. Footnotes also remind the reader of earlier discussions of people or relate stories about the people not told in the letters themselves. Samuel Laws, president of Westminster College in 1860, later became president of the Gold Exchange in New York City and hired Thomas Edison. Emily Quisenberry, who sent the oldest son of Sue Machette Scott a get-well note in 1882, died with her two sons in a house fire four years later. William Hockaday Wallace, whose oratorical victory is reported in an 1870 letter, became a prosecuting attorney who identified Jesse James's body in 1882. Anne Bates Hersman, the wife of Margaret Machette's grandson, was the granddaughter of Abraham Lincoln's attorney general. Detailed documentation is provided for the introductory matter to each chapter. However, city, state, and federal records, along with cemetery records, obituaries, unpublished documents, and material from general reference books are not listed in the footnotes to the letters unless they provide unusual information about a person or event. Sources are listed at the end of the book.

Because political and larger social issues were often not mentioned by the writers, each chapter begins with an essay that describes contemporary events for that time period based on the headline news of the paper these people read, the *Missouri Republican*, which became the *St. Louis Republic* in 1888. Despite the newspaper's name, it fiercely supported the Democratic Party. This collection also relies heavily on the extant issues of the *Telegraph*, *Gazette*, and *Sun*, all Fulton newspapers. Although the names of the St. Louis and Fulton papers underwent minor changes over the years, for consistency's sake, these are referred to as simply the *Missouri Republican*, *St. Louis Republic*, *Fulton Telegraph*, *Fulton Gazette*, and *Fulton Sun*.

In addition to describing the news of the period, each introductory essay also discusses dominant themes in the letters. The introduction to chapter 1 is a discussion of the Presbyterian church, to which most of the family members belonged, and the Civil War. Chapter 2 offers a rhetorical analysis of the love letters written by Sue Machette and Harvey Scott. Chapter 3 discusses the domestic life of the middle-class home-maker, and the last chapter is on Victorian sentimentalism, especially regarding death. To help readers follow the Machette family throughout the book as members were born and died, each chapter begins with a genealogical chart, which shows who was in the family during that decade of the volume. A complete genealogy is listed in the Descendants chapter.

the *P*resbyterian church and the rebellion

1860–1869

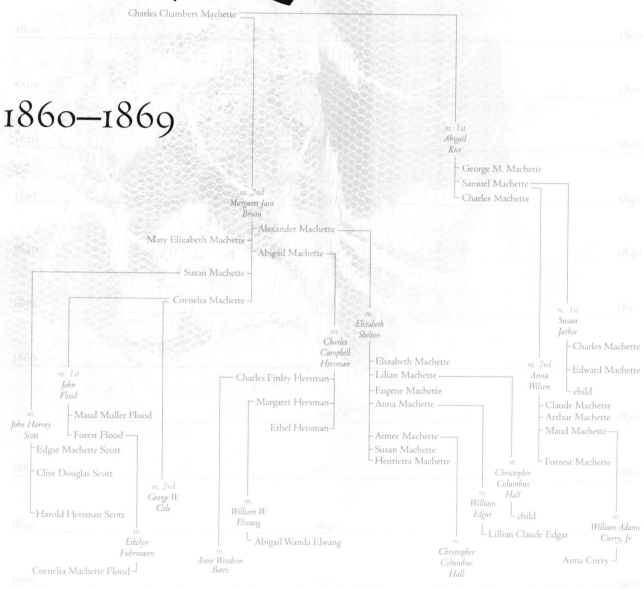

Charles Chambers Machette

m. 1st
Abigail Rice

George M. Machette
Samuel Machette
Charles Machette

m. 2nd
Margaret Jane Bruin

Alexander Machette
Mary Elizabeth Machette
Abigail Machette
Susan Machette
Cornelia Machette

m. 1st
Susan Jarboe

Charles Machette
Edward Machette
child

m. 2nd
Anna Wilson

Claude Machette
Arthur Machette
Maud Machette

m.
Elizabeth Shelton

Elizabeth Machette
Lilian Machette
Eugene Machette
Anna Machette

Aimee Machette
Susan Machette
Henrietta Machette

Forrest Machette

m.
Charles Campbell Hersman

Charles Finley Hersman
Margaret Hersman
Ethel Hersman

m. 1st
John Flood

Maud Muller Flood
Forest Flood

m.
John Harvey Scott

Edgar Machette Scott
Clive Douglas Scott

Harold Hersman Scott

m. 2nd
George W. Cole

m.
Ethelyn Fuhrmann

Cornelia Machette Flood

m.
William W. Elwang

Abigail Wanda Elwang

m.
Anne Woodson Bates

m.
William Edgar

m.
Christopher Columbus Hall

Christopher Columbus Hall

child

Lillian Claude Edgar

m.
William Adams Curry, Jr.

Anna Curry

CHAPTER I

Machette Family
January 1, 1860

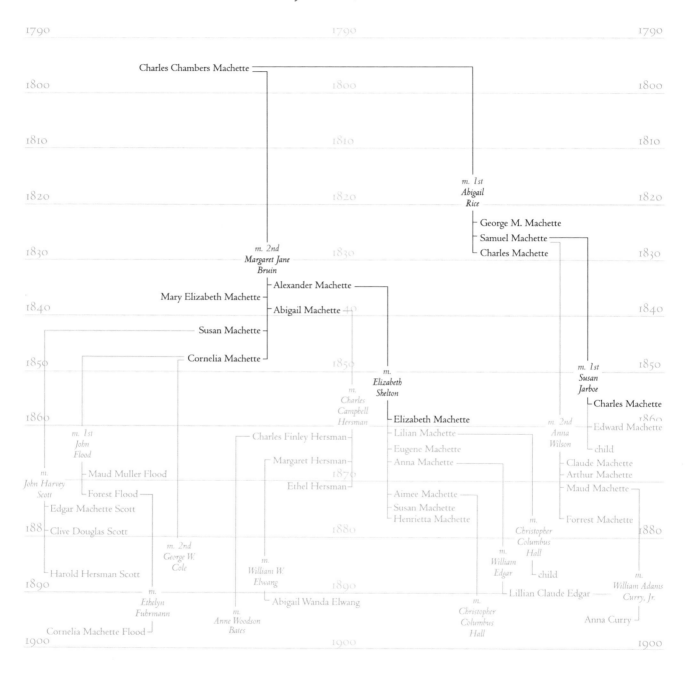

1790   1790   1790

Charles Chambers Machette

1800   1800   1800

1810   1810   1810

m. 1st
Abigail
Rice

1820   1820   1820

George M. Machette
Samuel Machette
Charles Machette

m. 2nd
Margaret Jane
Bruin

1830   1830   1830

Alexander Machette
Mary Elizabeth Machette
Abigail Machette

1840   1840   1840

Susan Machette

Cornelia Machette

m. 1st
Susan
Jarboe

1850   1850   1850

m.
Elizabeth
Shelton

m.
Charles
Campbell
Hersman

Charles Machette

1860   1860   1860

Elizabeth Machette

m. 1st
John
Flood

Charles Finley Hersman

Lilian Machette
Eugene Machette
Anna Machette

m. 2nd
Anna
Wilson

Edward Machette

child

Margaret Hersman

Claude Machette
Arthur Machette

m.
John Harvey
Scott

Maud Muller Flood

Ethel Hersman

Maud Machette

Forest Flood

Aimee Machette
Susan Machette
Henrietta Machette

Edgar Machette Scott

Clive Douglas Scott

m.
Christopher
Columbus
Hall

Forrest Machette

1880   1880   1880

m. 2nd
George W.
Cole

m.
William
Edgar

child

m.
William Adams
Curry, Jr.

Harold Hersman Scott

m.
William W.
Elwang

Lillian Claude Edgar

1890   1890   1890

m.
Ethelyn
Fuhrmann

Abigail Wanda Elwang

m.
Anne Woodson
Bates

m.
Christopher
Columbus
Hall

Anna Curry

Cornelia Machette Flood

1900   1900   1900

Fulton, Missouri, where the Machettes lived in the 1860s, was settled in the 1820s and 1830s. The seat of Callaway County, Fulton sported a number of industries and businesses in 1860 including one bank, one brewery, one hardware store, one fancy goods store, two livery stables, two drug stores, two steam-operated flouring mills, two grocery stores, two hotels, three jewelry stores, three harness shops, four carriage and wagon shops, and eight general stores. The city offered six stage routes to other locales in Missouri, and the *Telegraph*, a newspaper established in 1845, brought the news to citizens.[1] Fulton was also the location of Westminster College, a school for men founded as the Fulton College by the Presbyterian church in 1851 and renamed Westminster College in 1853. In 1860, Samuel S. Laws, the college's first president, was still in office. The Female Seminary, established in 1850 by William W. Robertson, a Presbyterian minister, was located in Fulton, too, although it would close during the Civil War. Two other institutions opened in the 1850s: the Asylum for the Education of the Deaf and Dumb, under the direction of William Kerr, and the State Lunatic Asylum No. 1. Letters in this collection refer to Laws, Robertson, and Kerr or members of their family.

When Margaret Machette came to Fulton, she joined the Presbyterian church, which had been established in 1835 by nine women and four men, including Margaret and Daniel Noley, Martha Buchanan, and Emily Boone Henderson, all friends and acquaintances of the Machettes. One of these charter members, Emily Boone Henderson, was the daughter of Jesse B. Boone and granddaughter of Daniel Boone.[2]

Because Margaret Machette was a member of the Presbyterian church and a landlady to students attending a Presbyterian school, it is not surprising that the first letter in this volume alludes to a controversy raging in the Presbyterian church in Columbia, Missouri, twenty-five miles west of Fulton. The importance of the Presbyterian church to the Machettes can be seen in other ways as well. In 1863, Margaret Machette's daughter Abbie married Charles Hersman, a professor and Presbyterian minister. In 1864,

1860–1869

---

1. *The Missouri State Gazetteer and Business Directory* (St. Louis: Sutherland & McEvoy, 1860), 89–91.

2. Ovid H. Bell, *This Large Crowd of Witnesses: A Sesquicentennial History of the First Presbyterian Church, Fulton, Missouri* (Fulton: Ovid Bell Press, 1985), 4–5. Ann Douglas, *The Feminization of American Culture* (New York: Alfred A. Knopf, 1977), 97, states that ministers in the northeast region of Victorian America "preached mainly to women."

Margaret Machette's son Alexander created a local scandal when he left the Presbyterian ministry to become a Baptist minister. In 1865, her youngest daughter, Cornelia, publicly professed her faith as a Presbyterian. The letters written by the Machettes in the 1860s thus demonstrate how the doctrine and politics of the nineteenth-century Presbyterian church intersected with the family.

The first Presbyterian church in the United States was established in the late seventeenth century, and in 1717, the Synod of Philadelphia was established, bringing together the governance of forty Presbyterian churches. Many of the first Presbyterians in the United States were Huguenots, Calvinists who had fled religious persecution from Catholics in France.[3] According to family history, the Machettes were originally French Huguenots, so it is not surprising that Charles Chambers Machette was a Presbyterian in St. Charles. His wife, Margaret, joined the Presbyterian church in 1841, seven years after she married.

In 1837, dissension in the Presbyterian Church in the U.S.A. (PCUSA) over the church's role in the political realm and its relationship with interdenominational missions led to a division and the subsequent formation of the Old School and New School of the Presbyterian church. For a time, the Old School included both northern and southern churches; however, the issue of slavery, which had already divided northern and southern Baptists and Methodists, caused increased tension in the Old School by 1860.[4] As citizens of the United States watched the Presidential campaign of 1860 and contemplated the effects the results would have on holding together the United States, northern and southern members of the Old School Presbyterians considered whether the church should split again, this time into regional factions.[5]

It is likely that discussions about a "split in the church at Columbia," which Margaret Machette alluded to in her October 4, 1860, letter, centered on political differences between northern and southern sympathizers. At the centennial celebration of the Columbia Presbyterian Church, Judge North Todd Gentry did not provide specifics about the controversies within the congregation, but he noted, "From 1850 to 1860, the Columbia Presbyterian church suffered from the bitter political and religious debates, as did other churches.... Fortunately, the cooler heads prevented open rupture, though many times the feeling on both sides was just what it should not have been."[6]

Politics in the Presbyterian church came to a head in 1861 when the General Assembly of the Old School voted to support the federal forces at Fort Sumter. At that point, the southern churches broke from the northern churches to form the Presbyterian Church in the Confederates States of America. In 1865, after Lincoln's assassination, the Old School Assembly declared that southern ministers had to admit they had sinned in promoting secession and slavery.[7] The southerners refused and formed instead the Presbyterian Church in the United States, more often known as the Southern Presbyterian Church.[8] To avoid a split within the church, the Fulton Presbyterian

3. Walter L. Lingle and John W. Kuykendall, *Presbyterians: Their History and Beliefs* (Atlanta: John Knox Press, 1978), 65, 67.

4. James H. Smylie, *A Brief History of the Presbyterians* (Louisville: Geneva Press, 1996), 87–91. *Dictionary of the Presbyterian and Reformed Tradition in America*, ed. D. G. Hart (Downers Grove, Ill.: InterVarsity Press, 1999), 246–248.

5. Lefferts A. Loetscher and George Laird Hunt, *A Brief History of the Presbyterians*, 4th ed. (Philadelphia: Westminster Press, 1983), 104.

6. *Addresses Delivered at the Centennial Celebration of the Founding of the First Presbyterian Church, Columbia, Missouri, October 17, 1928* (Columbia, Mo., 1928), 22.

7. Loetscher and Hunt, *Brief History*, 105–106, 113.

8. Lingle and Kuykendall, *Presbyterians*, 77.

Church formally associated with neither the PCUSA nor the Southern Presbyterian Church in the years immediately following the war. In 1874, it joined the Southern Presbyterian Church.[9]

It was the doctrine of baptism that led Alexander, Margaret Machette's son, to become a Baptist minister. On March 19, 1864, Margaret Machette bitterly referred to her son's conversion as "the downfall of sprinkling," an allusion to the difference between Presbyterians, who sprinkled water for baptism, and Baptists, who immersed the entire body in water during the baptismal ritual. The Presbyterians' ritual of baptizing infants was rejected by Baptists, who believed that baptism (by immersion) should follow a profession of faith and thus was not appropriate for infants and small children. As he stated in his June 3, 1864, letter, by rejecting the Presbyterian ritual, Alexander was also rejecting "the Popish perversion of the Instrument of Baptism." Although Alexander was kindly disposed toward other Protestant religions (see his comments on January 17, 1878), he would make another anti-Catholic remark on January 9, 1893, when he declared that "Romanism is getting more bold, and I fear that many who have refused to accept the truth will be swallowed up by it."[10] Anti-Catholicism was common among Protestants of the nineteenth-century, although Alexander's Huguenot background might have well fostered his disdain.

Nineteenth-century Presbyterians supported a public profession of faith, but they linked it to membership in the church instead of baptism. The Presbyterian profession of faith figures in the March 1865 letters when it was reported that Margaret's sixteen-year-old daughter, Cornelia, professed her faith at a local revival. Revival meetings were common during this time period, and the Fulton Presbyterian church held eight revival meetings between 1860 and 1876. In March 1865, when Nealie joined the church, the revival produced twenty-six new members.[11]

Among Presbyterians, church members were expected to have a sound education in the Bible. The Sunday or Sabbath school, which is described in the 1860 letters, was a way to provide that religious education to young Presbyterians. Presbyterians, following Calvinistic doctrines, had a broad commitment to education, believing as they did that an educated population served well both society and the church.[12] Consequently, the Presbyterian church developed many seminaries and colleges, including Westminster College in Fulton, whose students were Margaret Machette's boarders. When Westminster College was dedicated in 1853, Dr. Nathan Rice, mentioned in the first letter in the collection, gave a speech in which he said that Christianity, education, and liberty were "The Three Great Interests of Man." He concluded his address by stating, "Christianity and Education are the two great pillars which support the Temple of Liberty."[13] Westminster College students studied such subjects as history, geometry, declamation and composition, grammar, rhetoric, ancient literature, English literature, theology, philosophy, logic, chemistry, astronomy, botany, political economy,

9. Bell, *This Large Crowd of Witnesses*, 14–15.

10. Philip Schaff, an important Protestant church historian of the nineteenth century, separated Catholicism, which he believed was allied with Protestantism, from "Romanism," which he identified with papal authority and condemned. It is possible that Alexander Machette made a similar distinction, although, according to Stephen R. Graham, most Protestants in the nineteenth century did not; see Stephen R. Graham, *Cosmos in the Chaos: Philip Schaff's Interpretation of Nineteenth-Century American Religion* (Grand Rapids: William B. Eerdmans, 1995), 68.

11. *History of Callaway County* (St. Louis: National Historical Co., 1884), 519.

12. *Dictionary of the Presbyterian and Reformed Tradition*, ed. Hart, 88–89.

13. *History of Callaway County*, 341.

and geology. For many years, Westminster had an academy or preparatory school as well.[14]

The Presbyterian church also had seminaries in Allegheny, Pennsylvania, and Chicago, both of which Alexander attended following graduation from Westminster College in 1859. After Margaret Machette's son-in-law, Charles Hersman, taught at Westminster College and then served as its president, he taught at Presbyterian Theological Seminary in Columbia, South Carolina; served as chancellor of Southwestern Presbyterian University in Tennessee; and retired at the Presbyterian Union Theological Seminary in Virginia.[15]

Margaret Machette's Presbyterian leanings may explain, at least partly, why she sent her daughters away to school even while facing economic hardships. Although church doctrine placed women in a subordinate role to men, Presbyterians supported the education of women to better serve God and family. In 1852, Abbie Machette attended the Fulton Female Seminary, founded in 1850 by the Presbyterian minister William W. Robertson.[16] Here young women could take precollegiate courses in reading, writing, arithmetic, and history, as well as collegiate courses in algebra, logic, history, chemistry, grammar, geography, moral philosophy, and Bible antiquities. In 1860, both Abbie and her sister Sue attended Lindenwood Female College in St. Charles, Missouri.[17] In 1866, Nealie, the youngest Machette daughter, attended Monticello Seminary in Godfrey, Illinois. Although none of Margaret Machette's daughters worked outside the home after marriage, the letters that her daughter Sue wrote after 1902, the date of the end of this collection, demonstrate how education opened up for her the world of fine literature, biography, and history and gave her the background necessary to discuss national and world politics.

Many of the people referred to in the 1860 letters and afterward were educators. Addison Van Court Schenck, mentioned on April 30, 1864, was the first president of Lindenwood College in St. Charles, serving from 1857 to 1862.[18] Michael M. Fisher, mentioned frequently in the letters, taught at Westminster College and founded Bellewood Female College in Kentucky. He later taught at the University of Missouri and was serving as president pro tem when he died in office in 1891.[19] William Dabney Kerr, the father of a friend of Sue and Nealie Machette, brought state-supported education for the deaf to Missouri in 1851.[20] In the late 1860s, Sue Machette taught at Clay Seminary in Liberty, Missouri, which was run by James and Lucy Love. On February 20, 1870, Nealie's husband described the trees that William Clagett, a student, had

14. Westminster College, now coeducational, was the site of Winston Churchill's famous "Iron Curtain" speech in 1946. Mikhail Gorbachev, Margaret Thatcher, and Lech Walesa have also spoken at Westminster.

15. Charles Hersman graduated from Westminster College in 1860.

16. *History of Callaway County*, 365.

17. In the early 1830s, Mary and George Sibley opened Lindenwood College for young ladies in St. Charles, Missouri. Mary Easton Sibley was a supporter of women's rights and a friend of Susan B. Anthony. See Leona Morris, "Mary Easton Sibley," *Show Me Missouri Women: Selected Biographies*, ed. Mary K. Dains (Kirksville, Mo.: Thomas Jefferson University Press, 1989), 73.

18. Lindenwood Seminary opened in the 1830s but was not chartered as a college until the 1850s; see *History of St. Charles, Montgomery, and Warren Counties, Missouri* (St. Louis: National Historical Company, 1885), 315–316.

19. "Michael Montgomery Fisher," in *The National Cyclopaedia of American Biography*, 8:187. Judge North Todd Gentry, 24, noted that when the Columbia Presbyterian church did not have a minister during "the stormy times of 1861," Fisher, also a minister, traveled by horseback between Fulton and Columbia to preach every other week, "never missing an appointment in spite of the inclement weather and almost impassable roads."

20. Richard D. Reed, *Historic MSD: The Story of the Missouri School for the Deaf* (Fulton, Mo.: Richard D. Reed, 2000), 7.

planted on the grounds of Westminster College. Much later, when the Presbyterian church could not agree on establishing a university at Dallas, Clagett gave his plans to the Methodist church; they became part of Southern Methodist University.[21] On June 24, 1874, Sue mentioned the grand reunion, sponsored by Frederick Thomas Kemper, to celebrate the thirtieth anniversary of the founding of his school in Boonville, Missouri.[22]

Presbyterians, of course, were not the only supporters of formal education for women and men. With the ascendancy of the middle class, education in general enjoyed a robust growth in the United States in the nineteenth century. On February 23, 1879, Alexander Machette, who was concerned about financing his daughters' formal education, referred to the school of Alexander Frederick Fleet, who was president of the Baptist Female College in Lexington, Missouri.[23] In 1865, Alexander himself was an educator in Kentucky (see Alexander's letters beginning November 20, 1865).

While the Presbyterian church figures from the very first in this volume, the Civil War (or War of the Rebellion as it was called by some) is not mentioned until October 29, 1863, two and a half years after the war began. There are, unfortunately, no extant letters between January 14, 1861, and April 1, 1863, during which the war began and battles were fought at Bull Run, Shiloh, and Antietam. From 1863 to 1865, however, the war, while not a central focus of the correspondence, was clearly affecting the world the letter writers inhabited.

Missouri, although a border state, played a significant role in defining issues that would eventually lead to civil war. When Missouri sought admission to the United States as a slave state, the petition led the nation as a whole to consider how many states could be slaveholders and how far west slaveholding states could extend. The problem was temporarily settled with the Missouri Compromise of 1820, when Maine was admitted as a free state and Missouri as a slave state; the compromise also determined that the rest of the Louisiana Purchase north of 36° 30' north latitude would not permit slavery. In 1857, when the United States Supreme Court declared that Dred Scott, a Missouri slave, did not have the rights of citizenship and was not entitled to his freedom, tension between abolitionists and anti-abolitionists increased.[24]

In 1860, when these letters begin, more than one-quarter of the population of Callaway County, where Fulton is located, were slaves, and many voters in the county hoped that the Presidential election would preserve the Union *and* slavery.[25] To further this end, the greatest percentage of voters in Callaway County cast ballots in 1860 for John Bell who, as a Whig on the Constitutional Union ticket, supported this position. Stephen Douglas, nominated by the northern Democrats, came in second, and John

---

21. William H. Clagett, unpublished papers from the Presbyterian Historical Society in Montreat, North Carolina.

22. First established in 1844, the school had various names, including Kemper Family School and, more recently, Kemper Military School. When his school was closed for a few years, Kemper taught at Westminster from 1856 to 1860. James Addison Quarles, *The Life of Prof. F. T. Kemper, A.M., The Christian Educator* (New York: Burr, 1884). The oldest military school west of the Mississippi, Kemper closed in 2002.

23. J.C. Maple and R.P. Rider, *Missouri Baptist Biography* (Kansas City: Western Baptist Publishing Co., 1914), 2:106–107. Other Baptist colleges founded in Missouri in the nineteenth century included William Jewell College, Stephens College, and Southwest Baptist College.

24. The 1854 Kansas-Nebraska Act, by nullifying the Missouri Compromise and permitting slavery to be determined by settlers of new territory, also played a significant role in bringing about the Civil War.

25. In Callaway County in 1860, 636 citizens owned slaves, and the average slave owner in the county owned slightly more than four slaves. McCandless, *History of Missouri*, 2:60.

Breckinridge, nominated by the southern Democrats, came in third. Only fifteen of 2,632 voters in Callaway County voted for Abraham Lincoln.[26]

In early 1861, after Lincoln became President and southern states seceded from the Union, Missouri held a convention to determine the state's policy regarding secession and slavery. One member of the convention was Judge Joseph Flood, whose son would marry one of Margaret Machette's daughters. The convention resolved to oppose Missouri's secession from the Union and to affirm slavery. When Fort Sumter was fired upon in April 1861, Missourians split over what the state should do. Some leaders urged secession, others supported armed neutrality, while still others supported the Union.[27]

The state did not secede, and it held a precarious position as both a slave state and a state occupied by Union troops during the Civil War. When Governor Claiborne Jackson, a Confederate supporter, was forced from office in July 1861 and formed a secessionist government outside of Missouri, Hamilton Gamble, a Union supporter, became governor. By 1864, the Radical Union party was in control of the state government.[28]

Although more Missourians fought on the Union side than the Confederacy, there were strong pockets of southern support in the state.[29] On the western edge of the state, citizens on both sides of the border were terrorized either by the abolitionist Kansas jayhawkers or by the anti-abolitionist Missourians known as Quantrill's raiders. In response to the skirmishing and the murder of 150 people in Kansas, Brigadier General Thomas Ewing of the United States Army issued General Orders No. 11 on August 25, 1863.[30] It required citizens of northwest counties in Missouri, who were assumed to be supporters of Quantrill's raiders, to leave the area. As a result of this order, the Reverend Joseph Wallace was forced from his home and moved to Fulton where he taught at Westminster (see October 29, 1863).[31] His son, William Hockaday Wallace, who graduated from Westminster College in 1871 (see February 20, 1870), later wrote about terrorism in western Missouri before the family was forced to leave: "Men were hung to trees or in their barns, or called from their homes in the night time and shot. Meantime the torch was vying with the sword. A burning house could be seen across the prairies in the night time at a distance of at least twenty-five miles. One night I looked out of a second story window and counted twenty-two houses on fire." Little Callie Abbot mentioned in the March 30, 1864, letter would, as Caroline Abbot Stanley, publish the best-selling novel *Order No. 11* in 1904; she dedicated her novel to

---

26. *History of Callaway County*, 421. Douglas won the state, Bell came in second, and Lincoln fourth. Parrish, *History of Missouri*, 3.

27. John C. Crighton, *A History of Columbia and Boone County* (Columbia: Computer Color Graphics, 1987), 145–147.

28. Gamble supported slavery when he first came to office but later realized the necessity of emancipation. Parrish, *History of Missouri*, 3:6–10, 30–34, 87–94, 114.

29. Missouri contributed 109,000 men to the federal side and 30,000 to the southern side. Lorenzo J. Greene, et al., *Missouri's Black Heritage*, rev. ed. (Columbia: University of Missouri Press, 1980), 76. One reason that more Missourians fought on the Union side was because slavery had been decreasing over the decades. McCandless, *History of Missouri*, 2:57, states that the percentage of slaves in Missouri "dropped from a high of 17.8 per cent in 1830 to 9.8 per cent in 1860."

30. Ann Davis Niepman, "General Orders No. 11 and Border Warfare during the Civil War," *Missouri Historical Review* (January 1972): 185–210. Parrish, *History of Missouri*, 3:99–101.

31. William E. Parrish, *Westminster College: An Informal History, 1851–1999* (Fulton: Westminster College, 2000), 31.

William Wallace's stepmother, Jessamine, because she had helped the author with details of the novel.[32]

Citizens of Callaway County tended to be fierce supporters of the South. In fact, the county became known as "the Kingdom of Callaway"; that is, the citizens symbolically seceded from the state and the Union. One account of this name is that *Kingdom* was used after Callaway citizens repeatedly tried to seat southern supporters in the Missouri legislature while the state was occupied by Union troops. Another account is that *Kingdom* was used after a group of men prevented Union militia from Pike County from invading the county in the fall of 1861.[33]

Kingdom or not, Callaway County, with the rest of the State of Missouri, was expected to support the Union effort. For example, Missourians were required to enlist in the federal army. As students left Westminster to enlist in both the Union and the Confederate armies, the college had so few pupils left that it was in danger of closing (see the letter for March 30, 1864).[34] One student who did not join was John Harvey Scott, a boarder of Margaret Machette and eventually Sue Machette's husband. In 1864, Harvey escaped conscription in the Union army when his father paid someone to serve in his stead. A letter from Harvey's family stated, "Your substitute cost $715 and a Negro at that." On October 25, 1864, Harvey's father, William Scott, warned him to stay out of the Confederate army as well: "The Federals are ruining every man [in Monroe County, Missouri] that has a son in the Southern army. They have taken every negro from most of them.... I am convinced they will...destroy every man that has a son in this rebellion. My son, I hope you will keep in your school until you get through if possible. The time has come when we had better be as still as possible so you can keep in school and what ever you do keep out of the Southern army, for as soon as you or Joe [Harvey's brother, also a student] goes into the brush I will be ruined."[35]

To support the federal army, Missourians were expected to pay a military tax. This tax was in response to General Orders No. 232 and Circular No. 27, both dated July 19, 1864, and ordering states to pay bounties for more volunteers in the federal army.[36] Not only Margaret Machette's complaint about the tax but also the receipt itself survive (see December 29, 1864, and January 1, 1865). Although the military tax for 1865 was only three dollars, it represented nearly two-thirds of the taxes she owed. Furthermore, it came due at a time when money was dear. Missouri had been financially weak before the war, and the Civil War further depressed the economy.[37] Willard P. Hall, who became governor in early 1864 when Governor Gamble died in office, pleaded with the Secretary of War, Edwin Stanton, to grant Missouri more time to collect taxes to pay the bounties.[38] Many people in Callaway County were not able to save their property during the war. By the middle of 1864, issues of the *Fulton Telegraph* were filled, column after column, with notices of bankruptcies. Margaret Machette did not go bankrupt;

32. William Hockaday Wallace, *Speeches and Writings with Autobiography* (Kansas City, Mo.: Western Baptist Publishing, 1914), 248, 254.

33. *History of Callaway County*, 99. Ovid H. Bell, *The Story of the Kingdom of Callaway* (Fulton: Ovid Bell Press, 1952), 20.

34. Westminster was one of the few colleges in Missouri that did not close during the war, but only Harvey Scott graduated in 1865. Parrish, *History of Missouri*, 3:81–83.

35. The Scott letters about paying a black man and not serving in the Confederate army are not included in this collection.

36. *The War of the Rebellion*, series 3 (Washington, D.C.: Government Printing Office, 1900), 4:515, 518.

37. McCandless, *History of Missouri*, 2:162.

38. *The War of the Rebellion*, series 3, 4:644–655.

however, the $1.50 to $3.00 that Westminster students paid weekly for boarding was insufficient income, especially when the college had only a handful of students. In 1864, she mortgaged her property (see December 29, 1864).[39]

Particularly galling to southern sympathizers was the Iron-Clad Oath, a clause in the 1865 Missouri State Constitution sponsored by the Radical Unionists. Missourians who were unwilling to swear that they had not supported the southern cause could not vote or even serve as ministers or teachers. Abbie's husband, Charles Hersman, who was both a minister and a professor, resigned from Westminster rather than take the oath (see the February 2, 1865 letter). In 1867, the United States Supreme Court declared unconstitutional the provision denying southern sympathizers the right to practice their profession. However, not until the election of 1870, the same year the Fifteenth Amendment gave black men the right to vote, did the oath cease to play a prominent role in Missouri elections.[40]

But all that comes later. In 1860, when this collection begins, Margaret Machette, a widow, was running a boarding house for young men attending Westminster College in Fulton, Missouri. Alexander, still a Presbyterian, had recently married Lizzie Shelton and was studying for the ministry in Chicago. Abbie and Sue were attending Lindenwood Seminary in St. Charles, and only Cornelia "Nealie," Margaret Machette's eleven-year-old daughter, remained at home.

---

39. These figures appear in Westminster's 1853–1854 catalog; the fee included fires, lights, and washing.

40. William E. Parrish, *Missouri under Radical Rule: 1865–1870* (Columbia: University of Missouri Press, 1964), 48–49, 74, 309.

Fulton, Missouri
October 4, 1860

*From Margaret Bruin Machette
and Cornelia Machette to Susan
and Abigail Machette*

My Dear Girls

I received your letters last night and was glad to hear from both of you. I am very glad you have written to Lizzie. I received a letter from them this week. Lizzie was not very well. She had taken cold by getting caught in the rain. She attends Doctor Rice's lectures with Alex. She is enjoying rare opportunities. It [is] not every preacher's wife [that] has such. James McAfee was here last evening. His father and mother are in Illinois. Mr. Mutchmore was in Fulton with him. There is likely to be a split in the church at Columbia, and they were down to see Mr. Laws on the subject.[40] I do not know what the trouble is....

6th... Nelia got a letter from Mr. Hersman last night. He was well. Dear girls, the chance of visiting you is small. I will if it is possible, but don't flatter yourselves too much. We are all quite well. Nelia is in town visiting Fannie Evans....[41]

Accept a heart full of love and good wishes from
Mother.

My Dear Abbie

... Tell Sue [that] Mollie Kerr says she must write to her. Tell her I did write to her. She must write me a little scratch before she can receive one from me. Abbie, I got a letter from Mr. Hersman. He is well and well pleased....[42]

your affectionate sister [Nealie]

Margaret Bruin Machette, photo on glass under a gold frame.

40. Margaret Machette's son Alexander was studying at the McCormick Theological Seminary in Chicago under the Reverend Nathan L. Rice. Earlier in 1860, Alex had married Elizabeth "Lizzie" Shelton, daughter of Meacon and Anna Berger Shelton. See the introduction to this chapter on the controversy at the Columbia Presbyterian Church. The Reverend Robert McAfee, father of James McAfee, helped to organize Presbyterian churches in Missouri including the Fulton Presbyterian Church in 1835. Samuel A. Mutchmore was minister of the Columbia Presbyterian Church. Samuel S. Laws, a minister and later an attorney and physician, was president of Westminster College until 1861. Laws was briefly imprisoned for refusing to take the oath of allegiance to the Union; he became president of the Gold Exchange, New York City, in 1863 where he invented the stock ticker and hired Thomas Edison as his superintendent. See Robert Conot, *A Streak of Luck* (New York: Seaview Books, 1979), 30–33.

41. Frances "Fannie" Evans, daughter of B.P. and Catherine Evans. Fannie and Sue Machette were lifelong friends.

42. Mollie Kerr, daughter of William Dabney and Susan Buckles Kerr; her father brought state-supported education for the deaf to Missouri in 1851 when he founded a school in Fulton. Charles Campbell Hersman, who was courting Abbie, graduated from Westminster in 1860 and then attended Princeton. In the words of George M. Marsden, *Fundamentalism and American Culture: The Shaping of Twentieth-Century Evangelicalism, 1870–1925* (New York: Oxford University Press, 1980), 22, "The Princeton Seminary was the bastion of conservative or 'Old School' Presbyterianism."

From John William Adams to his
cousin, Abigail Machette

Fulton, Missouri
October 6, 1860

Dear Cousin

... I have been here just two weeks, but it seems to me more like two months — not because I am not pleased, far from that. I am perfectly delighted with going to Coledge[43] ... [but] I am very low spirited this evening. You will simpathise with me I know, for prehaps you have been so some time through life. If I was a girl I would cry but that is against my principalls being as I am a boy.

Sam and Lucy did marry. You said they would last spring as you was coming home from Montgomery last spring. I was at the weading. There was not a great many there. Sam and Lu showed well that night. Lu looked very pretty. The supper was a nice one. There was a good many at the infare the next day, lots more than was at the weading.[44] I enjoyed myself finely at the weading and the infare both.... You will please excuse me if I fail to interest you for I am so absent minded this evening that I cannot think of one thing long enough to get it writen down.

I have just got back from town. I went over with Nealie. She went to visit some of the little girls. I am going after her after supper. I expect to get a letter from home to night and as night has approached I feel better.

Dr. James C. Ford was ... to the weading. Julia C. tryed to coax him back, but he would not have anything more to do with her than he could help.[45] She tryed to get him to talk, but he would only answer and then stop — served her wright, do you not think so? She asked him to go home with her from the infare and he had to do it....

From Susan Machette and
Abigail Machette to their mother,
Margaret Bruin Machette

Lindenwood College[46]
St. Charles, Missouri
October 13, 1860

Dear ma,

... The wind comes keenly and we shrink from its autumnish breath. It tells us that winter is coming on. It also tells me that I am minus sacques and undersleeves. Abbie wants to go to town very much this evening, and if she does go she will get our winter bonnets....

Give my love to Nealie and accept much for yourself....
yours affectionately
Susie

43. John William Adams, fourteen-year-old son of Edmund Finley and Eleanor "Ellen" Dutton Adams and great-nephew of Margaret Machette, was attending Westminster Academy, a preparatory school. After his father's death, his mother married David W. Nowlin, a teacher and Baptist minister. The errors in children's letters are preserved.

44. Samuel Nowlin, son of David W. Nowlin and his first wife, Elizabeth Berger, married his first cousin Lucy, daughter of Washington and Mildred Berger Graves. The mothers of Lizzie Shelton Machette, Sam, and Lucy were sisters. Infare, a reception for the bride in her new home.

45. In 1863, Julia Crockett, daughter of the Reverend William Wallace and Elizabeth Crockett, married David Graves, brother of Lucy Graves Nowlin. In his unpublished autobiography, David Graves, a teacher and Baptist minister, stated that James Ford was his "rival in courtship."

46. George and Mary Easton Sibley ran Lindenwood College for young ladies in St. Charles, Missouri.

Dearest Ma:

... I received a book called *The Still Hour* from Charley [Hersman] on Friday evening — have no doubt I shall find it very interesting — received a letter also.[47] Have you written to him lately?... Mr. Hersman is so perfectly delighted with Princeton. I am afraid he will conclude to stay his three years out without returning. If he should, what would poor me do? Would certainly have time to forget him in that time, don't you think so?

... Tell John Adams I will try to find time to write to him very soon. I was delighted to hear from him.... Ma, please don't stay home so closely. I think you would enjoy yourself much better if you would visit more. Now, my own dearest Ma, accept all the love and a sweet kiss from each of your daughters.

Your *loving* Abbie

Abigail and Susan Machette, daughters of Charles and Margaret Bruin Machette. On this tintype, the photographer added pink dye as rouge for their cheeks and one collar trim, and blue dye for the other collar trim.

Fulton, Missouri
November 15, 1860

From Margaret Bruin Machette to her daughters, Abigail and Susan Machette

Dear girls

I got home on Tuesday from Montgomery. I had a pleasant visit and delightful weather but it has almost broke me down. I have not felt as good for nothing this fall as I do today. It is the fatigue of traveling and half a day's hard work. I bought fifty pounds of butter and brought [it] home with me. It took me half a day to work it over and put it in pickle. I paid 12-½ cents per pound. I found Ellen very sick. That was why we went down. John got a letter stating that his mother was very sick. She was some better the day we left, but she is not out of danger yet. The doctor told her mother she would not be well till she was confined which will be in February....[48]

Bled McKinney as it was is dead. She died on Wednesday, the 7th of this month. She was sick but three hours. Her babe died a few minutes after it was born. She died with convulsions.[49] She is another of Lizzie's schoolmates that have gone home in their youth....

47. *The Still Hour* (1860), a best-selling book on prayer by Austin Phelps.

48. Children from the union of David and Ellen Dutton Adams Nowlin apparently did not survive infancy. Jane, also Mary Dutton's daughter, married Jacob Shelton, brother of Lizzie Machette.

49. Bled McKinney married Nathan Kouns in 1859. In 1855, Kouns served as one of three attorneys for Celia, a slave who killed her master after years of sexual abuse. Her attorneys pleaded mitigating circumstances; that is, Celia had the right to defend herself from rape, even if that rape was committed by her own master. Missouri law did not recognize such rights for slaves, and the judge did not permit such a defense. Celia was subsequently found guilty and hanged. See Melton A. McLaurin, *Celia, a Slave* (Athens: University of Georgia Press, 1991). Kouns wrote the novels *Arius, the Lybian* (1883) and *Dorcas: The Daughter of Faustina* (1884). He died in the Nevada (Missouri) Lunatic Asylum in 1890.

From Margaret Bruin Machette to her daughters, Susan and Abigail Machette

Fulton, Missouri
January 14, 1861

Dear girls

... On Friday I went to see Mrs. Burdett. She is very sick with typhoid fever. I stopped for Mrs. Bailey to go with me. I stopped to dinner at Mrs. Bailey's. She sent love to you both; we went to Mrs. Burdett's early in the day and stayed till twelve o'clock; Mrs. Burdett sent love to you, too.[50]

They had prayer meeting at the college every night last week. Did they have prayer meeting at St. Charles? You know it was the week set apart to pray for the heathens for missionary operations. I had a letter from Alex a few days ago. They are well. They were very sorry to hear of Susie's sickness.

The young men have prayer meeting every Sunday evening. They had it here on last evening, next time at Mrs. George's and next Mrs. Bailey's and then here again.[51] It is just the young men that board at these three places. They are very interesting meetings.

I have not heard whether Mr. Mutchmore is going to accept the call to preach for us or not. I heard they had made up over eight hundred dollars for him.[52]

I opened the apples this evening. They are rotting very fast. I am going to put them up in jars so I can have some when you come home. I am sitting in John's room. Mr. Hand is hearing Nelia's lesson and you know she won't let me hear her. John is getting his Latin lesson. I went to the college to preaching last night.... Mr. Van Doren and Sam are both sick....[53]

Bob McPheeters was with one of Hersman's cousins last night at church.[54] He sat up close to her, I tell you; Abbie, you are cut out, or as Hersman says when any one loses their sweetheart, they have had the fence thrown on them.

Dear precious daughters, take good care of yourselves and if you are sick let me know at once. I wish you would let me know how Sue is. Has she taken her bitters? Has she got any better? Now, don't keep me ignorant of how you both are....

From Samuel Machette to his half-sister, Susan Machette

Cottonwood Springs, Nebraska
April 1, 1863

Dear Sister

... I am well this morning. I have this day sold out the one-half interest I had in the train I brought out with me and will start for Omaha where I have some business to transact on the 3 [of] April.[55] After I get through with my business at Omaha, [I] will go to Kansas City and from Kansas [City] shall pay you a visit.[56] You may look for me

50. Martha Ann George Burdett and Frances Nall Bailey.

51. Margaret George, widow of Alfred George. Like Margaret Machette, she and Frances Bailey took in boarders.

52. After William Robertson resigned as minister of the Fulton Presbyterian Church, Samuel A. Mutchmore became its minister, serving until 1863.

53. James Hand, a Westminster student. William Van Doren, the first Westminster professor, taught mathematics between 1853 and 1861; Sam was his son.

54. Robert "Bob" McPheeters, apparently a former suitor of Abbie, became a judge.

55. Samuel Machette, son of Charles Chambers Machette and his first wife Abigail Rice, was a merchant in the Kansas City area.

56. Sue Machette was a tutor in Arrow Rock, in the western part of Missouri.

in two or three weeks from above date. I shall not be down any length of time as it will be necessary for me to return here on account of the interest I have in the beef contract with the government at this pass....

And so you think you are the homeliest of the Family. Well, I must beg leave to differ with you. Ma shall continue to think that I am the homely one. As we seem to differ in regard to this matter, I propose to wager a fine new whip to a pair of slippers worked by your own hands that I am the homely one and will leave it to whoever you may choose to judge between us. Now I consider this a bet I win as a matter of course so you will have to make the slippers. It may be, however, that you may win. If you do the whip shall be forthcoming.

You wish to know how old I am. I was thirty-seven the tenth day of last February. Charlie, my oldest son, was four years old in December last. Edward, my youngest son, will be three years old the last of June coming. You wish me to tell you who they look like. I have no time to tell you about them now. When I come down you will go with me to Kansas City and see them and judge for yourself. My wife's maiden name was Susan C. Jarboe, like yourself [of] French descent but a long ways from being French.... I shall here tell you adieu, Sister, until I see you which I hope will not be long.

Charles Campbell Hersman, a minister and professor, married Abigail Machette July 16, 1863.

Married on the 16 of July 1863 by the Reverend J. P. Finley
Abbie Machette to C. C. Hersman

Written on a sheet of paper by Margaret Bruin Machette

Fulton, Missouri
October 29, 1863

From Margaret Bruin Machette to her daughter, Susan Machette

My Dear Susie

Why is it you are so long letting me hear from you? I received your note saying you arrived at Mrs. Sappington's on Wednesday after you left home and you also said you would write in a day or so and let me know the particulars of your trip.[57] Consequently, I have waited till this evening hoping every day to get a letter.

Lizzie wrote to you the week after you left. She is at her father's. Her sister Mattie and Mr. Wells came for her on last Saturday week. Lizzie and babe were well when they left.[58] The babe has grown very much since you saw her. Your Brother has gone on search of his things. They were shipped for Mexico near three weeks ago but have not

57. Sue was a tutor in Arrow Rock for the children of Penelope Sappington, daughter of Governor John Breathitt of Kentucky. Penelope Sappington's father-in-law and her maternal uncle, John Sappington, introduced quinine for malaria and in 1844 published a medical treatise, possibly the first medical book west of the Mississippi. Thomas B. Hall, Jr. and Thomas B. Hall, III, *Dr. John Sappington of Saline County, Missouri 1776–1856*, 2nd ed. (Arrow Rock, Mo.: Friends of Arrow Rock, 1986).

58. Alex and Lizzie returned to Fulton from Westport, Missouri, where Alex had been a minister. He became minister of the Fulton Presbyterian Church after Samuel A. Mutchmore resigned. Alex and Lizzie's daughter Lilian was born in 1863. Lizzie's sister Martha "Mattie" was married to Thomas Wells.

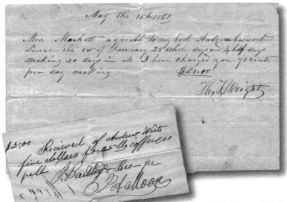

A May 15, 186, receipt for $21 to Margaret Machette from Henry T. Wright for thirty days' work by his slave Andrew after January 25, 1861. Andrew is also mentioned in Margaret's October 29, 1863, letter, at right, to her daughter Susan.

Margaret Machette had Andrew Wright buy her twenty-five pounds of coffee for $5.

arrived yet. We have had quite a deep snow and some hard freezing last week.

Andrew commenced making the molasses on the 21st which was Wednesday and on the next day the ground was covered with snow which continued to fall till in the night. They had [a] very cold time working with the cane. It turned out very poor. We have only 30 gallons of molasses. We have 20 bushels of potatoes put up. I have not received my apples yet. I engaged 12 bushels before the freeze. I hope they will prove good ones.

… They have put Mr. Wallace in the English department of the College…. Mr. Wallace has rented Innis Bailey's place. It's all stuff about his losing every thing by the jayhawkers. They have lost but two negroes, George and a man. [59]

Nelia is not going to school any more. This winter she will recite to your brother and Lizzie. I was out at Mrs. Wright's yesterday. They are making cider. I will send a keg out on Saturday to get it filled. She sends much love to you. [60]

I suppose Lizzie told you of Abbie's sickness. She was very sick for three weeks, poor child. Hers is a hard trial away among strangers who show her no kindness and him obliged to be in College so much of his time. [61] All the attention she got was when he was at home but I hope she is well now. They had concluded to return home at one time but I think he has concluded to remain the term out.

Dear Susie, you can't imagine how much anxiety I feel about you situated where you might sicken and die before I could hear from you. I disliked to have you leave when you did and every day makes me regret it more. If I could hear from you often I should feel better. I hear of that part of the country being full of soldiers which makes me more uneasy about your safety. [62] I hope you will be very careful of yourself. Live very near to God. He is my only hope for protection and oh that he will protect my Dear daughter….

Lu Shelton is teaching in David Graves' school at Montgomery City…. [63]

59. Joseph Wallace, minister and teacher, was forced to leave his home in Independence after General Thomas Ewing issued General Orders No. 11. Joseph Wallace's son, William Hockaday Wallace (see February 20, 1870, and the introduction to this chapter), wrote about this time in his autobiography: "One day a band of soldiers under Captain Pardee, belonging to the Kansas Regiment of Colonel Jennison, came to my father's. They sacked our home, taking everything of value which could be carried, clothing, blankets, quilts, silverware, bridles, saddles, harness. One of the negroes [a slave], Alfred, went with them. The other negroes, under the advice of Marshall [another slave], who was ever true to us and who stayed with us until he was forced into the Federal army, refused to go, although Big John and George left shortly afterwards. Five of the best horses were taken that day." See Wallace, *Speeches and Writings with Autobiography*, 253–254.

60. Innis, son of Benjamin and Frances Bailey. Elizabeth Jameson Wright; her husband hired out Andrew.

61. Charles Hersman, who married Abbie Machette in July 1863, was teaching at Carroll College in Waukesha, Wisconsin.

62. Joseph Shelby, commander of a Confederate cavalry, was at Arrow Rock, where the Missouri State Militia engaged his troops in a skirmish on October 13. The battle report of General Egbert Brown of the Missouri Militia, which was carried in the October 15 and 22, 1863, *Missouri Republican*, stated that the militia had thirty or fewer dead or wounded troops and the Confederacy had over 120 casualties.

63. Lu Shelton, sister of Lizzie Shelton Machette.

Fulton, Missouri
November 14, 1863

Dear Susie

... Your brother got home with his things the week before last and I was helping him unpack and straighten up. Poor fellow, it is a sad move for him. His things cost him near ninety dollars, and they are in a sad plight, bruised and battered shamefully. Lizzie's new bedstead is ruined. The side rails are lost and the bureau looks like it had been used for fifty years. Your brother says with the exception of his books he would have saved money to have thrown his things away.

... I had a letter from your Aunt [Mary] Dutton last week. She is very well.... Ellen Nowlin has better health than she has had for seven years.... Mr. John McAfee and Henie White are very sick. The school is suspended on account of sickness. Two of the young ladies have died. Typhoid fever is raging at Ashley. I did not learn what was the matter with McAfee but suppose it is typhoid fever as it is raging as an epidemic. I have two new boarders, a Mr. Major and Mr. Hockensmith, but I don't think Hockensmith will stay long. He has consumption and can't bear studying.[64]

Fulton, Missouri
December 10, 1863

Dear Susie

Your letter was received Saturday night. It found us well except the negroes Lucinda and Agie were both sick. We did not think Agie would live at that time but she is better now. She had inflammation of the bowels. There is a great deal of sickness in Fulton and many deaths. Miss Sallie Jameson died on the 11th of November of inflammation of the bowels — just two weeks from the day she died she was to have been married. She and Bettie were to be married on the same day.[65] Bettie was married on last Monday week. Both gentlemen were from Kentucky. They think the one that Sally was to marry is going crazy. Bettie left Missouri the day after she was married for New York on a bridal tour.

Miss Lizzie Broadwell died on Tuesday. She had pneumonia and typhoid fever. They are waiting for her brother to come before they bury her. Little Mollie George died yesterday morning of scarlet fever. She is to be buried today. There has been [such] a number of other deaths that I can't remember their names not being acquainted with them. Mrs. George is preparing to go to California in the spring. I don't know whether Mollie's death will change her plans or not....[66]

64. Watson Seminary in Ashley, Missouri, where Isaac White, father of Henrietta "Henie" White, taught, was a preparatory and teachers' training school. Samuel Watson (not Samuel Watson of Fulton) willed money to start the school. In his will, he also freed his slave Esther. John McAfee was principal at Watson Seminary; in 1875, he cofounded Park College in Parkville, Missouri. The July 11, 1851, *Liberty Tribune* stated that Newton Hockensmith's parents, sister, and three family slaves died of cholera in that year.

65. Sallie Tom and Bettie Jameson, daughters of John and Susan Jameson, a prominent Fulton family. Bettie married Benjamin Rogers. Their father was the head attorney for Celia, a slave charged with her master's murder. See p. 25, n. 49. above, for November 15, 1860.

66. Lizzie Broadwell, sister-in-law of Samuel Laws. Mary "Mollie" George, daughter of Margaret George, was about nine years old when she died.

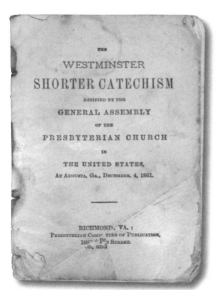

This catechism was printed in 1861, when Southern Presbyterians met in Augusta, Georgia, to form the Presbyterian Church in the Confederate States of America.

Miss Mag Scott's health is still poor. Ella and Miss Lizzie continue the school.... I heard that Addie Grant and Mr. Yates were to be married soon.[67] Mrs. Wright spent the day here on Monday. She sends much love to you. She is much distressed at Sallie Tom's death. You know she thought so much of her nieces.

I see very few of the Fulton people. They never come out to see us.... There is a number of strangers in Fulton this winter. The churches are well attended. I do not mean that every body goes to church, but we have large congregations every Sabbath. Your brother preaches to a full house every Sabbath and they pay marked good attention. He is studying very hard, poor fellow. He looks so thin he could not stand much sickness. Lizzie feels very uneasy for fear he gets sick. He visited Miss Lizzie Broadwell twice while she was sick. She sent for him the morning she died to pray with her. Lizzie went with him to see her. Your brother and Lizzie called to see Mrs. Nolley and Sally Davis the same day. They are both sick.

I received a letter from Abbie last week. She is still poorly. She told me that she would have to come home before the session was out. She expects to be confined in the spring. I have written to her to come before the weather gets too cold. Poor thing, I feel so sorry for her. She has had a hard time since she left home — has been sick every day and don't get half enough to eat. Just imagine to yourself that you had been sick for three weeks and was getting able to eat something and that I was to send you some cold sauce and cold baked beans and cold hard bread and rancid butter for your breakfast and you have an idea how she fares. She said her bed was not made up but twice while she lay sick except when Mr. Hersman made it. He even had to empty the chamber pot for her. I guess he is pretty well initiated in the mysteries of married life.

Nelia is in Montgomery County. She says she is enjoying herself very much. You know that it does not take much to please her. She gets to ride on horseback every day.... I told her when she went away she must write and tell me all the news. She says all the news she hears is about babies. She believes every body down there is going to have a baby in the spring!... Mr. Nowlin has been allowed to come home. They say he is looking very well....

I have four boarders. Mr. Dudley and Stonebraker are new ones. There is two others that spoke for board — Noah Flood and a Mr. Allen from Lafayette County. Mr. Major that rooms with Harvey Scott is a cousin of Noah Flood's. Mr. Hockensmith left in a day or two after I wrote you last — Stonebraker is not at all like his Uncle Denton. He is a great lady's boy. He went to [the] Robnetts' and stayed from Saturday evening till Sunday night, went to church with the girls twice on Sunday. I fear he is too fond of going to town to study much.[68]

You asked me if Ann George went to school.[69] She does and boards in town. I believe she pays her board by giving music lessons. She has her piano with her.... Mrs.

67. Margaret "Mag" and Elizabeth "Lizzie" Scott, daughters of the Reverend William and Sarah Tate Scott, taught in Fulton. Ella was perhaps Ella Wilson, daughter of William and Ellen Grant Wilson. Agnes "Addie" Grant, daughter of Mary Warren Grant and Israel Boone "Licking" Grant, married Benjamin Yates.

68. Clifton Ferguson Dudley and John Emery Stonebraker, Westminster students. Denton Stonebraker attended Westminster in the 1850s. Noah Flood, son of Judge Joseph and Eliza Major Flood, and John Harvey Scott, son of William and Jane Scott, both Westminster students. The Robnetts were probably the family of James and Sarah Ann Robnett.

69. Ann George, daughter of Margaret George.

Burdett says Ann will not practice for her, that she has not taken a lesson for some time. Molly had commenced taking lessons and was doing very well when she was taken sick. She was only sick five or six days....

You asked if Nelia studies hard. I think she does. Your brother says she gets on with her algebra and Latin finely. Lizzie and babe are well. They stay up stairs. I went up this morning and brought Lilian down about five o'clock. I wish you could have seen her. She was perfectly delighted — laughs and crows as much as a child of six months. She makes her mother get up with her about four every morning. She is a very good babe and perfect romp....

Your brother and Lizzie join me in love to you. Aunt Lucinda sends love and howdy to you. Agie says tell Miss Susie to come home and make some music.

Fulton, Missouri
January 13, 1864

From Margaret Bruin Machette to her daughter, Susan Machette

Dear Susie

... Nelia has not got home yet. The cold weather has prevented her coming. I have not heard from Abbie since before Christmas. We have had no company this winter. It would be very lonesome for you if you were at home this winter. Nelia wrote that she was enjoying herself very much, says she would not be in Fulton this Christmas for anything. Your Aunt gave her a candy pulling, says she had a fine time sparking the boys.... She will write you when she gets home and tell you her experience....

I have Lucinda this year, have to pay thirty dollars for her.[70] It's a large price but I don't feel like I could do all the work. Lucinda sends her love to you. Alex and Lizzie send much love.

... How did you stand the cold weather? I suppose the snowstorm reached you and of course was to your liking. I believe you admire snowstorms. It is thought to have been the coldest weather we have had for thirty years.[71] At any rate it came near freezing us to death here. Lizzie and your brother had to come down to my room and stay till it moderated. We lost all our plants. I brought everything into my room to keep [them] from freezing but it froze as hard in there as anywhere else. I had all the work to do that week as the negroes had holiday. We had but two boarders that week. It was fortunate for me — I tell you I made very little cooking do. I froze ice cream in the dining room by simply sitting the freezer on the floor and stirring the cream occasionally....

Fulton, Missouri

From Cornelia Machette to her sister, Susan Machette

Dear Sue,

... I remember what a great hand you always were to ask questions, so I will imagine you are here questioning me about my trip. Well, to begin, I had a *delightful* time,

70. Lucinda might have been a slave hired by Margaret Machette.

71. The *Missouri Republican* for January 3, 1864, reported that the temperature on New Year's Day was twenty-two degrees below zero, making it the coldest day "for at least the last thirty-one years."

Sometimes Cornelia Machette (inset) wrote on the same page twice—
horizontally and then vertically.

spent most of my time riding horseback. The family Aunt has living with her has a little pony, and they told me whenever I felt like riding the pony was at my service; they
are such nice people — *too* nice for that neighborhood though I think it has improved
a great deal. I stayed down there a month, then went to Montgomery City so as to go
with Lu [Shelton]. [I] think she is very pretty but not beautiful, like her very much,
enjoyed my self exceedingly down there; we stayed there three [days] — would have
come home sooner but the weather was too cold. I came home on the cars by my self
— met Ella Wilson at Mexico so we came together in the hack.[72] Home folks were
perfectly surprised when I came by my self....

While I was gone, Sue, I caught a beau. You said in your letter that yours couldn't
talk of nothing but horses, dogs and pretty girls. Mine was more intelligent. His topic
was Lorena, performs very well on the piano....[73] They say his parents are wealthy, have
a splendid piano; quite a recommendation, you know.

Now that I have finished telling you about my visit I will say something about home
which will prove more interesting to you, I hope. To begin again I went to a concert the

72. See p. 8 on the development of the railroad in Missouri.
73. "Lorena," piano music written by Joseph Philbrick Webster; a popular tune in the Confederate army.

other night. Mr. Tuttle got it up, had all the Sabbath school scholars in it.[74] It was gotten up for the purpose of getting a new library. I believe they made 53 dollars and after all the expenses were paid had 49 — will get a very good library, won't it? I told Mr. Dudley when they came he must get some and loan them to me; he was perfectly delighted with the idea. Speaking of Dudley — he is the biggest dunce I ever saw; no more thinks of knocking at Ma's door than he does of flying. He said the other day he wished he could hear Miss Sue play, was trying to get me but I wouldn't do it.

Stonebraker is another dunce. He took Lute Harrison to the concert the other night and when she got home she complained of being very tired, giving him a hint to go but he didn't take it. She gaped several times but still he made no move to leave so she grows desperate — gets his hat and shawl, lays them on a chair saying she is very tired, will retire, and he can go when he pleases. Now to [tell] of it, he is only about 16 — her, nobody knows how old she is. Noah Flood is talking of going to California in the spring.[75] He is in bad health, I believe. The girls often speak of you. Mr. Stonebraker said I gained 10 pounds while I was gone — am 5 feet 2 inches and a half. Montgomery is a great place....

Fulton, Missouri
February 7, 1864

From Abigail Machette Hersman
to her sister, Susan Machette

My Dear Sister!

... Don't you think I have been quite a *soldier*? Came all the way from Wisconsin alone. I thought it quite an undertaking, but was so *very* anxious to return I felt quite willing to venture. The saddest part was to leave Mr. Hersman so lonely. He expects to be home in seven or eight weeks. You can imagine how long the time will seem. Susie, I am enjoying myself very much indeed. Have done nothing else but eat since my return, but when you take into consideration how long I have been fasting, this seems somewhat excusable — doesn't it?

... Mrs. Brooks invited us all over there last Tuesday to spend the day.[76] We went of course and enjoyed ourselves very much indeed. Mrs. George and Mrs. Burdett were there also. Susie, I hope you will excuse this short letter! I am not feeling well and could do no better....

Fulton, Missouri
February 21, 1864

From Margaret Bruin Machette
to her daughter, Susan Machette

My Dear Daughter

... Abbie is with me at this time. Her health is good. She expects Mr. Hersman home the first of April. She is making up little clothes for her boy she says. She looks very fine and large. Nelia was wonderfully shocked when she first saw her.

---

74. In 1867, Warren Woodson Tuttle, Sabbath school superintendent, opened the first store in Fulton that sold only groceries.

75. Noah Flood moved to Nevada and then to California where he practiced law.

76. Lavinia and E.M. Brooks ran a boarding house.

Mollie Shelton as it was has a fine son. Jane Shelton has a daughter, calls it Ella Lee. Kate Roper has a son, calls him John....[77]

I have my ice house filled. The ice is not over three or four inches thick but very clear and good. It cost me eleven dollars.

Lizzie and I and your brother went over to town last week to have Lilian's likeness taken but she would not sit still long enough. I had mine taken but it is a poor thing. I could not change the locket so I sent you my likeness in a case. Ann George was here last week. She has grown coarse — is not as pretty as when you left. Mrs. Burdett has moved to her mother's place. She sends love to you. Old Mr. McAfee preached for your brother last Sabbath. Jim's wife has a daughter. He is going to Kentucky to live. The old man does not like it much — thinks Jim ought to stay with him. Jim calls his daughter Mary Moore after his mother....[78]

My Dear, I want to see you very much. What will you do about Lizzie's trunk? She will want it when she leaves. Your brother will be in Boonville in April at Presbytery. If you could meet him there you could leave the trunk with him. You could get you one in Arrow Rock.

Do take good care of yourself, my own precious daughter.

From Margaret Bruin Machette to her daughter, Susan Machette

Fulton, Missouri
March 19, 1864

My Dear Daughter

Why so long silent? Abbie and Nelia have both written and had time to receive an answer. I have been very uneasy for fear you are sick. We are having so much sickness and so many deaths in Fulton that I am more anxious about you than formerly. There was three deaths last week. Old Mr. Renshaw died on last Sabbath. Mrs. Nolley died on Wednesday and Mr. Licking Grant on Tuesday night. They took Mr. Renshaw to St. Louis to bury. Mr. Grant and Mrs. Nolley's funeral was preached at eleven o'clock on Thursday by Mr. Robertson in the church.[79] It was a sight not often seen, two old people, members of the same church. They were both brought in and placed in front of the pulpit while Mr. Robertson preached the sermon. The Freemasons buried Mr. Grant in Fulton. Mrs. Nolley was taken back home till Friday morning when she was taken to the country and buried. I have not heard what was the matter with either of them.

Lizzie and Alex have been to her father's visiting. The friends are well. Little Margaret Bruin as we always called her is at your Aunt's. She has been married near two years and is a widow. She married a Mr. Rice, nephew of your uncle Walter Rice. She has a little boy eleven months old, a very delicate child. She brought him

---

77. Mary "Mollie" Shelton, sister of Lizzie Machette and Jacob Shelton, had recently married Thomas Hammond. Jacob Shelton's wife Jane was the daughter of Mary Bruin Dutton and hence Margaret Machette's niece. Kate Roper, daughter of David Nowlin and his first wife Elizabeth Berger Nowlin, married William Roper. Her son John, who worked for the railroad, died in 1886 in Oregon when he was run over by a train.

78. Jim McAfee, son of the Reverend Robert and Jane Moore McAfee. See October 4, 1860.

79. Margaret Tate Nolley, a founder of the Fulton Presbyterian Church in 1835. Israel Boone "Licking" Grant married Mary Warren in 1831, the same day that Mary's two sisters Martha and Miriam also married. After Licking and Miriam were widowed, they married each other. (See December 10, 1863, on the marriage of Licking's daughter Addie Grant.) The Reverend William Robertson founded Fulton Female Seminary in 1850. His daughter Sarah was a lifelong friend of Sue Machette.

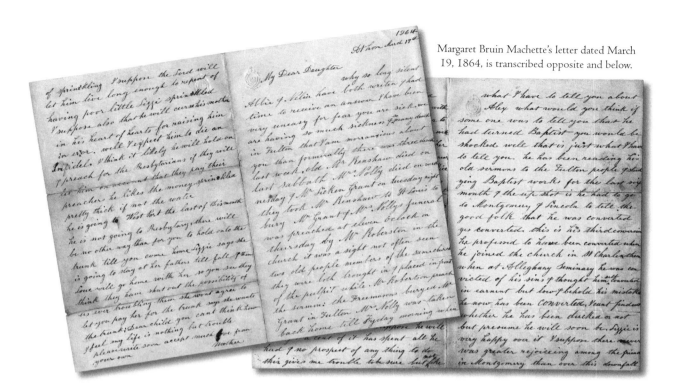

Margaret Bruin Machette's letter dated March 19, 1864, is transcribed opposite and below.

to the country for his health. Lizzie says she is very handsome. Her husband died in the federal army.[80]

... We are looking for Mr. Hersman home in three weeks. It has been a sorry time for him. They have not paid him his salary. I don't suppose he will ever get a cent of it, has spent all he had and no prospect of any thing to do. This gives me trouble to be sure but not like what I have to tell you about Alex.

What would you think if some one was to tell you that he had turned Baptist? You would be shocked. Well, that is just what I have to tell you. He has been reading his old sermons to the Fulton people and studying Baptist works for the last six months and the up shot is he had to go to Montgomery and Lincoln to tell the good folk that he was converted, yes converted. This is his third conversion. He professed to have been converted when he joined the church in St. Charles. Then when at Allegheny Seminary he was convicted of his sins and thought himself converted in earnest but low and behold his mistake — he now has been converted.[81]

I can't find out whether he has been ducked or not but presume he will soon be. Lizzie is very happy over it. I suppose there never was greater rejoicing among the friends in Montgomery than over this downfall of sprinkling. I suppose the Lord will

80. Little Margaret "Mag," the daughter of Margaret Machette's brother, John Bruin, married Joseph Rice on June 19, 1862; Malin was born in the spring of 1863. Joseph Rice, a lieutenant in the Federal army, died of disease on December 15, 1863. Sir (his first name) Walter Rice was probably the brother of Charles Machette's first wife, Abigail Rice.

81. The Sheltons from Lincoln County and the Duttons from Montgomery County were Baptists. Alex Machette attended the Presbyterian seminary in Allegheny, Pennsylvania, before his marriage.

let him live long enough to repent of having poor little Lizzie sprinkled.[82] I suppose also that he will curse his mother in his heart of hearts for raising him in error. Well, I expect him to die an Infidel. I think it likely he will hold on and preach for the Presbyterians if they will let him on account that they pay their preachers. He likes the money sprinkled pretty thick, if not the water.

He is going to Westport the last of this month. He is not going to Presbytery. There will be no other way than for you to hold onto the trunk till you come home. Lizzie says she is going to stay at her father's till fall and then Lu [Shelton] will go home with her, so you see they think they have shut out the possibility of us ever troubling them. She won't agree to let you pay her for the trunk — says she wants the trunk. Dear child, you can't think how I feel — my life is nothing but trouble....

From Cornelia Machette to her sister, Susan Machette

Fulton, Missouri

Dear Sue

... Night before last and last night the people of Fulton were honored with concerts from a ventriloquist. I went the night before. Mr. Scott was my gallant. I had more fun than I ever did in my life before. The gentleman that acted was the handsomest man I ever saw and dressed most splendidly. I can't describe what all he done. We went there [at] half past six [and] returned at 10 — were highly entertained all the while. I must tell you [about] the last play. First he commenced talking to someone in a hat — represented it to be a little boy. His name was Charlie. He asked him why he didn't come up and see the people, and he said there was an old man there that wouldn't let him. The ventriloquist then proceeded to look into the matter himself, so he asked the old man what he was doing there. He told him it was none of his business so they quarreled a while till at length the ventriloquist told him he was a-going to look into his bundle. The first thing he brought out was a little pair of stockings. The next a little shirt, then a dress. Laid over the hat was a baby's dress and scarf, then such a cry the baby set up you never heard. The man tossed it in the hat [and] sang to it. Still the child continued to cry. At last he took out a very large doll. He let on to be scared nearly to death of the sight and took it behind the curtains. Then [he] appeared, told us all good night, and disappeared.

Last night it was raining so that I could not go. Dear Sue, how I wish you could be here next for every other night Professor Minor is going to lecture on astronomy.[83] Everyone seems to think it will be a great thing. Although I have never studied it, yet I expect to attend thinking perhaps it will do me some good after while....

You asked in your letter, dear Sister, if I read much — I have not done much of it this winter in the way I used [to do] fall reading. Have read several of Scott's works, a good deal in Byron and different poems, [and] Goldsmith's *The Deserted Village* and *The Vicar of Wakefield*. Am now reading *The History of Greece* — like it very much — and have read a great deal of trash besides.[84] You asked me too if I visited much — not a great

82. Little Lizzie was Alex and Lizzie Machette's daughter, born before Lilian and buried in Westport where Alex had been a Presbyterian minister.

83. Benjamin Blake Minor, president of University of Missouri when it was closed by the state in 1862, supported himself by lecturing on astronomy.

84. *The Vicar of Wakefield*, *The Deserted Village*, and *History of Greece* by Oliver Goldsmith (c. 1730–1774).

Margaret Machette's children probably enjoyed reading as much as their mother, as noted in Cornelia's letter to her sister Susan, opposite. Margaret subscribed to some of the most popular periodicals, including the *New York Observer*, *Harper's*, and *Peterson's*, as well as religious periodicals such as the *St. Louis Presbyterian*.

deal though more than I used to, though I don't like Fulton any better than I used to. All the attraction it contains for me is my dear Parent, Sisters, and brother Charley but he being away and you it is dreadful....

Fulton, Missouri
March 30, 1864

From Abigail Machette Hersman to her sister, Susan Machette

My dear Sister:

... Brother and Lizzie left bright and early and now we are quite alone once more. They went over to Mexico in a wagon — Lizzie will take the cars there for her father's, Brother for Westport. I do not know how Lizzie will go to Westport! She may possibly stay with her friends until next fall. Susie, you cannot imagine what a *great* relief it is to have them gone. The more I see of Lizzie the less I fancy her. Ma just waited on her like a servant the whole time, and she never seemed to feel any gratitude whatever. You can imagine how very trying it must have been to me, to see our dear Mother making herself a perfect servant to *a stranger*. But enough of this now, Susie — I have much to tell you when you come home.

The time seems long until you return, but we will try and not think of it. When I first returned from Waukesha, it seemed an *age* 'till Mr. Hersman's return, but now only two weeks and he will be at home. We are all very anxious to see him! Nealie can scarcely talk of anything else....

Susie, you remember Thurmond, don't you? Well, he has gone to Danville.... The Profs disliked very much to give so good a student up. The number of students in college here is very small this session; several left at the close of the first term. I fear they will have no college next year....[85]

Mr. Fisher and wife called out yesterday evening — they were both very well. Mrs. Fisher has quite a music class — [including] the two Abbots (Nannie and Callie)....[86]

Nealie is standing before the glass combing her hair! She says, "tell Susie to measure the length of her hair and send me. I want 25 cents if it is as long as mine." You

85. Nicholas Thurmond left Westminster to attend Centre College in Danville, Kentucky, and later joined the Confederate army.

86. Michael M. Fisher, professor of Latin language and literature at Westminster, and his wife, Anna Atwood Fisher; she would die in October. Ann "Nannie" and Carolyn "Callie" Abbot, daughters of Rufus and Mary Rebecca Hart Abbot. As Carolyn Stanley, Callie would later write the best-selling novel *Order No. 11* (1904), on the 1863 federal order requiring Southern sympathizers in western Missouri to leave the area.

know her hair is *very* short. Lizzie trimmed it for her again yesterday. I forgot to mention that Brother took all his furniture over to town last Saturday and sold it. He did pretty well, I believe. Susie, you need trouble yourself no further about the trunk. I heard Ma say she would pay them $12 for it and let you keep it.

Susie, did you think [it] very strange of Brother's becoming an "Immersionist"? You cannot think how distressed Ma has been about it. He treated Ma so badly about it, too! [Alex] went down to Montgomery and told them, but never has said a *word* to *Ma* on the subject. Ma saw a portion of a sermon of his while he was absent which excited her suspicions, and so when they came home she asked Lizzie one day who they expected to baptize Lilian. She replied — *Mr. Finley.*[87] Now, how do you suppose she could tell such a falsehood? She went up stairs after while (to talk to Brother, I suppose) and came back, [and] told Ma that Alex had changed his views as to the proper mode of baptism. Susie, you had better look out — no doubt they will be trying to make a Baptist of you.

... Susie, as soon as you get through reading this, throw it into the fire. There are things in this I would not wish anyone else to see....

From Susan Machette to her sister, Abigail Machette Hersman

Arrow Rock, Missouri
April 5, 1864

My dear Abbie:

I have just finished reading your welcome letter. I should have been so much disappointed if I had not gotten it. I was waiting in Mrs. Sappington's room for Mr. Marmaduke who always brings out the mail.[88] When he came I asked him if he had any thing for me. He said he believed he had and held it out of my reach while he read very deliberately my name and asked me if I had any idea of changing it soon. I assured him I hadn't. He told me there was a certain "young man" coming to see me soon: the information did not frighten me badly, as he often gives mysterious hints of said gent. I imagine he is a myth as such a thing as a young man is out of the question in this region of [the] county. I was congratulating myself that Mr. Marmaduke had gotten no joke on me, but he has one now — the worst kind, too, about a *stinking* old widower. It happened thus:

Mrs. Marmaduke and I were in town shopping and we went into a new store and I didn't know the keepers of it from Adam. It fell to my lot to be waited on by the widower; and Mrs. Marmaduke came home and told it worse than it was, though to be sure he did cut a good many antics. While I was in Arrow Rock I saw Miss Lou though only for a short time.[89] I do love her so much. I got me a calico dress, right pretty I think. I intend to make it by myself. I will try to cut it myself though Mrs. Sappington would do it very willingly for me, but I want to learn how. It was 28 cents a yard. I got me a splendid pair of hoops for $2.50. They are very small. I think my old

87. John P. Finley, Presbyterian minister and professor of Greek language and literature at Westminster, 1862–1864. He presided over Abbie and Charley's wedding.

88. Mr. Marmaduke, possibly a son of Lavinia Sappington Marmaduke, sister-in-law of Penelope Sappington and widow of Meredith M. Marmaduke, Missouri's governor in 1844. Another son, John S. Marmaduke, a graduate of West Point and officer in the Confederate army, was Missouri's governor when he died in 1887.

89. Lou Atwood, music teacher and sister of Anna Fisher, who had been the wife of Michael M. Fisher. See March 30, 1864.

ones have done remarkably well to last this long. I do not intend to wear any new ones till summer.

Tell Nealie she must not cut her hair off any more. "They say" none but small children wear shingled hair now and every one that can get long hair wears it. I sent ten dollars to Lutie V — who is in St. Louis to get me a braid. She said she could get me a handsome one for that. It seems rather high, doesn't it? But Miss Lou says it is very reasonable as hair is double the value it was. [I] was just obliged to have one. Nealie asks how long my hair is. I believe it is about as long as the longest of yours, that is long enough to tie a braid to.

Did Ma pay Liz for her trunk? If she did I will send the same to Ma. But I do not see how she could ask $12 for it seeing she only gave $10, though perhaps trunks like musical instruments improve from use....

By the way, we have such sweet little pets — rabbits — all the children have one and so have I. They are so gentle and sweet. They bring them to school and carry them in their sleeves, but I forbade them bringing them any more as it takes their attention off their books.

... I look at Ma's picture and try to imagine I am with her, but it is not the reality. Well, it is only three months till I am with you, providence willing. By the time you get this, Mr. Hersman I expect will be with you....

Susan Machette, as a teacher, was aware that children need encouragement to learn and focus on their studies. When she and her siblings were small, their mother rewarded them with certificates of merit as encouragement.

Fulton, Missouri
April 10, 1864

*From Margaret Bruin Machette
to her daughter, Susan Machette*

My Dear Susie

... Nelia wrote and waited to put her letter in with mine, but when Abbie received one and you had not answered hers she threw it in the fire saying if you thought more of Abbie than her you would get no more letters from her.

I have been cleaning house, changing carpets, and getting Abbie's room fixed before Charley came.[90] They have the room over mine. He came last tonight in about an hour after she received your letter. I have not heard from Lizzie yet. I got a letter from Alex last night.

... Mrs. George leaves Fulton the last of this month for California. She and Ann send much love to you. Sally Davis is very sick. They thought she would not live through last week, but they think she is some better now. I paid for the trunk. They said that trunks were worth more now, that I could not get such a one for fifteen dollars. I am looking for Mag Rice up this week. I want the time to pass rapidly now till you get home.

Don't let that young man run off with you. By the way, I think you are a favorite of old widowers. How many little responsibilities has he?...

90. In the spring, carpets were replaced with mats; in the fall, the process was reversed.

From Abigail Machette Hersman
to her sister, Susan Machette

Fulton, Missouri
April 18, 1864

My dearest Sister:

The most *important* piece of news to communicate this time is the return of Mr. Hersman. You were correct when you said that you supposed your letter would find him here. He has not been well since his return, nor for some time before. I do not think he could have *survived* a much longer stay in "Yankee-dom." You can well imagine I am *thankful* to have him home once more. Now if we only had our darling Susie with us, [we] would be happy! But alas! [we] cannot always have our every wish gratified, and must endeavor to wait patiently a few months longer.

Only the last sheet of Alex Machette's "famous epistle" survives. In it, he reported that he was "perfectly satisfied now upon the subject of Baptism."

… I suppose, Susie, you have received Ma's last letter: what did you think of the *other* famous epistle? You may depend he received a *scorching* in reply. Sue, the whole town are talking about Alex becoming *a Baptist*. A great many, rather doubting the report, have asked us of its truth. It is on every tongue *and no wonder*.

Mr. Finley heard from him the other day and showed the letter to Mr. Hersman. Before he left here, [Alex] had several conversations with Mr. Finley on the subject, and Mr. Finley advised him just to remain quiet for a time, hoping that he might come to his senses again. But no indeed! He had no idea of listening to this really sensible piece of advice but must go and blaze it abroad, and *requests in Mr. Finley's letter to be dismissed from the Presbyterians altogether.*

Susie, now candidly, did you ever hear of such a fool in all your life?

Lizzie is at her father's. She has not condescended to let any of us hear from her since she left. I trust for her own sake she will write to Ma! [I] cannot imagine how she could ever forget what Ma has done for her and Lilian. She is as ungrateful a piece as ever lived I suppose. I really have no desire of meeting with her again. She told me before she left that she believed (judging from the way Ma took on over Alex's change) Ma thought one's soul's salvation depended on being "*sprinkled.*" Now don't you think that was a piece of impudence?

… Susie, Uncle Andrew starts to California next Monday. Are you not sorry to hear it? Poor fellow, he does not want to go at all. But prefers doing so to joining the army.[91] Ma is busy making him some calico shirts to take with him. Ma feels that she will be

91. In November 1863, black men, free or slave, were required to enlist in the Union army. By August 1864, approximately five regiments of black troops had been formed in Missouri, and many other blacks had left the state to avoid the draft; *War of the Rebellion*, series 3, 3:1034 and 4:577. See p. 7 on Andrew's escape from the draft.

almost broken up when Andrew leaves. Poor Ma, it does seem as if her portion was *trouble* in this world. I do everything in my power to cheer and comfort her! God only knows how much I wish I had something more than mere sympathy to give her....

Fulton, Missouri

From Cornelia Machette to her sister, Susan Machette

Dear Sister:

I received your dear letter the other day, was delighted to hear from you. I had come to the conclusion that you had forgotten me or thought my letter not worth answering. It was very simple I acknowledge, but the best I felt like doing. You don't *know* how badly I hate to write, Sue. It's worse than drinking a cup of *coffee* with *oil* in it — still I take a pleasure in writing to *you*, if you will *answer* them.

... You spoke of my going to Monticello next year.[92] I should like to very much, provided I would only have to pay 100 dollars. I commence reciting to Mr. Hersman this week; will study algebra, astronomy, Latin, and grammar: the grammar is something right new — he thinks it the best thing he ever saw. Don't you get very tired of teaching?

I [would] give any thing to see you in the schoolroom, to see how much dignity you have. How does your pet rabbit get on — be sure and bring it home with you. The boys went out the other day and caught a squirrel. We put it in your cage and forgot all about it till next evening when the boys got it out to shoot at. They gave it a mortal wound. Then when it went to run, Dudley got after it with a stick — and such fun they did have. At last they killed it and took it round to Lucinda to cook. We had it for supper. When brother Charley was [taking a] helping [of] it he said to Stonebraker — "well, Stonebraker, you beat this thing enough to make it soft," and it made me really sick; for I saw how they worried it to death.

... I'm thinking we'll have a little niece or nephew soon — take warning, Sue, and learn how not to brag what you're *not* or *are* going to do when you get married — see how *Abbie* has turned out. What do you guess it will be? *I* guess it a *boy*. All send their love. Aunt Lucinda says tell Miss Susie not to fall in love with some old widower and marry him up there....

Fulton, Missouri
April 30, 1864

From Margaret Bruin Machette to her daughter, Susan Machette

My dear daughter

How much I should love to have you home this evening. I feel quite lonely. Nealie is in town. She went in yesterday to attend Sally Davis's funeral. Sally died Wednesday evening. She died very suddenly. She was eating her supper and took a coughing spell which ruptured a blood vessel and she died in two minutes. She had been sinking for some time but was able to sit up the day she died. Nealie will not be home till tomorrow evening. Tomorrow is communion. Professor Fisher preached this

92. Monticello Seminary for young ladies in Godfrey, Illinois, opened in 1838.

morning. Mr. Hersman will preach tomorrow evening. Mr. Hersman heard while in town this morning that John Kerr was dying. He has been sick for a great while. Mollie is at home. They sent for her. Ed is in Tennessee. Poor Dolly will be a young widow.[93]

Mr. Hersman received a letter from Alex this morning. He is to preach for the Baptist church in Westport. I suppose Lizzie goes up next week. I received a letter from Lizzie on Tuesday. She says Lilian can stand alone and has one tooth. She thinks that Lilian will walk by the time she is nine months old....

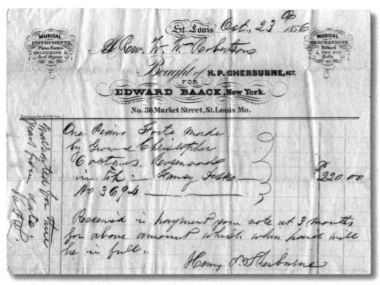

This 1856 receipt suggests that Margaret Machette's piano was bought by the Reverend William W. Robertson on her behalf.

You ask if the piano is in tune. It is not. I could not raise the money when the man was here in the winter. I hope some one will come along soon. I will try and have it done.

May 2. The weather continues very cold. My garden is very late. All that I have planted is up but the rabbits are taking my peas. I don't expect I shall raise one. Mr. Hersman preached last night. I walked in twice yesterday. John Kerr is to be buried at three o'clock this evening. Mr. Schenck preaches his funeral.[94]

Anna and Van Schenck joined the church yesterday morning. There was three children baptized at the same time — Mrs. Burdett's Jimmy, Mrs. Fisher's Laws, and Mrs. Wallace's little boy.[95]

... Abbie is very poorly, has not been able to sit up but very little for near a week. I don't know how soon she will be confined. I hope soon, though. She is so helpless. She is not half so stout as Lizzie was last summer.

Dear daughter, take good care of yourself. I hope the time will pass rapidly till you get home. Miss Mag Scott is still sick.[96] She has not been out all winter....

Written on a sheet of paper by Margaret Bruin Machette

Charles Finley Hersman born May 16th 1864

93. John and Edwin Kerr, physicians; sons of William Dabney and Susan Kerr. John's widow, Dolly Tate Kerr, later married William Marshall and died in childbirth in 1878.

94. Addison Van Court Schenck, former President of Lindenwood College and professor of metaphysics and sacred literature at Westminster from 1862 to 1864.

95. Anna and Van Schenck were probably the children of Addison Van Court, Schenck's brother. As a brakeman in 1883, Laws Fisher, son of Michael Montgomery and Anna Atwood Fisher, died after slipping between rail cars, severing both arms and one leg from the body. The Wallace boy was Addison Alexander, son of Joseph Wallace and his second wife, Jessamine.

96. Margaret "Mag" Scott died in August 1864 at the age of twenty-eight a few days after the death of her sister Lizzie Scott, who was thirty-four. See the December 10, 1863, letter on their school.

Westport, Missouri
June 3, 1864

*From Alexander Machette to his
sister, Susan Machette*

My Dear Sister.

    … Lizzie and I are pleasantly situated. We are boarding with a Mr. Shotwell who lives on Dr. Parker's place. The place is a very pleasant one — the yard full of trees and flowers. We have 2 rooms, a study and family room.

    Lizzie and I rode down to the cemetery last evening to see our dear little Lizzie's grave.[97] I intend marking it with a tombstone as soon as I can. We have myrtle, violet, and a white lily growing on the grave. Lizzie has not been well today. Lilian is well and fat as a little pig. She tries to talk and walk.

    I preach here regularly every Sabbath morning — and have 2 monthly Sabbath afternoon appointments in the country. I have good congregations here, about such as I had in Fulton. Have organized a Sabbath School since I came and superintend it myself. The Sabbath School numbers 70 and growing. Have also a fine Bible Class, composed of young ladies about your age.

    Have had a pretty hard time of it here on account of my Baptist views. My old friends here (Presbyterian) have nearly all turned against me, and do all they can (in the way of slander &c.) to injure me. But they are really doing themselves more injury than they do me. Of course, it is not strange that the people here should treat me thus, when my own nearest relatives disown me. These sad consequences were *anticipated* in some measure, so that I have not been wholly taken by surprise.

    I hope you will not treat this as Ma and Brother Charles Hersman have done my letters to them — that is, with silent contempt. I have no doubt you have heard some hard things against me. But you need not be afraid of me. I trust that I am not an Infidel, nor a Heathen, although I have rejected the Popish perversion of the Instrument of Baptism.

Fulton, Missouri
December 16, 1864

*From Cornelia Machette to her
sister, Susan Machette*

My *ever darling sister*

    It is with a feeling of extreme loneliness that I sit by my little table up in our room to night for the purpose of writing to you. It was my intention after supper to read or listen to Abbie read a novel called *Thaddeus of Warsaw,* so I hurried and got through with the dishes and just as we got ready here comes Brother from Harvey's room and instead of going to his own room flops himself down in a chair and commences reading *Great Truths of the Bible.*[98] Of course, Abbie insisted him reading it aloud, and sure enough he commenced. I got *mad,* returned the book to Mr. Scott and came off here to write you, dear Sue, feeling sure my letter would be welcome to you. Since you left I feel so very lonesome. I have no one to sympathize with me in my little troubles. Ma, you know, has enough of her own. Besides I can always confide in you better than any one else. Abbie, you know, is perfectly carried away with brother and the baby.…

---

97. Alex and Lizzie had a child, Lizzie, buried in Westport. See March 19, 1864.

98. *Thaddeus of Warsaw,* a popular novel (1803), written by the English novelist Jane Porter.

Dear Sue, we were more together the last year, and it was then I found out what a precious sister I had. It used to be that I loved Abbie the best (but that was only because I did not know you so well); indeed now, Sue, I love you next to Ma and *my God*. Although, dear Sue, I have always appeared so unconcerned on the subject of religion, still there has always been a longing to be better than I am, and had it not been for that fiend in human form (Alexander) I would have been a *Christian* but he the *gargoyle* opposed my joining the church on account of my youth. I believe now that if there ever was a true believer of God, I then was and hope before I am many years older to be again. Sue, you must always offer me up in your prayers, and then perhaps I one day may be a true sister in every sense of the word, as it is a great gulf separates us....

Saturday morning. I have just completed the laborious task of cleaning up *my* own *room*. I made up the bed, swept it from beginning to end, and you can imagine how nice it looks. It is a lovely morning, the sun is shining brightly, and it is as warm as a spring day. I have the window open and have just been listening to the church bell as it came swelling along on the air (quite poetic that sentence). It had a bad effect on me, for it made me feel so lonely. I was just thinking that if you only were here we would have such a nice walk to church, but as it is I do not like to go by my self.

There was a storm party one night this week.... *I of course* did not attend, though all the nice girls in town were there, had a very gay time I believe, as most of the boys were b—y.[99] Travis and Bill were and a good many more. I don't know whether the girls knew it or not. *I heard that.* It is not my intention to attend any of them for it sounds so common, and then it's not exactly the company I would like to be in. Ma would let me go if I wanted to.

Ella Reed plays on the melodeon for the Sabbath school and Mr. Baier helps her sing.[100] You know he has about as much music in his soul as my big toe has in the end of it. Miss Cox figures as largely as ever I believe. I think she is the greatest little *squirt* (as Jennie said about her brother) I ever saw. Reminds me of one of these frisky little pests, for instance. Mr. Tuttle wanted you to play, but we told him you were gone.

Sue, you may thank *your stars* that you got off when you did for if you had have stayed you would have blown away by this time. Every thing is so awful dry here, gets more so every day of the world I verily believe. But never the less I intend to try [to] keep body and soul together until next year. Then I expect to be *liberated* by going to the *land of Liberty*, and dwell in Love's establishment while there;[101] next time you write tell me all about your school, how you like it, and so on. Sue, you must get Jennie to write for you some, for it will be so trying on your eyes. I am sure she will do it. You know she is so sweet....[102]

Sue, I have just come from down stairs. I've got a letter from dear brother Sam. Poor fellow, his wife and child is dead. He had them with him when he wrote, bringing them to be buried at home....

99. The word is indecipherable. It might mean "intoxicated."

100. Ella Reed, daughter of Preston B. and Mary Tate Reed. Leo Baier graduated from Westminster in 1866; later became president of St. John's College in Little Rock, Arkansas.

101. A pun on the school where Sue Machette was teaching. Clay Seminary in Liberty, Missouri, was run by James and Lucy Love. In James Love's recollections, published in the March 17, 1914, *Fulton Gazette*, he was a teacher in Fulton in the 1840s when he was shot by the father of Nathan Kouns for whipping his son. Defended by John Jameson, Dr. Kouns was found guilty, but the governor remitted his fine. See November 15, 1860, on Bled McKinney Kouns' death.

102. Jennie Wilson, sister of Ella Wilson, was teaching at Clay Seminary with Sue Machette.

Abbie has just been up trying to get me to wait on the table, but I won't do it. She is always poking it off on me.... All send their love.

Samuel Machette, stepson of Margaret Bruin Machette, his wife, Susan Jarboe Machette, and their oldest son, Charles. Susan and their youngest child died in December 1864.

Fulton, Missouri
Sabbath evening

From Abigail Machette Hersman
to her sister, Susan Machette

My dear Susie:

... Oh, Susie, it is such a cold *cold* day! I am sure if you were here [you] would almost freeze. Today the boys did not attend church, so while they were at dinner Ma and I went round to clean the rooms, not having had any other opportunity, you know. Ma went in to Harvey's room — I in to Trave's. I did not find the room quite as untidy as usual (so I at first thought) but on looking down at the side of the bed some one had spit any quantity of nasty spit (oh, I can't tell you how *provoked* I felt). I could do nothing more than give utterance to some such expression as these — "the nasty, dirty creatures," &c. I hurried and swept the floor and proceeded to make the bed, when lo and behold! it had an occupant!!! You can well imagine my consternation upon making this discovery. Of course all that I had said had been heard.

I went back to my room then, and took a peep to see who could be absent. And who do you think it was, Susie? No other than "Big Bill." Ma went in and asked him what was the matter. He said that his throat was sore again. I think he is the greatest "take on" I ever knew. Susie, I do hope to goodness they will all leave Christmas. I despise them all....

Nealie has Finley and is insisting on my taking him, so I will be obliged to close....

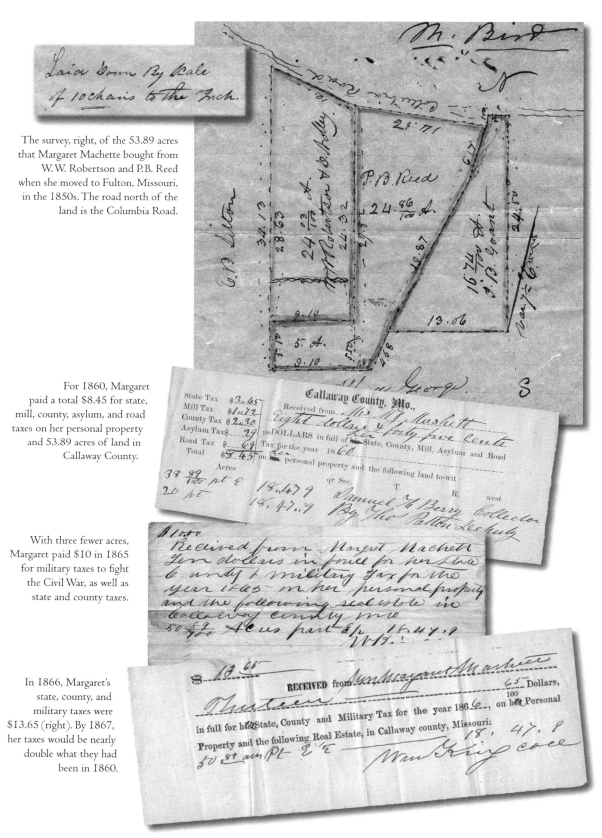

The survey, right, of the 53.89 acres that Margaret Machette bought from W.W. Robertson and P.B. Reed when she moved to Fulton, Missouri, in the 1850s. The road north of the land is the Columbia Road.

For 1860, Margaret paid a total $8.45 for state, mill, county, asylum, and road taxes on her personal property and 53.89 acres of land in Callaway County.

With three fewer acres, Margaret paid $10 in 1865 for military taxes to fight the Civil War, as well as state and county taxes.

In 1866, Margaret's state, county, and military taxes were $13.65 (right). By 1867, her taxes would be nearly double what they had been in 1860.

Fulton, Missouri
December 29, 1864

*From Margaret Bruin Machette
to her daughter, Susan Machette*

Dear Susie

… There has been no mail for near a week before on account of the ice in the river. We were very sorry you have not received any letters from home. Nelia has written three letters to you and I think Abbie has once. We are all well and alone. The boys went home on last Friday. Mr. Hersman would have gone but was not very well, and I was not sorry for it is so lonesome without some man about the house. It is a very dull Christmas for us. I don't hear of any thing going on in town. Mr. Hersman bought two turkeys. We had one on Christmas day. Mr. Brooks and Mrs. Brooks and the girls came over after church and ate dinner with us.…

Nelia and Abbie are learning to cook. They take it [all] day about. Abbie got dinner today. She roasted a turkey. It was very well done. Nelia makes splendid light rolls. If I was to leave home they could get along very well without me. Well, I had to stop just here to eat a turnip — wish you had one. Mr. Hersman is repairing fence. He has hauled the chip pile out on the garden. He intends having a good garden next year if he lives [here]. Little Finley is sitting on his pallet eating an apple. He has six teeth and is as great a romp as ever or more so. He will play till he gets sleepy and go to sleep on his pallet. I don't know what we should do without him.

Susie, if you were at home you would be very lonesome. There has not been any one out from town since you left. About two weeks ago Tuttle saw Mr. Hersman and told him to ask Miss Sue to please come in and play for them on the melodeon, that Ella Reed had been playing but she did not play with expression enough. He was very much surprised when your brother told him you was in Liberty. The Sabbath school has bought Schenck's melodeon, gave one hundred dollars for it.

Mrs. Burdett has moved out to Mrs. Young's place so I shall not get to visit her.[103] The last we heard of Mrs. George her health was much worse than when she lived here. Ann was in Denver City teaching.

Susie, I wrote to Mr. Watson for three hundred and fifty dollars [and] have lifted my note that Hook had and will pay Tucker the thirty I borrowed for you. I will give you my note for all I owe you with a mortgage on the land.[104] I paid my taxes. There is a military tax of three dollars levied on your head.[105] What do you think of that — every man and woman over eighteen and under forty-five have to pay. I will pay it this week for you.

Neither of the Bufords will return to school.[106] Christman will, I suppose, as he left his trunk. Have you heard anything from Alex or Lizzie?…

We have twelve beautiful little pigs. Mr. Hersman has them fastened up in the shed. I don't know which occupies his time most — the pigs or Finley. We all talk about you every evening and wonder what Susie is doing. I am so thankful your health is good. If [I] could know that you was well, I could bear your absence better.…

---

103. Perhaps Ann Young, widow of Judge Benjamin Young. The Youngs, Georges, and Burdetts apparently were related.

104. Probably Samuel Watson, Zadok Hook, and Daniel or James Tucker, prominent businessmen in Fulton.

105. The military tax was created to pay for the troops Abraham Lincoln ordered in July 1864. The Ninth District, where Callaway County was located, was expected to furnish and support almost three thousand troops. *Fulton Telegraph* (July 29, 1864).

106. The Bufords were probably Travis and Bill. See December 16, 1864.

I received a letter from Mag [Rice] a few days ago. Little Malin was very sick with lung fever....

From Margaret Bruin Machette to her daughter, Susan Machette

Fulton, Missouri
January 1, 1865

My Dear Susie:

I wish you a happy New Year. I should love so much to see you this morning. Abbie and I are here all alone. Mr. Hersman is at his Mother's, and Nelia is at church, went by herself, will stay all night, and take her singing lesson in the morning before she comes home. I went out to see old Mrs. Bailey with Mrs. Brooks yesterday afternoon. The old lady is very sick. She has broken very much since I was there before.[107]

... I told you in my other letter that you was taxed three dollars. It is a mistake. Your brother misunderstood Mr. Brooks. It is I that is taxed the three dollars military.

Wednesday 4th.... Mr. Hersman got home last night.... Harvey and Joe will be home Saturday.[108] Mollie Kellogg was at Harvey's Father's spending Christmas. She is at Hunstville teaching music. Little Finley has been quite sick for two or three days but is better this evening.

... You asked something about the college. I can't tell. It's very doubtful about its going on even the next five months. Your brother [Charley] has written to some friend near the school he was talking about but has not received an answer yet. If he can't get that school, I don't know what he will do....

From Cornelia Machette to her sister, Susan Machette

Fulton, Missouri

Dearest Sue:

... Now, Sue, just the blank idea of your saying that you are always cross and crabbiest when at home is ridiculous; if it is so with either of us, I claim it as being me. I know I am bad and spoilt, but then remember I am the *"baby"*....

Every thing is getting along finely from the "bird" up. Oh, Sue, I have become a splendid cook — get every supper all by my self, and "Abbie" gets dinner and "Ma" breakfast. So you can see we have it *nicely* arranged — takes a greatest off of "Ma's" hands.... Have only "Joe" and "Harve" to cook for. I have been nearly distracted to

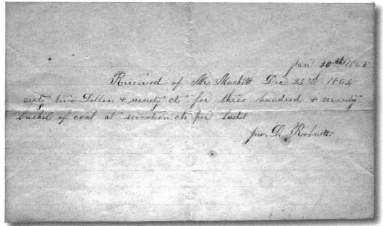

John D. Robnett sold Margaret Machette 370 bushels of coal at 17 cents a bushel.

107. Frances Bailey died later in 1865.
108. Harvey and Joe Scott were brothers.

have you here to help me enjoy *Pickwick Papers*; it is the funniest thing I *ever* read; they are *more* than they are cracked up to be.[109] If you possibly can, get them, for you and "Jennie" would have your own *fun*.

Sue,...I had a very nice "Christmas" take it all together, went to only one party. While there, [I] was talking to Mr. Sheley on the inexhaustible subject of novels, much expressed a wish to read *The Planter's Northern Bride*.[110] In two or three days after, here brother came with it saying Mr. Sheley sent it to me to read. I of course was very thankful and felt fully repaid for the *tedious* talk I had with him.

... I got a letter from "Andrew" the other day. He wrote so badly I could not make it out, except something about you being such a *pretty lady* &c.[111] Adieu, dearest sister.

Clay Seminary
Liberty, Missouri
January 16, 1865

From Susan Machette to her sister, Cornelia Machette

Dear Nealie:

I received a [letter] from brother Sam the other day. He...sent me a photograph of his wife: it was taken from one of hers taken soon after they were married. He said he would like to come and see me but that [he] would start for Nebraska City the next [day] (the 11th) and thence to the plains. Sam said he would like to have my picture. Jennie and [I] went down town Saturday and had our physiognomy taken. I will send mine to Brother. I do not think it is very good but Jennie does.

Since I wrote the above, Jennie went to visit one of her friends in town. When she returned she said she had such a good joke to tell me. She asked me if I didn't remember that fellow in the picture gallery — said fellow was a pert chap who waited on us. He was dressed pretty in uniform but we supposed that was a fancy of his. His part of the business was to fix our heads and adjust our drapery. Well, as I was going on to say, Jennie said her friend was telling that a certain accomplished friend of hers — a Lieutenant somebody — was up in the gallery when two young ladies called to have their pictures taken, and he whispered to the artist to let him wait on them. Of *course* we knew who the ladies were....

Jennie, you know, has such a faculty for getting into scrapes — and is so artless as to tell them, but we have a joke that really plagues her — that she doesn't allow me to tell, but I will tell you if you promise secrecy. You know in phrenology they speak of the different organs.[112] Well it seems Jennie had never spoken of them in that way. She was down in Mr. Love's study one night and was begging him for a lock of his hair. He asked her what organ she preferred it off of. Jennie looked disgusted and said, "off

---

109. *The Pickwick Papers* (1837), Charles Dickens's novel.

110. *The Planter's Northern Bride*, an anti-abolitionist novel (1854) written by Carolina Lee Hentz as an answer to *Uncle Tom's Cabin*.

111. See October 29, 1863, and April 18, 1864, on Andrew. Andrew was apparently successful in escaping conscription in the federal army. Although the 1847 Missouri Constitution forbade teaching blacks to read and write, free blacks and even some slaves acquired literacy. McCandless, *History of Missouri*, 2:196. Parrish, *History of Missouri*, 3:145.

112. Phrenology, the study of examining the contour and "organs" on the skull in order to determine a person's emotions and intellect, was developed in the early nineteenth century.

your head, of *course.*" It happened that same evening that Jennie and I were sitting by the fire — talking — I told her I believed in phrenology and was speaking of the different organs — when suddenly she clapped hands and threw back her head and gave other evidences of having the hysterics. She 'fessed up and we laughed at it a good deal.

Nelia, are you taking piano music lessons or singing from Miss Lou?... Tell Miss Lou I am going to take singing lessons next summer. Saturday I got me 4 yards of cotton to make me drawers, 40 cents a yard.

Mr. Love is such a good man. He told Jennie the other day that he was going to Kansas City and that he was going to take me to Westport. Not that I want to go but the intentions are all the same. I declare I don't know what I shall do. I don't want to tell him I don't want to go to see my brother. I would a sight rather see Sam....

From Cornelia Machette to her sister, Susan Machette

Fulton, Missouri
February 2, 1865

My dearest sister:

... You remember my speaking of the exhibition we were going to have given by Mr. Miller's school and the boys. Well, "Sue," I would have given anything I possess if you could only have been here. It would have done for you to laugh at for years. The girls all looked beautiful. That part did very well, but horror of horrors! *the music,* it was enough to make one's blood run cold and make their hair stand on ends....

Ella played for the first piece, "Smith's grand march," and Mollie Kerr played — perhaps you have heard it — "*The storm.*" I never heard it before — such rumbling, crashing, and banging no mortal ears ever heard gush forth before, and it was really amusing to see how the people were pleased. They would commence cheering almost before the piece was half finished. Well, now for a description of the "boys" — they got Ella and the girls to play for them, and I can assure you that "Ella" *immortalized* herself. Just let me tell you, two of the pieces she played and you will not doubt it — *she attempted* "Leap for life...."[113] It reminded me of a bull bellowing — do not let this comparison shock your sensitive nerves. And the other was "Fanfare melody." *Now she did play this splendidly.* Well, she struck every key she ought not to have done and banged and flourished to some purpose, you may depend, [and] would have to stop to get her breath at times. Still the instrument would keep up its grumbling — poor thing, I guess its heart strings were almost broken....

The boys [of the Westminster literary societies] acquitted them selves with honor. Every one agrees that the Philologics beat the other side badly, even the Philalethians own it.[114] I had a delightful time both nights; the first night I went with Mr. Scott, the next with brother and Abbie.

I went to a party the other night. It was at Mrs. Tucker's. I was invited by Miss Jennie Watson. It was given for her. The company with a few exceptions was very select. I

113. Ella, probably Ella Reed; see December 16, 1864. Thomas J. Martin wrote the musical score for "Smith's March" (1861) to honor General Persifor F. Smith, who fought in the Mexican War. John Hullah wrote the musical score, "The Storm" (c. 1860). Henry Russell composed "A Leap for Life" (1845).

114. Members of the Philologic Literary Society included Harvey Scott and Leo Baier. Members of the Philalethian Literary Society included William Carr Dyer, James Snell, and Van Schenck.

became acquainted with a good many of the boys, Mr. Flood among the rest.[115] Oh! Sue, they had such a charming supper, all kinds of cakes and candies and oysters and crackers and apples and ice cream &c., &c. — oh so much that I cannot enumerate it all. Joe went with me there. We had a long walk but were amply repaid for our trouble. There was snow on the ground — while [we] were there it rained a little so when we came home it was very slippery and coming down the hill I fell flat on my back. Joe commenced laughing and it made me so mad.[116]

By the by, Sue, I must tell you that the college came very near suspending Joe, and Harve went home, but they might have stayed for it is going to begin again Monday. Brother [Charley] resigned on account of the oath they had to take.[117] So has Schenck — the professors now are Messrs. Montgomery, Fisher, and Scott. Mr. Scott will be here Saturday, I believe.

… You asked me if I was taking Latin lessons. I am but as "Ma" will have only one boarder [I] will stop I guess and will not care much for I never wanted to take Latin lessons, but gave all manner of hints to take on some instrument but of no avail…. They all send a kiss and love to you and Jennie — write very soon.

Probably a parody on the literary societies mentioned in Nealie Machette's letter above, the Ninth Annual Bender of the Swell-Heads featured John Flood, who debated the question, "Does the rat with the shortest tail get in the hole first."

115. John Flood, brother of Noah Flood, graduated from Westminster College in 1863 and became a Fulton attorney.

116. The following year, Virginia "Jennie" Watson, daughter of Samuel and Martha Watson, married Newton Hockensmith, the student who had tuberculosis; see November 14, 1863. Mrs. Tucker, possibly Elizabeth Tucker, wife of Daniel Tucker. Joe Scott, brother of Harvey Scott.

117. As of July 4, 1865, Missourians were expected to take the Iron-Clad Oath that they were loyal to the United States and had not aided or supported the Confederate States. Those who refused to take the oath could not teach (see p. 22).

From Cornelia Machette to her sister, Susan Machette

Fulton, Missouri
February 12, 1865

Dearest Sister:

... Mr. Scott came the other day. Brother went back on his horse.... If they conclude to go [to Monroe County], I think I shall "go up the spout," for Finley is the sweetest child I ever saw, not one bit of trouble — quite a *recommendation*, you know.... I am going to make me such a pretty shuck hat next week. They are worn a great deal here, are just the shape of the boys' "caps." Kate Robnett and I are going to make ours together.[118]

Mrs. George I hear is very much pleased with her new home, says she can wash all day and then go visiting all evening so you see her health is improving very much. The Indians wanted to buy Ann. If I was her I would be afraid they might *steal* me. She has a great many beaus out there. Mrs. George says she doesn't have to buy any meat as Ann's beaus go hunting and supply her with it. They say the climate is delightful. Don't you wish we were out there? I think just such a life as that would be so pleasant. Mrs. George has laid her claim for three hundred and fifty acres and the family has done the same. If land goes up they one day may be quite wealthy. That would seem strange, wouldn't it?

Law, Sue, I wish you could get out of going to see Alex. I don't want them to think we love them so much....

From Margaret Bruin Machette to her daughter, Susan Machette

Fulton, Missouri
February 28, 1865

Dearest daughter

... You had better come by the river if you can as you have to travel alone, though I am not able to advise in the matter. I wish you could have company either way. If there was some one going to St. Louis that you could travel with to Mexico or St. Aubert[119] — it would be better than traveling alone.

Abbie received a letter from Mr. Hersman. He is not coming back to Fulton. He is going to farming with his brother George and preach to their church. He is coming for Abbie this week perhaps, and she is coming back to spend next summer with us. I can't well do without you at home now that Abbie will be away.

Mr. P.B. Reed died yesterday morning with Erysipelas.[120] His funeral will be preached at two o'clock this evening at the church.

You must exercise your own judgment in regard to coming home. If the roads were passable, I would try and send for you. If you lack means to come home on, write and let me know....

118. Louisa Katherine "Kate" Robnett, daughter of James and Sarah Ann Robnett. See December 10, 1863.

119. Both Mexico and St. Aubert had railway stations. The *Missouri State Gazetteer* for 1860 noted that Fulton was fifteen miles from St. Aubert on the Missouri Pacific Railway. The 1893–1894 *Missouri Gazetteer* (St. Louis: R.L. Polk, 1893), stated that St. Aubert, renamed Mokane, was the location of a new branch of the Missouri, Kansas, and Texas Railway, known informally at the K-T or "Katy Railroad."

120. Preston B. Reed, Fulton attorney and trustee of Westminster, sold land to Margaret Machette when she moved to Fulton. Erysipelas is a skin disease. See December 16, 1864, on his daughter Ella Reed.

Fulton, Missouri
March 12, 1865

*From Margaret Bruin Machette
to her daughter, Susan Machette*

Dear Susie

… Abbie and Mr. Hersman are here. He returns to Monroe this week, will leave Abbie till the roads get so they can come with a wagon for her.[121] I shall be lonely but can do very well. There will be none but Nelia and Mr. Scott with me, but then I won't have much to do. I want you to use your own pleasure about staying or coming. If you can stand teaching till the term is out, do so. If not, come home. Do nothing to injure your eyes.

I went to church this morning. It was communion. Mr. Robertson preached a very good sermon. The meeting will continue. You spoke [of] going to Kansas City. I wish you would go and see Alex. I want to hear from him. When you are in the city, you ought to go and see Sam's little boys.…

Fulton, Missouri
March 26, 1865

*From Margaret Bruin Machette
and Abigail Machette Hersman
to Susan Machette*

Dear daughter

… We have been enjoying a very precious revival in our church. I believe I mentioned in my last letter that there was a meeting in progress. It closes to night. Mr. Robertson has preached every night except two. Doctor Montgomery always made appropriate remarks afterwards.[122] I don't know how many have professed religion. There was about eighteen [who] joined the Presbyterian Church and doubtless there is some that will join other churches. Nelia was one of the first that joined. She was in great trouble for several days but now rejoices. She stayed with Mrs. Allen and Miss Lou Atwood during the meeting as it was too far to walk twice a day. There was prayer meeting at four and in the evening. I have great reason to be thankful that my dear daughters are Christian women, have chosen Christ in their youth. If I have trouble, I have joys far greater.…

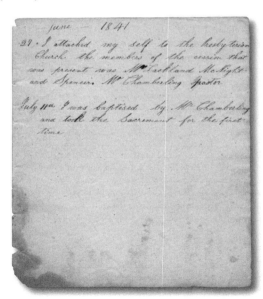

Margaret Machette, a wife and mother of three children, joined the Presbyterian church in 1841 and was baptized and received her first communion the same year. The church was to play an important role in her family's life.

121. Charley Hersman's family lived in Monroe County.

122. John Montgomery, minister and acting president of Westminster College in 1864.

Before Mr. Hersman left he hired a black woman to stay with me. She appears to be a very good woman She has three children. He pays her thirty dollars a year. She clothes herself and children.

… Give my love to Jennie and accept a heart full for your self from your own Mother.

Sabbath evening. My dearest Sister:

How we should love to see our darling Susie this evening! But the time, I trust, will not *seem* long ere we are once more united. Ah! Susie, is it not a glorious thought that there is a time — there is a place where these sad separations are never known. And, dearest Sister, how should we pray that our names may be at last numbered with those redeemed ones who are ever to rejoice in the sunshine of his glorious presence.

Susie, I have been waiting, thinking to have the pleasure of sending our photographs, but alas! as I often am, was doomed to be disappointed. Yesterday week (Saturday) Charley took Finley and I in to have our pictures taken, but Manchester would not take mine on account of my dress being too light.[123] He was willing to try Finley's, however, and we accordingly placed the little fellow in a high chair. The very first trial was a success. Just as soon as it is finished I will send you one. Am making me a new dress now and intend having mine taken as soon as Charley returns from Monroe. I cannot say when he will get back exactly — perhaps the last of this week. Poor fellow! He is now reduced to the necessity of making his living by the sweat of his brow. But I should not complain, for very, *very* much have we to be thankful....

Your loving Sister, Abbie

From Susan Machette to her mother, Margaret Bruin Machette

Clay Seminary
Liberty, Missouri
April 1865

Dearest Ma:

… You don't know what anticipation Jennie and I have of summer. It is our constant theme. If either of us gets vexed or put out [in] any way, which is not infrequently the case, the magic words "next July" put all care to flight.

You don't know what fine plans Jennie and I have. I would have told you before but I was afraid some how that she would get wind of it. I would not tell it now, as it seems a betrayal of confidence, but some of my plans enter into hers, and I will tell knowing that it will go no further. Well, Jennie proposes to step off the carpet next Fall. Her intended is a perfect gentleman — a Virginian and is wealthy — young and handsome. When he was out to see Jennie a month ago, I became acquainted with him. That was where my picture was. Jennie is always telling him something about me and he always sends me some message. My picture being unusually good as she thought, I gave it to her and she sent it to him. He returned it when he was here. He sent me his picture in his last letter to Jennie.

He sent me word that I must certainly accompany them on their bridal tour and as Jennie says I must, too, I intend to if I can. Dear Ma, to slight such a chance would be flying right in the face of providence. I'd not have such another in a life time. Jennie

123. Erastus T. Manchester, Fulton photographer.

says it's etiquette for the bride groom to bear all the expense so I will only be at the expense of getting a wardrobe. He sent me word that he considered me mortgaged property for he gave me his brother.

Jennie and I expect to have such a glorious time coming home. Her beau is coming out with a half dozen or so of his friends to invest in land, about the time school is out, and he will go home with us.

I sent a check down to Ella Wilson the other day to get my summer clothes. She is going to get Jennie's and she will send them up at the same time. I only sent for some kind of summer wrapping, a plain hat, a lawn dress — a traveling and Victoria lawn [dress], the latter because I am obliged to have some thing to wear under my thin white dress, and I thought I would get a skirt that I could wear as a dress. I would be so glad if some one would be passing so that you could send me my linen chemise up, for I shall need it very much, as the examination lasts two weeks and I have but two whole ones now. They wash with a machine here, and it is so hard on the clothes.

Dear Ma, what a comfort it is to you, as it is to all of us, that dear little Nealie has chosen the better part — how much pain and suffering there is here — how all earthly pleasures turn to bitterness when we possess them. And how blessed the hope that though we struggle along, not even blessed with each other's society, there we will be one day united in our father's home above. I suppose every one experiences disappointment here. In youth we are so hopeful and carried away with visions of the future. When sober reality comes how enervating the reaction. But we must learn it some time, and it is better in youth when we have strength to bear it....

There are a good many bushwhackers in the county already and some are anticipating a great deal of trouble and others think it will go farther north.[124] I hope so, I am sure....

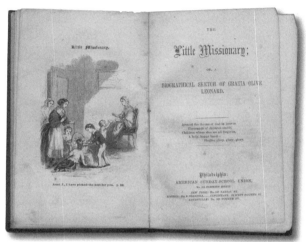

The Little Missionary, published in 1855, was a children's book belonging to the Machette family.

Fulton, Missouri

From Cornelia Machette to her sister, Susan Machette

Dear Susie:

... I am so glad you have such a fair opportunity [of] visiting "Virginia." Be sure and take advantage of it. Shan't talk, though Jennie's secret *is no secret*. I was in town and saw Mrs. Buchanan, and she related it all from beginning to — I was going to say end but she knew not when they were to be married.[125] She asked me if you had never said

124. The *Liberty Tribune* for April 7, 1865, reported on a skirmish between bushwhackers and citizens in Clay County. On May 19, 1865, the *Tribune* reported that Liberty citizens resolved to offer a thousand dollars "for the apprehension and delivery, dead or alive" of bushwhackers. The resolution was signed by James Love, secretary. See Richard S. Brownlee, *Gray Ghosts of the Confederacy: Guerrilla Warfare in the West, 1861–1865* (Baton Rouge: Louisiana State University Press, 1958), 233.

125. Martha Warren Buchanan, wife of William Buchanan and sister of Licking Grant's first and second wives. Jennie Wilson's maternal grandmother, Letitia Warren Grant, was a fourth sister.

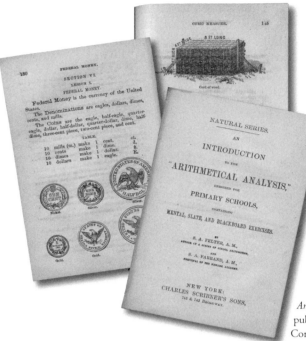

any thing about it. I of *course* was in blissful ignorance or *pretended* to be so. I believe her intended passed through on his way to Liberty.

You cannot imagine how very busy I am now — am taking instrumental lessons of "Miss Lou" and reciting arithmetic and algebra to "Harvey" — get along fairly so far — "Oh I wish I was smart" —

The union folks have a grand time here — illuminate about every night. Sue, I hope you are as strong a S[outherner] as ever. I for my part am stronger — my motto is "Take up for the weaker party," so even if I were Union, fear I should turn....

An Introduction to the "Arithmetical Analysis," published in 1863, shows the kind of lessons Cornelia may have had in arithmetic and algebra.

From Margaret Bruin Machette to her daughter, Susan Machette

Fulton, Missouri
April 12, 1865

Dear Susie

... There has been more rain this spring than for three years before. I have had to turn off the spouts to keep the wells from running over some ten days ago and still it rains. I have made no garden yet. We will have plenty [of] peaches if they don't get killed with frost. The trees are very full of bloom. I have rented the field to Mr. Brooks and Mr. James. I hope it will be a good crop year so that I may have plenty to feed the cows through another winter. The poor things look so starved this spring. The white cow has a calf and I hope we will soon have plenty of milk and butter. Mr. Hersman has not come for Abbie yet. The roads are so bad that he can't travel.

The good people of Fulton have had a good time rejoicing over the taking of Richmond and the surrender of Lee and his army. This night [a] week ago the town was illuminated and there was several speeches. Old Ansell made a speech in which he said he wished the confederacy was in *Hell* or something to that amount.[126] Doctor Montgomery followed in a speech and said that he endorsed all that Ansell said. Pretty well for a Presbyterian preacher, don't you think?

Nelia is practicing very well, and she commences reciting arithmetic and algebra to Mr. Scott this evening. I hope she will study hard.

Dear Susie, I count the weeks till you get home. Do you still expect your Brother [Sam] to come home with you? We all wish to see him very much. I should like to see

126. Thomas Ansell, who immigrated to Callaway County from England in 1828, was mayor of Fulton in 1865.

his little boys very much indeed. I hope you won't be disappointed in your anticipated pleasures next summer. I will try and finish your shimmies and send it to you. . . .

Kansas City, Missouri
Sunday

From Alexander Machette to his sister, Susan Machette

Dear Sister Susie:

... I have a special request to make of you — and that is that you will spend your next summer *vacation* with us. Lizzie and I would be exceedingly happy to have you with us. If you cannot spend the whole vacation, you can, at least, spend a portion. Can you not come over before that time and make us a little visit? We are keeping house now to ourselves and will be greatly slighted if you do not arrange it so as to spend some time with us.

Lizzie has not been quite well for a few days past, but is able to do all her house-work. Our dear little Lilian is fat as a pig, and I know you would think her *very sweet* — at least, *we* do. . . .

Perhaps you are wondering how it is that my letter is dated "Kansas City." I will explain — Brother Fuller (Pastor of the Church here) is absent for some few weeks, and arrangement has been made for me to preach for him on Sabbath night in his absence.[127] I preached in Westport on yesterday (Saturday) morning; also, as usual, this morning, and tonight here in Kansas City.

A very deep feeling exists in the minds of the people here on account of the infamous crime perpetuated at Washington.[128] Well may we ask, what are we coming to? Our only hope is found in that declaration of the Psalmist "The Lord reigneth"![129]

... Let me hear all the news from Fulton and from Home. . . . God bless you and watch over you is the prayer of your affectionate Brother

A Machette.

Fulton, Missouri
April 27, 1865

From Margaret Bruin Machette and Cornelia Machette to Susan Machette

My very Dear Susie

... I am happy that you receive letters from your brothers. Be punctual to answer them. Did Alex say any thing about visiting home this spring? Where is he living now?

I am very busy making garden. There has been so much rain this spring that I am very late. I planted all day yesterday and will again this evening. I have onions, peas, beans, beets, parsnips, potatoes, cucumbers, and melons planted. My tomatoes and sweet potatoes are ready to set out. I want to have something to eat when you get home. I have thirty-six little chickens. If they live they will be large enough to fry when you come home. You say you think so much about home folks — not any more than we do about you [for] sure. Finley's pictures are not finished. Abbie will send yours as

127. Jonathan Fuller, Baptist minister.
128. Abraham Lincoln was assassinated on April 15.
129. "The LORD reigneth" is used in Psalms 93, 96, 97, and 99.

soon as [they are] done. When you go to Kansas City, you must go to see Alex and Lizzie.... Give my love to Jennie and accept a heart full for your self from

your Mother.

Dearest Sister,

... Had you heard that Noah Flood was married?[130] They say it is so. I did not hear any of the *particulars*. Sue, I hope you will excuse this dreadfully written [letter] for the clock is just striking 12 — and I have one hour to eat my dinner, finish this letter, and walk in to take my lesson. By the way, speaking of taking my lesson reminds me that [I] have not told you about Miss Lou's visit to us the other day. She came and all the children.[131] How I wish you could have been here. We had a delightful dinner, all kinds of vegetables and very nice dessert.

... Sue, you must not tell Brother Samuel any thing about me, only that I am horrid ugly and have about half sense — now I am in earnest — I am terribly tanned and sun burnt, and you know when you get so in the spring you get over it only by the next winter. Give my love to him and a kiss, and tell him for me that he will find nothing but a cross, high tempered little sister in me — that I have all the temper of both families except the very small portion that he and you share....

from your devoted Sister
Nealie

From Elizabeth Shelton Machette to her sister-in-law, Susan Machette

Westport, Missouri
April 29, 1865

Dear Sister Susie:

Your long, interesting and much appreciated letter was received a few days since, and I do not now attempt a reply, for as the letter was to your Brother, I will leave that for him to do, but simply write to let you know that I have prepared a small box for you.... There is nothing very tempting in the box, but still I hope you will derive a little satisfaction from it.

How I wish you could be with us at meal times, when I have *something real good*. I thought of you to night as we sat down to a table supplied as follows: Nice Java coffee, "chopped beef," fresh fish and hot light rolls with the delicious home made butter, "maple syrup" and nice cold milk. I wish I could send along a plate of my butter and a pitcher of cream and some good hot coffee. But you must come and see me soon, and I hope I may be fortunate enough to have something good when you come.... We are more comfortably fixed than ever before, by the kindness of our friends. I had a fine cow presented me when I went to housekeeping, which furnishes us with all our milk and butter and 95 cents worth [of] butter for market every week.

Susie, I want you to see Lilian so much. She is so very interesting to us that I imagine she would be to you, or any one. I some times wish her Grand Ma Machette could see her. She can say "Aunt Susie," "Aunt Abbie," "Aunt Nelia," and "Grand Ma Machette" quite plain. She knows Abbie's and Nelia's pictures and Ma's the very moment she sees them. She says almost every thing. I would love so much to have Abbie's and the baby's

130. Noah Flood married Mary Moss in 1865; she died of tuberculosis in 1869.
131. Lou Atwood was taking care of the children of her deceased sister Anna Fisher.

pictures. I want to see the baby so very badly. I must have yours and Nealie's photographs. I am going to have one taken from Ma's ambrotype and I want you to beg Abbie to give me hers.[132] I have Charley's and have a space opposite left for hers.

O Susie, I sometimes feel like you all do not care any thing for us at all any more — and you do not know how it hurts me at times. For awhile I will get over those feelings and feel quite indifferent — and then again I feel like I can't stand it at all. But I trust that we may "all see eye to eye" and "know as we are known," "when that great and notable day of the Lord shall come."[133] I am so rejoiced to hear of Nealie making her public profession of faith in Christ. I do truly trust it is a saving faith she professes, for I had thought some time ago that Nealie felt some interest on the subject of religion. My love to her and all at home when you write....

This unidentified girl is one of Alex and Lizzie Machette's six daughters.

Fulton, Missouri
April 30, 1865

From Margaret Bruin Machette to her daughter, Susan Machette

Dear Susie

... You asked something about the college. It is still in existence, but I doubt if it continues longer than this term. They are not able to pay the professors, and Doctor Montgomery says he won't stay, and Fisher intends to leave for Europe this fall — that is, if he can. Mr. P.B. Reed's estate won't pay 25 cents on the dollar that he owes and he owes the college 25 hundred dollars, the very money that ought to have been paid the teachers. There is Lyle and Mr. Finley that have not received their money yet, and they still owe Mr. Hersman a hundred dollars.[134] I tell you there never was a more rascally set of men than the Fulton men....

Fulton, Missouri
Sabbath evening

From Cornelia Machette to her sister, Susan Machette

Sweet Sister:

You cannot imagine how very lonely I feel this beautiful evening. Dear Abbie and sweet darling little Finley have left. They went on the cars — left Friday. When you

132. Ambrotype, an early kind of photography with the negative on glass.

133. Isaiah 52:8: "Thy watchmen shall lift up the voice; with the voice together shall they sing: for they shall see eye to eye, when the Lord shall bring again Zion." I Corinthians 13:12: "For now we see through a glass, darkly; but then face to face: now I know in part; but then shall I know even as also I am known." Acts 2:20: "The sun shall be turned into darkness, and the moon into blood, before that great and notable day of the Lord come."

134. After Reed's death, his family moved to Pleasant Hill, Missouri. His daughter Ella married James Duncan there in 1870. John Newton Lyle, Westminster professor of mathematics and natural science.

Cornelia Machette, the youngest
of Margaret Bruin Machette's children

think for a moment you will not wonder at my loneliness. I am separated from both of my dear sisters and have no young companions to cheer my lonely house. I have, it is *true*, no *right* to *complain* — have all the blessings I could desire with the exception of being separated from you. Sue, *dear* Sue, you have no idea how wicked I am. Instead of getting better, I seem to get worse. Sometimes I attempt to examine my self, but it only discourages me. I have such an evil temper it is my constant dread. I pray for power to control it and hope by waiting patiently my prayer will be answered. Susie, you too must pray for me but enough of this strain....

I have concluded for a change [I] will wear a bonnet — will have your hair bonnet fixed. You, of course, will not care as it is too old to do you any good. I will have it by next Sabbath and expect to feel like a scared rabbit. It will be trimmed in the ribbon I had on my hat last year so you see it will not cost me much. Miss "Cox" and Mollie have one. They are very unbecoming. Miss Cox looks like a little *witch*. Mollie looks like an elephant would with one on. "Ella" W— has a beautiful little bonnet and looks very sweet in it.

I have made up my best dress. It fits me quite neatly — have one of the wide belts — made it myself as I had not the change to get me one. I do not like them but have to wear it on account of the fashion.... Cecelia S — is the prettiest girl in Fulton — has a lovely little bonnet.[135] What is "Jennie" going to wear this summer, her hat or bonnet? [I] guess she will not give up getting married, hope not at least on your account. Oh what a charming visit you will have — you will and must and shall go, that is if my word has *any* influence. "Ma" is well and is I believe living on the anticipated joy of being united with her children again in the summer. Oh! just imagine — brothers Sam, Charley, Sister Abbie, and Sue all, all will be here next summer. What joy!...

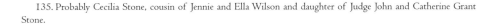

*From Margaret Bruin Machette
to her daughter, Susan Machette*

Fulton, Missouri
May 17, 1865

Dear Susie

Yours of the 5th was received last evening. It found me busy washing the windows in my room. I put down the towel until I was through reading your letter twice and then Nelia took the letter from me for fear I would wear it out. I then remembered that I had not finished washing the window. We have been cleaning house this week, but you never saw such whitewashing in your life. I had to stop the work. It looks like you had taken a rag and daubed the wall instead of [using] a brush. I have been planting potatoes today and my hand trembles so that I can scarcely write.

Abbie left for Monroe last Friday week. She went in the hack to Mexico and from there on the cars to Renick where Mr. Hersman met her. It was an open top buggy she

135. Probably Cecelia Stone, cousin of Jennie and Ella Wilson and daughter of Judge John and Catherine Grant Stone.

went in, and she was in a very hard rain, got very wet. I am quite anxious about her. She had a dreadful cold when she left, and I fear her getting wet has made her sick. I heard that Doctor Wilkerson and Miss Lou Baker are to be married tomorrow morning....[136]

I am so glad that you have had such a nice visit. How does Lizzie and Alex look? Did they ask about us? Is Lizzie on the road or is she nursing Lilian yet?[137] Are they coming to visit us this summer? When you write, tell me all about them.... How long is Samuel going to stay with us when he comes? I want to know so I can have Abbie and Mr. Hersman here at the same time. I should love to have Alex and Lizzie, too. I think it would be so nice to have you all at home at the same time. You must bring both of the little boys, Charlie and Eddie. Tell Samuel that I want to see the children so much that if he thinks it won't make them sick please bring them....

Fulton, Missouri
June 10, 1865

From Margaret Bruin Machette
to her daughter, Susan Machette

Dear Susie

This morning finds me very well. Nelia is in town. She went to the picnic yesterday, and as the girls met this morning to sing she did not come home last night. As it is threatening rain, she may not come till tomorrow after church. She stays with Miss Lou mostly. I sent Martha in this morning with her calico dress. She wore her white one yesterday. I am very much afraid that Nelia is seriously out of health. She looks wretchedly but won't give up....

... I forgot to tell you that Kate Van Doren was dead. She died of consumption. Mrs. Jinna Overton has gone to California.[138] She started the day before the letter was received with the news of Kate's death....

Sunday morning. Dear Susie, yesterday I told you that Nelia had not come home. About six o'clock in the evening I was sent for to see her. She was taken suddenly very sick and out of her mind. She remained so two or three hours, but after taking morphine she got quiet. She was at Doctor Stone's. I stayed all night with her. She is much better this morning. Doctor Scott brought her out home this morning. [He] thinks it debility and overexertion.[139] The trip to the picnic and the singing was too much. I shall keep her at home now. They will have to get on with out her. Don't be uneasy. I will let you know how she gets on. I hope that rest will make her all right. Tell Jennie her friends are all well. I saw Ella this morning....

---

136. Achilles Wilkerson, participant in the California gold rush and physician, married Lou Baker.

137. Margaret seemed to be asking if Lizzie was pregnant, perhaps assuming that a woman who was nursing could not become pregnant. Lizzie was pregnant at the time.

138. Virginia "Jinna" Barnett Overton, widow, was a sister of William Van Doren's first wife. Van Doren had moved with his family, including his daughter Kate, to California, where he died in 1877. See January 14, 1861.

139. Elijah T. Scott and W.B. Stone; both physicians. See December 10, 1863, and April 30, 1864, on Elijah Scott's sisters, Mag and Lizzie Scott.

From Susan Machette to her sister, Cornelia Machette

Liberty, Missouri
June 11, 1865

Dear Nealie:

One month from today I hope to be with the dear ones at home. We did not go to church today, though there was preaching at the Methodist Church. Jennie and I have our clothes put away just ready for the examination, and we do not want to dishabille them till then. We are preparing to pitch in to the preparation for the examination which is only two weeks off....

Jennie's beau will be here in two weeks. I am so glad for he is such a nice gentleman. Jennie is expecting to make quite a sensation when we get home. I suppose dear old Fulton will be asleep. The examinations being over, Little Miss Cox will doubtless be on the "qui vive" to find out every thing concerning Jennie's engagement as there is a bit [of] romance connected with it, which I suppose every one will get wind of....

I sent you a belt last week. You must make a lining for it like mine. Just take a piece of cloth, double it [as] wide as your belt and run cases for splits about an inch apart. It fits to your form so much better than paste board. Jennie and I packed our clothes — I mean our winter dresses and cloaks — in a good box, so we have plenty of room for own lawn dresses in our trunks....

What room will we sleep in this summer? We ought to all stay up stairs. It is so nice and cool up there. I have thought so often of a night in July last that you and I sat up quite late. It was so warm — at the front door — and [we] watched the moonlight and cracked jokes &c.

From Abigail Machette Hersman to her mother, Margaret Bruin Machette

Monroe County, Missouri
August 17, 1865

Dear Ma:

... Finley is getting on finely. Yesterday he was 15 months old! You know he always does something *smart* the 16th of every month, so yesterday he got up twice and stood alone in the middle of the floor. I think he will be walking now in a very short time. He makes a great effort to talk. When I'm up stairs, he will say, pointing to the stairs, "downstairs" very plainly indeed. Every thing he is told to say he makes every effort to do so.

... I have got such a nice quantity of pickles together and by the time I go over, my barrel will be full. Have made some of the nicest damson and grape preserves you ever saw. Will make about two gallons of pear preserves before I come and will also bring you enough to can. If you make a little peach preserves I think we will have about enough.

I made my grapes up with the nicest crush sugar; the damsons I made up with clarified brown sugar. I made the latter up yesterday and saved enough out for supper. I thought Charley and Will would never get done praising it.[140] Will said when he got married he intended to have preserves every day. We have a great many tomatoes — they are ripening very fast. Would you like to have some dried? That will be the only

---

140. William Hersman, Charles Hersman's brother.

way I can put them up. We will have any quantity of butter beans if I stay to gather them....

Dear Ma, I do want to see you all so much, but the time will not be long. Joe Scott has returned from Kentucky. He says they are having terrible times there: negro troops every where....[141]

La Grange, Kentucky
September 29, 1865

From David Graves,[142] teacher, to Susan Machette

Dear Friend,

... I have taught now three weeks and have 37 pupils, which I think is doing very well. Owing more to the number of classes than the number of pupils I have been compelled to employ a teacher in the Primary Department, but still I am in need of another Assistant to take two or three classes, as I have more than I can well attend to. The classes I should like to give up are 6th Reader and 4th Geography and Primary Grammar. I would then have enough left to keep me busy even should there be no more classes formed. I would have Arithmetic, Trigonometry, Algebra, Geology, Evidences of Christianity, Moral Science, Sacred Rhetoric, Secular Rhetoric, Latin and Greek. Though by engaging another teacher I should be taking away considerable profits to my self, yet for the interest of the school I must employ another teacher.... There are a great many young ladies here and quite a number of them are in school and I think I may get up a very good music class. I will make to you the following offers which you may reject or choose from at pleasure —

1. Thirty dollars a month.
2. The entire proceeds of the music class for the first five months and ½ of the proceeds for the second term.
3. One-fifth of the entire proceeds from Latin and music lessons for the sessions.

These offers do not include the paying of your board which will cost you about $16 per month. I have made you just as liberal offer as I think I possibly could make without making too great [a] sacrifice for the sake of music. I hope you will adopt some one or reject all the propositions I have submitted and that I may see you soon in Kentucky or hear that you can not come. Should you come, it may be that after while I could do better for you, as my school should increase. My prospects are still very

The Reverend William W. Robertson, a friend of Margaret Machette and the father of two daughters, strongly supported higher education for females.

---

141. Joe Scott wrote his brother Harvey that he left the University of Missouri where he was studying Latin because he "was in danger at Col[umbia]," possibly from being forced to serve in the Union army. From Louisville, where he was a teacher, he wrote his brother on April 22, 1865: "Since you wrote, Richmond has fallen, Lee surrendered, and probably Johnson; many brave men have been killed, and Abraham Lincoln assassinated. If I live to write to you again, what changes will occur before I take my pen for that purpose, God only knows." Because black troops generally entered the war later than whites, a greater number were still serving their terms of enlistment at the end of the war. Ira Berlin in *Freedom: A Documentation History of Emancipation 1861–1867* (Cambridge: Cambridge University Press, 1982), 733, writes, "In October 1865...Kentucky and Tennessee accounted for another 22,000 [black Union soldiers]."

142. David Graves, cousin of Lizzie Machette; married to Julia Crockett. See October 6, 1860.

encouraging. I secured 9 additions in one day — Tuesday. I look for a large number more next Monday.

... Write immediately and come [as] soon as you can get here.

From Mary Bruin Dutton[143] to her sister, Margaret Bruin Machette

Montgomery County, Missouri
October 12, 1865

Dear Sister

... Our friends have all got back to Montgomery. Sam and Mary Jane was there when their Father and Mother died.[144] Their sickness was remitting bilious fever. From what I have seen in sickness I would call it congestion....

Sister, you wished to know if I ever thought who of my friends I would meet that was numbered among the dead. I have often thought on this subject. My chief meditations are those when I think of the goodness of God to me in giving me my dear children. When he sees fit to take them in the midst of affliction, I am made to rejoice to think of the meeting. When we are done with this troublesome world, we all shall meet in Heaven. God [will] have taken none but those we have a hope of meeting there and I will know them. There we will know them as they are known here [but] not in these vile bodies and [in] the height of our joy we will meet our Savior there — where we will meet the redeemed of the Lord. My fond anticipation is, if I can be clothed in his righteousness, I will meet many of our friends there, Christian friends and neighbors there.

If you could have seen Ellen when she was put in her coffin, she looked so pleasant. If she could have spoke, it would have been "my savior smiles and bids me come." In all the afflictions she had passed through, she never was so patient as in the end. Mr. Nowlin seemed to have a presentiment of his death. They said before he left Illinois he would say, "I don't think I have long to live." He was so anxious to get back home, to die at home. Ellen told me this. He was not conscious of what he suffered. For 3 days and nights at any rate he never spoke nor seemed to know any one. We have an assurance that he was reconciled to God's will. Mr. Roper gave satisfactory evidence of his acceptance with God.[145]

Sister, I could tell you many things that we witnessed — the husband and wife both sick in the same room. When the friends saw he was dying, [they] proposed to take him into another room, but she was not willing to have him moved so he died where she could hear all his death groans. At one time she asked why Lizzie was fretting so and she was asked if she [did] not know Mr. Nowlin was dying.[146] She said she didn't think he

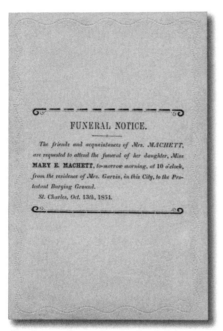

FUNERAL NOTICE.

The friends and acquaintances of Mrs. MACHETT, are requested to attend the funeral of her daughter, Miss MARY E. MACHETT, to-morrow morning, at 10 o'clock, from the residence of Mrs. Garvin, in this City, to the Protestant Burying Ground.

St. Charles, Oct. 13th, 1854.

Death was always close at hand. Margaret Machette kept copies of funeral notices, including one for her oldest daughter, Mary Elizabeth, who died in 1854, shortly after she turned 17, and before the family's move to Fulton.

---

143. Margaret Machette's older sister, Mary Rebecca Bruin, married John H. Dutton (1790–1856). Their children were James, Bruin, John Harrison "Harry," Jane Shelton (who was married to Lizzie Machette's brother Jacob), and Eleanor "Ellen" (the mother of John William Adams who wrote the October 6, 1860, letter).

144. Sam Nowlin, son of David Nowlin, and Mary Jane Adams Wells, daughter of Ellen Dutton Adams Nowlin, were at the deathbed of their respective father and mother.

145. William Roper, husband of Kate Roper and son-in-law of David Nowlin. Roper died later that year when he was twenty-eight. See February 21, 1864, on Kate Roper.

146. Elizabeth "Lizzie" Adams, teenage daughter of Ellen Bruin Adams Nowlin.

would go first. She thought she would be the first to go, but she lived until Friday morning during which time she talked very satisfactory to the children, told Sam to not forget the promise he made his Father to take good care of his sisters and requested Mary to take Lizzie and take care of her. Mr. Nowlin left a will and they will abide by that. All that was Ellen's will be for her children. Sam will move to the old home and take charge of that.

I received a letter from Jane [Shelton] last Saturday. She is very much afflicted in her feelings in the death of her sister. She said it seemed so hard to think she was so near and could not see her and did not know she was much sick until she was dead and buried. If she could have been there to see her and hear her talk it would not have grieved her so much.... Jane said she had done better this time than she ever had before. She has a very healthy child. They call him Emmett....

Fulton, Missouri
October 18, 1865

*From Margaret Bruin Machette
to her daughter, Susan Machette*

Dear Susie

... I was glad to hear that you got to Mr. Graves without accident or trouble. From what you say about board I fear you won't make enough to pay your board. You must be sure to let me know how you are situated all the time. You must look well to your own affairs, not put too much dependence in strangers. Remember how much rests on you [when there is] no one to take care of you so far from home. Be particular about your associates. A lady is judged by those she lets wait on her.

Did you see Alex in St. Louis? I received a letter [from] Sam.... You must write to him at once and tell him about your going from home. Mr. Fisher got home from Synod last night. The college came out all right. They raised seven hundred dollars at once to fix the campus, have put a man in the English school — everything that the Professors could wish....

Louisville, Kentucky
November 2, 1865

*From Alexander Machette to his
sister, Susan Machette*

Dear Sister Susie:

I drop you a line just to inform you of my arrival in Kentucky. I expect to leave here in the morning for Bowling Green to visit the church in that place, possibly also some other localities in this state. I would be exceedingly happy to see you, and also David Graves and family. I will try on my return to slip out and see you, say next week. I hope you are pleased with your situation. Suppose you learned already about our fine boy. We call him Eugene.

I learned, since I left Troy, of the death of David W. Nowlin. Truly they are a bereaved family.

Having nothing of special interest, and as I am writing in a *cold* room I will close.

From a journal written by Susan Machette

La Grange, Kentucky
November 7, 1865

I will hold forth tonight on the text "wonder under what unlucky star I was born." Tonight I find myself in Kentucky. The last I wrote in my journal was in Liberty. I had no more idea of being in Kentucky than in the moon. Who knows where I will hail from next. I started from home the 9th October. I reached here the 11th. I commenced teaching the following Monday. Began with three pupils, have now 6 — encouraging, isn't it? Well, if I don't succeed here I'm not bound to stay here. Though I should prefer doing so. I don't like to go back so soon — it will look like I was not successful which would not be far wrong.

November 16, 1865

I have been living in the anticipation of the club meeting. I'm such a little fool. I happened to have a compliment passed on [to] me — it so elated me that I have been dreaming of how I'm going to read so fine next time. I know that I am going to make a botch next time.

From Alexander Machette to his sister, Susan Machette

Lincoln County, Missouri
November 20, 1865

Dear Sister Susie:

The letter I received at Louisville, forwarded by you from La Grange, informed me that our little boy had been laying at the point of death. Of course, I lost no time in returning home, found the child very delicate indeed. I fear we shall not have him with us long, He suffers greatly day and night. Lizzie and Lilian are in fine health.

I found Taylorsville a quiet pleasant little place. The church there desires to obtain half my time, and also that I should take charge of the school. I expect to hear from them by the first of next week. The probability is then that I shall move to Taylorsville. If so, I expect to labor to build up a first class school. I cannot tell yet, but I think there will be a good opening for a *music teacher* by the first of February. I would like, at least, if you would not make any permanent engagements beyond that time until you hear further from me. Lu [Shelton] will probably assist me in the literary department, and with you to teach music, how pleasant it would be. Don't you think so?

The friends here generally are well. Aunt Dutton is here on a visit.... I hope that you may have a pleasant time, and be sustained in your heroic efforts so far from home.

Alexander Machette, the eldest child and only boy of Margaret Machette. Alex and Lizzie had already lost one child. Eugene, referred to in this November 20 letter, just a few weeks old, would die before year's end.

Taylorsville, Kentucky
December 13, 1865

*From Alexander Machette to his
sister, Susan Machette*

Dear Sister Susie:

I drop you a line to let you know that we are again in Kentucky. Whilst in Missouri, I made a visit to Fulton and found all well there. Ma returned with me to Lincoln County to see my family before we left Missouri. I would have taken Lizzie and the children up to Fulton had it not been for the baby. His health was and still continues to be very delicate — so much so that I fear we shall never be able to raise him. The dear little fellow is nothing but skin and bone — has no flesh and does not seem to improve at all.

Lilian is as well and playful as ever. Sister Lu is with us. She and Lizzie are both very busy making up carpeting. We expect to get to housekeeping next week, and will be ready to receive you by Christmas if you see proper to favor us with a visit. I want you, Susie, if you can afford the expense, to come and spend Christmas week with us. I think you would be pleased with our village, and we would be delighted to have you with us. In case you should conclude to come, you must write and let me know what morning you will be at Louisville, and I will have the stage to call for you at the depot and bring you straight on to Taylorsville the same day. The stage leaves Louisville every morning for Taylorsville. It *professes* to leave at about 8 o'clock, but it is nine or ten sometimes before they get started. Now the train from La Grange comes into Louisville quite early in the morning, and if I knew what morning you would be at Louisville, I could have the stage to call at the depot for you. What do you say to this arrangement? . . .

All join me in love to you and earnest wishes for you to spend Christmas with us.

Fulton, Missouri
December 18, 1865

*From Margaret Bruin Machette
to her daughter, Susan Machette*

Dear Susie

I have just received a letter from Lizzie dated the 12. She said they arrived at their new home on this day the 7th, the same day that I got home. Her poor little boy is not expected to live. Poor Lizzie, I do feel so sorry for her. She says she feels like she could not give it up. The dear little heart has never seen a well moment since it was born.

Dear daughter, this leaves me in good health and I hope it will find you in health and happiness. I suppose you are at Mr. Graves by this time. Give my love to Julia and her family. Alex said he was going to have you to spend Christmas with him. He went to see Nelia as he went to Kentucky. She was very much pleased to see him, and he was just as much pleased to see her. Lizzie says she never knew him to rejoice more over a visit. He says she is a perfect lady and a beauty so you see she must have improved.

Susie, Sallie Robertson and Thurmond are married. I did not hear what day they were married but it's recently. Ella Wilson did not go with Jennie, so Miss Lou Atwood told me. Mr. Wilson told Mr. Hersman that he had heard from Jennie that she was well. I suppose he thought we were anxious to know.[147]

147. Sallie Robertson, daughter of the Reverend William and Mary Robertson, married Nicholas Thurmond, who graduated from Westminster in 1867. He became a Westminster professor and later a judge. Jennie Wilson, daughter of William Wilson, married Isaac Johnson, the same day her cousin Cecilia Stone married James Johnson. Sue Machette apparently did not accompany Jennie on her wedding tour.

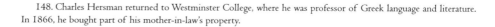

WESTMINSTER COLLEGE,
FULTON, MISSOURI.

THE ENGLISH SCHOOL in this Institution has been entirely remodeled. The design in its present form is to fit young men thoroughly for a College Course; to fit those desiring it for teaching, thus taking the place of a Normal School; and, in the last place, to furnish our students the facility for a good Business Education.

The following is the course of study in this Department.

PRIMARY CLASS.
Webster's Spelling Book; Wilson's 2d and 3d Readers; Ray's Intellectual Arithmetic; Warren's Primary Geography; Butler's Primary English Grammar Spencer's Penmanship; Declamation.

JUNIOR CLASS.
Webster's Speller and Definer; Wilson's 4th Reader; Written Arithmetic (Ray); Common School Geography begun (Warren); English Grammar, (Butler); Penmanship (Spencer); Elocution; Map Drawing.

MIDDLE CLASS.
Smith's Speller and Definer; Wilson's 5th Reader; Arithmetic (Ray); Geography Completed (Warren); English Grammar; Composition (Quackenbos' Small) His. United States (Quackenbos); Penmanship; Elocution; Punctuation (Wilson); Physiology [Cutler.]

SENIOR CLASS.
Webster's Dictionary; English Gram. [Kerl's Comprehensive]; Parsing in Milton; Physical Geography [Warren]; Book Keeping [Fulton & Eastman]; Composition [Quackenbos' Large]; History United States [Quackenbos' Large]; Punctuation; Philosophy and Chemistry [Primary]; Geology—Hillside—Higher Arithmetic—Ray.

The Board have made such arrangements as will, it is believed, meet the wants of the Department as thus organized. Those who complete the course will receive a Certificate of that fact. The next session opens on the 29th of January, 1866. For information, address the undersigned or any member of the Faculty. **M. M. FISHER,**
Secretary of Faculty.

☞ The other five schools of the College Proper, are in full operation.

You wished to know how the College is getting on. It is flourishing finely. There is eighty students in attendance. [I] guess Mr. Hersman is permanently fixed here. I think he would like to buy this place, and I sometimes think of letting him have it....[148]

Dear Susie, do take good care of yourself. If you go to Alex you must wrap up good for there is great danger of taking cold traveling. You have the advantage of us if you can get calico for 25 cents. It is 35 [cents] here. I don't know of any thing that is cheaper than when you left. I have to pay 16 dollars for a barrel of flour, and I believe it was 13 when you left....

This announcement for the January 1866 term promised that Westminster College, which had nearly closed during the Civil War, would be "in full operation."

From Cornelia Machette to her sister, Susan Machette

Monticello Seminary
Godfrey, Illinois
January 1, 1866

Dearest Sister:

It is on the first day of the year that I received your dear letter and have seated my self with the determination of answering it immediately. I am so sorry to see that you have spent so dull a Christmas. I have had a delightful time taking it all together. Christmas night we had a candy pulling here. There were several strangers here, but all ladies excepting one and he was a brother of one of the teachers — an "old *Batch.*" He paid me quite a compliment that night. We, of course, played a good many games and among others we played one in which points were sold. In selling them they came across Mr. H's knife and to redeem it he was told to bow to the prettiest, kneel to the wittiest and kiss the one he loved best; he bowed to one of the teachers, and kissed his sister, and came away across the room and knelt at my feet. He paid me a good deal of attention all evening, much to the amusement of the other girls. We went on Thursday night to the "sociable" and paid ten cents to go — had a nice supper and saw a good many boys. Saturday night we had kind of "tableau" in which Mr. H and myself figured.

... I have had my brown dress made up, and I flatter myself that it is quite becoming. I do really wish I could have my picture taken for you, dear Sister, but I don't see

148. Charles Hersman returned to Westminster College, where he was professor of Greek language and literature. In 1866, he bought part of his mother-in-law's property.

how I can for I have but five dollars and that is to pay for my dues and express on my box which [will] take it all but a few cents and then I soon will have to have a new pair of shoes, as mine now are nearly worn out. Those leather ones were no earthly account and "Gymnastics" has very nearly put the gaiters through. It's dreadful hard on shoes here. We take so much exercise &c.

I have joined the Society. I thought it would look little and mean if I did not — it was only 50 cents to become a member. Then so much is expected of a member of the church. So many of the girls are not professors that it is now [a] constant delight to pick at those who make such professions. I do not think it will draw my attention from my lessons because if it had that tendency they would not have gotten it up and besides they have all joined it. It is a "home mission" entirely for the minister (is in Missouri, south western part). I am real home sick today. It is New Year's day and yet I can't realize it to think that another year has flown and yet how little *I* have improved.

... Sue, I think if Sam ever offers to assist you again, you had better accept it. I do dislike to see you wearing your life out the way you now are....

Taylorsville, Kentucky
January 6, 1866

From Alexander Machette to his sister, Susan Machette

Dear Sister Susie:

Why have you not answered my last? Since my last was written we have known what it is to see our dear little Eugene laid in the grave. He breathed his last on the morning of December 21st. He never knew what it was to be well. Our loss is his gain.

... How are you doing now at La Grange? How many scholars would you require to come to Taylorsville?...

Taylorsville, Kentucky
January 12, 1866

From Alexander Machette to his sister, Susan Machette

Dear Sister Susie:

... As to the number of music scholars to be obtained here, it is impossible to tell now exactly what can be done. There are several that we can count upon. Others probably will be obtained when school opens that we do not know of now. At any rate, I will make you the following offer — I propose to *board* you (washing excepted) and give you besides twenty dollars ($20) per month to teach from first of February to first of July....

I think you would find it very pleasant here. Good society &c. Lu is very anxious to have you come. Let us hear from you by return mail.

        Your Brother,
        Alexander

P.S. I excepted the item of *washing* because Lizzie is doing her own work, and of course she will have her hands full.

From a journal written by Susan Machette

La Grange, Kentucky
January 20, 1866

I am unsettled at present. The session will be out in two weeks. I do not know what I shall do then. I hope that I shall not be *fool* enough to remain here unless under more flattering circumstances. I declare I could not stand it much longer. I have no privacy at all, a nasty young one forever squalling, two rude men always talking, whistling, and singing. I do not visit any yet — poor pay. Wonder what the future has in store for me? I got a letter from home today. Abbie tells me they are getting on badly there. If I quit teaching and go home, we will live on for a few years — get deeply in debt, and what next I'd like to know? Nealie is doing well at Monticello. I was weighed today — 130 pounds. The climate seems to agree with me, though I do not feel any better. Received [a letter] from Alex not long since. He said perhaps I could get a class there at Taylorsville. I do not much expect I will get it....

From Abigail Machette Hersman to her sister, Susan Machette

Fulton, Missouri
January 24, 1866

My darling Sister:

How do you come on by this time, Susie? We all feel so anxious to hear from you. I only write now to let you know that we are all pretty well, with the exception of old Aunt Mary. She is lying very low with pneumonia, poor old woman. I have no idea [if] she will ever recover. She was telling me yesterday what she wanted done with her things. Said she wanted Miss Abbie to have her two best calico dresses to make her a comfort. If old Aunt Mary dies, I fear Ma will never be able to get such another excellent servant. The Dr. (Wilkerson) has no idea of her ever recovering....

From Abigail Machette Hersman to her sister, Susan Machette

Fulton, Missouri
January 26, 1866

Dearest Sister:

... Susie, *to tell the plain truth*, I think Graves has acted very badly indeed. You know he *insisted* upon your coming — did every thing in the world to induce you to go to Kentucky and, now that he has got you there, does nothing to retain your services, or render your stay a comfortable and pleasant one. Well, never mind, I know such a man can never prosper. He may for a time, but it will not continue.

Ma sends you some money, so that you may return home if you deem it best. Of course you must under present circumstances. I would not stay with Graves unless he could offer greater inducements. Susie, if you undertake to start home, make Graves attend to placing you under some one's charge. It may be that some one may be coming to Missouri, as far as St. Louis say, and there put [you] on the cars for Mexico, [so] you would have no further trouble. I wish with all my heart that you were only safe at home. I think we would have a very pleasant time. We could visit together more than we have ever done.

Margaret Machette bought dry goods from Daniel
and James Tucker, brothers and prominent businessmen
in Fulton. The receipt from 1860 (top) includes
105½ yards of fabric and trimmings, the most
costly being Irish linen at 60¢ a yard.

Warren W. Tuttle, superintendent for the Sabbath
school at the Presbyterian church, owned a dry
goods store and later a grocery store. Margaret
kept a running account with Tuttle.
This receipt (center) covered 1861-63 and
included day hauling of ice and corn.

Sue Machette, who wrote about making her
own dresses, bought 15 yards of poplin on
this 1865 receipt (bottom) from J. & P.
Shannon Importers in Kansas City, Missouri.

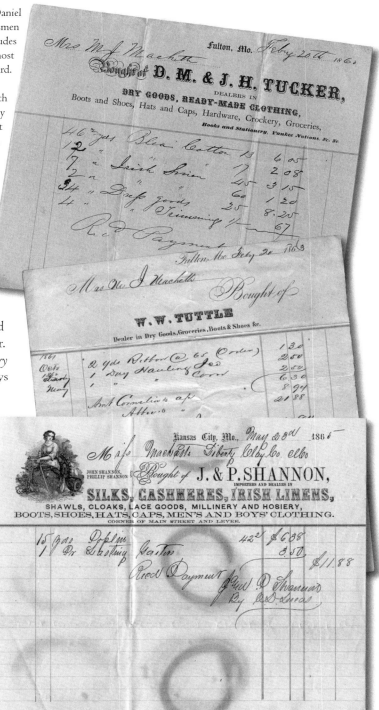

Miss Lou and her Ma are both in
Fulton. They get out to see us every now
and then. I have been to see Mrs. Wilkerson and
Mollie Henderson, and intend going over to Mr.
Burdett's shortly.[149] I think there are some *very*
pleasant people about Fulton. Mr. Hersman says
I have just got to visit more this next five
months. Intend doing so, and have already
made a pretty fine beginning. My horse is
a splendid one to ride. I just jump on her
and ride to Miss Lou's and then walk over
to town, unless I wish to go to the store
and then I ride up to the store in grand
style, where there is always some one to
assist me down. Was in at Miss Lou's the
other day, and she tried every way to ride
out home behind me, but found it *impossible*. I love Miss Lou very much indeed. She
got into the saddle once, and you can't
think how funny she looked.

Ma says she thinks you ought to write to
Mr. McAfee before you leave Kentucky.[150]
You know he is so kind, might think hard
if you left without writing to him.

… The boys are still with us, and I
hope if any new scholars come in, Ma will
be able to get Scott's room filled. Charley

---

149. Mary "Mollie," daughter of Alexander and Hadassa Henderson, had attended Lindenwood Seminary with
Abbie Machette.

150. See February 21, 1864, on James McAfee's moving to Kentucky.

is in very fine spirits about the college. He will have the chair of Greek alone [for the] next five months....[151]

Ma sends you 15 dollars so that if any thing happens to detain [you], you will have enough. I would not pay Graves one cent on my board but let the teaching go to pay him.

Finley sends a sweet kiss to Aunt Susie. He is talking very nicely now. You can understand a great deal he says.

From Margaret Bruin Machette
to her daughter, Susan Machette

Fulton Missouri
February 1, 1866

Dear Susie

... I am so glad that you are going to stay with Alex. I hope you will be better situated there than you were at Dave's. I had sent you fifteen dollars to help you come home on rather than stay there any longer. You must write and tell me all about the examination and exhibition and about your trip to Taylorsville and how you like the looks of the place and people. I have no news to communicate. My health is quite good, and it's well it is for it seems that I am the only one that can stand to do all the work of this family. Old Mary is some better but improves very slowly. I doubt very much whether she does much this winter. She has been so sick. She is an excellent servant when able to work. I have but four boarders this five months. There is not as many students in college as [the] last five months. They are mostly from town and near town. They have Judge Flood in the English school now.[152] It's some relief to Mr. Hersman.

Dear daughter, I hope you will be able to assist your brother in building up a good school. Now is the time to make good impressions on the minds of the people. If you all work together, you may make it a paying concern. Try and impress it upon Alex that it's not best to be too amiable as that is worse than being too severe. From the experience you have, you can assist him very materially. I hope he may do well where he is. It's hard to have you all so far off but there is nothing to be done here.

I had a note from Nelia this week. She is very well. Mr. Hersman sent her a hundred dollars to pay her school bill with. We are doing as well as usual — looking forward to the time that you will both be at home again with us. I hope Alex and Lizzie will come home with you next summer and Miss Lu Shelton and Lilian also. Tell Lilian she must not forget me. Bless her little heart, I can see her now so sweet and pretty. Finley is the greatest boy you ever saw. He is talking quite plain, calls for Aunt Sue every day. I am sure if you were up stairs and peep through that hole at him, he would know you. When ever your name is called, he looks up there and says "Aunt Sue."...

I am having straw put on the ice. At first I thought I would not have the ice house filled but upon second thought concluded to have it done. It cost 13 dollars to fill it....

151. Harvey Scott moved to the Whaley House, a hotel in downtown Fulton. William Parrish, author of *Missouri under Radical Rule*, in correspondence to the editor, stated that Charley most likely took the Iron-Clad Oath in order to continue to teach at Westminster. Edward Bates, Lincoln's attorney general and a leading citizen of St. Louis, opposed the oath and argued that people should feel free to take the oath if they had not carried arms against the federal government and if they believed they were loyal to Missouri and the country (Parrish, *Missouri under Radical Rule*, 44–45). In 1894, Bates's granddaughter would marry Charley Hersman's son, Finley.

152. Judge Joseph Flood, the father of Noah and John Flood, was professor of English language and literature until 1867.

Fulton, Missouri
February 13, 1866

*From Abigail Machette Hersman
to her sister, Susan Machette*

My dear Sister:

... Sunday between 3 and 4 in the morning, Charley and I were waked up by Ma rushing into the room exclaiming, "oh! children, get up for Mrs. Boulware's house is on fire!"[153] We were not long getting to the door, I assure you, and there, sure enough, the whole house was wrapped in flames. And what made it all seem all the more *terrible* was that not a thing was to be heard — every thing was perfectly quiet.

There was no one here but Mr. Hersman and Joe to go over. They dressed themselves as soon as possible and hurried over. They found no one there but the old Lady and two of her little grandchildren. The old man had gone to the country the day before. Mrs. Boulware and the children had carried out a few things and what Mr. Hersman and Joe got out, which was a very small number, was all that was saved.

The old house was not long burning down. How it originated has not been ascertained. Just to think, Susie, both Mrs. George's and Mr. Brooks' old places are burned to the ground — it seems so strange.[154] I hope they were not set on fire by any person, for were this the case, I should fear our time would come next.

They put Mrs. Boulware in a feather bed and brought her over here; Mr. Hersman came running in and told us to prepare a place for the old Mrs. Boulware, that she was as crazy as a loon. She remained with us until yesterday afternoon when the old man had her carried over to town. I never was thankful of any thing in all my life. Aunt Mary being sick it was really inconvenient to have her here. The old man did not return from the country until yesterday. I know you would have been highly amused to have seen them meet. He kissed her not less than half a dozen times....

I am making my silk dress. Send me word how to make the sleeves. Susie, I wish you could see dear little Finley. He is just the prettiest, sweetest, and smartest little thing you ever saw, I'm sure....

Kansas City, Missouri
February 14, 1866

*From Samuel Machette to his
half-sister, Susan Machette*

Dear Sister

Yours of January 20th has been to hand for some days past. My object in writing now is not so much to answer yours as to inform you that I am to be married on the 6th of March to Miss Annie Wilson of this place, a young Lady with whom I have been acquainted for the last seven or eight years. I shall start for Saint Louis on the same evening I am married and will visit your Mother as I return from Saint Louis. I am in hopes that I will find you in Fulton when I reach there.

153. Theodoric Boulware, a Baptist minister born in 1790, was among the first pioneers in Callaway County. The *Liberty Tribune* for July 18, 1862, noted, "During the summer of 1860, Mr. Boulware traveled by rail and otherwise over 3,000 miles preaching from one to three sermons each day." The Reverend Boulware's first wife died in 1854 and his second in 1857. In 1865, he married Ann Young, possibly the Mrs. Young mentioned on December 29, 1864. He moved back to his native Kentucky in 1866 because of the Iron-Clad Oath and died the following year.

154. Apparently the home of Mrs. George, who left in Fulton in 1864, as well as the home of Mr. and Mrs. Brooks, who also left Fulton, had recently burned.

From Cornelia Machette to her sister, Susan Machette

Monticello Seminary
Godfrey, Illinois
February 23, 1866

My own darling sister:

    … Our grand "gymnastic review" came off last night, and I feel pretty well used up. I have been in bed the most of the day. I have not been to my classes but learned my lessons all the same. I could have possibly, I suppose, have crawled down and recited, but I thought it much better to take care of my self at once so as to prevent any thing like a week in bed.

    … I wish I was at home this evening. I feel so badly — my back aches so much and my side is so sore. I have never been unwell since I came here and do not see any prospect of being. I only feel badly from over tasking my self with last night's exercises. I wish I only had your soft little hands in mine and your loving voice in my ear whispering words of love and encouragement and feel your loving arm around me, how happy I should be. I think I would recover from my weariness with out delay. I have to write an old composition to morrow — how I dread it. I believe I might write them for ever and still not improve.

    I have gotten into the Concordia Society at last. My self and 5 others were all that have been admitted as yet. This is quite encouraging, I am sure! But some times I get so discouraged. When ever I have a very hard lesson to learn, I have no loving Mother or sister to encourage me.… I guess I will make Ma poor by sending for shoes. It is preaching and you which does it.[155] We get shoes and they do not last one month. You can not get excused from it either no matter what your parents say. It is considered to [be] essential to health.…

    Good-bye, dearest sister, and may God watch over and protect you from all evil.

From Margaret Bruin Machette and Cornelia Machette to Susan Machette

Fulton, Missouri
March 18, 1866

My Dear Susie

    … I have delayed writing till Sam and his wife and Nelia came. They got here on Thursday. I know you want to hear how I like her. Well, my private opinion is she is very much of a lady, one that will suit Samuel exactly. She is not a Christian, but I hope she will become one in time. I think Samuel has made a good choice. I think he has shown as much business tact in getting a wife as in making money. She is a Reb of the first waters, was in a southern hospital, detailed to nurse the wounded. Has gone through some hardships during the war. Had two brothers in the southern army — one was killed and the other badly wounded. She is an orphan, has one sister and one brother. Owns considerable property in Kansas City and I think is of a very amiable, loving disposition.[156]

---

155. That is, Sue and Charley paid for Cornelia's schooling. Charley Hersman was a Presbyterian minister in addition to being a professor.

156. Anna Wilson Machette's mother, Deborah, died in 1852 and her father, Thomas, in 1860. One of her brothers was Richard Wilson, possibly the Richard Wilson who was wounded in 1862 at Corinth, Mississippi. *Kansas City Globe* (February 10, 1890).

Nelia is not looking well but I hope rest will do her good — seems very glad to get home. Annie calls you all sisters — seems to feel perfectly at home — says she would give any thing if we only lived in Kansas City....

Give my love to Alex and Lizzie and all the family.... Accept a heart full of love from

> your Mother.

Dearest sister:

... Sam is a great tease and has been at me ever since he came. I like him very much. He wishes you were here so much, and so we all do. I admire his wife so much. She is quite pretty, has a beautiful form. I did not go to church today, did not feel able to walk. I will commence Latin with Brother [Charley] soon and in this may get through in two years. I do not think it will be any loss to me not remaining [at Monticello] this year. I have you to return my thanks to for this opportunity of getting home. I now feel almost happy. Mrs. Dr. Wilkerson had a "young one."[157]... Little Finley sends a kiss — he is a perfect little "angel." Good-bye, dearest sister. Write soon to your

> Loving
> Sister N—

Samuel Machette was 18 years older than his half-sister Susan and 22 years older than his half-sister Cornelia. Sam was 40 and a widower with two sons when he married the 26-year-old Annie Wilson.

Fulton, Missouri
March 29, 1866

From Abigail Machette Hersman to her sister, Susan Machette

Dear Susie:

We, that is Ma and I, are getting uneasy about our little Sue, lest she has become too much interested in someone of those Kentucky Gents. If such be the case do not take us too much by *surprise*, but write and inform us sometime before. I think I shall have to strike up a correspondence with Lizzie, *so that in case you do have an admirer* I may be able to keep posted up.

We were all much pleased with Sam and his Bride. She made herself perfectly at home and seemed to like us all very much indeed. We did every thing in our power to render their visit a pleasant one. Charley hired a hack and we all went out to the asylum.[158] They enjoyed it very much. Annie dresses elegantly! She had one of the sweetest bonnets I ever saw.

Little Finley admires your picture greatly, does nothing but carry it round, kissing it all the time. I'm sure he would know you, were you to come home!...

157. Lou Baker Wilkerson, whose forthcoming marriage was reported on May 17, 1865, gave birth to Thomas. Lou would die in 1871.

158. State Lunatic Asylum No. 1 or the Asylum for the Education of the Deaf and Dumb.

In 1860 William McIntire, a local butcher, sold Margaret Machette beef and tallow on credit through the year for $59.36. In February of 1861, he gave her $20 credit for corn and fodder, leaving the balance of $39.36.

In October of 1865 Margaret paid the Bartley dry goods store $2.75 for a pair of shoes and 50¢ for spectacles along with her sewing needs.

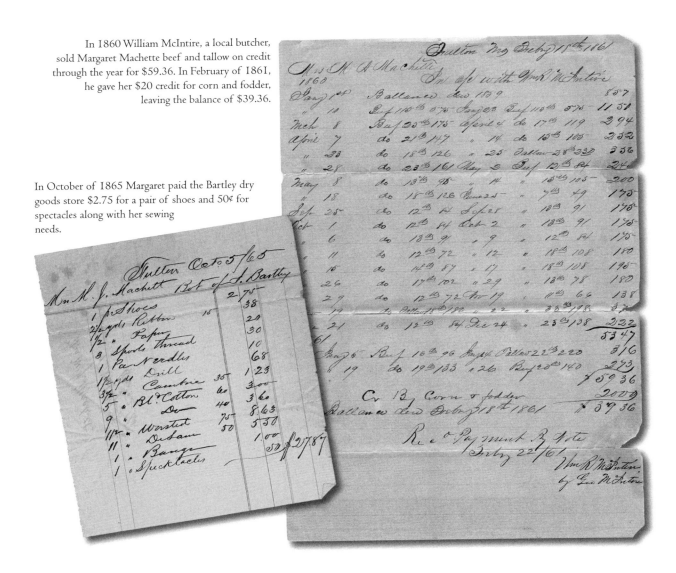

From Margaret Bruin Machette to her daughter, Susan Machette

Fulton, Missouri
April 22, 1866

My Dear Susie

... I am so sorry you are suffering with your eyes. Pray don't use them sewing or reading. If your Brother could get you the yellow root, you ought to make you some eye water. Simmer the yellow root in water till the strength is out, then add a little sugar and salt and whiskey. Strain and bathe your eyes often with it....

I suppose Abbie and Nealie told you all the news except that The Henderson and Miss Sheley were married.[159] They have been married two weeks last Friday morning.

159. Sarah Sheley, daughter of Judge James K. Sheley, married Theodore "The" Henderson, son of James S. and Emily Boone Henderson and great-grandson of Daniel Boone.

They went to Mr. Sheley's farm. I don't know where that is. I suppose they thought The would do better in the country than in town. Miss Lou is still at Fisher's. I don't much expect she will go to Boonville. Ella Wilson is in Fulton and I heard that Jennie was to visit Fulton this summer.

Susie, I have made part of my garden and expect to finish this week. I have no sweet potatoes. I wish Alex would express me some for seed. I have bought me thirteen fine sheep and eight lambs. I paid fifty dollars for them. I am going to spin the wool for carpeting this year. I will keep the sheep till we make a sufficient quantity of bed clothing and carpets to last me and my family a great while. I hope they will prevent my having to pay such large meat bills. I paid McIntire one hundred and twenty-nine dollars for meat from last March till December.[160] I hope to have bacon enough to last till my chickens are large enough to kill. I have one hundred and twenty-four young chickens. The turkeys have not commenced setting yet.

We have finished cleaning [the] yard. It looks perfectly beautiful. The grass is so green, and the cherry trees and that little plum tree are perfectly white with bloom. The cedar trees have grown so much. The ones that Mr. Hersman has put out are very small. The flowering almond is in bloom and the lilacs are very full of bloom and the snowball is completely covered with buds to bloom. The limb that I bent down last year has taken root and I cut it off and set it out this spring. It is growing and will have two blooms on it. The farmers are very busy putting in their crops. Everything promises well if we have a healthy season, but if the cholera rages we can't count on anything.[161] I wish my family were all together in case the cholera does come. It is not probable we will all live through it.

Tell Lizzie that I will answer her letter soon and Alex's. Also give my love to each one of the family. Tell Miss Lu Shelton I hope she will make us a visit this summer. . . .

Tell Lilian that if she was here this morning she could see the little lambs and chickens and the calf all full of life. The little chickens look so pretty running through the green grass. The calf attempts to chase the lambs. The old buck sheep has tremendous crooked horns and looks very savage but is very docile.

---

cholera remedy

Red pepper, one teaspoonful in one-half pint of hot water. In this dissolve one tablespoonful of salt. Of this give frequently until relieved.

One teaspoonful charcoal and four of sulfur given in teaspoonful doses every three or four hours said to be good.

Written on a piece of paper by Margaret Bruin Machette

---

160. William McIntire, butcher.

161. The April 20, 1866, *Missouri Republican* noted that some people thought cholera came every seventeen years. Because epidemics had occurred in 1832 and 1849, 1866 was expected to be dangerous as well. Machette family correspondence from 1833 describes how the mother, father, and sister of Charles Machette died of cholera that year after they moved to St. Charles to escape the cholera epidemic in New York City. James T. Barnett, "Cholera in Missouri," in *Missouri Historical Quarterly* (July 1961), 351, states, "In 1849 the estimated deaths [in St. Louis] were 4,500 to 6,000 from a city of less than 70,000." He further notes, "The bacterial cause of cholera was not established until 1883."

From Cornelia Machette to her sister, Susan Machette

Fulton, Missouri
May 6, 1866

Dear Sister:

. . . It has done nothing but rain, rain since I came home. There has been only three clear Sabbaths since, I believe. I intended fixing up quite nice since this morning and go to Sabbath school, but could not on account of this weather.

I have gotten me quite a pretty little hat. It is fine white straw trimmed in white ribbon and black lace and a large pink and brown rose, and to finish off with a graceful black veil one yard and a half long which is attached to one side of it. It is also very becoming.

Abbie has a beautiful bonnet. The material is black illusion trimmed with buff ribbon and pink and buff flowers. It is an elegant-looking affair and perfectly becoming to her, as everything else is. Have you gotten you one yet?

. . . Fannie Evans was out here the other day and spent two days and a night with me. We had a gay time coming out. I had remained all night with her, and she was to come home with me. The next day was very cloudy and had every appearance of rain, but come out home I would. Mr. Evans had the horse saddled, and after many injunctions to ride fast and not let the rain catch us we started — Fannie in the saddle and me behind. We had but time to get in front of the college when there came up an awful rain. We were not more than half way home and instead of keeping on we turned back — as the horse was very wild we were afraid to go out of a slow pace. How it [was] lightning and thundering and raining — you can imagine how simple we looked taking it so easy. And to cap it all we met nearly all the boys who very politely offered us a dozen umbrellas. This frightened the horse so that it started in a lope and never stopped until we reached home. I was almost frightened to death. We afforded a great deal of amusement for people in general, I believe. Ella Reed and Mollie Henderson were out Friday evening — they were both very pleasant.

. . . We are all very well and happy together: there is but one thing to mar our pleasure and that is your absence. I am the ugliest little mortal you every saw, short hair, flush face and long nose — too ugly to exist very long. Miss Lou has gone at last. I do not think Fisher grieves very much over her absence, and I do not blame him. . . .

From Margaret Bruin Machette to her daughter, Susan Machette

Fulton, Missouri
May 26, 1866

Dear Susie

. . . Miss Lou is in Boonville with the children. Susie, it beats all you ever heard the way she has made a fool of herself. She wants Fisher to let her come back home. He told her he had no home, and as for living as he had done for the last eighteen months he never would do it again — that is pay for her waiting on him and his children with a vengeance. He intends getting a wife as soon as he can and I don't blame him.[162] She has spent all her time in trying to get him to marry her and now he will marry some

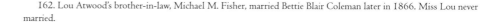

162. Lou Atwood's brother-in-law, Michael M. Fisher, married Bettie Blair Coleman later in 1866. Miss Lou never married.

one else and she can shift for herself. If she had acted properly she might have had money laid up. As it is she has nothing and no home and her friends are all hurt with her for staying with Fisher. You must burn this as it must not be told. Give my love to each member of the family and accept a heart full for your self. Lilian's picture does not flatter her. I am very glad to get it....

Lilian Machette, daughter
of Alexander and Lizzie Machette

Fulton, Missouri
May 27, 1866

*From Cornelia Machette to her
sister, Susan Machette*

Dearest Sister:

... We will have a very nice time here [for] "commencement." I presume a good many of the "old students" will be here. They are going to have the "young ladies" play for them this year, I believe, but I would not take any part in the performances. I have been having a very nice time lately. I assisted in an "old folks' concert." There were about a dozen "young ladies" and as many "gentlemen" who took part. We met every night for about a week and a half to practice.

At last the concert came off. I was dressed up in old style and looked very ugly. I enjoyed the evening very much. Jennie Cox and I sang the "A.B.C. duet" together, and I think done it full justice. We all had a gay time on the stage, were in disguise. I remained with Fannie while we were practicing; among my other escorts which I had was "John Hockaday," found him very good company.[163] I am now anticipating a pleasant visit to Sam's. He wrote saying he intended, when he returns home, sending for me. I have gotten a very pretty pink calico dress. I made it most all my self. It is of course a beauty. I shall feel quite strange in such gay colors. You know my taste is very grave. My dress is very becoming they say.

You asked me what I meant by saying that about Miss "Lou." I meant this. Miss Lou took no pains to conceal her love for Fisher from any one, much less from the gentleman himself, I guess, so it became the talk of the town concerning them. He, I suppose, took the surest means to get rid of her and sent her to Boonville. I was in town the other day and Miss Mattie Watkins and my self were talking about them. She

163. John Hockaday, son of Judge Irvine O. and Emily Hockaday, was an attorney.

said that "Miss Lou's" adoration for Mr. Fisher amounted to idolatry and so we all think.[164]

... Ma is now engaged in making quite a nice carpet, will have it done some time I guess. I can never get used to doing without my piano. I miss it so very, very much. It seems like some one of the family is gone....

From Abigail Machette Hersman to her sister, Susan Machette

Fulton, Missouri
June 3, 1866

My darling Sister:

Ma sat down with the intention of writing quite a letter, but on account of one of those trembling spells she very frequently has she was unable to do so....

You ought to see dear little Finley now. He is talking so sweetly! — very frequently asks about Aunt Susie. I know you will be surprised but I haven't weaned him yet. I think of doing so very soon, as I think it will go very hard with me to nurse him in hot weather. You know he is over 2 years old now. Finley is growing very fast, is large enough for a child of three years.

Tuttle had a Sunday school picnic last Friday! Nealie and Fannie concluded to spend the day out here together; they did so and seemed to pass the time off quite pleasantly. Mr. Hersman and I went out to the picnic, stayed until dinner and then returned. There seemed but little enjoyment, or at least such was *our* impression at the time. Joe went out also, and came home thinking it did not pay to attend "Picnics."

... Harve Scott is very much in love with Fannie Evans, and from what Nealie says I expect Fannie likes him pretty well. Wouldn't it be too funny if they were to marry? Fannie is too sweet a girl for him to marry....

From Margaret Bruin Machette to her daughter, Susan Machette

Fulton, Missouri
June 10, 1866

Dear Susie

... I received a letter from Sam's wife last week. She and the little boys were well. She did not know when Sam would be home. She calls him fair Sammie. I also received letters from Mrs. Brooks and Mrs. George. Mrs. Brooks is very much pleased with her new home. They were all well. Mrs. George and family were well.... Ann was married the 4th of April to a Mr. Sears — is living in Denver.... Mrs. George, Allie, and John Wilson are living about 6 miles from Canon City on a farm. She says it is the most beautiful place in the Territory. They call it Mountain Spring Ranch. Dear Susie, we all want to see you but none more than your Mother. Benny George preaches at our church this morning. Abbie and Mr. Hersman have gone to hear him....[165]

---

164. Martha "Mattie" Watkins, music teacher.

165. Ann George married Jasper Sears. Alfred "Allie" George was Ann's brother. John Wilson was possibly Ann's maternal uncle. Benjamin Young George was probably Ann George's cousin and Ann Young's grandson. A Presbyterian minister, he became a Westminster professor of Latin language and literature in 1871. See February 13, 1866, on the burning of the homes of Mrs. George and the Brookses.

Well, Susie, I have been out and hived a swarm of bees and will try and finish this scribble and prepare dinner. Old Mary has gone to church. Finley and I are here alone. Susie, I have near three hundred chickens, some nearly large enough to fry. Wish I could send Lizzie one hundred for they do consume so much corn meal.... Susie, Finley came in just now and I asked him what I must tell Aunt Susie. He said tell her, "make haste and come home and see my new shoes." He says his new shoes make him three feet high.... I shall not get my carpet done before you get home. I will try to hurry up as fast as I can....

Fulton, Missouri
June 29, 1866

From Margaret Bruin Machette to her daughter, Susan Machette

Dear Susie

... Mr. Hersman and Abbie will not leave until you get home, that is if you don't put off coming too long. Well, college has closed and everyone [has] gone to their homes well pleased. I don't expect they ever had as harmonious [a] session as the one that has just closed. The speakers in both societies did fine and the graduates had good speeches. There was a very full board in attendance and quite a number of the old graduates. There was a fine supper given them at Mrs. Kerr's last night — Mr. Hersman and Abbie and Nelia were there.

I am sorry you was not at home. We have had company every day this week.... Mrs. Hersman and old Mr. William Scott took dinner with us....[166]

Fulton, Missouri
July 12, 1866

From Cornelia Machette to her sister, Susan Machette

Dearest Sister:

... I went to a party the other night at Mrs. Lawther's — had a very pleasant time indeed. I went to one at Mrs. Kerr's parties during commencement.[167] I do not think I ever spent a more delightful [time] in my life, had a charming supper &c. — ate quite heartily, of course....

I am now busily engaged in making preparations for school. I will return to Monticello next year, will make it my last year at school. Then warn! would advise you as a friend to be looking out, for "little sis" will be on the carpet and no longer in the back ground....[168] Fannie Evans and I have sent on and engaged a room together, and so she and my self will the first of September march for dear old Monticello. Do not think I ever regretted any thing more than the thought of this being my last year at school. After that, [I] guess I shall fully realize the trouble and trials of this weary life

166. Charles Hersman's mother, Margaret, and Harvey and Joe Scott's father, William, were siblings.

167. Virginia Dyer Lawther, daughter of Samuel Dyer and wife of Hans Lawther. Susan Buckles Kerr, wife of William Dabney Kerr and mother of the Machette girls' friend Mary "Mollie." Samuel Dyer was one of the earliest settlers in Callaway County, coming in 1821, and his daughter was born in Callaway County three years later. See October 4, 1860, and April 30, 1864, on Mollie Kerr.

168. "On the carpet" or to come out socially. See Sue Machette's letter for April 1865 on stepping off the carpet, or getting married.

of ours — a long life is some thing which I have a horror of. I agree with "Moore" — let us aim but remain what he is, and no hell is worse.[169] Really, dear Sister, I do not think there is any pleasure in this life, unless it is in trying to serve our Maker, but even this makes me miserable, for I discharge my duties so poorly....

Note written by Margaret Bruin Machette

Mary R. Dutton departed this life on Tuesday the 14th of August 1866.

Written on a sheet of paper by Margaret Bruin Machette

Margaret Hersman born Sept. 25 1867

Nealie may have worked from this illustration to design her wedding gown. She used many yards of fabric and trimmings for her gown.

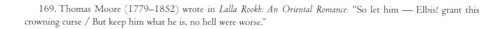

169. Thomas Moore (1779–1852) wrote in *Lalla Rookh: An Oriental Romance:* "So let him — Elbis! grant this crowning curse / But keep him what he is, no hell were worse."

The wedding portrait of Cornelia
"Nealie" Machette and John Flood.
Married July 10, 1868.

Maud Flood born Oct. 25th 1869

*Written on a sheet of paper by
Margaret Bruin Machette*

Deep afflictions and dear times

1870–1879

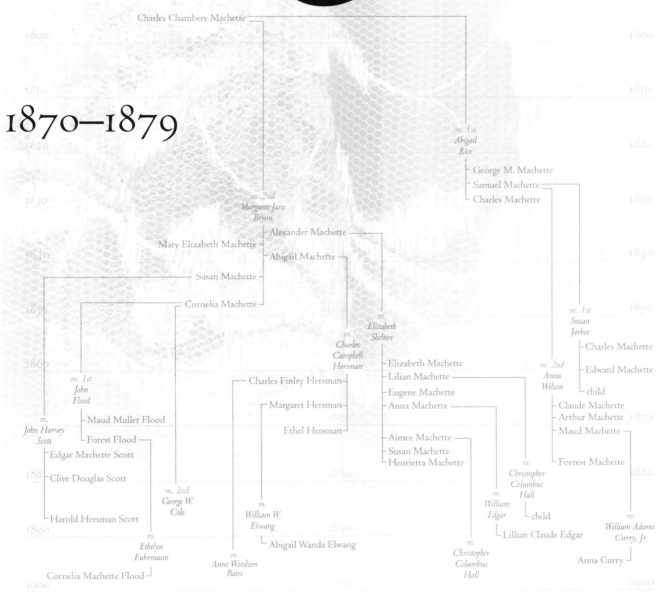

Charles Chambers Machette

m. 1st
Abigail
Rice

George M. Machette
Samuel Machette
Charles Machette

m. 2nd
Margaret Jane
Bruin

Alexander Machette
Mary Elizabeth Machette
Abigail Machette

Susan Machette

Cornelia Machette

m.
Elizabeth
Shelton

m.
Charles
Campbell
Hersman

Elizabeth Machette
Lilian Machette
Eugene Machette
Anna Machette

m. 1st
Susan
Jarboe

Charles Machette
Edward Machette
child

m. 2nd
Anna
Wilson

Claude Machette
Arthur Machette
Maud Machette

Charles Finley Hersman

Margaret Hersman

Ethel Hersman

Aimee Machette
Susan Machette
Henrietta Machette

m. 1st
John
Flood

Maud Muller Flood

m.
John Harvey
Scott

Forest Flood

Edgar Machette Scott

Clive Douglas Scott

Harold Hersman Scott

m. 2nd
George W.
Cole

m.
William W.
Elwang

Abigail Wanda Elwang

m.
Christopher
Columbus
Hall

child

m.
William
Edgar

Lillian Claude Edgar

m.
Christopher
Columbus
Hall

Forrest Machette

m.
William Adams
Curry, Jr.

Anna Curry

m.
Ethelyn
Fuhrmann

m.
Anne Woodson
Bates

Cornelia Machette Flood

Chapter 2

MACHETTE FAMILY
JANUARY 1, 1870

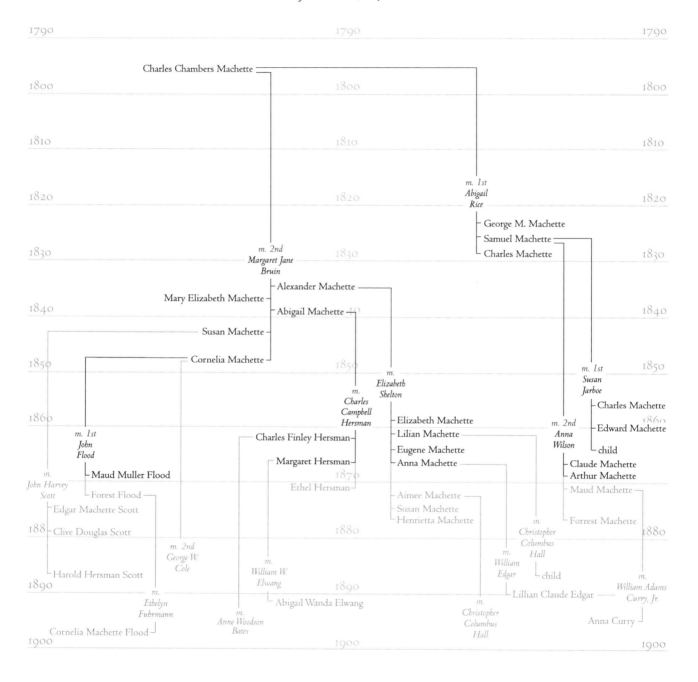

Ⅰn the spring of 1870, the *Missouri Republican* described the "Grand Celebration by the Colored Citizens" over the ratification of the Fifteenth Amendment; grandfather clauses and poll taxes in many parts of the country, however, would effectively keep black men from exercising their right to vote.[1] In late 1870, the newspaper reported that President Grant supported suffrage for women, but by January 31 of the following year, the matter was referred to the states where it stalled.[2] At the very end of the decade, the front page of the newspaper proclaimed that Thomas Edison had perfected electric light, which Edison claimed would make the invention an effective substitute for oil and gas.[3] An ironic yet fitting depiction of the contrasts and contradictions of this decade were two headlines published in the *Missouri Republican*, one on July 5, 1876, and the other a day later:

The Centennial Celebration
One Hundredth Birthday of the American Republic
The Whole Country Aglow with Patriotic Enthusiasm

Terrible Slaughter of United States Troops in Montana
The Gallant Gen. Custer Among the Slain
Three Hundred and Fifteen Other Soldiers Killed

The Centennial Exhibition in Philadelphia, which was attended by Fulton citizens, including Sue Machette Scott's husband (see the August 20, 1876, letter), celebrated the country's independence and scientific ingenuity. Displays at the Centennial included the steam engine, telephone, and typewriter.[4] At the same time, the Battle of the Little Bighorn, where the Sioux fought against being forced onto reservations, demonstrated that "the whole country" was *not* "aglow with patriotic enthusiasm."

A disaster facing Missourians in the 1870s was a drought and grasshopper infestation in the western part of the state. According to Margaret Machette's own eyewitness account on May 30, 1875, livestock in the area were so starved "they seem[ed] to stagger as they walk[ed]." In response to

1. *Missouri Republican* (April 12, 1870).
2. *Missouri Republican* (December 29, 1870, January 31, 1871).
3. *Missouri Republican* (December 22, 1879).
4. Schlereth, *Victorian America: Transformations*, 2–3.

the crisis, Missouri Governor Charles Hardin proclaimed a day of prayer and fasting so "that Almighty God may be invoked to remove from our midst these compelling calamities...."[5] The editor of the *Missouri Republican* ridiculed the proclamation: "To suppose the pestiferous insect can be cast out, as were the devils of old, by fasting and prayer, is an exhibition of stupendous credulity which nothing can excuse." The editor argued, instead, for better stewardship of the land. The *Fulton Telegraph*, on the other hand, defended the governor: "We, in rural districts, have not yet gotten far enough along in the road of progress, to dethrone God from governing his own world and to scoff and sneer at a Governor of the State for believing and acting upon the plain statements of the Bible."[6] The debate over Hardin's proclamation typified the larger discussions that were occurring in Victorian America as many Protestants moved away from the Calvinism of their Puritan ancestry and toward increased faith in self-determination.

The 1870s were also the time of Jesse James's notorious exploits. During the Civil War, Frank James rode with Quantrill's raiders, the anti-abolitionist group that terrorized Kansas citizens and, though the evidence is less clear, his brother Jesse also appeared to have connections to a guerrilla band.[7] After the war, Jesse and Frank James turned to robbery in the Midwest. On September 1, 1874, Nealie's father-in-law, Joseph Flood, reported that he missed by one day being on a stage coach robbed by the James brothers. Jesse James would be killed in 1882, and his body was identified by prosecuting attorney William Hockaday Wallace, a former Westminster student (see the February 20, 1870, letter). Wallace stated of Jesse James's manner of death, "It was one of the most cowardly and diabolical deeds in history. Jesse James was a wonderfully lawless, blood-thirsty man, but that gave the Ford boys no right to assassinate him."[8] Bob and Charles Ford pleaded guilty, and the governor of Missouri pardoned them unconditionally. Wallace later prosecuted Frank James, but he was acquitted.

Fulton, too, had its lawlessness, and on August 31, 1873, Nealie wrote about the murder of the sheriff and the lynching of a mule thief. As is typical in these letters, her emphasis was not on the lawlessness but on the domestic scene, specifically the situation the sheriff's daughter, Ophelia Law, found herself in after her father's death.

The Reverend William Robertson's Fulton Female Seminary closed during the Civil War, but the Synodical College for Young Ladies—also founded by the Presbyterians—opened in 1873. Advertised as a continuation of the earlier Fulton Female Seminary, the college offered a chapel, recitation rooms, parlors, and rooms for boarders and faculty.[9] Westminster College, the jewel of Fulton, continued, although it was in a financially precarious position in the 1870s. In 1868, Nathan Rice, who was mentioned in the October 4, 1860, letter as Alexander's teacher, became president of Westminster and minister of the Fulton Presbyterian Church. He would remain as Westminster's president until 1874, when Michael M. Fisher, who is referred to in the 1860 letters, became acting president.

Fulton had its polite society, a society that the Machettes both participated in and disparaged. One of the most socially prominent families was the Hockadays. John

5. *Fulton Telegraph* (May 21, 1875).

6. *Missouri Republican* (May 26, 1875). *Fulton Telegraph* (May 28, 1875). The grasshopper plague ended in 1877. Duane G. Meyer, *The Heritage of Missouri*, 3rd ed. (St. Louis: River City Publishers, 1982), 429.

7. William A. Settle, Jr., *Jesse James Was His Name* (Columbia: University of Missouri Press, 1966), 25–30.

8. Wallace, *Speeches and Writings*, 280. William Hockaday Wallace's maternal grandfather and John Hockaday's father were brothers.

9. *History of Callaway County*, 367–369.

Hockaday, whom Nealie referred to on May 27, 1866, as her escort, was the son of Judge Irvine and Emily Mills Hockaday. Symbolic of the family's status and aspirations, the Hockaday House, built around the time of John's marriage to Edith Cox in 1867, was an imposing Victorian mansion atop Hockaday Hill.[10] John Hockaday served as Callaway County's prosecuting attorney, and in 1874 he was elected attorney general of Missouri. In 1875, he was featured in the *Republican* as the host of Jefferson Davis, the former and still-heralded President of the Confederacy. (Nealie's husband, John Flood, was also a member of the committee that invited Davis to Missouri.[11]) According to Nealie's letters in the summer of 1876, John Hockaday had further political aspirations, even setting his sights on the Presidency. His ambitions were thwarted, though, by his failure to win the gubernatorial nomination.

At the same time, the political aspirations of Nealie's own husband seemed to be on the rise when he received the nomination at the Democratic Senatorial Convention for the state legislature in the summer of 1876. In the fiercely Democratic Callaway County, winning the nomination was tantamount to winning the general election.[12] John Flood, however, would not be able to fulfill his early promise either. He became ill in August 1873, and by 1877 he had been diagnosed with tuberculosis. Searching for relief, the Floods became part of the westward migration. Missourians had participated in other westward migrations. A group of Callawegians including Edwin Curd, Robert Tureman, David Whaley, and Achilles Wilkerson—all friends and acquaintances of the Machettes—went to California in 1850 to seek their fortunes as part of the California gold rush.[13] In the 1860s, the Georges, friends of the Machettes, moved first to California and then to Colorado (see letters from December 10 to June 10, 1866). In the 1860s, John Flood's own brother, Noah, moved to Nevada and then to California where he practiced law. In November 1864, when Noah was living in Carson City, Nevada, he wrote his brother John: "There are robbers here who watch the road for these teamsters as they return from Virginia City and relieve them of their ready cash. Last night one poor fellow was returning here when these outlaws hailed him with 'Your money or your life.' He being a foreigner could not understand them, was shot on his wagon.... Girls are played out here. Very few who are virtuous.... By a late proclamation of Lincoln's this is now a state. The Abolitionists expect to carry the state for Lincoln."[14]

John and Nealie first went to California, but by January 1878 had settled in Colorado, which had become a state two years earlier. The Floods were part of a larger movement that occurred in the 1870s and 1880s, that of "lungers" who believed they could recover their health in the West. Accounts of the robust health of Indians, the medical advice of doctors who equated good health with the climate in the West, and published testimonials on the regenerative powers of the western climate prompted this migration.[15] According to Sheila Rothman in her book on tuberculosis in the

10. Phyllis J. Strawn, *"Kings Row" Revisited: One Hundred Years of Fulton Architecture* (Jefferson City: Missouri Heritage Trust, 1980), 14.

11. *Missouri Republican* (September 11, 1875). *History of Callaway County*, 447.

12. By 1875, the Radial Unionists, who were responsible for the Iron-Clad Oath, had lost their hold in Missouri. Parrish, *History of Missouri*, 3:291.

13. *History of Callaway County*, 383–385, 733, 738.

14. The letter from Noah Flood is not included in this volume.

15. Thomas Dormandy, *The White Death: A History of Tuberculosis* (New York: New York University Press, 2000), 117.

United States, "By 1900 fully one-quarter of the migrants to California and one-third of the newcomers to Colorado had come in search of health."[16]

While the 1870s proved to be a difficult decade for the Floods, for Nealie's sister Sue it was a time of romance. From February 1873 to their marriage on August 13 of the same year, Sue Machette and Harvey Scott wrote each other over fifty love letters. Harvey, who was discussed in the 1860s letters as a student and boarder in Margaret Machette's home and Charley Hersman's first cousin, remained at Westminster College as a mathematics professor. In the late 1860s or early 1870s, Sue Machette returned to Fulton after teaching in western Missouri and Kentucky. They each rented rooms in the Whaley House (as did the Floods for a time), and by early 1873 they were in love.

As Karen Lystra explains in her book on love letters of the nineteenth century, love during this time period was perceived as a process a courting couple went through.[17] In the interest of conserving space, not all of the love letters are included in this collection and most that are included are abbreviated, but what remains demonstrate the process that Sue and Harvey went through in their courtship. (Some readers might prefer to read the letters first and then return to this discussion; see p. 98 to p. 115.) Key parts of Sue and Harvey's courtship were

- wonderment as they marveled over their first kiss and newly awakened passion for each other,
- increasing familiarity sought by Harvey and granted by Sue,
- declarations (words of love, gifts or tokens, and kisses) of love and commitment,
- obsession,
- tests by one to confirm the commitment of the other followed by reassurance from the other that any tests could be successfully overcome,
- hope for the future tinged with despair that something would prevent their marriage.

Throughout this process, the lovers drew a relationship between romantic love and Christianity. Lystra notes that middle-class, nineteenth-century American lovers "relied heavily upon Christian structures and symbols" to explain their passion.[18] In love letter 17, Harvey wrote that he prayed that Sue would become his wife because "I believe that I could serve Him [God] better *then* than now."[19] Sue concurred, writing that once they were married she would "be a better woman and serve Him as I never did before" (love letter 31). Both were willing to swear on a Bible of their devotion to each other (love letters 14 and 22). Sue referred to the "sacredness" of her letter writing to Harvey, and once she wrote a love letter on her brother-in-law Charlie's sermon paper, as if her declaration of love were the kind of declaration a minister would make about God's love (love letters 4 and 6).

At the same time that Sue and Harvey used Christianity to explain and even justify their love for one another, they were mindful that romantic love displaced their

16. Sheila M. Rothman, *Living in the Shadow of Death: Tuberculosis and the Social Experience of Illness in American History* (New York: Basic Books, 1994), 132; see also 133–136, 151.

17. Karen Lystra, *Searching the Heart: Women, Men, and Romantic Love in Nineteenth-Century America* (New York: Oxford University Press, 1989). Jill Dawson, in her introduction to *Kisses on Paper* (Boston: Faber & Faber, 1994), 4–5, identifies the following themes in love letters: rejection and desolation, invitation or consummation, temptation and frustration, and adulation.

18. Lystra, *Searching the Heart*, 257.

19. Unlike most of the other letters in the collection, the love letters usually begin without a date. To facilitate the discussion of these letters, they are numbered from 1 to 33. All the letters were written in Fulton, unless otherwise stated.

love of God. According to Lystra, this too was common in the nineteenth century.[20] Sue admitted that she sounded "like a heathen" for wanting to go to prayer meeting just so she could sit by Harvey (love letter 8). In the same letter when she wrote that her love for Harvey would bring her closer to God, she admitted that love made her forget her "duties to Him" (love letter 31). Harvey admitted he too spent more time in church thinking of his beloved than listening to the sermon, and he confessed that the tokens of love that she had given him taught him "to worship *graven images*" (love letters 3 and 11).

One manifestation of romantic love of the nineteenth century, Lystra writes, was the desire for privacy: "Insisting on seclusion, they often read and wrote love letters as if they were in a conversation that might be overheard. When alone, they kissed their love letters, carried them to bed, and even spoke to them."[21] Sue perhaps best explained the desire for privacy and seclusion when she wrote, "Do you know—since we have been sweethearts I don't like society at all. When I am not with you I had much rather be alone or just with the home folks" (love letter 18). A desire for privacy, of course, extended beyond writing and reading love letters to wanting to be alone with each other. One day, after Harvey had left Fulton to see his mother and ailing father, Sue wistfully recollected the times they would meet in the hallway, presumably the hallway of the hotel where both of them lived: "[W]as ever anything *so sweet* as those *dear stolen kisses*, when you had to look one way and I another to see who was looking?" (love letter 26). In his response to that letter, Harvey too remembered those times: "How sweet it was to meet you in the Hall and kiss you when *we thought* no one was looking. Next year I can love my Darling with none to molest us" (love letter 27).

It is evident from these expressions of love that sexual passion was a part of the feelings of both Harvey and Sue. Lystra observes that the middle class in the Victorian age entertained both "public prudery and candid private correspondence." In fact, she continues, "the public constraints on sexual expression actually encouraged the growth and intensified the experience of private eroticism."[22] Both Sue and Harvey felt caught between Victorian propriety and the desire to be alone. In an early letter, Sue regretfully told Harvey that "Nealie says I must not receive gentlemen callers in my room . . . [that] I must make this sacrifice to propriety" (love letter 8). Harvey accepted the decision but admitted, "It's a great temptation to wish there were no such thing as *propriety*" (love letter 11).

Throughout their courtship, both lovers expressed growing sexual passion. In an early letter, after describing Sue's kiss as "an oasis, a green spot, in my life," Harvey playfully asked, "When will I come to the *next* 'green spot' in my life journey, my Susie?" (love letter 9). A few weeks later, he was more forward: "Am most tempted to act the part of a *desperate lover* some night and tap at *your window*. Would you let me in? Would you, sure enough?" (love letter 23). Sue, more circumspect as one would expect a middle-class woman in the nineteenth century to be, would wait some time before mentioning their kisses and in the first instance she intimated possible regret that Harvey might be like other men who "do not want to kiss ladies they expect to marry" (love letter 12). However, later she too also enjoyed recollecting their kisses. Furthermore, after Harvey wrote that their marriage must be postponed, Sue wrote back in

20. Lystra, *Searching the Heart*, 8.

21. Lystra, *Searching the Heart*, 4.

22. Lystra, *Searching the Heart*, 6, 91.

despair, "Am I never to have an expected pleasure realized?" (love letter 33), surely an allusion to sexual passion.

What gives the love letters drama, a plot of sorts, are the tests that both Harvey and Sue had to pass to prove their love. Testing, Lystra writes, was a "ritualized" part of nineteenth-century lovemaking.[23] In April, beginning with love letter 18, the lovers went through a series of tests, which moved from playful banter to heartache. This part of their courtship was particularly important because it seemed to result in Sue's establishing a more or less equal relationship with her future husband.

While Harvey indicated time and again that he gloried in feeling helpless and obsessed by his relationship with Sue, she seemed to fear feelings of helplessness and obsession. Early in their letter writing, she confessed, "I don't like being in love much though. It places one's happiness in another's hands" (love letter 6). Perhaps because Sue, who turned twenty-nine during their courtship, had many years of living independently or because she knew that wives in her culture were expected to hold a subordinate position to their husbands—whatever the reason—found romantic love more painful than Harvey did. This pain seems to explain why she held her ground on the tests Harvey asked of her in April and why she protested, "Sometimes I think you do not love me. That is when you treat me like I was a little *kitten* or something to be played with" (love letter 22). Sue could accept romantic love and its passion only if Harvey would treat her with respect and dignity. That Harvey would give her what she wanted seems implied by a comment he wrote near the end of their courtship when he offered to help her with her trousseau: "I would *like* to help you mark your clothes and be in your way generally. Could you not send me some *sewing* to do, one of your new dresses to make, for instance?" (love letter 27). Lystra argues that love letters of the nineteenth century demonstrate how couples found ways "to bridge some sex-role divisions while they were in love."[24] Harvey seemed to be bridging these divisions in this letter; rather than ask some great sacrifice of her, he was willing to relinquish his male role to assume her domestic duties—to, in effect, domesticate himself.

In the letters written after the end of this volume—letters Sue and Harvey wrote to their grown sons and to each other—Harvey demonstrated his respect for his wife as a partner. Their later correspondence shows that Sue and Harvey worked together in the garden and yard, and they made decisions together about their children. This is not to say that Harvey and Sue were not defined by their gender. Sue was responsible for cooking and cleaning, and Harvey was responsible for providing the family income. In letters written after 1902, Sue as nurturer was the primary correspondent to the children, while Harvey played a more pragmatic role, especially in advising his sons about financial matters. Nonetheless, the later letters suggest that neither role was subordinate to the other, and the roles Sue and Harvey assumed often overlapped. The love letters, instead of just being a light confection of hopes and kisses, became a medium the lovers used to establish mutual respect in a marriage that would last for fifty-five years until Harvey's death in 1928.

---

23. Lystra, *Searching the Heart*, 157–158.
24. Lystra, *Searching the Heart*, 9.

Fulton, Missouri
February 18, 1870

From Cornelia Machette Flood to
her sister, Susan Machette

Dearest Sister:

... I am very well now, but have had another spell of this "weed" and Maud nursed the cold from me and is not very well. I do wish you could just see the sweet little darling. She has improved so much. Her complexion is splendid and her eyes are very dark blue. Her little features are the same, only more perfect, and her hair has come back so thick and dark as at first. She is just as fat as [she] is pretty. I have got her little stockings and little flannel bodices. She kicks and talks from morning till night — can almost sit alone and the other day amused us very much by saying "Papa" twice very plainly. She can smack her little mouth so loud as to be heard all over the room. She is kissing at us all the while. I do hope she may keep well, but the whooping cough and measles are both in town. I trust she may not take any of the diseases.... You asked me if I had gone out any yet. No, I am afraid of getting the whooping cough as they go every where when they have it.

... You told me to use your bonnet frame. I am much obliged, but will not need it, so it will be nice and new for your use when you come home. I shall be so glad if you were here. Floodie now has a great deal of writing to do and does not retire until 10 o'clock and Maud goes to sleep at 6 o'clock, so I have a great deal of time to read or sew, and if you were here we could take up some course of reading together....[25]

Mother and child: Maud, daughter of Cornelia
and John Flood, born October 25, 1869

Fulton, Missouri
February 20, 1870

From John Flood to his sister
Sallie Flood and sister-in-law,
Susan Machette

Dear Sallie and Susie

... [Abbie and her family] are all well and the children grow rapidly. Have not taken the whooping cough yet. Nealie is much confined in dread of the same. She took a horse back ride a few days time, but has not made a call or been to church yet. I will be glad indeed when she can go round some, as she enjoys the same, and has stayed so close at home so long. We intend taking frequent horse-back rides when the weather gets pleasant again. It is quite cold today, however! Ma received Alex's letter yesterday — glad to know his school is encouraging.

Poor Denny — we have been expecting the sad news, but sorry indeed to hear of his death. Young Newland has left College with consumption. So you see Foreman is left alone. That makes three in the past year which sickness and death have robbed those two higher classes of. Wallace got the prize! But there is ever considerable dissent from the decision. Three of the professors, if not more, thought Shaw should have had

25. Nealie called her husband, John Flood, "Floodie." He was an attorney in Fulton.

it. Some thought Trimble! Clagett had just fairly immortalized himself (physically speaking). He has planted out 320 elm and ash trees in the college *"campus."*[26] Charley says the work is well done.

I have two opportunities to rent Ma's farm, but I guess *"old Man Samuel Watson"* will take it.[27] One man went to look at it yesterday to buy. I hope soon to make some favorable disposition of it. We had a letter from Ma and Pa this week. They were expecting you both out soon. Maud is growing rapidly and is not more trouble than when you were here....

John A. Flood, a Fulton attorney
and husband of Cornelia Machette

*From Margaret Bruin Machette
to her daughter, Susan Machette*

Fulton, Missouri
April 3, 1870

My Dear Susie

Yours was received on Friday evening. The rain last week made the roads so bad that the mail failed to come for one or two evenings. Little precious Maud — [I] can't tell [you] how sweet she is but just imagine all the sweet things you can think of and she is still sweeter than all. I hope she is entirely over the measles now and will escape the whooping cough. Abbie's children have not had either yet. Maggie is not well. I hope it's nothing but cold. She runs out all day on the wet ground. The only wonder is that she is not sick all the time.

... Since Miss Lizzie Rice left they have no one to play on the melodeon [at church]. Some times the German preacher gets there in time to play for them. They will be glad when you get home. I do not know whether Dr. Rice's family will remain in Fulton or not during vacation. [28]

Mr. Hersman is hard at work when out of school. He has cut that tall hedge and staked it down like the one north of the house. It looks much better.... I believe I spend more idle time now than I ever did in my life. I feel bad to think of it. The most I have done since you left is to trot back and forth from Nelia's to Abbie's. I spent last

26. All Westminster College students. With Portius Eugene Denny dead and Fred Newland ill (he died in 1878), only Alexander Hodge Foreman graduated in 1870. William Hockaday Wallace won the Westminster oration prize at the Junior Exhibition over Thomas W. Shaw and John M. Trimble. The title of Wallace's speech was "Home." Later he would prosecute the Jesse James gang. See p. 18 and p. 88; also see the footnote to October 29, 1863, on Wallace. According to Clagett papers at the Presbyterian Historical Society at Montreat, North Carolina, the Reverend William Clagett gave his plans to the Methodist church when the Presbyterian church could not agree to begin a university in Dallas; these plans became part of Southern Methodist University.

27. Around 1871, Margaret Machette sold her property and moved in with Abbie Hersman's family. Sam Watson, father of Jennie Watson Hockensmith. See December 29, 1864.

28. In 1871, Lizzie Rice married James Henderson, brother of Mary "Mollie" Henderson. Lizzie's father, Dr. Nathan Rice, became president of Westminster College in 1868. See October 4, 1860, and January 26, 1866.

week at Nelia's and this [week] is for Abbie if I can stay away from Maud so long. Mr. Flood will be very busy this week it being [a] court [session]....

I have returned from preaching, heard a fine sermon. The Sunday evening lectures now are from Revelation, the seals and vials. I should be glad if you was at home to enjoy them with us.

Are you not going to Sam's? I hope you will. I shall be sorry if you don't go to see Sam and the children. The check came safe. I think I will get me black silk and make me a long shawl or scarf to wear with my new dress. I wish you could get some pretty colored yarn to knit stockings for Maud and Maggie for next winter. One pound will be enough. Lizzie had such pretty yarn for her children....

Kearney, Missouri
August 26, 1870

From Sallie Flood[29] to her sister-in-law, Cornelia Machette Flood

My Own Darling Sister

This has been a sad, sad day to us all here at home. We have just returned from the graveyard where we laid in the cold ground the form of our little idol.[30] It is hard to give the lovely little creature up, but she is a happy, bright angel now. She would have been a cripple if she could have gotten well, for she had a terrible rising on her hip, and you all can not imagine how she suffered for five long weeks. She knew every thing until last Sunday, would hold out her little bony fingers begging for water, then offer to kiss for it. At times we could hear her piteous moans way out in the yard, and three times we stood around to see her die, but we thought she was getting better until Sunday. Every sign was favorable, only that fearful cough, when she began to choke and could not drink, then over her eyes came a wild glare, and they were never closed again until in death.

She had so many spasms and suffered so much that it is a glorious thing God took her to Heaven as soon as he did. When we saw her through the glass at the grave, her little head had turned some to one side — that made her look cute like she used to. After she was dead she reminded me so much of little Maggie. I did not know how much I loved her until she was sick. She was so smart and affectionate and had so many cunning ways. Every one says that she was taken from us because we made her our idol. Little Maud is all the baby we have to love now....

Kearney, Missouri
June 18, 1871

From Eliza Major Flood, to her son and daughter-in-law, John and Cornelia Machette Flood

Dear Children:

I am here all alone.

In your sad bereavement you have all the sympathy parents can give. We have had such a trial for a time I felt as one [who] could not be comforted. Long ago I felt it

---

29. Judge Joseph Flood, his wife Eliza Major Flood, and their youngest children, Sallie and Annie, had moved from Fulton to Kearney, Missouri.

30. Mary "Mamie" Yates (born May 19, 1869), niece of Sallie Flood; daughter of Dr. William and Mary E. Flood Yates.

Maud Flood, daughter of John and Cornelia Machette Flood, born October 25, 1869, died June 13, 1871

A lamb rests atop Maud's gravestone in Hillcrest Cemetery (photo by Margaret Baker Graham).

was wicked to want her back from her home on high.[31] Dear sweet little Maud, I shall never forget her lovely smiling face when I kissed her good-bye. Her grand Mama was holding her in her arms at the door. I gave her a second kiss and said, "Good-bye. Sweet thing, I fear I shall never see you again." I told the family when I came home I never expected to see the sweet little thing again. I would have been so glad could I [have] seen her once more.

Nelia, don't grieve after her. She is so much better off than you or I. She is in heaven with her Savior. If you were permitted this morning to be in her presence in glory, could speak to her in person, ask her to come back to this world of suffering and sorrow, she would say, "now, now, Mama, this home is so much better than yours and Papa's. A little while you and Pa will be here." Oh happy thought, the time will soon come and we will be with our babes in that happy land and live forever with the Lord.

I feel so glad your Pa saw her. He just bragged so much on her. He told us when he came home she was the prettiest and smartest and sweetest child to him in the world. When he read your letter [that] sweet little Maud had just died, he wept as if his heart would break. Sweet little creature, she is so much better off. Oh how hard it is to give her up. I am so sorry for John. She was such an idol with him. Poor Nelia, how hard it will be with her to give up an only child. Children, she was lovely and sweet. It's so hard for us to be reconciled in all things to our lot....

Children, I wish I could see you. If tears and sorrow would avail, you would have many a sympathizing one. Children, I can't express to you my sorrow. One consolation you know, you are the parents of an angel in glory — consoling thought. She is gone. She can't come back. You can go to her. You won't always feel as you now do. Time will

31. Eliza Flood was probably referring to her daughter Euphrates, who died in 1852 when she was sixteen months old. Joseph Flood wrote John and Nealie: "We feel to sympathize with you, in your deep affliction, from the very bottom of our hearts. We have passed through the same affliction before you in the loss of our sweet little Fraty."

make you better reconciled. We were so glad she did not suffer like poor little Mamie did. Of all the objects of suffering, she was the greatest we ever saw. Her Mama gave her up better than I could have done. She saw her suffer so long. We dressed her ourselves. She kissed her and said, "Farewell, sweet little Mamie, you are done with this world and suffering." She was a dear sweet little thing. I often go to her grave.

I know how you feel. All of her little acts and words, smiles and steps are before you. Wherever you look you see something to remind you of her, the little chair and cup, her bonnet and shoes, the cradle and buggy, the little dog, and a thousand little instances will remind you of her. You will find your selves listening for her, looking for her — a little while and you will be with her.

When will we see you? Our love to all. A kiss for yourselves. Write often. Excuse this disconnected letter. It's from your
          Mother.

Ethel B. Hersman born December 4th, 1871

From a Bible belonging to Susan Machette

Finley in learning his catechism lesson deeply pondered over the answer that we are made of dust.[32] He came to his Mother one day and said, "Mamma, when I die you must look in my dust — you'll find a button there. I swallowed one."

Note written by Susan Machette

Forest Flood born January 16th, 1873[33]

From a Bible belonging to Susan Machette

Forest, son of John and Cornelia Machette Flood

32. The answer to the question on the body of man is that "we are dust … and that, in this our fallen state, we are to return to the dust again." *The Westminster Assembly's Shorter Catechism Explained, by Way of Question and Answer*, part I (Philadelphia: Presbyterian Board of Publications, 1845), 62.

33. At first, Nealie's son's name was spelled "Forrest," perhaps after Edwin Forrest, an important American actor who died in 1872, or after Nathan Bedford Forrest, a Confederate general. After a time, one "r" was dropped; for consistency's sake, "Forest" is used throughout.

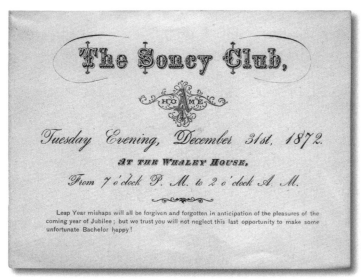

Sue Machette, taking advantage of tradition, invited Harvey to a Leap Year party in February 1872. This Soncy Club party might have been another Leap Year invitation to Harvey. "Soncy" means "of good fortune."

Love Letter 1, from John Harvey Scott to Susan Machette

February 23, 1873

Miss Susie:

Must I now ask your forgiveness for this intrusion and say, "I am very sorry to interrupt you and hope you will excuse me?" Or will not your natural goodness of heart find an ample apology, if one be wanting, in my deep solicitude to hear from you?...

Do you know that the year 1873 has lately become the first of years to me? And that the first day of that year is the 6th of February? It is to me what the hegira is to the devout Mohammed, and the M[asonic] Hall is my Mecca.[34] Around it cluster my dearest recollections, and from it will radiate remembrances to gladden the darkest hour. When I think of it, I can scarcely persuade myself that I have not been the victim of some magic spell, and that after all, when the potent charm is broken, the beautiful dream will have vanished. But I have in my possession one proof that it was not *all* a dream. That earring, you know. It has been my chief consolation and is, as it were, a living representation of my Lady-love.

I *believe* I made love to it. I am sure I kissed it — more than once — for its *owner's* sake. But I expect that you want it, and so *reluctantly* send it to you. Now, as a reward for my *generosity* in returning it so soon, will you grant me one request? Please send me that *picture* of yours of which you spoke....

Love Letter 2, from Susan Machette to John Harvey Scott

Professor,

... The 6th will always be held in dearest remembrance. I think that is Aladdin's Lamp you keep in your mysterious Hall — by aid of which I discovered a *jewel*.

When I took the earring out of the envelope I couldn't think what you meant till I read your note. You want to exchange it for a picture. You know I would give you one

34. Harvey was a Mason. In his love letters, he linked romantic love to religion as nineteenth-century American lovers tended to do, but in this first instance the link is to the Islamic faith rather than Christianity.

willingly if I had a respectable one. I burned up several the other day — they were such absurdities. If there is one left you can have it — I will look and see. The boy did not wait for an answer to yours. I will try and find Paul and send this....

———

My d— Miss Susie,

Just imagine the *next* to the last word *omitted*, and the dashes in the second word filled up, and the address is complete — as I would like to have it. I couldn't resist the temptation to begin my note as above. As the elder Mr. W would say, "It is a more tenderer" form of address than "*Miss* Susie." Besides, the word Miss has an air of frigidity about it now that unpleasantly reminds me of less favored days. To *my very sensitive* mind it is also suggesting of *distance* and a comfortable degree of *coolness*.

For all these very good reasons, I know you will excuse me — I mean not get *mad* at me for commencing as I would *like* to have done. I do think you treat me very badly. I declare I have dreamt of that watch pocket for a week or more and am almost crazy to see it. Please do send it and let me be "joined to my idols." You have already taught me to worship *graven images*. The watch pocket will make me an "out and out" heathen.

...Good-bye, and if it be not asking too much of you, think of me some times....

Love Letter 3, from John Harvey Scott to Susan Machette

———

My Dearie —

I would have liked the commencement of your note better without the *Miss*. I hope you won't call me so any more — that is, won't call me Miss Susie. I think you an "awful sweet" to send me the box and note....

I...am in Sallie's room[35] — I thought I was going to have the evening to myself but Sallie has returned and I hope you will make her responsible for this disjointed chat — I can't write to you when anyone is by. I hate to write before her and not tell what I'm writing and yet I would not for it would detract from its sacredness, might I say.

As to the watch pocket — I looked at it once or twice today and wanted to send it to you — but it did not look pretty a bit and I didn't have the heart to send it. I will send it in the morning, though, begging you to consider that I couldn't get any material in town to make one that I wished to and so had to make it with what I had at hand. I will just let you have this till I can make you a better one.

I wish you would write to me often — I wear one note out before I get another and that ought not to be. You ask me to think of you sometimes. I think too often of you, I 'spect. I think about you once a day and that is all the time. I will stop now.

Love Letter 4, from Susan Machette to John Harvey Scott

———

My own Susie,

... Now I am all alone, with nothing to distract my attention save a sweet face which, somehow, is always before me, and which is present even in my dreams. Oh, how I love that face — I call it my "guardian angel."

Love Letter 5, from John Harvey Scott to Susan Machette

---

35. Sallie Flood married Robert "Bob" Tureman, a banker, in 1872. Harvey Scott, the Floods, the Turemans, and Sue Machette all apparently had rooms at the Whaley House.

I can not tell you how glad I was to get that short note. I prize it above other letters you have written me, because it came from you *freely* and *voluntarily*. I would give anything for another like it, only longer. Will you not write me another *to-morrow* or next day and tell me in it that *you do love* me? I would like to see that *declaration* in *writing*, for somehow it does seem too good to be true. I would like to read it over and over again 'till the sweet conviction was fastened on my mind.

May I write to you every 6th? *every Thursday*? But I can not wait from one Thursday to another. I love my Susie too much to keep quiet all that time. When with you, time flies, oh, so rapidly. Away from you, "like a wounded snake it drags its slow length along."[36] You have become so absolutely necessary to my peace of mind that I believe I will rejoice when Monday comes.

I dare not lay my sacrilegious hands on that watch pocket. I send it back to you to make it larger, but don't keep it a moment longer than is required to fix it. When you write me that letter to-morrow, send me a piece of that dress you are making — a very little piece will do....

Love Letter 6, from Susan Machette to John Harvey Scott

Dearest —

Don't think I'm going to give you a sermon because I'm writing on sermon paper. I am at Abbie's and can't find any thing else to write on. I called you dearest because you are dearer to me than anybody in the wide, wide world, for don't I think more about you and have sweeter thoughts of you than of any one else? And I'm sure you have it more in your power to give me pleasure or pain than any one I know. So you must be very good to me (I'm sure you are) for I couldn't bear that you should be displeased with me or neglect me. You ask me to write "I do love you." Well, I do love you. I don't like being in love much, though. It places one's happiness in another's hands. Don't you think so?

How easy it is to talk on paper. I have wanted to say all this to you — but am always tongue tied when I am with you or a little frightened maybe.

You ask if you may write every Thursday &c. I'll think you treat me badly if you don't write oftener. If I don't see or hear from you ever day or two, I think you do not love me. They do treat me too badly at my table — that is, Brother John, Nealie, and Sallie. Every time I look up to try to see you they always say something ridiculous to make me laugh — so that I hardly ever get to speak to you....

I was so delighted to get your letter this morning. I was awake a long time last night thinking — I think George regards himself quite in the light of confidential friend. He put his head in at my door this morning and grinned saying — "Ain't up yet and I got a letter for you."

... I send you a piece of my dress....

Love Letter 7, from John Harvey Scott to Susan Machette

My own dear Susie

... If you just could know what angels of mercy those little notes of yours are, you would not be so sparing of them. If you only knew what genuine happiness the last one brought and how I almost envied that poor inanimate "sermon paper" for being

36. A line from *Essay on Criticism* by Alexander Pope (1688–1744).

the first to catch those words so dear to me, you would have sent me another before this time. 'Twould have been an act of Christian charity and mercy to have sent it.

I've been trying an experiment: To see whether I could *wait four days* without hearing from you. So far as waiting the four days is concerned, I regard the experiment as a disastrous failure. Apart from that, it taught its lesson. I find I cannot wait longer than *one day comfortably*. The second day I found to be both long and tiresome; the third was absolutely unbearable; and the fourth — well, I don't know what would have happened. I just can't wait any longer. Now please write me a nice sweet letter like the last.

When can I come to see you? To-morrow night and go with you to prayer-meeting? The watch pocket is all right now. I recognized that new dress Sunday morning — admire your taste as displayed in the selection.

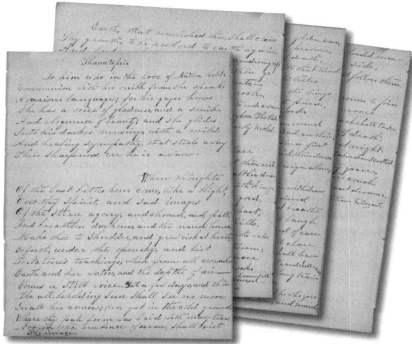

Harvey Scott, who enjoyed quoting poetry, copied in a notebook "Thanatopsis," William Cullen Bryant's famous poem in the Romantic tradition.

Darling —

… Tomorrow I shall have pleasant anticipations of seeing you. I shall enjoy prayer meeting so much — I was going to say because I can sit by you — but that sounds like a heathen. I want you to come to call on me so much — Nealie says I must not receive gentlemen callers in my room — since I must make this sacrifice to propriety, could I not see you in the parlor some evening? What do you think? …

You must not try any more experiments — such as waiting four days — it's real cruel to me.… I am glad you like my calico — I don't care whether any one else does or not.… Write to me soon again, if it is only to tell me you have not forgotten me.

Love Letter 8, from Susan Machette to John Harvey Scott

March 17, 1873

My own dear Susie,

When can I have you for my own, in fact?

An hour or more ago I came from the Masonic Hall. Do you think I go there often? Well, I find it very difficult to sit at this end of the hall from 7 to 10 or 11 o'clock, book in hand, my thoughts all the while at the *other end* of the hall. I say it is hard to be pouring over some musty old book when my *heart's idol* is so near by. The fact is, I can't study. I don't believe I have done anything of that kind since you have

Love Letter 9, from John Harvey Scott to Susan Machette

been here. My time is too fully occupied with thinking of you, to have any to spare on old dry books. And I had just as well recognize this further fact, that I never will be any more account until — well, until this present scene of things is changed and I can have my Susie all my own.

Then, after the *novelty* of the *situation* had worn off, I could study. I would try to do any thing for *your sake*.

I remarked above that I had been to the Masonic Lodge to-night. But I have been back over two hours and have spent a good part of the time *thinking*. Can you guess what about? I know you can not and so I will tell you. I was just reviewing *last Saturday night*. How pretty you were and how sweet. I can see you *now* just as you looked then — the picture is photographed on my mind. And then that kiss you gave me! I would give any thing in the world for *another*. Even the *memory* of it could not be bought. That night was an oasis, a green spot, in my life.

When will I come to the *next* "green spot" in my life journey, my Susie?

… Susie, if you *could* only love me as much as I do you, I know the reality will be more pleasant than the anticipation. Can you do that?

But I have written enough this time. Forever blessed be the man that invented writing. Good-bye.

Love Letter 10, from Susan Machette to John Harvey Scott

Darling:

… Wouldn't you like to know when I do not think of you? I could not tell of such a time, save when I am sound asleep. Then I dare say I dream of you.… I am tempted to wish I was an enchantress as you accuse me of being — I'd assume the appearance of a *book* that I might be with you always. It does seem right hard when I love to be with you so dearly that I only occasionally catch glimpses of you. Next time you go to Brother Charley's I want you to let me know. I could go any time.

You ask "if you could only love me as much as I do you." You know I haven't the gift of language to express my feelings, but briefly — I'm like the owl, my Dear, I keep a mighty thinking. If I am not able now to persuade you, by words, that I love you devotedly — [in] the days that are to come, I hope my life will prove the sincerity of my affection for you.…

Love Letter 11, from John Harvey Scott to Susan Machette

March 21, 1873

My own sweet Susie —

… Just think of it: Here I am not half a hundred feet from you, and yet *you* had just as well be in the *moon*, so far as my seeing you is concerned. I believe the moon would be the more preferable situation of the two. I could *then* sit and look at you all night long which I can't do *now*.

Even from a boy, I have had the most ardent sympathy with old Tantalus of mythological notoriety.[37] But his punishment sinks into utter insignificance when compared with mine. His sufferings were his just reward for an offense committed against the "immortal gods" — mine is a sacrifice to "propriety." It's a great temptation to wish

---

37. Tantalus, son of Zeus; tortured forever in Hades for tricking the gods.

there was no such thing as *propriety*. But I won't wish that, even though in its relentless-ness it forbids my going to see you in *your own room* when I would give my eyes to do so. I *feel better now* after reminding you again of your very *kind* and *friendly invitation not* to come to see you — there....

I wonder what there is in that quiet, innocent face of yours that is so perfectly fas-cinating to me. I tried to study out that problem last night at *church*. I thought of that face a vast deal more than I did of the sermon. And the more I thought of it, the more I loved it. I could only make this out clearly, that I did love my Susie more than lan-guage can express or thought conceive. And then I wondered whether she loved me thus; whether she loved me better than any body in the "wide wide world." The fact is I heard precious little of that sermon. It won't do for me to go to church with you, that is sure. Had better stay at home than act like a heathen. Oh! how long it does seem before you will be *my* Susie — before I can call you my dear sweet w——. But even then I could not love you more than I do now....

Dearest:

... I have not gotten over the effects of blues.... I suppose one's imagination sug-gests all sorts of horrible things. Don't yours?... The fact is I listened to some com-mon sense advice yesterday drawn from practical experience which made me think very much about Miss Lizzie B. I almost wish you had not told me about that. The burden of said advice was that men are deceivers ever and that men do not want to kiss ladies they expect to marry &c. &c.

I can't tell half that was said — but it was all disinterested and well meant and because they wished me well and because they know more than I do, but I must not think or write any more about it for I shall spoil the day. I beg you to believe that they have the best opinion of you. It is only the low estimate they put on poor human nature.

I'd rather [by] far have my own romantic views. I do love and trust you so, and when you tell me I shall be your "dear sweet wife," I believe you, and wish it for my own sake as well as yours.

I fall more in love all the time with my sweet little watch — I haven't let it stop yet. Its ticking shall only be to me the lan-guage of truth and constancy, and I could not bear to hear it if my heart beat not sincerely in love to you.

... You will be sure to be at Abbie's tomorrow night. I want so for time to fly fast till then. I am always so happy when I am with you — married folks say they think more and more of each other every day they live — seems strange, doesn't it? — hearts grow larger I imagine. There's the dinner bell and I must close — write to me often.

Love Letter 12, from Susan Machette to John Harvey Scott

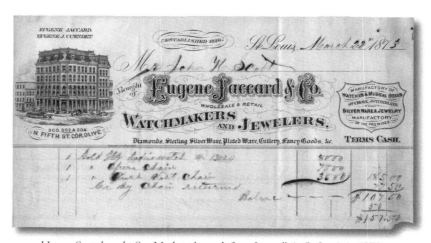

Harvey Scott bought Sue Machette's watch from Jaccard's in St. Louis in 1873.

Love Letter 13, from John Harvey Scott to Susan Machette

Dear Susie —

... I never told you the *exact* and *full* truth about my love scrapes. I did in the case of *Miss Lizzie*; but not in the case of *Miss Mollie*.[38] It was not because I wished to conceal any-thing from my darling that I did not tell her; but simply because it was an experience of my boyhood years and it was anterior to the time of my knowing you, I thought you would not be interested in it at all. I thought once that I loved Mollie — I was a boy then and just as *crazy* as boys usually are — I found out afterwards that it was all a mistake and so I broke it off.

I love my Susie, though, with the love of a *full grown man* which can never change — no, *never, never, never.*

Love Letter 14, from John Harvey Scott to Susan Machette

April 1, 1873

My own darling Susie —

... Above all things I had rather read a love letter *from* you; excusing that, I had rather write one *to* you. I never knew the *poverty* of the English language till I attempted to tell you *how much* I loved you. I'm sure there are not words enough in my vocabulary to tell how dear thou art to me. "For speech is weak such love as mine to tell."

... I think I never loved you so much before. I feel that my capacity to love increases the more I know you. Into what deeper depths of love do you intend to lead me, my darling? Am I not yours entirely and are you not yet satisfied with your conquest? But go on, and let me love you more and more. It's sweet to love when we are loved....

Now I am going to prove to you that all men are not *deceivers*, and that my *heart* and my *tongue* speak the *same language* and that my *life will do so.* When you say, "I do love and trust you so &c.," I long to convince you that your trust is well founded and that your confidence and love will never be violated. Does not my Susie believe me? I know she *must*, and so will have the *blues* no more *forever.*

... Let me conclude with a verse I read just now from my favorite poet, Burns—

> I swear and vow that only *thou*
> Shall ever be my *dearie!*
> *Only thou*, I *swear* and *vow*,
> Shall ever be my dearie![39]

I can put my hand on a *Bible* and repeat that verse. *Could you*, if you had written it to *me*? Sweet dreams and Good night.

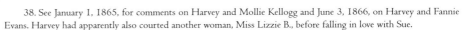

HUSBAND AND WIFE.

This clipping of Gerald Massey's poem on idyllic marriage was preserved in Harvey Scott's notebook.

---

38. See January 1, 1865, for comments on Harvey and Mollie Kellogg and June 3, 1866, on Harvey and Fannie Evans. Harvey had apparently also courted another woman, Miss Lizzie B., before falling in love with Sue.

39. From "Wilt Thou Be My Dearie?" by Robert Burns (1759–1796).

April 6, 1873

Dear Harvey —

You ask me to write to you before church — else you will have the blues. I will *commence* this note at least — as I would do anything that I thought would please you. If I do not have time to finish now, I will do so this afternoon. I wish I could tell you how *good* and *dear* and *sweet* and *handsome* I think you — you wouldn't have the blues at all today. Won't you believe it because I tell you so! I love you more and more every day I live. I never heard of satiety in love — don't believe there is such a thing. I don't know how much love my nature is capable of — but I must love you very, very dearly, as every thing you do seems right to me — I don't see any faults in you at all — and I know that no one is faultless so it must be because I love you so. . . .

I think my watch and chain the prettiest I ever saw — you don't know how I prize them as dear souvenirs of my Darling. . . . The church bell is ringing and I will leave. . . .

April 9, 1873

Dear Harvey:

Don't you feel bad for the way you did last night — I'm sure you ought but you didn't look like it at breakfast — were in the finest spirits, if I may judge from appearances. I admit things are sometimes deceiving — let us trust they were in the present instance.

I haven't felt good a bit, though I did promise I would forget and forgive. One can't always do as one would wish. I'm sure I only wish to remember how good and sweet you are — which I always do, but a dull pain is ever present now — it is the consciousness of the mutability of affairs mundane.

I knew an old bachelor once who was forever repeating:

> Alas! how easily things go wrong,
> A sigh too much—a kiss too long—
>   Then follows a mist and weeping rain,
>   And life is never the same again.[40]

Wouldn't you like to know for certain what the "ships from the unknown seas" have for us — whether they bear the same portion to you and to me? . . .

I've been blue today. As antidote for the same I went down to see Mrs. Sheley — met Mrs. Brown then — she noticed my pretty chain and remarked that it was the very latest style &c.[41] She looked at me so very hard I am sure I must have looked very [self] conscious. As often as I look at my watch I always think of you as faithful and true. When you are tender and kind to me, I cannot cherish a thought that is not true to you. I am afraid if you were otherwise I should be naughty and — and — do something I might regret.

40. A slight rewording from George MacDonald's *Phantastes* (1858).

41. Mrs. Sheley, probably Kate West Sheley, who married James K. Sheley, Jr., in 1868. Mary "Mollie" Kerr married John T. Brown, a physician, in 1868. Kate and Mollie were cousins. See October 4, 1860, and April 30, 1864, on Mollie Kerr. See April 22, 1866, on Kate's sister-in-law, Sarah Sheley Henderson.

John Harvey Scott, photo on glass over a
gold frame and enclosed in a decorative case.

Do write to me and tell me lots of sweet things — How
much you love me, how often you think of me and what you
have been doing since I met you, &c. Harvey, I haven't a happy
thought the whole long day that is not connected with you....

Your own Susie

Dear Harvey: I had just written to you when yours came —
I was in Nealie's room and George came for me and I came
and found your note containing assurances that you still love
me — my heart is a great deal lighter and I shall sleep a great
deal better tonight for it. I do love you better than any one in
the wide, wide world and very readily forgive you the pain you
gave me last night, especially in consideration of the fact that
you do believe in me a *little* more. I wish you did so, altogether
— I am afraid you will be trying some more *experiments* which
I don't like.... I think it was so sweet in you to write to me this
evening and to send me the orange....

*Love Letter 17, from John
Harvey Scott to Susan Machette*

April 10, 1873

My dear Susie —
    ... Your last [note] made me feel sad and glad at the same time. You know you gave
me a *little scolding* in the first part of your note: that made me *sad*. You also awakened a
sort of melancholy sympathy for the old bachelor who was always repeating those
dirge like lines. And then again when you mention the "ships from the unknown seas,"
I never think of the future except my ideas cluster around my Susie as the central figure. From the 6th day of February till this day, I have never suffered myself to think of
the possibility of those "ships" bringing to you *one* portion and to me *an-other*. I may
not have acted wisely in this, but I confess that I cannot bear to think of living without
you. And my most earnest prayer to the good Father is that He may make you mine
that I may love and cherish you for ever. For I believe that I could serve Him better *then*
than now.

    But your letter also made me glad at heart. When you say that you have not a
"happy thought" that is not connected with me, you make me as nearly contented as I
can be now. But I do think that I *deserve* to be thought of *thus by you*. If I could tell you
how often and how lovingly I think of my darling, I am sure that she would admit that
such love merited none other than a most fervent love in return....

    My Susie is *every thing* and *every body* to me. I think of her by day, and in the silent
hours of the night I love to lay awake and think of her. I think of her first in the morning and sweet thoughts of you are the last to leave my mind at night. Does my darling
doubt my love? I wish you knew how often your pretty face presents itself to me during the day. How often I kiss the picture you gave me. And here let me remind you
that, while I made certain promises which I mean to keep, *you made a promise too*. You

said I might kiss you when we were alone together and put my arm around you. *I won't forget your promise....*

―――――――

Dear Harvey

 I have been busy with my new dress to day — that is why I have not written to you as I intended to do; and I don't suppose I will get to finish this, for I will have to get ready to go to Mrs. Curd's — which will bore me beyond expression.[42]

 Do you know — since we have been sweethearts I don't like society at all. When I am not with you I had much rather be alone or just with the home folks. I will have to go, though, whether I wish it or not. Brother John made the engagement for me, first to play croquet this afternoon but it being rainy Mr. Walthall asked me if I would go this evening.[43] O Mercy! don't you feel sorry me. I wish it would just rain like every thing. I hate croquet of all things — I'll have to play parlor croquet this evening if it rains.

 When are you coming to see me? You have got to tell me when — this week. I could scarcely get you to come here last week. I'll think you don't want to see me, and of *course* don't *love* me if you do not come *very soon*. But — you *do* love me and will come. What would I do if I had not the happiness to know this? What an awful thing it would be, to love you as I do and *not know* that you loved me. Although I do feel certain that my darling is all mine, sometimes I do feel wretched. I imagine that it is too good to be true or maybe that I have done something to displease him — which I wouldn't do for the world if I knew it and could help it. I wish sometimes you would ask me to do some great thing that could prove conclusively how much I love you — I can't think what such a thing would be. I'm sorry I said this; now, for I dare say you will set your wits to work to think up something to torment me about, just for mischief. Mind you, I shall be on my guard hereafter. You promised you would be good. Remember. I think you did right badly the last time but you did so sweet at last I could not remember it against you.

 Do write to me — and come to see me.

―――――――

April 15, 1873

My dear Susie:

 In one of your notes received some time since, you speak of *"discontinuing"* a piece of work on which you were engaged, in order to pay your first duty to the one you love best. But in your *last* note, you tell me that you put off writing to me because you *were busy with your new dress.*

 I presume, then, that you love your *new dress more* than you do me! At any rate, you did not wish to *discontinue* it as you *would have done once.* I am sorry that your promise to write to me interfered in this instance — maybe in others — with duties considered by you as of more importance, and, perhaps, also, more interesting. Am afraid I shall

Love Letter 18, from Susan Machette to John Harvey Scott

Love Letter 19, from John Harvey Scott to Susan Machette

―――――――

42. Harriet Webster Curd, who married the banker Isaac Curd in 1865.

43. Croquet came to the United States in the 1860s and was soon very popular. Mr. Walthall, probably one of the sons of William Walthall, a Baptist minister, and his wife Matilda.

feel embarrassed after this in asking you to write to me at all. I confess that I find my dearest and sweetest pleasure, first in being with you and talking to you, and then in writing to you. I don't know a duty that I would not gladly sacrifice — so far as my inclinations go — to write to you.

... Just here the entrance of Mr. L put a stop to my writing. After he left I was most too sleepy *to finish* and so had to defer it till this time Wednesday.

When you kissed me so sweetly this morning, I almost regretted what I had already written, for the first part of this note was accomplished last night. But when I thought of *some other things*, I resolved to let it stay. I wonder if you do love me as much as you say, and if you would *really* be willing to make some *great sacrifice* in order to prove it conclusively. Do you happen to remember that you were just on the point of getting *mad* at me the other night when I asked you to *prove* to me that you love me by doing something to which you were averse? I find then that the *"great thing"* I must select in order to try your love must be *just such a thing* as *you want* to *do* and no other. There is not much credit in doing what one wants to do, you know. Why, I believe that had I persisted in my demand, you would have broken our engagement without hesitation. Does this prove the sincerity of your love?

... Please write to me very soon and answer the *charges* I have brought against you in this note *if you can*. That is, if your *new dress* does not prevent your doing so. Also, send a piece of *that* new dress....

Love Letter 20, from Susan Machette to John Harvey Scott

Dear Harvey

When I told you yesterday morning to send me what you had written — that I would not be mad &c., I did not really suppose it would be as unjust and evil as it was. I don't say that I am mad but I can't but be a little indignant that you insist on thinking me inconsistent, deceitful and false when I am conscious that my actions have been prompted with a desire to please you and that I have not been wanting in love and duty to you in a single instance, since we have been engaged. I agree with you that I rested too secure in the belief that you loved me — I do not err today, however.

I would give a great deal to really to know whether you find our relation as lovers too *insipid* to dispense with lovers' quarrels, or whether you are tired of the engagement altogether or might I hope that it was the effect of dismal weather and blues that caused you to be so unkind. I know this much, you cannot thoroughly love one you *trust* so little as you do me — You cannot believe that I love you, else you would not continually wound me as you do. There is not a person in the world that has the power to do so, *but you*. I hadn't the heart to read your letter more than once — I threw it on the table — got in bed and cried myself to sleep — you can't blame me, can you? For you were not here to kiss me into forgetfulness of wrongs.

You ask me to answer charges you bring — which I think it is very easy to do. First you make a great deal out of my saying that I was too busy with my dress to write. What do I want with a pretty dress if it is not for *your* benefit, I'd like to know. I want you to consider that all the stitches in said article are thoughts of you and if you should discover any thing particularly killing in its effect, when finished, my intention *only* is — *believe* me — that you shall assume a new pair of *fetters*. Then my dress was not the only reason of my not writing. I was so vexed at that idiot Mr. W that I could not write sooner. I am sure I think all this is [a] much better excuse than getting "too sleepy to write."

As for a "great sacrifice" in order to prove my love, I honestly think I would make any reasonable sacrifice, but I hope you know that would not involve principle for then I could not have *self-respect* — neither could I have *yours*.

You say if you had done so and so I would have broken our engagement without hesitation. There is nothing on earth that could induce me to do so — I say this most *solemnly.* I was going to say there was but one thing that could make me do it — that was if you did not love me — but that would be your doing, wouldn't it? So I can say with a good conscience that I can never sever our engagement which is most sacred to me, more so than any thing in the world. It does seem to me that your love is absolutely essential to my happiness. I never thought I would be so weak, I love you so much, that I could not make your affection for me a means of torture....

I send you a piece of my offending dress. It looks as dismal as this miserable weather to me. I did not know before, till you told me so, that I was in a hurry for your visits to be over. And I deny that too. I always do enjoy your visits so much and am so sorry when the time comes for to go.

Your unhappy Susie

April 17, 1873

Love Letter 21, from John Harvey Scott to Susan Machette

My own dear unhappy Susie —

After the general *blowing up* contained in your last, I feel much as though I had come out of the contest *second best.* The first in your letter was *rather* severe. I hardly think mine deserved *such* a censure and I cannot persuade myself that you *mean every thing* you say — Upon my honor, what I said was designed rather to solicit some *strong* expression of love from you than seriously to question your love. Had I known that it would have wounded you, I would not have written it I am sure; for I did not believe *more than* a *small fraction* of it at the time. Now, I do not believe any of it — scarcely — I cannot explain myself better than by saying that my letter must be taken in a "pickwickian sense."[44]

Let me ask you in all candor, *do you believe* I would be engaged to one that I *thought* did not *love* me? I told you that I wanted you to be my *dear sweet wife.* I *meant* it, *honestly* — *sincerely.* I *still mean* it. I look forward to that time with a greater desire than I can explain to you....

I do love my darling and *she knows it.* I love my Susie with a love fine, strong, and never dying. I would like to have been by you to kiss away the

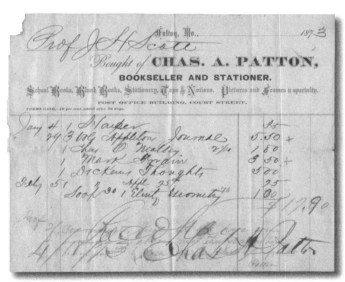

Harvey Scott bought works by Charles Dickens and Mark Twain. Other receipts from the 1870s indicate that he also bought works by Thackeray, Scott, Irving, Darwin, Tennyson, Shakespeare, Dryden, Dante, Wordsworth, and Homer.

44. "Pickwickian sense," a reference to *The Pickwick Papers* (1837), Charles Dickens's novel.

tears and make you forget your wrongs. If you will send back that *hateful* letter of mine that was the cause of those tears, I will *burn* it....

Love Letter 22, from Susan Machette to John Harvey Scott

My dear Mr. 'Fessor:

I hope this note will not be as unfortunate as the last — that is, I hope I won't say anything to make you *mad*. You made me feel so bad and gave me a little heart ache last night. I heard the clock strike ten, eleven, twelve, but you don't believe anything I tell you. I wonder if you do not sure enough. Sometimes I think you just *'tend*, like the children say, to make me repeat what I have said — I judge you by myself — for I just love for you to tell me "I love you." It is *never* an old story. If Major W has a Bible in his parlor, I will lay my hand on it and do as you asked me if I would last night.[45] I know this much — if I didn't love you, you couldn't make love to me — I never saw any one that had the courage to do that — yet.

Sometimes I think you do not love me. That is when you treat me like I was a little *kitten* or something to be played with....

Love Letter 23, from John Harvey Scott to Susan Machette

April 22, 1873

My darling:

... It is well enough, I expect, that we did postpone our assignation. The present gives promise of a bad night.... What if the night after this should be a bad night, too? It would be just too much to stand, wouldn't it? I think in that...case you would have to let me come and see you in your little corner room. Do you know I have the greatest desire and curiosity to see you in that same room? I can imagine nothing more *comfortable* and sweet than to be all alone with you in *there* and make love to you. Am I ever to have that pleasure? Am most tempted to act the part of a *desperate lover* some night and tap at *your window*. Would you let me in? Would you, sure enough?

... How I do love to kiss you! And how I love you just because you will let me kiss you. Every single kiss makes me assume a new "pair of fetters," more effectual than those forged by new dresses. And speaking of kisses, by the way, reminds me that you owe me *two dozen*, which you are to pay *to-morrow night*. You did owe me two dozen, but by the time of our next meeting, the *interest* — I charge you *one hundred per cent* — will have run the number up to *four dozen*.

My darling, how I do want to see you to-night. Why must I sit here all alone hour after hour and you so near by? Do you want to see me as much as I do you? Of course not. Else you would come to see me or allow me to come to see you. Can you tell me wherein consists the difference between seeing you alone in the parlor and seeing you alone in *your room*? I wonder if there is not some humbuggery in all these *over-nice distinctions*. If you will pardon the humor displayed, I will wish them in — *Boston*, for to-night.

... How I long for to-morrow night. After that, I reckon I will wish for *Friday* night. If dreams come from a multitude of thoughts, I will dream of my darling. Awake or

---

45. Major David Whaley, proprietor of the Whaley House.

asleep she fills my every thought. I sometimes get vexed when I think how much I love you and how *poor and tame* the *words sound* by which I try to tell you my love.

May 11, 1873

Love Letter 24, from John Harvey Scott to Susan Machette

My *own* darling Susie —

. . . You say I have never mentioned to one of your family anything about our proposed marriage. It is true that I never have. I acknowledge it freely; but I *utterly deny,* as you seem to insinuate, that my silence on this subject was prompted by any want of love or fidelity to you. As I hope to stand acquitted before that last and highest tribunal, I solemnly declare that my purposes to you from the very first 'till this time have been *honorable* and *nothing* wanting in *love.* In fact, I have several times determined to speak to some of your people about it, but have simply put it off from time to time.

Why didn't you tell me to speak to your Mother about it? I think you might make free enough with me to speak without embarrassment on this subject. Besides, I am not certain but what it was *your place* to *request* me to do so. I would have done it freely and most willingly. But you shall not have occasion to complain on this score any more. Who must I speak to about it? To your Mother, I suppose. Well, so it shall be. Will you go with me to see her at any early day? The sooner the better. Or must I go alone? Please tell me if you will go with me and when you will go. . . .

Harvey Scott sent his love letters in small envelopes (4.5 x 2.5 in.), sometimes writing notes on the outside, such as the one above where he wrote, "I love to wake you up so early in the morning —."

May 29, 1873
Thursday

Love Letter 25, from John Harvey Scott to Susan Machette

My Darling—

Do you remember *our first* Thursday? I have just been thinking about it, and wondering whether you would not like to *see once more* the place where first I kissed you. I told you that we — the Masons — were going to have a nice "Strawberry Festival" up there just one week from to-morrow night. Do you want to go?. . .

Tuesday

Love Letter 26, from Susan Machette to John Harvey Scott

Dear Harvey:

I had intended going to Ma's this morning to get to work but the rain prevented [it]. Imagine your "Baby" with a rainy day before her and her *Darling* far away — nobody to kiss and pet her. It makes me perfectly heartsick when I pass down the hall and meet no loving looks from your corner. Indeed every spot about here turns with dear loving memories and suggests tender thoughts of my sweetheart. I did not stay in

Harvey clipped Millie W. Carpenter's poem, "A Lover's Idyl," for his notebook.

Love Letter 27, from John Harvey Scott to Susan Machette

my room last night — I was afraid I should get *blue* — I stayed [at] Sallie's — Mr. Tureman was absent on business.

After you left yesterday morning I went in to see the ladies that were calling. They stayed till nearly dinner time.... I find myself taking a vast deal of interest in the Post Office since I look to it for a message from you, Harvey. O I hope I shall get a letter to night! I looked at the moon last night and wondered if you saw it — I thought you must be at Moberly, and would write to me from there.

You said I would not tell Mr. Ben that I would not go with him; yesterday evening he came in to see brother John when I was there, and he kept talking about getting something to bathe my eyelids with, &c.[46] I thought it was a good chance and told him, "I don't like you any way and you needn't think you are going with me any-place." He knew I meant it and so I will not be troubled any more....

It is about ten now — I suppose you are at home now with the dear ones. But you won't forget your dear one here, will you? Won't I be glad when I can go with you to see them. Darling, I want to see you *so badly*. How I wish I could go out into the hall and receive a kiss — (was ever anything *so sweet* as those *dear stolen kisses*, when you had to look one way and I another to see who was looking?) — and tell you that *I love you all* and *more* than I could *possibly tell* and that I love no one else but you &c....

Give my love to the home folks. With all my heart I am your own

Susie.

Evansville, Missouri
July 6, 1873

My Darling—

Yesterday afternoon, just before supper, I rode down to Evansville to get a letter from you, and there, sure enough, I found it waiting for me. I had been there several times before for that same letter and had most despaired of hearing from you this week. I believe I never was more glad to get any-thing. To day, Sunday, would have been both long and lonesome without it; but with all its assurances of love, I have felt forti-fied and strengthened against every emergency....

Darling, I do know we will have just the nicest kind of a time when we are married. Only a few weeks off: how I wish they were gone and that you were *now* what I *so much* long to make you, my own dear wife. I will be all impatient 'till that time. How am I to pass away these intervening weeks? I left Fulton Monday. It seems a long time already. How can I dispose of the next two or three weeks? — If I could only meet you at cousin Abbie's, that would do.[47] I would *like* to help you mark your clothes and be in

46. Benjamin Tureman, brother of Robert Tureman and brother-in-law of Sallie Flood Tureman.

47. Charlie Hersman and Harvey Scott were first cousins; hence, Abbie was "Cousin Abbie" to Harvey.

your way generally. Could you not send me some *sewing* to do, one of your new dresses to make, for instance? And speaking of dresses, I have not forgotten that you promised me a cravat from those same dresses. Darling, I am most dying for one loving, sweet kiss. And to put my arms around you once more would be happiness itself.

It is pleasant and sad at the same time to think of all the ever to-be-remembered meetings we have had about the Hotel. They are pleasant because they speak of my Darling's love to me, and sad to me *now* because those precious interviews are gone for awhile. How sweet it was to meet you in the Hall and kiss you when *we thought* no one was looking. Next year I can love my Darling with none to molest us....

But I must go to bed now, as Mother wishes me to go to Moberly for her to-morrow — a ride of near 20 miles there and back. As I am but little used to riding, it will make me very tired, I *"spect."* The roads must be very bad, too, for it has been raining here for some days.

... How thankful I will be when we are married and may good angels guard us in that dearest of all earthly relations.

July 6, 1873

My dear, dear Darling:

I am perfectly heart sick to see you this morning — if it would bring you back I would take a good hearty cry — but I must not do this, must I? For how blest I am — I have what I prize of all things earthly — *your love!* I was waked up by a storm this morning about three o'clock, and laid awake a long time thinking about you, Harvey, how I could not bear the thought of living without you and of that awful day when there will be a parting and I felt that I could scarcely live if there was not hope of meeting in the land of the Hereafter. I never prized the "present moment" as I do now, and I feel that I should be and am happier than ever before, and I am sure this feeling will be increased infinitely when we are married.

... I will send this as facsimile of my mind at present — consider both chirography and composition! There never was any body so afflicted as I — to think of having such a *dear, noble, darling, handsome, precious Sweetheart* as I have and have to be separated from him — it is enough to break one's heart....

Love Letter 28, from Susan Machette to John Harvey Scott

... Do you remember this is the 6th — just five months since that blessed 6th of February. If it shall please you that we shall be united 6th August — it will be 6 months then since we were lovers. Sometime we will together go over our courtship — do you know, I cannot read over your old letters to me while you are away? I dare not think much of the dear times we have had together, for fear I should die of the *blues* or *cry* my *eyes* out. — I never wanted to see any body so *badly in all my life.* Can't you come over very soon to see me? I will hurry and get through my work so I can *devote my whole time to you.* I will take my dresses to Mrs. Ward tomorrow and then I will go to Ma's and then I will go down town and get me a calico dress &c. Good-bye, Darling — How I wish I could *kiss* you as I did last Sunday.

Love Letter 29, from Susan Machette to John Harvey Scott

Love Letter 30, from John Harvey Scott to Susan Machette

Evansville, Missouri
July 14, 1873

My Darling

This has been the most sorrowful day I ever spent at home. The Doctor says Pa cannot get well; we do not expect him to live through this night. At best, he cannot live but a day or two. The sorrow of my family makes me sick at heart.

Love Letter 31, from Susan Machette to John Harvey Scott

Darling

I have been thinking of your sad return home — of what pleasant anticipations you had of the same. How little do we ever know what the future has in store for us. My mind is filled with horrible presentiments today. I think how religious I should be — how good, since God has bestowed such mercies on me — and yet I know I am so forgetful of my duties to Him. The last five or six months I have thought of scarcely any thing but you. I wonder if it is right — if I realize the happiness I have expected and do expect with you — it will be different from most of my expectations in life. May God in his great mercy grant us a happy union. I think like you that I will be a better woman and serve Him as I never did before. How *blest* I will be, Darling, when you are *all* mine — you are now, Dear, all save your presence, ain't you?

It will be the proudest most joyous day of my life when I promise to *love you forever.* I have promised that long ago. I mean when I promise before "Angels and men."

Love Letter 32, from John Harvey Scott to Susan Machette

Evansville, Missouri
July 31, 1873

My Own Darling—

I have wanted to write to you for four or five days but in truth have not had *time* or *opportunity.* When I see you I will tell you why. The sickness of my Father has prevented me from going to see you this week as I intended. I expect now to go the first of next week. I do hope that nothing will prevent [it]. I can say in truth now that I *am almost dead* to *see you.* My Mother wants me to put off our marriage for a week; that is, 'till the 13th instead of the 6th. The very dangerous illness of Pa has so disarranged things as to make this desirable.[48] We hope that by the 13th he will be so far recovered as to be up and about. With you, I presume it will make no great difference; but I am so sorry to have to put it off a week longer. I do so want to have you all my own. I don't do a thing but think of my sweet Darling. I want to kiss her and put my arms around her and call her my own dear wife. I'll have that privilege soon, I pray....

48. William Scott died in 1874.

August I, 1873

Dear Harvey:

Am I never to have an expected pleasure realized?... I am sitting all alone in my room — the house is so still. The moon is shining and every thing is so sweet out, but some how it gives me the heart ache and I have shut it out. So often I have sat by my window and dreamed of this moon that would make me so happy and how it is shining so peacefully, and I feel disturbed — how can I help it, Dear?...

My linen came home tonight from the wash — I had worked up so many pretty thoughts in it about *you, Darling.* I couldn't keep from crying when I put it away. I hoped you would be here to see it with me. The dreadful thought haunts me, Darling, that maybe you don't love me as well as you thought you did when you were with me. If such would be the case I pray a merciful God to let me die. *Darling, do* write to me that you have not changed. I can't believe it possible in so short a time. I wonder if it was wrong to write what I did above. I did not mean to be rebellious — I hope I shall always say God's will be done. Darling, I want to see you....

Love Letter 33, from Susan Machette to John Harvey Scott

Susan Machette Scott in what is believed to be her wedding portrait. The photographer added gold touches to Susan's two-heart ring and around the edge of her neck broach on this tintype photo under a gold frame.

John H. Scott and Sue Machette were married by Rev. W. W. Robertson, August 13th, 1873, at Whaley's Hotel, Fulton, Mo.

From a Bible belonging to Susan Machette Scott

Fulton, Missouri
August 19, 1873

Dear Brother and Susie:

... You both left on Wednesday, and on Friday Floodie's father took him home with him, so I have been quite lonely — had it not been for my precious little Babe, [I] would have found it hard to have borne. Have received several letters, sweet letters, from my Floodie since he left. He will not be back before the first of September, has been right sick since he left. I should have gone with him but we were afraid to venture out with "the mans."[49] If my darling should be much ill and taken, then O my God help *me!*...

From Cornelia Machette Flood to John Harvey and Susan Machette Scott

49. "The mans," Nealie Flood's son Forest.

Forest Flood, son of
Cornelia and John Flood

No one that I can hear of was taken much by surprise except Arthur Tureman.[50] He said, "Why, Mama, Aunt Susie and 'Mr. Fessor' married — why I didn't think *they* would ever marry...." Your wedding was a success and so must your lives be. Love God and one another and all will be well with you. The best that I can wish for is that you may be as happy as I have been and a great deal more deserving.

I have been rocking the cradle every page I commence writing; but will do better next time. The Fair is in progress and so is the Theater. Every thing goes on well and the "moon hangs high." Forest is perfectly charming and wishes the Fair to continue always....

From Sallie Flood Tureman to her brother's sister-in-law, Susan Machette Scott

Fulton, Missouri
August 31, 1873

Dear Sister

... So you are having a nice time — am glad to know it, and hope that such may ever be your lot. Sister Nealie has not been here for some time now. Brother John sent for her in one week after he left. The telegram almost frightened us to death. He has been very sick since he went up there, and they write that he has fallen off very much but still they think that it is mostly from the effect of medicine. Brother Will says that it was all caused from brother John not being doctored in time. Brother and sister Nealie both think that Brother Will can cure him, and I do sincerely hope that he may....[51]

I will be so glad when you come home. I hardly know how to get along without *you all*. If I hadn't the very best husband in the world I couldn't. Mrs. Henderson died last night and will be buried tomorrow.[52]

50. Arthur Tureman, stepson of Sallie Flood Tureman, born May 1867.

51. John Flood was being seen by his and Sallie's brother-in-law, Dr. William Yates, the father of Mamie Yates, whose death was reported on June 18, 1871. Samuel Morse first tested the telegraph line in 1844. McCandless, *History of Missouri*, 2:150, writes, "Telegraphic connections with the East via Louisville first reached Missouri in December of 1847 and Chicago a short time later. Until technical problems could be resolved, telegraph messages had to be ferried across the Mississippi at St. Louis."

52. Emily Boone Henderson, daughter of Jesse B. Boone and granddaughter of Daniel Boone; mother of Theodore "The" whose marriage to Sarah Sheley was reported on April 22, 1866.

You have seen the papers and know what is the all absorbing topic. Colonel Law did not leave Ophelia one cent or he made no will and the law cut her out. The other wounded man is bound to die very soon. You just should have been here that awful day. To *us* it was almost as frightful as the battle of Waterloo.[53]

Don't you think Old Miss Matt Patton and Mr. Willis are married! I am glad that the babies have a nurse but I pity her, don't you?[54]

Miss Mollie Dobyns has returned with a new black grenadine dress and her hat has lavender strings. She looks killing, I tell you. Mr. Tureman was struck at first sight. It was quite lively during the fair, but I did not go much for you know my opinion of fairs.... Mr. Porter don't seem to be paying his *distresses* to Miss Fannie any more. Brother Ben says that there is no thing left for him now and Miss Fannie but to take each other since you played off on him and Professor on her....[55]

Montgomery County, Missouri
September 28, 1873

From Margaret Bruin Machette to her daughter, Susan Machette Scott

Dear Susie

... I am glad you have a pleasant room. Don't buy very extravagant furniture. If you ever wish to sell the loss is so great. I do hope the College will prosper so that Professors Scott and Hersman will feel settled in Fulton. You think that Mr. Flood's health is improving. Has he heard any thing of the virtues of the Loutre spring, the old gum spring at the foot of the Loutre hill? You all know where it is. The Danville people think it [is] possessed of great medical properties — persons haul the water fifteen or twenty miles and use it. The spring is fixed up nicely. Jacob says that Nat Shelton has been greatly benefited by the use of it.[56] I wish Mr. Flood would try the water. Perhaps it would benefit him.

Julia Graves asked a great many questions about you — said she never would forget your kindness to her in Kentucky. She has four children. The oldest girl has red hair — all very pretty children. Julia said when Jimmy Graves saw your marriage notice in the paper he called his wife and told her Miss Susie Machette was married.[57] She answered, "yes and your underlip will hang down for a week." He always told his wife that you would be his second wife....

---

53. After Kessler, a mule thief, helped his son escape, a mob descended upon the carriage escorting him from the Callaway County Courthouse to the prison in Jefferson City. Kessler was hanged by the mob a mile from the courthouse. The sheriff, George Law, and a guard were shot. Law later died of his wounds, leaving his daughter Ophelia stricken and the town horrified. The *Fulton Telegraph* for August 22, 1873, reported that Ophelia Law was so "shocked, when she heard the dreadful intelligence, that for nearly twelve hours fears were entertained that she would not live."

54. Martha Patton was forty-three when she married the Reverend Henry Willis, a widower.

55. According to her October 12, 1906, obituary in the *Fulton Gazette*, Mary E. "Mollie" Dobyns, after expressing Southern sympathies in St. Louis during the Civil War period, was arrested in St. Louis and banished to Canada. Neither Ben Tureman nor Fannie Whaley, daughter of David Whaley and his first wife, Jeanette Darne, ever married.

56. Nathaniel Shelton, brother of Jake Shelton and Lizzie Machette; a circuit court judge.

57. James "Jimmy" Graves, brother-in-law of Julia Crockett Graves. David and Julia Graves had returned from Kentucky to Montgomery County, Missouri. See October 6, 1860, and October 29, 1863.

From Margaret Bruin Machette to her daughter, Susan Machette Scott

Montgomery County, Missouri
October 16, 1873

Dear Susie

... I am quite well at this time and am enjoying my visit very much — have been to two quiltings, have seen all the friends, and will try and get home before cold weather. Mrs. Shelton is at Jacob's on a visit, is looking very well, takes the death of Mr. Shelton very hard.[58] Poor old lady, I feel so sorry for her. Jane and family are well. She and Jacob want me to spend the winter with them — says there is no excuse now [that] Mr. Scott will take care of you. I have about six visits to make. It will [take] about two weeks after this and then home....

From Susan Machette Scott to John and Cornelia Machette Flood

Fulton, Missouri
June 14, 1874

Dearest Brother and Sister:

This has been a rainy Sunday. The people came home from church this morning through a hard rain — I did not go. They said Dr. Rice preached a splendid sermon. I should have liked to go tonight but it looked much like rain. I knew I would get all my Sunday dry goods spoiled — so concluded I had better stay away. Dr. Montgomery addresses the R[eligious] I[nquiry] Society tonight. I dare say he will give some thing good. They say a good many have come to commencement.

Dr. Fisher is here. He told Major D[obyns] he would not come here unless he was made president. I think from what I hear he will leave no means untried to accomplish this. So far as the faculty are concerned they would much prefer him to Dr. Rice. I suppose the latter will resign, though he has not stated so to the faculty. Professor Rice waits on Sue Hockaday constantly — takes her buggy riding and all that. Katie Taylor told some one not long ago that "Uncle John had given Miss Sue a diamond engagement ring."[59] I haven't heard of any large entertainments to be given. The church sociable was at Mrs. Lawther's last week. They had no refreshments, Ma said. She supposed the elite had taught the members how to eat and would continue their instructions in other matters.

... Who do you reckon is stopping at the Hotel? Mr. and Mrs. Schenck — she seems to be all right now.[60] They had not heard whom we married. They look just as they used to before she lost her health. They say Annie Schenck is teaching and Van preaching....

Tuesday night. Harvey has gone to the Exhibition. I did not care to go.... The bad discipline seems to be known all over the state. Dr. Montgomery was trying to find out

58. Lizzie Machette's father, Meacon Shelton, had died earlier in 1873, and her mother, Annie Berger Shelton, was visiting Jacob and Jane Dutton Shelton.

59. Michael M. Fisher, who had resigned from Westminster in 1870, was contemplating returning. Major Edward Dobyns, father of Mollie Dobyns by his first wife, had lived in St. Louis as a wealthy slaveholder and ardent Democrat. St. Louis had strong Union supporters during the Civil War, which led to the Dobynses leaving the city and eventually settling in Fulton. "Professor Rice," John Rice, professor of English and history at Westminster and Nathan Rice's son. Sue Hockaday, niece of John Hockaday. Kate Taylor, daughter of Colonel Thomas Benton and Ellen Rice Taylor and niece of John Rice.

60. The Reverend Elias and Anna Schenck, parents of Van and Annie. The 1860 census identified Mrs. Schenck as "insane." Elias might have been a brother of Addison Van Court Schenck. See April 30, 1864.

Westminster Hall, which
burned in 1909

M.M. Fisher's photograph from his
book on Westminster College,
published posthumously in 1903

Nathan Rice, who resigned as president
of Westminster College in 1874

John Harvey Scott,
mathematics professor at
Westminster College

from Dr. Rice his notions of government. The Dr. told him that before this present year
they tried disciplining the boys — but it resulted only in getting [the] ill will of people.
This year he had not tried any thing of this sort and had gotten along *just* as *smoothly!*

I am glad the Session is out — you have no idea of the vexous things that were ever
coming up. Like when Harvey examined his Algebra class, he refused to pass but three
of them and several of them would not speak to him on the street, they got so mad at

The Philologic Society offered Westminster students an opportunity to practice their oratorical skills.

him. Mrs. Wallace and Harvey struck up an acquaintance on the strength of this — She hailed him as he passed and he expected a scolding, but she thanked him for being so faithful to her boys and in short Harvey came home quite in love with her.

Mrs. Whaley says you must *send* her all the *flower* seeds you can collect — or bring them Fannie says. Crock Whaley says that out west there are so many poisonous insects to bite one that you ought to keep soda on hand, always, to put on the bites, to kill the poisons.[61] You must try this if any thing bites dear little Forest. Harvey and I were wondering how you would manage to keep him in one room, after his having such a fine time riding.

Every body says Dr. Montgomery's address was splendid save Dr. Rice, who told Brother Charley that it was a failure.

June 20th Saturday.... We have not packed up yet, will do so next week and go to Monroe, so I expect you had better direct your next letters to me at Evansville, Monroe County.

The college is to go on next year with the four Professors of last year.[62] Dr. Fisher will take Dr. Rice's place. He is just president pro tem. There was more interest and excitement about the college this year than I ever heard of before. Dr. Rice was determined not to give up his place. He sent in his resignation but had his friends to tell that he did not expect it to be accepted. On commencement night he made the same old speech he has been making the last five years — only more so. Every one thought it perfectly absurd. I don't believe any body wanted him to stay, but the Kerrs, Hockadays and Nesbits.[63]

Last Wednesday Ed Kerr came up to Harvey and was telling that they ought not to accept Dr. Rice's resignation &c. When John Sam Baker came up, too, and slapped him on the shoulder and said, "Scott, the best thing I have heard lately is old Doctor's resignation" &c., Ed looked kinder foolish.[64] The Rices gave a Senior party — none of the Professors were noticed by invitation. I wish I could see you to tell you all about every thing — paper is such a round about way of telling any thing. I wish I could know what you are doing now....

61. Crockett Whaley, brother of Fannie Whaley and son of David Whaley and his first wife, Jeanette. David Whaley and his second wife, Martha, ran the Whaley House. The Floods spent the summer in California, hoping for a cure for John, who had tuberculosis, see p. 89.

62. The four professors were Charley Hersman, Harvey Scott, John Rice, and John Lyle.

63. Prominent Fultonian families of William and Susan Kerr, John and Edith Hockaday, and Judge Thomas B. and Mary Nesbit.

64. Ed Kerr, physician and son of William and Susan Kerr. John Samuel Baker, physician and brother of Lou Baker Wilkerson, whose marriage was reported on May 17, 1865.

Fulton, Missouri
June 24, 1874

*From Susan Machette and John
Harvey Scott to John and
Cornelia Machette Flood*

Dear Brother and Nealie:

You see we are still in Fulton; we thought to have left by this time — but the Board, with their usual consideration, left without saying a word about salary of last year. Brother Charley and Dr. Fisher went to Boonville to Mr. Kemper's grand reunion.[65] They will be back by next week — so Harvey thought best to wait till then to hear something.

Professor Joe Cook came in on the cars this afternoon — has been to Columbia to commencement there — the speech Voorhees from Indiana [gave] was the great thing to hear but he failed entirely.[66] John Hockaday and Professor Rice attended the same.

Joe Cook says Professor Rice stands the best chance for the chair [of] English literature [at the University of Missouri]. Wouldn't that be *glorious* for Westminster? The Board are so anxious to get rid of him — they would have turned him right out if they could have gotten the professors just to say the word. Mrs. Wilkerson told Mrs. Dobyns they (the Rices) were the worst taken down people she ever saw — when the Board accepted the doctor's resignation, already he had accepted the place in Danville....[67]

Mrs. Rickey's boy died Monday morning. I think it had the measles. Mrs. Boulware's little baby died the same day — you know it has always been sick. Mrs. Atkinson has a boy a few days old.[68]

This is the 24th — a great day with the Masons. The Negroes are celebrating it at the fair ground. Three carloads of negroes came in this morning to attend — about thirty black Masons marched through the streets to the music of the negro band. We had dinner at 11 o'clock to let the darkies go.

Mrs. Dobyns sent me such a beautiful bouquet today, 14 different kinds of flowers in it. Mollie Brown called on me yesterday — asked a great deal about you all.

July 2, Thursday.... We heard from home that Mod expected to be sick about this time, so deferred our visit.[69] Harvey has ordered some new furniture — I expect we will get our room fixed up.

         [Susie]

July 6, Monday morning. Susie desires me to finish her letter, so I will begin by saying that Professor Rice did not get the place he applied for in the university. Now I have a few items of news to give you of a later date and will commence with the least important first.

---

65. In 1844, Frederick Thomas Kemper founded a school in Boonville, later known as Kemper Military School, which closed in 2002. Giving one of the speeches at the reunion, Charley Hersman spoke on the value of acquiring truth in the pursuit of education.

66. Daniel Voorhees, then an Indiana Congressman (Democrat) and later United States Senator, spoke on "The Influence of the Physical Sciences on the Progress of Civilization."

67. Professor John Rice apparently was seeking a position at the University of Missouri at Columbia. His father, Dr. Nathan Rice, had taken a position at Danville Theological Seminary in Kentucky; he would die in 1877. Elizabeth Dobyns, second wife of Major Edward Dobyns and stepmother to Mollie Dobyns.

68. Sallie Rickey, daughter of Dr. Thomas Howard and wife of Joseph Rickey. Anna Boulware, wife of Isaac W. Boulware, an attorney for Celia, the slave who was hanged for killing her master. Linda Jameson Atkinson's father, John Jameson, was Celia's head attorney. See p. 25, n. 49. See also December 10, 1863, on Linda Atkinson's sisters, Sallie Tom and Bettie.

69. Mary "Mod" Scott, sister of Harvey Scott, married Robert Burton, 1872; their daughter Jennie was born in 1874.

On Saturday, July 4, the negroes had a big time here. Did not know there were so many negroes in Callaway County as marched through the streets of Fulton on that day. They had a dinner somewhere out about the Lunatic Asylum. It was amusing to see them: all ages, sizes, sexes, with all the colors of the rainbow displayed in dress. On Saturday night, the whole of Fulton assembled on the banks of the town creek to witness the celebration of Hockaday's bridge — a burlesque on the St. Louis celebration.[70] The anvil was fired for an hour or two almost continuously, only stopping for music or a speech. Then there were torches gleaming out in the darkness here and there, and bolts of fire flying through the air in every direction, and other fire works.... So much for the celebration.

Now as to the last and most important part of this letter. On Sunday, July 5, 1874, at 5 o'clock p.m., a fine looking *young man* made his appearance in our room here in the Hotel. He weighs just 9 pounds and is pronounced by all who have seen him to be really a fine specimen of a boy. Susie and I think him just perfection itself. Susie and the boy are both sleeping now and are doing finely....

[Harvey]

From Margaret Bruin Machette to her daughter, Susan Machette Scott

Fulton, Missouri
August 25, 1874

Dear Susie
... Dear little Edgar, I want to see him so much — have been so lonesome for you since you left. I went down and opened your room the week after you left. The water had not been thrown out of the urn and pitcher. I did that and brushed up the room....

M. M. Fisher is in Fulton on his way to St. Louis. He gives a distressing account of the want of rain — said he had traveled over thousands of acres where he could not see any thing green. Corn had dried up and fallen down before it had tasseled and there was no stock to be seen. Every thing looked most desolate. Some one by the name of Ross went from Fulton to Kansas where he owned land with the intention of improving [it] but the drouth was so distressing that he came back. Says there are places you could not buy a bucket of water and what the drouth had not killed the grasshoppers had eaten up. We heard that Dr. Rice was going to Kentucky to stay till after Christmas....

Edgar Machette Scott, the first of Harvey and Susan's children, grew to 13 pounds by September 1, 1874, when he was almost two months old.

70. St. Louis was celebrating the opening of Eads Bridge over the Mississippi River. The *Missouri Republican* for July 5, 1874, proclaimed the bridge "The Greatest Work of the Age Completed" and "Triumph of Art, Science, Industry and Perseverance." Spanning the Mississippi River for use by both trains and wagons, the bridge was, according to Parrish, *History of Missouri*, 3:218, "the first important bridge in the United States to use steel instead of wrought iron in truss construction."

Kearney, Missouri
September 1, 1874

From Joseph Flood to his son and daughter-in-law, John and Cornelia Machette Flood

Dear Children

... I returned from Lexington last evening. Annie and Lidy seemed well pleased.[71] We were just 24 hours too late to be robbed by the James Boys at North Lexington.[72] We rode in the same bus that they robbed the day before. You saw a correct report in the paper.

I am sorry it is so we can't come down next week and stay some time but we can't. I have some engagements that will conflict. I want to make my annual settlement next week and have agreed to meet a commissioner to settle railroad claims &c. &c.... We are well as usual. Let Sallie see this — it is for all. I received her kind letter also this morning and will answer soon. We feel very lonely now — all of our children gone from us. I wish we could see you all more frequently....

Fulton, Missouri
November 22, 1874

From Susan Machette to her mother, Margaret Bruin Machette

Dear Ma:

... Nealie takes Forest to Sunday School to Mr. Tuttle's class — he has 75 in his class. Edgar is improving all the time. I gave him a piece of news paper to play with while I write, but he got his hands all black and I had to wash them and give him to Harvey. There was a church sociable at Mrs. Kerr's last week; there was scarcely anybody there — no one went from the Hotel.

Nealie finished her new calico — it looks splendid. I have seen some of the prettiest calico this fall I ever saw. Mrs. Watson has a black and white check trimmed with goods with larger check. It is trimmed with squares, bound, like this, set on the edge of [the] over skirt and basque. Emma Snell has one with the goods set this way and bound.[73]

People seem to be wearing their old dresses this year. I have not heard of any new fine ones. The favorite hat is beaver. I have not fixed up my black dress yet or my hat either — I go out so seldom and I am kept so busy with Edgar.

Do you think Mrs. Bratton told Nealie last week that she heard I had been confined! and asked if it was so. She has been sick you know. Mrs. Atkins is going to wait on Sallie. Sallie looks very large — I suppose will be sick about the 1st [of] December.[74] Mrs. Henderson is making her baby clothes. They say Professor Rice and Miss Sue Hockaday are to be married soon.[75] Harvey got the Baby such a pretty gold pin for his bib. Dr. Rice is going to come back next week and will stay two months.

71. Lidy, possibly Lida Davis, born in 1858. The niece of Joseph Flood, she was a year younger than his youngest daughter Annie. Lidy and Annie were probably attending school in Lexington, perhaps at the Elizabeth Aull Female Seminary. Lida Davis died in 1875.

72. The *Missouri Republican* for September 1, 1874, reported that the James gang had robbed two stagecoaches or omnibuses of $800, see p. 88.

73. Mrs. Watson might be Francis "Fannie" Tucker Watson, who in 1872 married James Watson, son of Samuel and Martha Watson. Emma Snell, sister of James Snell, an attorney who married Fannie Evans in 1874.

74. Herbert, son of Sallie Flood Tureman, was born January 1875.

75. John Rice and Sue Hockaday married later that year.

... I don't want Edgar to forget you — he is just as sweet as he can be — he is a good fellow to laugh when amused. His calico dress fits him now without drawstrings. I am going to knit some this winter — I have some to do for Harvey and Edgar kicks out of his stockings so I shall soon have to knit for him. Edgar...would be over the colic I believe if he was free from cold....

From Margaret Bruin Machette to her daughter, Cornelia Machette Flood

Montgomery County, Missouri
November 29, 1874

Dear Nelia

... The third snow of this season is on the ground now. The people say it is the deepest that has been since '54 and '55 when it drifted over the fence tops. It is thirteen inches deep now and not drifted. It fell on Friday. This being the fifth Sunday there is no preaching in the neighborhood.... Mr. Robnett preaches at Zion next Sunday. There is preaching at Zion once a month, at Providence once, and at Price's Branch twice a month. There is no Sunday school that I know of....[76]

I have not heard from Alex since he left here.

This leaves me in good health. I don't know when I will be home. I do hope this will find you all well and the good Lord will keep you and care for your wants is my daily prayer. Tell Forest that I have some beautiful red yarn for to knit him socks and will send [them] to him when I send Abbie's yarn. Jane is weaving rag carpeting and when that is out of the loom she has jeans and flannel to weave for her family.... I hope Mr. Flood's health keeps good. Above all guard him against taking cold....

From Margaret Bruin Machette to her daughter, Susan Machette Scott

Montgomery County, Missouri
December 13, 1874

Dear Susie

... It is raining this morning and I shall not go to church today. This makes the second Sunday we have stayed at home on account of rain, [the] distance to go being six or seven miles.... Jane and Jacob went with the older children but I preferred staying at home with the little ones....

Jacob killed hogs yesterday. Jane is in grease up to her eyes today drying up her lard and making sausage meat. The children are at school and Jacob is helping her. As soon as they get through with the grease they are going to kill their geese and chickens for market. The whole neighborhood is engaged in hog killing and preparing poultry for market. I think there is more spinning and weaving done in this part of the country than has been done for a great while before. Jane has a piece of jeans ready to put in the loom — twenty yards for herself and ten for Harriet and then she will weave white linsey for herself....[77]

76. Mr. Robnett, probably John D. Robnett, a Baptist minister. See February 12, 1865, on his sister, Kate Robnett.

77. Harriet, wife of Bruin Dutton and daughter-in-law of Mary Bruin Dutton. The drought in western Missouri, mentioned in the August 25, 1874 letter, did not extend to the eastern part of the state where the Sheltons lived.

Montgomery County, Missouri
January 10, 1875

From Margaret Bruin Machette to her daughter, Susan Machette Scott

Dear Susie

I have just got home from preaching. Mr. Smith preached an excellent sermon. There was not many out on account of the cold. We have very extreme cold and have had for several days. On Friday afternoon there was a storm of wind and snow. It came on as suddenly as a summer thunder storm and continued all night. Jacob had just come with the last load of ice and had unloaded when the wind commenced blowing and it was all that they could do to keep the horses from running away with the wagons before they could unharness and the cold continues. We did not suffer today with cold. There was a quantity of straw in the wagon and we were well wrapped up — Jacob, Jane, Nellie, Cooper,

A subscription to *Illuminated Lessons* (weekly) was 10¢ per year or 2¼¢ per quarter. These Bible lessons for children included a story and questions on the back with a hymn and Scripture verses on the front of the card.

Ethel, daughter of Abbie and Charles Hersman, was born in 1871. This photo was taken when she was 2 years, 9 months old.

and myself. I was out visiting two days last week — on Wednesday at Doctor Crockett's and Thursday at David Graves' — both pleasant places to visit....[78]

I hope you are all well. I do want to see the boy very much. I try to imagine how he looks but I know I can't. Does he sit alone yet? How is Mr. Flood's health? Does Nelia and Forest keep well? When did you see Mr. Hersman and Abbie and the children?...

The people seem in good spirits. On every hand they are preparing for a busy year to come. There are a great many persons in the county trying to rent and the farmers are building houses on their farms to rent. It is astonishing to see the thousands upon thousands of hogs that are brought from the southwest and other parts of this state to sell and to be fed, there being no corn or any thing to feed on at home. This part of the state has been favored with fine corn crops and are realizing good prices for their corn....

---

78. Nellie and Cooper, children of Jacob and Jane Dutton Shelton. William Wallace Crockett, physician and Presbyterian minister; father of Julia Crockett Graves, who was married to David Graves. See October 6, 1860.

From Margaret Bruin Machette to her daughter, Susan Machette Scott

Westport, Missouri[79]
May 30, 1875

Dear Susie

... I have been to church this morning but few [were] out considering it is such a fine day. The people from the country were not at church. Perhaps their horses are too near starved to drive. You have not the most distant idea, you can't have unless you witness it with your own eyes, the destitution, the distress there is in the counties where the hoppers have eaten every green thing, where the drouth last year cut the crops short and all were hoping and depending on what they could raise this spring.

Now you may ride out in any direction, and the fields, meadows, and pastures are as bare as a blade of anything green as the middle of your streets are in midwinter. The trees have now been stripped of their leaves. The people are cutting down trees in the wood to let the stock get the leaves. Lizzie and I drove into the City yesterday afternoon to see Mag Crockett before she went to Montgomery to see her Mother as we wanted to send some word to Jacob Shelton.[80] We drove by the market square and the most we could see was loads of wood and the poorest horses that I ever saw — poor things, how they manage to pull a half load I don't know. I have no doubt but usually there is more marketing offered in two weeks in Kansas City than has been there this whole spring. The most distressing sight was the poor people trying to get to where they can get something for themselves and stock to eat. They are passing through Westport every day driving horses and cows so poor that they seem to stagger as they walk. Those that have money can buy corn and hay to feed their stock, and persons in the City can get vegetables that is brought on the railroads.

Next Thursday is the day appointed by the Governor as a day of fasting and prayer. Will the people of Fulton observe the day? The churches united in observing it in this place. There will be preaching at eleven and three o'clock....[81]

From Samuel Machette to his stepmother, Margaret Bruin Machette

Kansas City, Missouri
March 16, 1876

Dear Mother

I have a letter from Henry dated Ypsilanti, Michigan, March 10th, asking me to write him and give him his age.[82] As you have a record of the age of all of Mary's children, will you please give me the year, month, and the day Henry was ushered into this world of trouble and vexation.

79. Alex and his family moved back to Westport. Possibly his school in Kentucky had failed.

80. Margaret "Mag" Crockett, sister of Julia Crockett Graves.

81. For more information on the drought in western Missouri, see p. 87.

82. Henry was a slave of the Machettes when they lived in St. Charles. In 1907, Sue Scott wrote, "About Pete at Lexington — Pa owned his Mother and three or four children — her husband was a French negro and his folks moved to St. Louis and she wanted to go with him and take Pete who was lame or delicate and she wanted 'Miss Margaret' to keep Henry and Milly. I didn't know he drifted to Lexington. Sam used to go to see him and said he was prosperous.... He was a play mate of Abbie's and was so good, I have heard." The record of the children's ages is not in the collection (perhaps it was sent to Sam); however, there is the following receipt from the estate of Margaret Machette's husband:

Hire of Boy Henry from January 1, 1853 to Oct. 1853. 9 months at 10$ per month. $90.

Hire of Sister Milly from March 1st 1853 to Oct. 1853. 7 months at 4$ per month. $28.

I wrote Sister Nealie a few days ago stating that our little daughter was very sick with scarlet fever.[83] I am glad to inform you she is out of all danger and rapidly regaining her health. Annie, the children, and I send love to all of the family.

Fulton, Missouri
July 23, 1876

*From Susan Machette Scott to her
mother, Margaret Bruin Machette*

Dear Ma:

I went up to church this morning, but as both preachers were absent, the people went to the Methodist church — I concluded to go on to Abbie's.... I think they are going to have such a nice house — The frame is up. They had a good week for work — at least not rainy — though so *hot!* I concluded I would work it off. I have made myself a calico dress and Edgar one and Harvey a pair of drawers. I got the pattern of the latter from Butterick and they fit him better than any he has ever had. I am going to make up his flannel drawers and anything that he needs so that I can have the Fall for my own sewing. Abbie made Brother Charley a pair of pants last Friday. I am going to try my hand on a pair tomorrow. Harvey thinks those you made him [are] such a comfort — but he has not enough to change. He has to wear them constantly this warm weather.

Nealie and family are all well. We laughed a good deal at the politicians returning from Jefferson [City]. They came back looking as meek and harmless as possible, especially Dr. Wilkerson and Professor Rice. Politics is something new to Dr. Wilkerson. I suppose his efforts consisted chiefly in urging every body to rush to Jefferson and do something for Mr. Hockaday. As they were expected to bear their own expenses, it was expecting too much, especially as they did not care two straws about the matter. The Hockadays present a funereal aspect — except Mrs. Edith is trying to make out like she "doesn't care"! while all the time she is making it clearer that she does.[84]

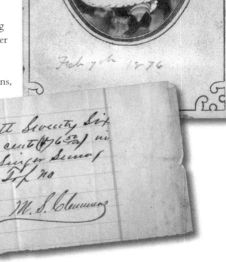

Edgar Machette Scott (photo taken on February 7, 1876, when Edgar was just over nineteen months old)

The Scotts purchased a Singer sewing machine for $76.50, twenty years after Isaac Singer had begun his work to improve the sewing machine. Susan made clothes for her husband and sons, as well as herself.

---

83. Sam's daughter was named Maud, the name of Nealie's deceased daughter.

I went out calling last Friday on the Rices, Curds, Lawthers and Browns. Met Mollie Dobyns at the Rices' — she has not been to see Abbie or I either. I heard that she has gotten a situation to teach in Florida. It will suit her as she likes the South....

From Cornelia Machette Flood to her mother, Margaret Bruin Machette

Fulton, Missouri
August 1, 1876

Margaret Bruin Machette, left, and her youngest child, Cornelia Machette Flood

Dear Ma:

... Every thing is going on as usual and we are enjoying so many of the bright blessings of God that it makes me most tremble for fear we do not walk softly enough before the Lord. Floodie was over to Sallie's today. They are as usual except Mrs. Clatterbuck. She is very near her last and, poor, good, old lady, may God be very near to her in the dying hour.[85] Susie and Edgar [are] as usual. Brother Harvey has gone over home for a few days. Little Maggie stays with Susie in his absence. Abbie and Brother's house goes on finely. It is such a great thing for you that Brother took you home with him. Abbie has just lots to shift from one place to another and every thing in such confusion that I really trust it would have made you sick. It will be one of the neatest little places in town when completed.

Forest grows right straight up, never saw a child grow so fast and is as sweet as ever. He and Edgar still have their spats but soon make friends. Finley is working like a Turk this summer trying to make money for his bank.

Mrs. Curd got very distressing news from her brother in Arkansas, Mr. Loughborough. It is supposed he committed suicide though nothing positive is known about it. His wife had come home to be confined, and he was down at home and found dead with his shot gun beside him and shot straight through the heart. It is all a mystery. I feel so for his poor wife and children. The Lord protect us from sudden affliction. I was up to see Lillie and Mrs. Curd this evening.[86] They feel dreadfully.

Are you all well, and how are you enjoying your visit? You must not be uneasy about us, but enjoy the society of the loved ones you are with. You know we can not all be together at once and all the time but God watches over us just all the same. Blessed be his name.

84. John Hockaday married Edith Cox in 1867. He was Missouri Attorney General from 1874 to 1876; John Hockaday was apparently seeking a higher political office. In her May 27, 1866, letter, Cornelia described him as her escort.

85. Mary Tureman Clatterbuck, mother of Robert and Ben Tureman and Sallie's mother-in-law.

86. James Loughborough was married to Mary, sister of Harriet Webster Curd. Lillie Webster was another sister.

Mrs. Hockaday looks flourishingly dressed more than ever — guess she thinks it no more [use] saving [her] finery for the [governor's] mansion.[87] Some one told Floodie [that] Hockaday wanted the position of Senator. Poor thing, it's a pity he can't be prominent some way. Before the election came off, some of his big kin rubbed their hands and said they expected to live to see the day that John Hockaday would be president of the U.S. Guess they do not feel so now, for he was most awfully beaten and they all feel terribly mortified over it....

Fulton, Missouri
August 10, 1876

From Susan Machette Scott and Margaret Hersman to Margaret Bruin Machette

Dear Ma:

... How much I wish you were here! Harvey went to the Centennial, at least started for the same, yesterday morning. He will be away till the last of the month. If you were only here I could enjoy your company. We all talk a great deal about you and want so much to see you. I will be so glad when Brother Charley's house is done. They work quite slowly. They will have on one coat of plastering this week, and I suppose they will get through with it in another week — it is going to be so pretty and pleasant. Your room will be such an improvement on your old one; it is so large and nice and you have a little south hall opening out from it, which is so private. As soon as your visit is out, I think you will have to come home.

When Harvey returns I expect we will go over to Monroe and spend a few days — which I think will be very pleasant. Bob Burton has a spring wagon and we can spend the time between Mod's and the old place. Harvey says it looks very lonely there, now.[88] The crops [are] poor. Mod's baby is not weaned yet!...[89]

Maggie Hersman is staying with me at night — she is a great deal of company to me and Edgar. Edgar is getting along very well — has cut all of his teeth, I believe. I wish you could see him — his favorite expression is "all right" or rather "all wight."

I think I shall work my loneliness off. I have just completed two night shirts for Harvey — have lately made him three pairs of drawers and a pair of linen pants. I had no trouble with the latter at all. I shall be very glad when the next three weeks bring my Sweetheart back again. I think the trip will improve him. I hated for him to settle into the routine of school without some recreation.... Jim Snell has moved into Russell's house by the Hotel. They eat at the house opposite. Their baby is very delicate....[90]

Susie

August 11, 1876

Dear grandma

I have just sit down to write to you to see if you are well we are well how did annie like her doll[91] I am staying with aunt susie while uncle harvie is gone aunt susie is learn-

---

87. John S. Phelps, Democrat, was elected governor of Missouri in 1876.

88. Harvey's mother had died in 1875 and his father in 1874.

89. See p. 121, n. 69.

90. Fannie Evans married James Snell in 1874. Their only child, William, died in 1888.

91. Anna, daughter of Alexander and Lizzie Machette.

The Machette grandchildren: Finley Hersman, Edgar Scott, Margaret Hersman, and Forest Flood

Margaret Machette's grandchildren learned letter writing early in life and often wrote special letters to their grandma. The children visited and stayed with one another's families frequently. Pictures were a common way to document the children's growth and share their lives with other family members.

Margaret "Maggie" Hersman's letter to her grandmother, shown below, is transcribed on p. 129–30.

Finley Hersman and his sister Maggie wearing her winter collar and muff. Finley was one year younger than his cousin Lilian, below left.

Lilian, left, daughter of Alex and Lizzie Machette, wrote to her cousin Maggie Hersman, who was four years younger (letter above right is transcribed, p. 133).

ing me notes on the piano. Be shure and Bring annie home with you I want to see her so Bad Edgar can say aunt Nelia the house is all most done I will Be so glad when it gets dune so you can come home mama is going to let me have lots of little girls on my Birth day it comes the 25 of septemBer Be shure and Bring annie home with you so that she can Be here on my Birth day it is the 25 of September Edgar says to tell you alright Aunt Nealie has shure a preiz little Bird she cals it Dick

                [Maggie]

Fulton, Missouri
August 20, 1876

Dear Ma:

    . . . Yesterday Forest was running to me on the bricks and run a needle into his foot. It had a thread in it. The needle run in so far the string would not pull it out but broke and the Doctor had to cut it and get it out with an instrument. It was very severe on him but he got so many pretties for the same I think he meditates getting another in soon. His papa bought him peaches and watermelons and a new wheel barrow and Finley gave him a white rabbit. I am so thankful the whole needle came out and it was not worn. He is feeling quite well this morning. Floodie brought Forest such a lovely little canary bird a few weeks ago. He loves it so much, and so do I. We named it Dick after our old bird you used to have. . . .

    Floodie went over to Mexico the 10th and was nominated by acclamation on the first ballot.[92] Some people in this town look like they would be rejoiced to see us in the "bottom of the sea." Sallie's mother-in-law is dead. . . .

From Cornelia Machette Flood to her mother, Margaret Bruin Machette

---

Fulton, Missouri
August 20, 1876

Dearest Ma:

    . . . I am in hopes Harvey will get home the last of this week. He went from here to Washington City and got to Philadelphia last Monday night. He only writes to say how he is reserving particulars till he comes back.[93]

    We have not heard from you for a long time — I hope you are well. We are all well except little Forest. He has been suffering much with a breaking out like Ethel used to have and yesterday morning he stuck a needle in his foot — it took Howard and Rootes both to get [it] out; it came out whole.[94] The needle was entirely in when found — just the thread sticking out. He is getting on very well this morning — was out at the table for breakfast. Edgar is getting on very nicely, is ever so saucy — stamps his foot at Mr. Whaley and says "go way, old papy."

From Susan Machette Scott to her mother, Margaret Bruin Machette

---

92. John Flood, nominated at the Democratic Senatorial Convention in Mexico, won in the general election and served in the state legislature. In the fiercely Democratic Callaway County, winning the nomination was tantamount to winning the election.

93. Harvey Scott was attending the United States Centennial celebration in the East, see p. 87.

94. Thomas or his brother John Henry Howard, both physicians, and George Rootes, a dentist.

Receipt for the carpets Margaret Bruin Machette bought
for her daughter Abbie's new house

Tuesday. Mr. Ewing has run off from his wife again.
They say Wells is the rival this time — it was his partner
before. I just heard of it Sunday morning and in the
afternoon I was coming from Abbie's and I saw Wells go
in to [the] Ewings'! She screamed and had the neighbors
in as before. I heard that Mrs. Dedman stayed up with
her all night!…

I just received your postal. I am so sorry to hear that
you are not well. Abbie and Brother Charley were
delighted with their carpets. She has them both made
ready to put down. I think them beautiful, so does
Nealie. I think Abbie has written — perhaps you did
not get her letter. You never saw any thing like the confusion they are and have been in; they would have had a
pleasanter and easier time if they had been camping. I
have been really thankful for your sake that you made
your visit when you did. They will scarcely get straightened up by school time.

… I have five dollars for you. Do you want it now, or
after while? Do try and get well, dear Ma. I always think
of you, and *pray God's richest blessings* on *you*.

---

*From Susan Machette Scott to her
mother, Margaret Bruin Machette*

Fulton, Missouri
September 1876

Dear Ma:

Edgar and I are alone again today. Harvey went over home yesterday — we had
thought of going, too, but gave it out. He will be back the last of this week so as to be
ready for school. He considered his trip to the Centennial a success. He got to see a
great deal that was new to him, and it is very pleasant recalling the same — though
fatiguing at the time he saw them. He spent nine days there — went at six in the
morning and stayed till six in the evening and *worked hard* sight seeing all the time. He
wore the heels of his shoes nearly off standing so much. Edgar was so glad to see him
when he returned. He acted just like a grown person would when they are overcome
with emotion — his lips quivered and he could not speak for some time.

The Fair is just over — very well attended I believe. I went out one afternoon. Harvey took Edgar three afternoons — he was very much entertained. He was very much
interested in a balloon ascension. Mr. Noah Flood and wife are here — came last
Tuesday — she is quite pretty.[95] I haven't seen much of them yet as they have been
attending the Fair. Edgar is getting along very well — is getting right fat and talks
more all the time.

95. See p. 89 on John Flood's brother Noah. Mary Dunphy, Noah Flood's second wife, sued him for divorce in
1893 citing "intemperance." Three years later, Noah, a San Francisco attorney, was fined $100 and served a day in jail
for striking an attorney in a courtroom. He died in California in 1910. San Francisco *Call* (March 30, 1893; September 20, 1896; October 8, 1910).

I was at Abbie's yesterday afternoon. I am helping her make carpet rags — I quite like it. I asked her about Maggie's patterns. She has not been making her anything lately — and says she can't see that she has grown any — so I suppose if you can guess at how much her patterns ought to be enlarged you will do as well as Abbie could....

Edgar has just waked up and I will have to close my letter. I am sorry your knee is still lame. You will have to get some bees to sting you. Abbie has a carpet down in her room now. I expect she will wait till they are through painting before she puts down the others. Brother Charley is working very hard to get things straightened up before school. The birds have almost ruined the grapes this summer. Write soon —

Fulton, Missouri
September 11, 1876

From Finley Hersman to his grandmother, Margaret Bruin Machette

Dear Grandma,

This morning (Monday) I entered school. There are going to be a good many students this year. I am in practical arithmetic, Clark normal grammar, fifth reader, and writing and drawing.[96]

Yesterday (Sunday) while papa and I were gone to church, and mama was in the house, some boys came and took about a bushel of grapes and two or three dozen pears. It was very fortunate that mama had gathered a few Saturday for some preserves, as that will be all we can get.

Tommy Buckland goes to school too.[97] Tommy is Mrs. Dobyns' cousin from St. Louis. We all want you to come home very much. Write soon.

    Yours aff.
    C. Finley H.

P.S. You must be certain and write a letter entirely to me as I have not had a letter for a long time.

Westport, Missouri
September 22, 1876

From Lilian Machette, daughter of Alexander Machette, to her cousin, Margaret Hersman

Miss Maggie Hersman:

My dear little Cousin, I have just finished you a little jacket. I tried to get it done to send with your dress, so that you might receive it on your birthday and would have finished it in time had not my wool given out and I had to send to the city to get more and [it] being Fair week I could not get more until last night; consequently I did not get it done in time; however you can consider it as a birthday present, the material from Grandma and the work from your loving cousin who sincerely hopes you will be pleased. All send love to the dear ones at Fulton.

96. Stephen Clark's textbook, *The Normal Grammar, Analytic and Synthetic* (1875).

97. After Thomas "Tommy" Buckland's mother, Mary E. Buckland, died in 1876, he and his sisters, Mary and Sadie, lived for a time with Major Edward and Elizabeth Dobyns.

From Alexander Machette to his mother, Margaret Bruin Machette

Westport, Missouri
January 9, 1877

Dear Ma:

I have just finished up the evening "chores" as the Yankee would say, and right gladly do I sit down before a good warm fire, for it is wintry enough out of doors. Snow [is] quite deep and falling rapidly. Lizzie and I have just got in from milking. Dear old white cow is a perfect prodigy. Cold weather seems to make but little difference in her milking — a great bucket full in the morning and a good chance at evening. Lizzie is just as fond of making butter as ever and of course just as *stingy* with her cream.

. . . I preached the funeral of old Sister Goforth last Friday afternoon. . . .[98] I talked with Mrs. Goforth the day she died, and inquired as to her state of mind. She replied very promptly, "I know in whom I have believed" &c. She seemed to have but one regret at dying — that was leaving her aged companion. . . .

Lizzie's flowers have survived the cold weather so far.

A great many children in town have been having measles, but our children have escaped as yet, and I hope will not have them this time. They are trouble enough this cold weather when well. We are all getting on about as usual, and I hope this will find you all well. Let us hear from you often.

From Alexander and Elizabeth Shelton Machette to Margaret Bruin Machette

Westport, Missouri
January 17, 1877

Dear Ma:

I have just weighed our brahmas. One weighed *eight*, and the other *six* scant. They are fine chickens, but very poor. The winter had been so severe that we have had to keep the chickens all in the stable, and they have been but poorly attended to.

It was announced that there would be preaching at the Cumberland Church last Sunday night. Lilie and I went to hear a traveling preacher but he was detained and did not get in so (as usual here in such cases) they called on me to fill the vacancy, which of course I could not refuse. When I was about half through the stranger preacher came in. When I had finished, I called on the stranger to close the meeting, which he did, making an excellent prayer and some very good remarks. . . .

Heard from Samuel's last Saturday. Anna and Charlie [Machette] came out and took dinner. Charlie stayed till Sunday evening. Samuel sent Lilie a bird cage containing two beautiful canaries, of which she is very proud. . . .

[Alex]

Saturday. . . . We spent a quiet happy Christmas. The children had some very nice presents. I had a beautiful cashmere dress and a nice shawl, besides *many nice eatables*. I

98. Eliza Goforth, wife of Thomas Jefferson Goforth, Westport's first mayor in 1857. The Goforths spent part of the Civil War in Illinois when General Orders No. 11 forced Southern sympathizers to leave western Missouri.

was so happy to know that Susie's shawl pleased her — was so afraid it would not suit — have not seen a nicer one this winter.

Our church is getting on as usual. They hope to build a house this year. We went to hear Mr. Madeira last Sabbath.[99] He did preach such a good sermon. I love to hear such a dear good man preach. Mr. Machette's sermon in the morning and his in the evening were two of the very best I ever heard. I thought of you and of how you would have enjoyed them.

Charlie and Maud Machette spent two or three days [of] Christmas week with us. They seemed to enjoy it *so* much. Charlie said to me, "Aunt, it is almost like heaven out here — so quiet and nice." Says he thinks girls are nicer than boys.... Maud was very quiet and sweet and did not want to go home at all. Cried herself to sleep when she got there and the first thing she told her Pa was that "Aunt Lizzie and Uncle Alex would *not allow* such a thing as a *boy* about their *house*." Anna said Sam *just laughed*....

How are your flowers this time? Is the pit a success? Mine are doing splendidly growing and blooming. Every one who comes in exclaims, "oh how lovely your flowers are." Does our little calla still flourish?

Ma, you asked about the preparation I use for the skin. I suppose you mean the *zinc*—

Elizabeth "Lizzie" Machette
and one of her daughters

> 10 cts worth oxide zinc
> 10 cts worth glycerin
> 10 cts worth rose water

> Put zinc in a mug or bowl and pour boiling soft water slowly and stir, Ma, till you have a pint. Then add glycerin and stir and when cool add rose water and bottle. It is good for almost any eruption and for galling or chafe heat — or any thing of the kind. I often use it as whitening for the babe....

Sabbath eve. Sister Anna [Machette] and Brother John [Flood] have just gone. He has been visiting the orphans' home and stopped at Sam's. Anna came out with him in a carriage to call on us. He is looking so well. I do not think I should have known him at all. I think Nelia might have come with him and visited us. He is one of the handsomest men I ever saw.

                    [Lizzie]

Westport, Missouri
February 19, 1877

*From Elizabeth Shelton Machette
to her mother-in-law, Margaret
Bruin Machette*

Dear Ma

... Mr. Machette and Lilian are attending the funeral of Mrs. Hamilton's little grandson this morning. He died of membranous croup. The family are pretty distressed. I cut all the bloom off my heliotrope and a quantity of small rose geranium heart and made the sweetest garland I ever saw for the little coffin. My heliotrope is white when the bloom is fully out and the sweetest scent I ever saw. It will soon bloom

---

99. Addison Dashiel Madeira, Presbyterian minister in Kansas City and Independence, Missouri.

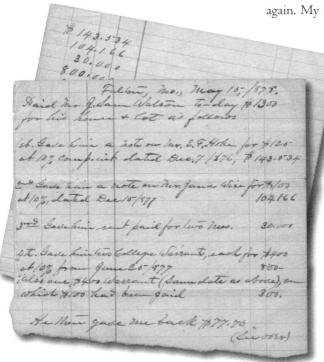

A few months after Sue "talked of housekeeping," the Scotts purchased a home from Sam Watson. The price of the house and lot was $1,300.

again. My flowers all are looking lovely and will soon have a quantity of bloom. I have seven varieties of pink geranium and two of rose. The new rose geranium I got of Mrs. Allen is so much sweeter scented and prettier than the common. My large calla has a large lily on it. My little "Lady Fern" has grown to be quite a large plant and the begonias are a "joy forever." The "lily of the valley" has not come up yet but the bleeding heart is doing nicely....

Ma, if Abbie has any thing nice in garden seed that you know I have not, I would be grateful for any thing she can spare. Has she any nice tomato seed? I fear I have lost mine — have looked and looked and can't find those I saved last summer. Don't you think it most time to sow them in boxes? Ma, I am making carpet rags as fast as I can. I wish you were here to tell me how much to prepare and how to fix them. I do not know when I have enough. It makes me cough too badly when I am working at them [so] that Mr. Machette made me put them away. Mr. Machette has gone to the City to get me a new cook stove this afternoon. Our old one has just gone to pieces so we can't cook at all on it.

You said Susie talked of housekeeping. I feel sure she will find it much harder on her than boarding. You asked what we thought of the little picture [of Edgar]. I believe Mr. Machette thinks it looks like him only so much fatter. I think it a fine looking little fellow. Not as much like Susie as I expected — looks very much like his Papa. How much I should love to see Nealia's, Susie's, and Abbie's children and ours all together once. I guess their dear Grand Ma would like to witness such an array of her posterity for a *little* while, too. They would make things almost *too jolly* to have them together for long. The boys would have to *keep quiet* with *seven* girls toward them. If they all live to be grown and should ever meet in one gathering, what a good time they would have.[100]

Etta is just as much afraid of a *boy,* as she is of "Cash." She won't let Charlie Machette look at her mean. Our dog Cash is a fine fellow, has just such a bushy tail as Dash had and nearly as large and much more watchful. We think a great deal of him now. Etta is pulling at me to take her up. She walks every where she pleases and is so sweet.

How do the people stand the idea of having Hayes for President? They might have known who would be President when they went into the "Commission" arrangement with those old black Republican judges. I felt like slapping the *Democrats' jaws* for that when they did it. Why they placed confidence in any of old Grant's judges I could not see.[101] It is *too provoking.* But any thing for peace.

100. The seven girls were Margaret "Maggie" and Ethel, daughters of Charley and Abbie Hersman; Maud, daughter of Sam and Annie Machette; and Lilian, Anna, Aimee, and Henriette "Etta," daughters of Alexander and Lizzie Machette.

101. In the 1876 election, both Rutherford B. Hayes and the Democratic candidate, Samuel Tilden, were declared winners. To resolve the issue, an electoral commission of fifteen legislators and Supreme Court justices was formed. The last person selected to the commission was Supreme Court Justice Joseph Bradley, a Republican appointee,

... Ma is quite well now but does not talk of coming up. Sister Mollie's health is worse.[102] She has made a trip or two to St. Louis to a physician who is trying to do something for her. Ma feels she can't come so far away from her while we are all well and she so afflicted. Oh! I feel it is almost *too hard* that I can't get to go and see my poor dear sister once more. I try to school myself to endurance without a murmur but it is hard to do it.

... *All* send love *to all*. And an extra portion to dear Ma, from your

Lizzie.

Fulton, Missouri
July 4, 1877

From Margaret Bruin Machette to her daughter, Cornelia Machette Flood

Dear Nelia

I received the postal last night — am sorry Alex did not get to see you and Mr. Flood. I presume he must have called at the wrong hotel. Did Annie call with Sam to see you? Am very thankful that Mr. Flood is improving in health. I do hope he may soon be restored to good health and Forest and yourself continue in health and happiness....

9th.... I was down at your house last week; you must not expect me to spend much time there. You can't imagine how very lonesome every thing is without your dear selves there. All the things are safe. Mr. Finley told Mr. Hersman that he could not find the oil can and his lamp was out. I went down and gave him the lamp that was in the other room and emptied the oil out of the parlor lamp in his lamp and then set the empty tin can on the sink in his room so he could find it next time....

11th.... Mrs. Fisher and Lizzie called on Abbie yesterday in style, becoming the upper ten. Had the babe and nurse but left them out in the carriage with the driver. They go to Columbia the first of September. Mr. Fisher tells different stories as to his leaving — told one party it was money and told Mr. Robertson that money had nothing to do with his going; he has got some of his best friends down on him.... Ed Kerr thought that John Rice would be the man to fill Fisher's place....[103]

Fulton, Missouri
July 8, 1877

From Susan Machette Scott to John and Cornelia Machette Flood

Dear Brother and Sister:

... We miss you very *very* much — and look anxiously for news from you. While we are sweltering through the heats of summer it is pleasant to think of you in a more

---

and many Democrats felt that he had unfairly tipped the election in Hayes's favor. Democrats were also angry at southern Democrats in Congress who acquiesced to Hayes's election, apparently in return for certain favors. The February 17, 1877, *Republican* described Hayes as "his fradulency" and branded Justice Bradley "a Judicial Hypocrite." "Black Republican" was used to describe members of the Republican Party who supported ending slavery. Kenneth E. Davison, *The Presidency of Rutherford B. Hayes* (Westport, Conn.: Greenwood, 1972), 43–44. John Hope Franklin, *Reconstruction after the Civil War*, 2nd ed. (Chicago: University of Chicago Press, 1994), 206–208.

102. See February 21, 1864, on the birth of Mollie Shelton Hammond's child.

103. After Michael M. Fisher's second wife died, he married Eliza Gamble in 1874. Abbie's husband, Charles Hersman, became president of Westminster; he served until 1887.

Sue Machette Scott gave piano lessons to bring in extra income.

The Scotts shopped at the store of James E. Watson. Watson's wife, Fannie, was a lifelong friend of Sue Scott. Perhaps the hobby horse bought on June 8 was for Edgar's third birthday.

genial clime.[104] We will spend the summer at home except a week, which I expect we will spend in Monroe County. They have been writing to us from there to "shut up" and spend the summer with them, but we can't think of leaving all our tomatoes and okras of which we have the promise of abundance.

As for town news, there is little.... The papers say Dr. Fisher has accepted the University chair — though he does not say so and seems uncertain what is best for him.[105] Some of Dr. Fisher's friends in town talked of getting up a purse for him to induce him to stay, but I think they failed — Mr. Tuttle said he talked to some and one half of them did not care whether he stayed or not. The Faculty would like very much for him to stay....

Last Thursday was Edgar's birthday — he was three years old — he enjoyed himself tremendously all day long. Mrs. McNairn spent the day with us, also Ma and Brother Charley and family, at least those that were at home. Maggie was away visiting and so was Finley.

... Tell Forest "Billy" is "all right" — is as saucy as can be — offers to fight Harvey and I if we interfere with his *rights* — such as scratching up the flower bed.

From the small scrapbook of Susan Machette Scott

Mrs. McNairn's Salve

Take a piece of bee's wax the size of the first joint of your thumb. Shave down in 1 pint of sweet oil. Put on the fire till it melts. Take off and while cooling add 10 cents worth of bergamot, and stir till cool. This is good for boils, sores, corns, hair oil &c.

From Alexander Machette to his mother, Margaret Bruin Machette

Westport, Missouri
December 21, 1877

Dear Ma:

Your nice little present of a pair of chest protectors were received in due time, and I ought to have acknowledged their receipt before this....[106]

---

104. Hoping that John Flood's health would improve, the Floods moved to Colorado. See p. 89 on tuberculosis, the disease he had contracted.

105. Fisher taught at the University of Missouri at Columbia. In 1891, he became president pro tem of the university but died that year in office. John Rice taught at Westminster until his death in 1920.

106. Chest protector, a vestlike garment often made of flannel.

The latest sensation in Kansas City is the meeting now in progress under the preaching of a lady evangelist, Mrs. Van Cott.[107] As a general rule I do not approve of such things, but I suppose there are exceptions to all general rules. At least, I am compelled to admit, after hearing Mrs. Van Cott, that she is one of the most eloquent speakers I have ever heard. The meeting is increasing in interest, and already many have been saved.

… This leaves us well except Etta — she is complaining some. Have you heard from John since he went to Colorado? I trust he will derive great benefit from the trip. He and his Pa were kind enough to spend a night with us. We were very glad indeed to see them. Let us hear how he is getting along.…

Denver, Colorado
January 13, 1878

From Cornelia Flood to her mother, Margaret Bruin Machette

Dear Ma:

… Now I can give you the good news that we are settled in our "cozy little home," and how I do wish you could step in as of old and see just how it looks for yourself. I will begin and tell you all about the same. The house to begin with is a tiny little frame of the neatest appearance possible — white in color with green shutters. It has three rooms.… The front room is the one that has a bed and wash stand and stove and two rocking chairs and pretty mingled yarn carpet — the room [in] back is the dining room with table, bed and washstand.[108] The room back of that is the kitchen with [a] nice little cellar underneath and this completes the whole. I have a snug cook stove. It is [a] coal stove and bakes nicely. The coal here is not dirty like that you have and has no big cinders.

Floodie seems to feel better this morning. He has frequent bad spells, dear one. I do hope and pray that he may get well. Forest is in "ecstasies" over house keeping. Will make him some ice cream on his birthday. He wishes so much for his little cousins to be with him on that day. Forest is sitting beside me in his little rocking chair and says, "tell Grandma [that] Papa got me a little chair and I love it so much and in three more days is my birthday and wish Grandma was here then."

We got our things in fine order and thought lots of the dear ones that sent and packed them. They all came in first class style, not a crack in the dishes or anything, but you would have killed yourself laughing at the blackberries and honey, such a mess. All spilled out and mixed together in wild confusion, with the corn. Out of the nine gallons, don't think there's more than 3 gallons [of] any account, but strange to say it all stayed in the little box and did not get on any thing.… As every familiar thing was taken out of boxes, [I wish you had been here] to hear and see little Forest scream with delight as his toys would come to light at last. A day or two after they came, he surprised me by saying, "Mama, Grandma don't tell lies, does she?" I turned around to chin him and he said, "Well, you know you said she would send my pretties and Grandma told the truth and sent them. Ain't she sweet, Mama?" He asked God to

107. Margaret Newton Van Cott spoke on "Little Things." A Methodist evangelist who spoke throughout the United States, in 1869 she was the first woman who was a licensed minister of the Methodist Episcopal Church. Rosemary Radford Ruether and Rosemary Skinner Keller, *Women and Religion in America*, vol. I (San Francisco: Harper & Row, 1981), 8–9.

108. The bed might have been a Murphy bed, which folded into a closet when not in use.

bless dear Grandma every night. We did not have to pay but $18.80 for our things delivered at home and all.

Pa, dear good man, insists on bringing my coal and water and making my fires and everything else that I find it hard to keep myself busy.[109] We get warm milk night and morning from my neighbor over the way, nice and warm for Floodie. And everything we have gotten in [the] way of eatables is of first class quality except corn meal and that is not good and they have no good ham....

From Alexander Machette to his mother, Margaret Bruin Machette

Westport, Missouri
January 17, 1878

Dear Ma:

I have been unable to study much today on account of neuralgia but will try and write a few lines. Lizzie received your [letter] last yesterday. I feel so sorry for Nealie and John, and daily pray that he may be restored again if it is God's will. Lizzie also received a letter last evening from Troy. Poor Mollie Hammond gets no better. I presume [she] will not survive long....

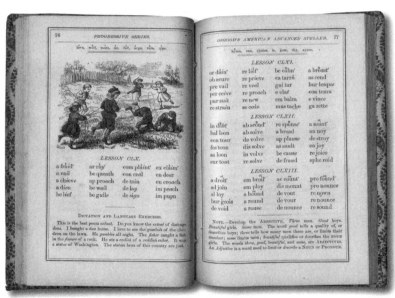

Osgood's American Advanced Speller, published in 1873, may have been used for home schooling.

The first term of Mrs. Elliott's school closes next week. Will stop the children, as the school is not so good as formerly. Do not know what to do with Annie and Lilie, as it is too far to send to Mrs. Lykin's school at the "Home," and too expensive to board them away from home.[110]

The "Murphy Movement," as it is called, has reached Kansas City, under the leadership of a Mr. Reynolds.[111] There is some talk of an effort in behalf of temperance here — it is certainly needed. We cannot afford but one little dry goods store, but have four saloons.

I would be glad if I had the means to visit you all, though I feel but little interest in the discussion of the Messrs. Ditzler and Wilkes.[112] As usual in such cases, I presume each side will claim the victory. I doubt if any real progress is made by such efforts toward the final settlement of the baptismal controversy. The better plan would be to put an open Bible before each individual, and let him under-

109. John Flood's father, Joseph, helped the Floods settle in their new home.

110. Alex and Lizzie's daughter Annie was probably named after Sam Machette's new wife.

111. The temperance movement, which was sweeping across Missouri, was named for Francis Murphy, a reformed drinker, who delivered his first speech on temperance in 1870.

112. In a debate in Fulton, J. Ditzler, a Methodist minister, spoke in favor of sprinkling as a baptismal ritual; L.B. Wilkes, a Christian minister, spoke against it. *Fulton Gazette* (January 18, 1878).

stand that he is at liberty to settle such questions for himself in the fear of God. One of the things which the Christian world has never been able to learn as yet is the idea of *Christian toleration*. Each one assumes for himself a sort of infallibility, and wants to enforce his own notions as yokes upon the necks of his fellow beings, just as it was with those Judaizers (in Acts 15:1) who "came down from Judea," saying: "Except ye be circumcised, ye cannot be saved." Away with such a spirit; and "Grace be with *all* them that love our Lord J. Christ in sincerity."

I recollect once the Methodists were starting a protracted meeting and announced a prayer meeting for Monday morning. Prompted by a kindly feeling, I went. As I entered the house, there were only three or four ladies assembled. One of them said: "Brother Machette, I hope you will get to be a Methodist yet"! I replied: "If to be a *Methodist* means to be a *Christian*, I hope I am one already"! I despise such contemptible "Sectarianism"; and yet that is the spirit that rules the day. It is not enough for a man to be a Christian — not enough that he makes God's word his guide, and prayerfully studies it every day to know God's will — not enough that he sacrifices *all* upon God's altar, and conscientiously follows Christ according to the best light that God gives him — all this goes for nothing. He is nobody, unless he thinks just as *we* do in every peccadillo. Is that the spirit of Christ and the Gospel? I think not. Fortunately, I have come to the bottom of the page, and (as the preacher said) will have to "bring my remarks to a close."

Westport, Missouri
January 28, 1878

From Elizabeth Shelton Machette to her mother-in-law, Margaret Bruin Machette

Dear Ma:

Your last was received some days ago, but I have found no time to write you until now. Really I am kept under such incessant toils I scarcely know how time passes. Lilian and Anna are both so busy at school now that they are but very little help to me, and I do everything — do not hire a single thing done. I have just gotten rags prepared since New Year to make 30 yards [of] carpeting and now must go back to my sewing and get ready for spring. I have shirts to make for Mr. Machette, besides a full supply of underwear for all the children. So you can see there is no rest for the wicked.

I have letters from home, almost every week of late. Dear sister Mollie is gradually sinking — I fear will not last more than a month or two longer. I wish I could go to see her, but I can't. It seems so hard that others can have the means to go where and when they please, and *I* must not even see a poor, suffering, dying sister.

This is such a pretty bright day, but so dreadful muddy — very few out at church. Ma, it looks so hard to see such talent as Mr. Machette's so little appreciated. His light is surely hidden under a bushel here. His sermon today was splendid and so few to hear it. The Presbyterians all go to the City to hear Mr. Madeira now that he does not preach out here any more. All except old lady Riechester — she goes to hear Mr. Machette. She sends love to you every time I see her, poor old soul. I think she is a real good old woman.

… Am sorry to learn of Abbie's losing her plants. Mine are looking beautiful — 3 callas in bloom and other plants full of buds. I wish I could give Abbie one of my callas. We have had to get up and keep fires 2 or 3 nights — with that exception my flowers have been no trouble. My chickens have laid all winter, just like spring. We have used eggs freely and sold a great many. If the weather stays this way I will set all that go to setting..., so as to have plenty of spring chickens. I often wish we had more room, so I could raise turkeys and pigs. We could then almost live at home with our good cow.

We are very much cramped as it is, in more ways than one. Here is Lilian now who ought to be in a first class school cramped down with Mrs. Elliott while others, her inferiors, can enjoy privileges they are not capable of appreciating. Her Pa says she is fully up with the junior classes in the best institutions in the land. He has dissected her course by the catalogue of Monticello, and she is in the second term of the junior year there. She is splendid in algebra, has completed *Robinson's University*.[113] And will finish mathematics [in the] next five weeks, also the natural sciences. You would be surprised at her improvement. She will go to Liberty in vacation and be examined by Professor Hughes and apply for a situation as a teacher and teach until she gets the means to send her self through school. I wish she could teach where she has relations to care some for her, but we do not know where the poor little thing's lot will be cast. Sometimes I wish we all could go out west some where, where Mr. Machette, Lilian, and myself could all teach and run a school, so we would not have to be separated from her. I wish I could see you, Ma. They're many things I could tell you and talk to you of that I would not trust to paper. We feel perplexed and troubled sometimes, but I try to keep up a cheerful spirit and do the best I can to hold up my husband. He feels *so much* the manner in which he has been treated and the want of ministerial affiliation. We miss Mr. Madeira so much. He is a good, kind, generous Christian, one who loves all God's dear children what ever their name.

We are so sorry of Brother John's not improving....

From Margaret Bruin Machette to Susan Machette Scott and Abbie Machette Hersman

Montgomery County, Missouri
May 16, 1878

Dear Susie and Abbie

... Susie, I am sorry I was away and could not help you about moving — am glad you have a home of your own so Harvey won't be worried moving again soon. How does Edgar like his new home? I begin to want to see the children. Abbie, I am uneasy about Finley, hope he won't get hurt with the horses at his Uncle's. I went home with Mary Jane Wells last Sunday week, intended to spend a week with her but Jacob and Jane was sent for to go to see Mollie Hammond, and I came back to stay with the children. Mollie died on Monday evening — was buried Tuesday of last week....[114]

From John Flood to his sister-in-law, Susan Machette Scott

Denver, Colorado
September 6, 1878

Dear Susie,

Pa left us very unexpectedly for home yesterday.... He intended to stay until Bob and Sallie went (Bob has been here about a week) but he was complaining for a few

113. Horatio Robinson's *University Algebra* (1847). Nealie attended Monticello Seminary.
114. Mary Jane Adams Wells, daughter of Ellen Dutton Adams Nowlin. See October 12, 1865.

days, and was home sick any way, and he concluded all at once to go, and went. I feel that he will be all well by the time he gets home. He has made many little sacrifices for Sallie and I the past year.[115] He is truly a noble Father.

Mr. Richardson was here. He only spent 2 days in Denver. His wife was with him. He had a spell of fever at Manitou which cut his visit to Denver short. The cause of his sickness was the same old one, "went too high in the mountains." His wife looked remarkably well. I was glad to be able to furnish them my horse and buggy whilst they stayed. Nealie asked him to have prayers before he left, and such a good prayer, so appropriate, so feeling, so full of faith. It did us good and we enjoyed his coming so much. You could see his visit was unselfish, and his sympathy and kind feeling genuine. Bob and Sallie leave for home in about 10 days. She and boy are much improving, but Bob has no thought of leaving them here. Langdon looks like a new man. He goes home when they do. They all come in time, and their improvement is marked. I was not so well after my trip to the mountains. I took severe cold, but I feel better now. This is a nice day and I hope to improve steadily. I will stay at home, too.

When I got back from the mountains Saturday, I learned that Joe Cook had returned to Denver in my absence and was at the point of death. I immediately went to him without waiting for dinner and remained the afternoon — and as much as I could with him until he died Sunday night. Monday at noon we sent his embalmed body (to Clinton, Missouri, where his wife lives) in a beautiful case. He looked better after he was dressed for the case than he did when he first came here.

He had every attention at a good hotel, and being a Mason the Masons were very attentive, and although Joe's brother had telegraphed to spare no pains and expense and to send the body home, the Masons had already given orders for him to lack nothing. Of course, Joe was a complete stranger here and had he had millions it would not have bought such attention as he had. From 1 to 4 Masons were with him all the time, and a prominent man here, an alderman in good fix, was with him all the time and when he died saw the body at once taken to the undertaker that there [would] be no delay in embalming, lest it could not be done — this too at midnight. He told me that over 600 Masons had been sent home in like manner in the 16 years he has been here. Of course the Masons bore the expenses of but few, but then such attention from kind hands in a strange land and without money or price is something to be appreciated.... As you knew Cook I thought this might interest you —[116]

This leaves Nealie and Forest quite well. Fruits of all kinds have come down. Can get tomatoes for a [$]1.00 a bushel, and apples, pears, peaches all can be bought for 10 cents a pound. Watermelons are cheapest as they can be raised here. I got 2 nice ones today for a bit a piece. Such at first sold for 1.00 —

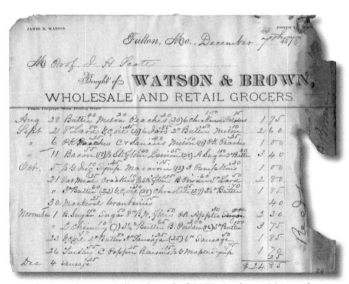

The Scotts' grocery bill at the end of 1878. Apples, at 30¢ a peck in Fulton, cost less than the Floods were paying in Denver.

115. Sallie Flood Tureman apparently was also ill; she would die in 1890.

116. See June 24, 1874, on Joe Cook.

A pocket-size Book of Job was vol. XVI in *The Holy Scriptures of the Old Testament* series by the Little Leather Library Corporation of New York.

FROM KANSAS CITY.

Only a line to let you know that the outlook for the Baptists is brighter than ever—brighter because a various, and in some respects a severe, discipline has taught us some valuable lessons. We have no pastor, only a supply. But I doubt if we ever had a pastor who "filled the bill" more perfectly than brother Powell is doing. He is studying the case, penetrating every home, and, like a good General, first organizing his forces. He is a plain, earnest, well-equipped Gospel preacher, having faith in the kind of preaching which has never yet failed to win for us the only triumphs which have been of any service to us. The attendance at the last communion season, and at our regular services, is the best evidence of his qualifications for this field.

I hear sad news from Westport. Bro. Machett has declared himself an open communionist. He has enjoyed the confidence of his brethren throughout the State from the time he left the Presbyterian Church, and his many friends are "taken back" at this strange folly. Had he expressed a regret for too hastily joining the Baptists, and announced his purpose to return to his first love, his Baptist brethren would have given him the hand of sympathy, and bade him follow his convictions like a true man; but they can only regard this movement of his within the Church as a signal of agitation which counts upon personal attachment and the sympathies of not over firm Baptists. Though this new departure will prove a shock to the little band at Westport, there is no doubt of the integrity of the body of the Church. Perhaps it will prove a salutary lesson in many respects. After years of pilgrimage in search of a rest of doctrine, it may be hoped that the Westport Theologian has found it. He will, I doubt not, be the only prophet of the kind in Missouri; and will therefore enjoy, in the estimation of the secret circular squadron of the East, a proud eminence.   J.

In this clipping, the writer refers to Alex Machette's support of open Communion as "this strange folly."

Beecher will be here next week.[117] I want Nealie to hear him without fail. I have heard him several times. Pa was anxious to hear him.

I wish you could just take one meal with us just to see Nealie's cooking, particularly her bread. Every body brags on it, and she does her work with as little ease as any one you ever saw. I milk, bring in the coal, and do all I can, but then I'm not much account.

From Alexander Machette to his mother, Margaret Bruin Machette

Westport, Missouri
January 20, 1879

Dear Ma:

... It seems my destiny to be involved in trouble. After a careful examination of the subject of Communion, I reached the conclusion that the practice of *"Closed* Communion" is not in harmony with the spirit of the Gospel.[118] If I had possessed a leathern conscience so as that I could have believed one thing, and connived at another, then I should have avoided trouble: but believing as I do, that a minister of Jesus should *speak the truth*, I find myself, once more, the object of persecution for truth's sake.

117. Minister and brother of Harriet Beecher Stowe, Henry Ward Beecher spoke about a more loving God than earlier Calvinism had preached; he also defended woman's suffrage. Five months before John wrote this letter, Beecher was in the headlines when Elizabeth Tilton confessed to "Criminal Intimacy with Reverend Henry Ward Beecher" (*Missouri Republican* April 16, 1878). In 1874 and 1875, Beecher had sued Elizabeth Tilton's husband, Theodore Tilton, for charging adultery. At that time, Elizabeth Tilton denied the charges, and the jury could not reach a decision. Beecher continued to deny the charges even after Elizabeth Tilton's confession. See Richard Wightman Fox, *Trials of Intimacy: Love and Loss in the Beecher–Tilton Scandal* (Chicago: University of Chicago Press, 1999); Halford R. Ryan, *Henry Ward Beecher: Peripatetic Preacher* (New York: Greenwood Press, 1990), 77–81.

118. Alex was objecting to the Baptist tradition of permitting only members of the church to participate in Communion.

I do not wish to be understood as complaining on that account. I had "rather be right than to be president"! It ought to be esteemed a privilege to suffer for conscience's sake. With God and truth on my side, I shall not fear what man can do unto me. Some think that I have acted "impudently" in "preaching the truth," and that I ought to have kept it all to myself and said nothing about it. Others think that I should have pulled up and moved off rather than be a disturber of the peace. But my conscience could be satisfied with nothing less than a bold declaration of God's truth, leaving consequences with Him. If it were to do over, I would not do otherwise than as I have done. God has not left me to stand alone. He has raised up strong friends who seem determined to stand by the truth. I trust you will remember me in your prayers....

Denver, Colorado
February 22, 1879

*From John Flood to his in-laws,
the Hersmans and Susan
Machette Scott*

Dear Charley, Abbie and Susie

... Nealie has *fully made* up her mind to make Denver her home. At least until Forest is of age and settled in life, and I most heartily endorse the idea of her remaining here with Forest. Both are in excellent health here. You never saw either looking near so hearty. Denver has excellent schools, magnificent churches, and its advantages are superior. Besides neither of us ever liked Fulton much. Aside from your 2 families there is nothing to go back to Fulton for and that should not control us in an important matter like this. Of course we don't want this generally known now as it might cut some figure in a legal way in winding up my estate.

I believe it best to raise Forest in this climate and Nealie is delighted with it. The Doctor says too it would be better to raise him here, in view of his possibility [of] inheriting my disease. She has a convenient little house here in a growing part of the City and Bob [Tureman] will manage her money and send her funds along as she needs it to live on. I think she takes a sensible view of it, and I heartily endorse it all — am earnestly requesting her to remain here. She always disliked Fulton more than I did and I don't blame her much. I have written you all firstly that you may know my views and that she and I most fully agree.

We saw quite a dispatch in the Denver paper that "Miss Georgia Arthur," a clerk in the P.O. at Fulton, Missouri, has been outraged in broad day light. But I took it as a joke, as I knew Arthur generally dressed as a woman in the boys' show. But it seems "she" was really dealt with. I think it a good thing. He is getting most too forward any way. Is a great tool of the Howard–Rickey crowd, and I suppose really in this matter J.H. Howard was the boss. He is terrible bad about such things. Miss Georgia has no doubt learned a lesson.[119]

119. The February 21, 1879, *Fulton Gazette* reported that an actress received a letter at the Fulton post office one afternoon around one o'clock. After reading the note, she became angry. Assuming that the letter writer was George Arthur, who was at the post office, she struck him with her riding whip. A week later the following appeared in the paper signed by "Outsider": "How is 'Miss Georgie Arthur, clerk in the post office' (at one o'clock), getting along?" John Henry Howard and his niece's husband, Joseph Kyle Rickey, apparently were part of a fast crowd. Rickey died by ingesting carbolic acid in 1904. The Gin Rickey cocktail, made with gin, lime, and carbonated water, was named after one of the Rickeys.

Well, I have said nothing about my health. I am feeling easier the last day or two, but I guess no real improvement. I haven't had on my clothes for near 4 weeks and am weak and appetite not good. The Doctor insists I will get about again but some how I can't think so. We have had a terrible winter on me. I never imagined I could become so reconciled. I just try to leave myself in the hands of Providence, and whatever comes is all right. I feel that "Jesus watches in tenderness over me" and that all is for my good. My lung does not bother me, but I have bad catarrh, and the chills and kidney infection worries me. I don't suffer, however, and I think it might be so much worse.... I would be glad to see you all, but I never expect to again....

From Alexander Machette to his mother, Margaret Bruin Machette

Westport, Missouri
February 23, 1879

Dear Ma:

I have been on a visit to Clinton, Henry County. It is a place of 3000 inhabitants on the M.K. and T.R.R. about 40 miles southwest from Sedalia.[120] The Church there has a very fine house and about 150 members. They have extended me a "call" to become their pastor. The salary offered is small ($800), but it promises to be a place of great usefulness. I think I will send my acceptance in a few days; and if I do, will enter on the work at once. Will not move my family until Spring opens out. They have half way promised to build a "parsonage," which if they do, will be quite a saving of rent as rent there is pretty high as compared with Westport.

Lizzie has gone to Liberty to visit her Ma, before her return to Lincoln County. She has been spending the winter with Lucy. Lizzie took the two younger children with her. I look for them back Tuesday.... I was in Lexington a few weeks ago. Visited Mr. Quarles and Professor Fleet — both have excellent schools and seem to be getting along well.[121] Hope this will find you all well and brother John still improving. Write as soon as convenient.

From Margaret Bruin Machette to her daughter, Abbie Machette Hersman

Denver, Colorado
March 2, 1879

Dear Abbie

The ground is covered with snow that fell yesterday morning. Friday afternoon we had one of the wind storms that this delightful climate boasts of, the sand so thick you could not see across the street. The cars on the Kansas Pacific road were five hours late on account of the wind. It is forty-five years today since your Father and I were married. Abbie, I wish if you still take the *Presbyterian* that you would send it to me after

120. The Missouri-Kansas-Texas Railroad, known as the K-T or "Katy Railroad."

121. After Lizzie's father died in 1873, her mother, Annie Shelton, lived with her children, including her daughter Lucy "Lu," who married Robert Semple in 1870. Semple became professor of Greek at William Jewell College when Alexander Frederick Fleet resigned in 1873. Fleet became president of Baptist Female College in Lexington, Missouri; he later taught at Missouri State University and then was superintendent of Culver Military Academy in Indiana. James Addison Quarles, graduating from Westminster in 1858, was president of Elizabeth Aull Female Seminary in Lexington, Missouri, and later at Washington and Lee in Virginia.

you read it at home. I have not seen a religious paper since I left home. Mr. Flood is about as well as usual, had a slight chill yesterday. My health is about as usual, not very strong at any time....

Denver, Colorado
March 11, 1879

From Margaret Bruin Machette to her daughter, Susan Machette Scott

Dear Susie

... John is better — has had no chills for over a week, is taking Smith's tonic and it is keeping off the chills. He is expecting to be able to be up soon, has a man spading his garden and sowing grass in his yard. The weather is bright and warm. Everyone thinks the hardest part of the winter is over. Still they will have cold weather through next month.

There is a great deal of improvement going on. The newspapers say that more than a thousand new houses will be built this summer. Rents have gone up. Mrs. Harrison has been paying 25 dollars a month the last year. She has to pay 40 a month this year for the same property. John is very fortunate in owning his house and lot. He is fortunate in money matters, too. I heard him tell his Mother his estate was worth fifteen thousand dollars.

If he keeps on improving I could be home by the time you need some one to stay with you if you want me.[122] I hope he may get up. He is so anxious to live till Forest is a large boy to be company for Nelia as he is determined she shall stay out here and I think she is more determined to stay than he is to have her. As for me staying I don't want to spend much time out here. There is nothing I like here as well as at home.

... I received a postal from Alex this week. He has entered on his work as pastor of the Baptist Church at Clinton, Henry County. They intend building him a house and his family will stay in Westport two months yet until the house is finished. I received a letter from Jane Shelton. They were all well. They had a good meeting at Zion in January. Nellie and Cooper both united with the church. Jane is greatly rejoiced. She has her three oldest children with her in the church now....

Dr. Crook's Wine of Tar was advertised as a cure for consumption. Here is a twenty-page book on uses for his medicinals.

122. Sue Machette Scott was pregnant.

From John Flood to his in-laws,
the Hersmans and Susan
Machette Scott

Denver, Colorado
March 26, 1879

Dear Charley, Abbie and Susie

This is the first time I have attempted to write sitting in a chair with my clothes on since last fall. I don't owe you all a letter, but I am here alone in my room. Nealie [is] in the next room on the bed where she has been suffering dreadfully with tooth-ache since Sunday night, now over 2 days. (Her face is terribly swollen. It is the same tooth that has bothered her so much. She must have it pulled as soon as she can.) She took cold Sunday standing at the gate in the cold wind without any wraps talking to Mrs. Albertson who would not come in. Ma is in the kitchen and Forest off at play. So I thought I would write you.

This is the prettiest day we have had this year. We haven't had many nice days, but are expecting them. Ma seems better the last few days. She has not been well since she came. And Nealie and I were afraid the climate was not agreeing with her, and told her the other day she could go home whenever she liked. She has been as good as she could be, and a great consolation to us, but we would regret it much if she were to die here. You know Pa contracted his disease here. He hesitated about coming and told me to telegraph him what I thought about it. I knew he wanted to come. (Sallie was then at his house on the way.) I telegraphed "Come by all means" and he came, and we all know the end. Ma I don't think likes the climate or country. And under all the circumstances we would prefer her to do just as she liked.... I don't want her health endangered for me as Pa's was.[123]

... I am perhaps talking too soon of my future, but for the past 3 weeks I seem to improve and it looks as if I would get around yet. If I live until fall I don't want to winter here, as I have been in bed these two winters, and I feel as I could not stand another such. If we or I don't go back to Missouri to try it, we or I may go South somewhere. Of course this is just some of my private thoughts. I wouldn't want every body to know....

I hardly know what to write to entertain you all. This place is being run over with newcomers and the City is improving rapidly. Rents and real estate have gone up much. Hundreds are coming here a day. Several whom we knew at home have called. I don't see what they are all going to do. Still residents say all who want work can get it at $2.00 a day. Two men who came out that I knew got work at once. There are thousands here and at Leadville who don't intend to work. Leadville is 150 miles from Denver. I reckon there is no doubt it is a rich mining country, but the snow is 2 feet deep there now, and likely to be until the 1st of May. We are expecting a snow storm here daily. Old settlers say we will have it....

From John Flood to his in-laws,
the Hersmans and Susan
Machette Scott

Denver, Colorado
April 8, 1879

Dear Abbie, Charles, and Susie

... Some two months ago a man here (we are satisfied who it was) wrote to Fulton in effect that I was in distressed circumstances without friends or money and would

---

123. Joseph Flood died of heart disease in 1878.

need the help of someone to be buried and even talked here of the Masons burying me, when I have always said I did not want to be buried Masonically. I do not like it.

To be plainer it was Henry Albertson who did the writing and his wife being in Fulton gave the finishing touches. They stirred up all the Lodges in Fulton who had meetings and wrote to the Lodges here very sympathetic letters to go at once and relieve me. Mason after Mason came in on us expecting to have to bring me things to eat and wait on me, and were much surprised indeed to find me in a comfortable fix with a house of my own and all I wanted, and also to learn the Doctor's order that I had too much company (and that two of those not Masons). One Mason who knew me last summer when he first came in wanted to know why I had not let my distress be known sooner. I told him I had nothing to do with this. That it was a meddlesome acquaintance who had stirred it all up. Of course when they learned the true condition of things, they did not deem it necessary to look after me.

Mr. Tuttle wrote me a letter of sympathy in connection with his wife — saying he had just this day heard of my *distressed condition*, and that arrangements would be made at once to relieve me. He could tell you all how the whole thing was gotten up I guess. I know Albertson was at the bottom of it. He as much as admitted it to me....

I have tried hard to collect my accounts but many won't pay me. I will lose near $3000 in that way, but I can't help it. My expenses will be very heavy owing to doctors' bills. My own expenses are more than the family's. They — mine — have been very heavy of late. I don't expect, however, to have to depend upon charity, unless things should be much worse than I anticipate....

Am not so well as formerly.[124]

Born Friday, 15 minutes to noon, on 2nd of May 1879. Present Dr. E. T. Scott, Mrs. Ford, and self:[125] Clive D. Scott

From the small notebook of Susan Machette Scott

Clive Douglas Scott, born in May, weighed 20½ pounds when he was six months old.

124. John Flood died in July 1879.

125. Assisting Dr. Elijah T. Scott was probably Martha Tate Ford, wife of Daniel Ford, harness shop owner and postmaster.

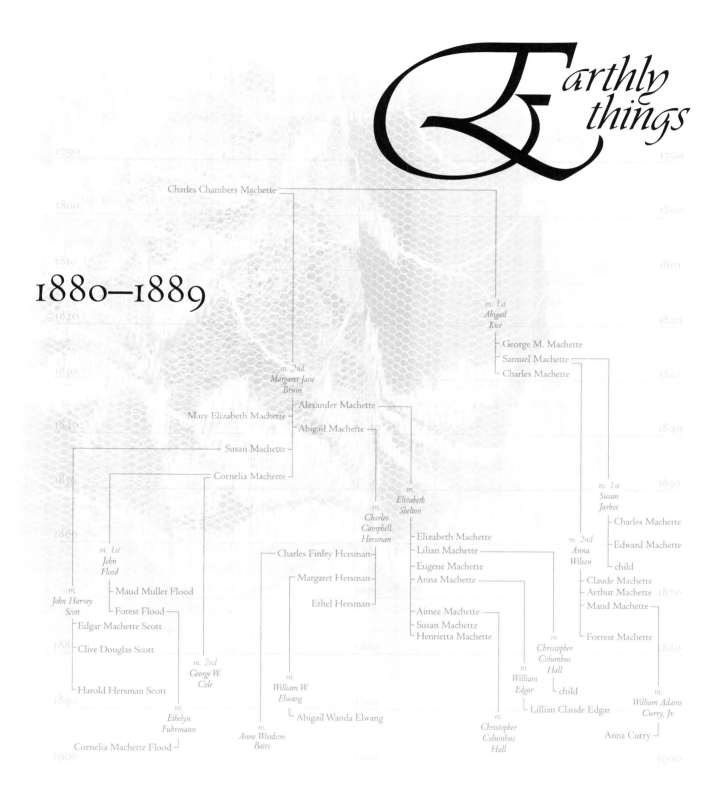

1790   1790

1800   1800

1810

1880–1889

1820

Charles Chambers Machette

m. 1st
Abigail
Rice

George M. Machette
Samuel Machette
Charles Machette

m. 2nd
Margaret Jane
Bruin

Alexander Machette
Mary Elizabeth Machette
Abigail Machette

Susan Machette
Cornelia Machette

m.
Elizabeth
Shelton

m.
Charles
Campbell
Hersman

m. 1st
Susan
Jarboe

Charles Machette

m. 2nd
Anna
Wilson

Edward Machette

child

Claude Machette
Arthur Machette
Maud Machette

Elizabeth Machette
Lilian Machette
Eugene Machette
Anna Machette

m. 1st
John
Flood

Charles Finley Hersman

Margaret Hersman

Ethel Hersman

Maud Muller Flood

m.
John Harvey
Scott

Forest Flood

Edgar Machette Scott

Clive Douglas Scott

Aimee Machette
Susan Machette
Henrietta Machette

Christopher
Columbus
Hall

Forrest Machette

m.
William
Edgar

child

Harold Hersman Scott

m. 2nd
George W.
Cole

m.
William W.
Elwang

Abigail Wanda Elwang

Lillian Claude Edgar

m.
William Adams
Curry, Jr.

m.
Ethelyn
Fuhrmann

m.
Anne Woodson
Bates

m.
Christopher
Columbus
Hall

Anna Curry

Cornelia Machette Flood

CHAPTER 3

Machette Family
January 1, 1880

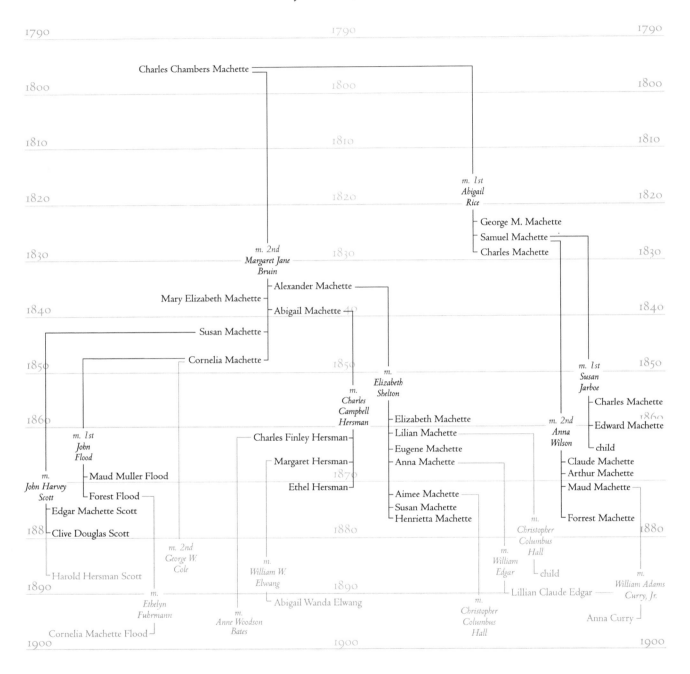

1790   1790   1790

Charles Chambers Machette

1800   1800   1800

1810   1810   1810

m. 1st
Abigail
Rice

1820   1820   1820

George M. Machette
Samuel Machette
Charles Machette

m. 2nd
Margaret Jane
Bruin

1830   1830   1830

Alexander Machette
Mary Elizabeth Machette
Abigail Machette

1840   1840   1840

Susan Machette

Cornelia Machette

m. 1st
Susan
Jarboe

1850   1850   1850

m.
Elizabeth
Shelton

m.
Charles
Campbell
Hersman

Charles Machette

1860   1860   1860

Elizabeth Machette

m. 1st
John
Flood

Charles Finley Hersman

Lilian Machette
Eugene Machette
Anna Machette

m. 2nd
Anna
Wilson

Edward Machette

child

m.
John Harvey
Scott

Maud Muller Flood

Margaret Hersman

Claude Machette
Arthur Machette

Forest Flood

Ethel Hersman

Aimee Machette
Susan Machette
Henrietta Machette

Maud Machette

Edgar Machette Scott

Clive Douglas Scott

Forrest Machette

1880   1880   1880

m. 2nd
George W.
Cole

m.
Christopher
Columbus
Hall

Harold Hersman Scott

m.
William W.
Elwang

m.
William
Edgar

child

m.
William Adams
Curry, Jr.

1890   1890   1890

m.
Ethelyn
Fuhrmann

Abigail Wanda Elwang

Lillian Claude Edgar

m.
Christopher
Columbus
Hall

Anna Curry

Cornelia Machette Flood

m.
Anne Woodson
Bates

1900   1900   1900

I n the last decades of the nineteenth century, Missouri was dramatically changed by the railroad. Paul Nagel states in his discussion of the railroad in Missouri, "The trail caravan, the steamboat, the pony express rider: all became obsolete in the wake of progress."[1] Kansas City, St. Joseph, and Joplin—all important railroad cities—experienced huge increases in population. Kansas City, which had a little over 4,000 people in 1860, had almost 56,000 in 1880, and by 1890, its population reached 132,716. St. Joseph's 1890 population of 52,324 was nearly six times larger than in 1860. Newly incorporated in 1873, Joplin had a population of 7,038 in 1880 and almost 10,000 people in 1890.[2] The train, a branch of the Chicago and Alton Railroad, came to Fulton at last. On one of its first runs, the train—as reported in the March 8, 1872, *Fulton Telegraph*—"sped on its way, over the yet unbalasted road, at the rate of twelve or fourteen miles per hour...."

The railroad, which helped to increase the profits of capitalists, became an impetus for the labor strikes that dominated headlines in the last quarter of the nineteenth century. Economic depression in the mid-1870s and the mid-1880s also fostered unrest among laborers as they fought for pay increases and the eight-hour day. In July 1877, the *Missouri Republican* reported that a national railway strike, which included St. Louis, produced "Unparalleled Scenes of Incendiarism, Violence and Plunder."[3] Similar headlines were used in covering the 1886 railroad strike that slowed commerce in St. Louis and Kansas City, and the 1894 strike targeting the Pullman Palace Car Company.[4] Violent strikes affecting industries other than the railroad included the 1886 strike in Chicago against McCormick Harvester and the 1887 strike in the sugar district of New Orleans.[5] In 1890,

1880—1889

1. Paul C. Nagel, *Missouri: A Bicentennial History* (New York: W. W. Norton, 1977), 69.

2. *Twelfth Census of the United States*, table 6. Although St. Louis also enjoyed population growth in the latter decades of the nineteenth century, it lost ground to Chicago. In 1860, St. Louis was the seventh largest city in the country, and Chicago was ranked eighth. By 1880, St. Louis was fifth and Chicago was third; in 1890 and 1900, St. Louis was fourth and Chicago was second. Christopher Schnell attributes the difference between St. Louis and Chicago to Missouri's failure to aggressively develop the railroad. See Christopher Schnell, "Chicago Versus St. Louis: A Reassessment of the Great Rivalry," *Missouri Historical Review* (April 1977): 245–265.

3. *Missouri Republican* (July 23, 1877).

4. *Missouri Republican* (March 11, 1886). *St. Louis Republic* (July 9, 1894).

5. *Missouri Republican* (May 5, 1886, November 12, 1887).

the United Mine Workers was organized, and soon the *St. Louis Republic* was reporting strikes against mining companies.[6]

As members of the middle class, Margaret Machette's children would have been fairly well insulated from the economic conditions facing laborers. Yet even they, hiring as they did women to work in their homes, dealt with the issue of domestic labor for hire. On May 21, 1889, Margaret Machette wrote that Abbie was having difficulty competing with the higher wages women were earning in nearby tobacco factories. Although Alex never made much money as a Baptist minister, his wife Lizzie sometimes had hired help (see the letter for August 16, 1882). Betty, a black woman, mentioned in Sue's journal for July 22, 1901, would work in the Scott household for decades. Census records indicate that Betty was probably Betty Miller, who could neither read nor write—a stark contrast to the highly literate Sue. Because Betty Miller was born in Missouri in 1849, she was likely born a slave.

In the 1880s, Margaret Machette's children were still raising their own families.[7] The surviving children of Alexander—Lilian, Anna, Aimee, and Henrietta—were at home in 1880. Lilian, the first of Margaret Machette's grandchildren to marry, would not do so until 1886. In 1880, Forest Flood was a schoolboy in Denver, where he lived with his widowed mother, Nealie. Abbie's daughters, Maggie and Ethel, were schoolgirls, and her son, Finley, was studying at Westminster, where their father Charley Hersman was the college president. Sue's son Edgar was a schoolboy, and Clive was a baby. Sue and Harvey had Margaret Machette's last grandchild and their third son, Harold, in 1887. Although relatively few letters were saved from this decade, enough exist to suggest something about the domestic life Margaret Machette's daughters lived as wives and mothers. Moreover, of particular value in discerning the home life of Sue Scott are three books she kept. One is a journal that Sue began in 1884 and kept almost up to her death in 1937. In a second book, a small scrapbook, Sue jotted down notes about her children and her gardening; she also wrote down or pasted in clippings of recipes and household hints, most of which were probably from the *New York Observer*, a religious paper to which the Scotts subscribed.[8] A third book is Sue's scrapbook on death and consolation.

The year Sue began her journal was the same year as the construction of the home the Scotts would live in until Harvey's death in 1928. At first their home probably had two rooms upstairs and two rooms downstairs with a kitchen attached to the back. According to Sue's journal, the downstairs was enlarged at least twice. When finished, the white frame house of the Scotts had a front porch where Sue would sometimes sit talking with visitors or greeting passers-by. The front hall opened on the right to a sitting room and on the left to the parlor, where company was received. Behind the parlor was the dining room.[9] At the end of the front hall was the library where Sue and Harvey

6. *St. Louis Republic* (April 3, 1891, July 3, 1897, September 17, 1900, August 20, 1902, October 16, 1902). The income of farmers also suffered as the railroad forced them to compete with wider markets and pay high freight charges (Christensen and Kremer, *History of Missouri*, 4:49).

7. Although Abbie, Sue, and Nealie had fewer children than many women of their generation, they were part of a trend toward smaller families. McDannell, *Christian Home in Victorian America*, 8, writes, "In 1800 the average number of children born to a woman before she reached menopause was 7.04. By mid-century, this number dropped by 23 percent to 5.42, and by the end of the century, to 3.56."

8. Many issues of the *New York Observer* are no longer extant, so publication cannot be confirmed.

9. In a 1906 letter, Sue described moving Harvey's bed to the dining room where he could sleep near a stove in the winter, and she intimated that the dining room furniture was moved to the downstairs sitting room/bedroom. Eventually, however, the library doubled as the dining room.

would read books and papers and write letters; Sue would also sew there while Harvey graded papers or prepared lessons. Between the library and the dining room was the bathroom, not much more than a long closet; the privy was in the backyard, and the Scotts did not have indoor toilets until 1910. At the very back of the house, behind the dining room, was the kitchen. Little more than a lean-to, it had a fireplace, cookstove, and small table where Sue and Harvey would often eat after the children were grown. When they first moved into the house, their son probably slept in one of the upstairs rooms while Harvey and Sue slept in the other. Later on, when Margaret Machette came to live with them, the sitting room was turned into Harvey and Sue's bedroom.[10] Margaret Machette's room became the room above the parlor, and the boys' room was above their parents' bedroom.

Sue and her sisters became homemakers when the Victorians' penchant for creating systematic order—for domesticating life—extended to domesticity itself. One important contemporary source on domesticity was *The American Woman's Home*, a book written by Catharine E. Beecher and Harriet Beecher Stowe. Published in 1869, the book was dedicated "To the women of America, in whose hands rest the real destinies of the republic...." Elevating homemaking to a domestic science, the authors explained why good ventilation in the home was crucial and how healthy food promoted good digestion. Another contemporary source on domesticity was *Good Housekeeping*, which began in 1885. As stated on its masthead, the magazine was "Conducted in the Interests of the Higher Life of the Household," and it offered advice on etiquette, cooking, cleaning, sewing and needlework, gardening, and child care. One of the clippings in Sue's small scrapbook offered household hints "From *Good Housekeeping*, always bright and useful...."

In Victorian America, even social obligations were well regulated through a system of calls and calling cards. Thomas Schlereth observes, "During its American vogue, 1870 to 1910, card leaving became an avenue for...carrying on all the communication associated with middle-class social life."[11] A woman new to a neighborhood waited to receive calls before making her own. A younger women waited to receive calls from an older woman. A woman with a higher social status made the first call to a woman with a lower social status. When a woman had a guest, the other women in the town called upon that guest before she made her own calls. Cards were used to announce visitors or to let members of the household know that someone had called during their absence. A wife's card was inscribed "Mrs. John H. Scott" or "Mrs. Jno. A. Flood," while a widow's card read "Mrs. Margaret Machette." The calling cards of the Machette women were plain white or cream-colored, but Sue's son Edgar had calling cards with colored drawings in the background, one of a boy pushing a girl in a swing and another of birds. All calls and cards were supposed to be returned within a week.[12] In her 1889 letters, Margaret Machette described the sometimes arduous process of making and returning calls while she was visiting her daughter Abbie in Tennessee.

10. The bed in the sitting room was a Murphy bed, which folded up into a closet when not in use. This allowed the room to function as both a bedroom and a sitting room. Many of the details about the interior of Sue's home come from letters written after 1902 and from the oral history of Mary Virginia Scott Baker, her granddaughter, who was born in 1920. When Mary Virginia was a child, she lived next door to her grandparents; she also heard family members speak of the house in earlier times. In 1986, Shirley Scott Payne, another granddaughter of Sue, had the old home torn down and built a new home on the site.

11. Schlereth, *Victorian America: Transformations*, 117–118.

12. Hester M. Poole, "Calls, Cards, Introductions, Invitations," *Good Housekeeping* (January 7, 1888): 109–112. Anna Sawyer, "The Etiquette of Calls and Cards," *Good Housekeeping* (February 1, 1890), 145–147.

The greatest responsibility that the middle-class matron had was to her home life—to be, in fact, "the angel in the house."[13] This concept of wife and mother was a vital part of the sentimentalism that Victorians valued. Marsden has noted, "The Victorians placed great value on both rationality and sentiment. Their era, characterized by the desire for order in society, was a technological one.... Yet it was also an age of emotion and romantic sentiments."[14] The sentimental portrait of the home was part of the trend away from strict notions of Calvinism. McDannell writes that "interest in domestic piety increased between 1830 and 1870," as "the traditional Calvinist notion of sin and salvation [was overturned] by advancing the spiritual dimension of the home."[15] Catharine Beecher and Harriet Beecher Stowe described the family as "the aptest earthly illustration of the heavenly kingdom, and in it woman is its chief minister."[16]

As the home's "chief minister," a woman had motherhood as her most important duty. Although the Reverend Theodore Cuyler, who is quoted in the general introduction, disparaged the move away from strict Calvinism, he also idealized motherhood: "God made mothers before He made ministers; the progress of Christ's kingdom depends more upon the influence of faithful, wise, and pious mothers than on any other human agency."[17] A February 8, 1872, article in the *New York Observer* extolled the role of mother: "She, alone, is the priestess who should minister at the altar where infant hearts are first taught the story of Bethlehem; where infant lips first learn to lisp the name of Jesus." In Sue's scrapbook on death and consolation, a clipping describes the story of Hannah from the Old Testament. Hannah, the mother of Samuel, devoted herself to caring for her infant son, took him to the house of the Lord when he was a child, and joyously led him to the service of God. The clipping concluded that mothers of the nineteenth century should do no less.

In Sue's remembrance written down on October 28, 1883, she described reading with her son Edgar the Bible lesson for children in the *New York Observer*. She also described helping him learn his catechism lessons. In the catechism, a series of questions and answers based on the Bible and ratified by the Southern Presbyterian Church, the first question is, "What is the chief end of man?" and the answer is, "Man's chief end is to glorify God, and to enjoy him for ever."[18] Other questions concerned sin and salvation, the Ten Commandments, and the Lord's Prayer. The private schools the Scott boys attended taught Victorian values as well. One passage in Clive's *The Pictorial Tract Primer* teaches the Victorian virtue of order: "Let order o'er your time preside, / And method all your business guide."[19] The other readings in Clive's primer

---

13. "The Angel in the House" was the title of a sentimental narrative poem published by Coventry Patmore, a Victorian English poet, and the title became a cliche to describe the ideal of the Victorian wife and mother.

14. Marsden, *Fundamentalism and American Culture*, 21.

15. McDannell, *The Christian Home in Victorian America*, xv.

16. Beecher and Stowe, *The American Woman's Home*, 19.

17. Cuyler, *Recollections of a Long Life*, 4. One reason for idealizing the role of motherhood is that it provided a justification for keeping women at home. Although Cuyler once asked a female evangelist to speak to his church, in his autobiography he also wrote: "The woman who neglects her nursery or her housekeeping duties, and her own heart-life for any outside work in the parish does both them and herself serious injury" (249, 290).

18. *The Westminster Shorter Catechism* (Richmond, Va.: Presbyterian Church of the United States, 1861).

19. Clive Scott's schoolbook was *The Pictorial Tract Primer* (New York: American Tract Society, n.d.). Inside the cover was written in Sue's handwriting: "Clive D. Scott, Nov. 14, 1883." Grade cards for Harold, Sue Scott's youngest son, show that he attended a preparatory school at Synodical College. On Harold's grade card, the first subject listed was "Bible."

are related to Christianity. For example, the section on letters of the alphabet draws from Christianity:

Aa
A, is for ADAM, who was the first man;
He broke God's command, and thus sin began.

Bb
B, is the BOOK, which to guide us is given;
Though written by men, the words came from heaven.

Cc
C, is for CHRIST, who for sinners was slain;
By him—O how freely!—salvation we gain.

Although the sentimental portrait of a mother nurturing her children's spirituality had some truth to it, it ignored or glossed over the secular and mundane that were also a part of raising children. In a 1908 letter to his son Clive, Harvey Scott wrote that he was sending him a complete set of Shakespeare. Harvey then wrote, "with the Bible, Shakespeare, a dictionary and our atlas, you have the very best this world can offer." In the Scott household, if the Bible was central to their lives, so, too, were certain secular texts.

Moreover, prayers and religious lessons were not enough to produce a moral child, and Victorian Americans, as they rejected earlier notions that children were just miniature adults, discussed how to raise children. Pets were encouraged as a way to teach children the need to care for others. Play too could foster moral development. One author for *Good Housekeeping* wrote, "The essential things to be taught them in play is to respect each others' rights, to protect the weak, and to be fair even in their sports. Moral courage should be cultivated in children by teaching them always to say boldly and do bravely what they believe is true and right, regardless of consequences."[20]

Discipline was of special concern in Victorian America. Instead of frightening children into obedience with tales of ghosts and goblins, mothers were encouraged to use didactic tales to teach children how to be careful and good. The May 20, 1875, *New York Observer* offers the example of a mother who, upon seeing her sons squabbling, told them of two other quarreling boys who foolishly and dangerously began hitting each other. The role that whipping or spanking played in the discipline of children was debated in Victorian society. On the one hand, a writer in *Good Housekeeping* stated, "It seems as if in this age of civilization that physical punishment ought never to be resorted to."[21] On the other hand, the January 27, 1876, *New York Observer* disparages the Society for the Prevention of Cruelty to Children, which had been formed in 1875, and argues that indulgence is a form of cruelty. Although condemning the punishment of "a child, in heat or with sudden violence," the article concludes that "the infliction of pain upon an erring child" is acceptable if precipitated by the parent's "calm, judicial, righteous judgment."

The Machettes apparently disciplined their children physically, although it is impossible to know how often that occurred. In Nealie's January 13, 1878, letter, she mentions that she was ready to "chin" or slap Forest, when she thought he was being disrespectful of his grandmother. In 1921, Abbie wrote her sister Sue about disciplining children:

---

20. Mrs. Eliza R. Parker, "Children's Manners," *Good Housekeeping* (August 7, 1886): 161–162.
21. "Disciplining Children," *Good Housekeeping* (August 7, 1886): 162.

Your children were at our house [in Fulton], of course, when we were so near, a good deal, but I never remember of any one ever thinking them in the way. Indeed, I felt as if they were mine. They had been taught *obedience,* at home—*a very important item I think.* I have never approved of using *"the rod"* too much but at the same time, as dear old Mother often said, "have a little switch *on hand* to use, when *necessary."* If I recollect correctly Ma used a little switch she kept on the mantle just behind the clock—*too often* for *my* comfort at least. She often said to others that "Abbie was not *a hard child to manage."* If I remember Sister Lizzie was *the leader* in all the "mischief" that was going on, and usually we got an equal share in the *punishment* administered—*probably we needed it.*[22] I am sure you think the same.

In a 1915 letter from Sue to her son Clive, then a physician, she advises him on how to manage a little boy with an eye injury. From this letter, it appears that Harvey might have used a switch on his sons but that Sue was more likely to follow the advice against whipping.

> . . . you'll have to tell him about the little boy in your eye and get him to look for his reflection in your eyes. I used to manage you little chaps that way and you would forget your notions. You used [to] take a notion not to eat at [the] table and I knew you would be hungry about the time everything was put away, so I would put down by your plate some bread and butter and wonder if a mouse would come along and take it and you would soon be eating heartily. Papa used to suggest a switch as a better argument!

Even though the middle-class homemaker typically had hired help, she herself also had an enormous number of housekeeping tasks to perform. In 1886, a year after *Good Housekeeping* was founded, it began a series of articles on a systematic approach to domestic chores: wash on Monday; iron on Tuesday; mend on Wednesday; clean silver, preserve fruit, or do extra duties on Thursday; dust, sweep, and clean windows on Friday; and bake bread and pies and clean the kitchen closets and cellar on Saturday.[23] Many of these duties are jotted down in Sue's journal and small scrapbook, but *Good Housekeeping* provides a more detailed description of how she might have spent her day. Cleaning a bedroom, for example, included putting knickknacks on the bed and covering them to protect them from the dusting and sweeping that followed. Damp tea leaves or newspapers were recommended to trap the dust. The heating stove had to be cleaned and blackened, the washstand and its porcelain washed, and the mirror polished.[24]

For washing clothes, rain water was recommended because of its softness. Linen, cotton, wool, and silk were all washed by hand. Clothes were to be boiled for up to fifteen minutes. Black pepper, vinegar, or ox gall were recommended as additives to the wash water to limit fading, and colored fabrics were washed twice. After clothes were rinsed in cold water, they were put through a hand-operated wringer or wrung by hand and then hung to dry. Shirts could be starched before or after they were dried. Clothes were dampened with a water sprinkler and rolled tightly before ironing, and

22. Mary Elizabeth "Lizzie," the oldest Machette daughter, died at boarding school in 1854.

23. Catherine Owen, "Progressive Housekeeping," *Good Housekeeping* (November 13, 1886): 2.

24. Catherine Owen, "Progressive Housekeeping," *Good Housekeeping* (December 25, 1886): 74.

the flatiron had to be kept hot on a stove. Dresses were to be ironed twice (once on the inside and once on the outside). Both a bosom-board and a longer ironing board were recommended.[25] Susan Strasser in her book on housework states, "One wash, one boiling, and one rinse used about fifty gallons of water—or four hundred pounds which had to be moved from pump or well or faucet to stove and tub."[26] Because washing and ironing were particularly arduous, the Machettes often had servants to do those chores.

The homemaker had other responsibilities around the house as well. For example, Sue jotted down in her 1890 journal the task of taking up and beating carpets.[27] She made almost all her own clothes, and for her husband and sons she made shirts, under-drawers, trousers, coats, pajamas, and even ties. Homemakers were expected to have recipes not only for cooking but also for making cleaning products, medicine, and pesticides, and Sue had recipes for all these products in her small scrapbook.[28]

In addition to working inside the home, women had outside chores to tend to. For many years, Sue kept chickens for eggs and a cow for milk. In her journal, small scrap-book, and letters written over the decades, Sue also described growing vegetables (pieplant or rhubarb, lettuce, peas, radishes, asparagus, okra, potatoes, beets, beans), fruit (raspberries, cherries, peaches, grapes, pears, strawberries, tomatoes), and flowers (chrysanthemums, violets, hyacinths, roses).[29] She also planted mushroom beds and kept beehives. Lizzie Machette, Sue's sister-in-law and a gifted gardener, grew callas, begonias, and geraniums.

The homemaker in a small town did not provide all her family's needs on her own, and Sue Scott had a variety of stores available to her in 1880. When she went to downtown Fulton, she could frequent general stores, grocers, a meat market, a millinery, a book and stationery shop, clothing stores, and the Callaway Savings Bank. A photography studio, druggists, shoemakers, and tailors were also available to her in Fulton.[30]

While homemakers in the latter half of the nineteenth century knew they had advances their grandmothers did not (for example, carpet sweepers, eggbeaters, and oil stoves), they also knew that stunning new changes were just around the corner.[31] In 1890, gas stoves were rapidly replacing oil and coal stoves.[32] Even more exciting, electricity, which was already being used to record dictation at the office and to run street-cars in the city, would soon be used to heat homes and provide hot water in the typical middle-class home. At the 1893 World's Fair in Chicago, visitors to the exposition saw coffeepots, chafing dishes, teakettles, and ovens, all powered by electricity.[33]

25. Mrs. Eliza R. Parker, "In the Laundry," *Good Housekeeping* (August 8, 1885): 11–12. Mrs. Lewis Swift, "A Well-Done Laundry," *Good Housekeeping* (February 18, 1888): 192–193.

26. Susan Stasser, *Never Done: A History of American Housework* (New York: Pantheon, 1982), 105.

27. See letters for November 29, 1874, February 19, 1877, and January 28, 1878, on making carpets.

28. Magazines and papers of the day also gave recipes for cosmetics and cold cream. See Lizzie Machette's recipe in the January 17, 1877, letter.

29. The April 18, 1872, issue of the *New York Observer* included an article on planting flowers to make homes into "paradises."

30. *Missouri State Gazetteer and Business Directory, 1879–1880* (St. Louis: R.L. Polk and A.C. Danser, 1879), 250–252.

31. Helen Russell, "The Good Old Days," *Good Housekeeping* (October 1894): 168–169.

32. N.D. Wright, "Heating," *Good Housekeeping* (February 15, 1890): 169–171.

33. A. Menlo Parker, "Electricity in the Home," *Good Housekeeping* (March 1894): 121–123.

In the meantime, much of domestic work was exhausting. Margaret Machette wrote of her fatigue after spending half a day working on fifty pounds of butter and of her hand trembling after whitewashing the house and planting potatoes (see November 15, 1860, and May 17, 1865). Lizzie wrote of making carpet rags until she was coughing so badly that Alex made her stop (see February 19, 1877). And in the letters written after 1902, Sue details much of her work around the house, including one time in 1906 when she spent the day making plum, peach, cherry, and blackberry preserves and, with the help of her youngest son, soldering them into tin cans. She then kept the bulk of her preserves, mailing "only about eight quarts" to her son Clive in St. Louis. For heating, cooking, and lighting, the Scotts relied on kerosene and coal. They did not have electricity until 1912.

Westport, Missouri
January 15, 1881

*From Alexander Machette to his
mother, Margaret Bruin Machette*

Dear Ma:

... I have been intending for several days past to write but have been suffering for about a week from neuralgia in the head. Have not been able to do anything scarcely for that length of time, and fear I shall hardly be able to preach much tomorrow. Lizzie and the children too have been having their share of epizootic and throat trouble. I am almost disgusted with our climate, and if I had an opportunity would be tempted to go where it is milder. Lizzie had a letter from her Ma recently. She is living now at Jacob's.[33]

... We all observed the "week of prayer" here as usual, but it has been too cold to protract a meeting successfully. We have been wanting to hold a meeting for some time, but the way does not seem to open up. Lilie is now busy teaching here at home — has several music scholars. Mr. Quarles offered her a place as assistant music teacher, but she preferred to teach here at home.[34] I should like very much to have her visit you next spring but cannot tell now whether it will be possible.

Remember me kindly to all the family, and accept much love from

Your affectionate Son
Alex.

Denver, Colorado
June 19, 1881

*From Cornelia Machette Flood to
her mother, Margaret Bruin
Machette*

Dear Ma:

... This leaves Forest and I in the best of health and happiness.... Our weather has been warm for some time — set in much earlier than usual. I sent you a paper with an account of Mrs. Cole's death.[35] After much and long suffering she at length passed peacefully away. Mr. Cole goes away in a few days to California. In them I have lost the best neighbors I ever had.

23.... Forest is in a terrible way about beating every thing around, running races a foot. I got some flowers from Floodie's grave and will send some to you. My flowers are not very abundant this year but every thing is green and nice....

Cornelia Machette Flood married her neighbor
George Cole in November 1881.

33. Lizzie's mother, Anna Berger Shelton, would die in 1889 at the home of her son Jacob.

34. See February 23, 1879, on James Addison Quarles.

35. George and Sarah Cole, neighbors of Nealie Flood in Denver.

From John Harvey Scott to his wife, Susan Machette Scott, and sons, Edgar and Clive

Eureka Springs, Arkansas
August 6, 1882

My dear Wife and boys

... Received a postal from you last night and was so glad to get it and to hear you were all getting on so nicely. Did not get the *Gazette* as here to fore — though you said in the postal that you had sent it. But it makes no difference as Miss Tish gave me hers and Miss Laura lets me have the *Telegraph*.[36] So you see we get all the Fulton news. Let

Susan Machette Scott with her sons, Clive and Edgar

Edgar Scott's chalkboard and eraser (photo by Margaret Baker Graham).

me say that I think a great deal of the two ladies just mentioned, and have become better acquainted with them than in all the years I have spent in Fulton. Miss Tish told me last night that if I got sick she would wait on me just the best she could. The water makes every one sick, *they say*, after using it a while. I just felt wretched with a sick stomach all day yesterday. Am better today, though not over it yet....

It is now nearly 5 o'clock and threatening rain — has been raining a little. Have not been to the springs today. Meet Mrs. Hook and Mrs. Christian there twice a day. Mrs. Hook must have forgiven you for not getting your hat from her.[37] She is just as pleasant as she can be — real jolly, and I like to meet her.

To morrow I will pack my trunk and prepare for leaving. I will have to go to the stage office tomorrow night, though I do not leave till Tuesday. Will be glad to get home; for after all "be it ever so humble there's no place like home." And there my dear Sweet wife and babies — it's worth leaving home for just to see how much I love them and how much they would be missed if I had them not. And then, too, just to see the poor afflicted ones here, suffering in all kinds of ways — my visit will not have been in vain if it teaches more resignation and thankfulness....

From Alexander Machette to his mother, Margaret Bruin Machette

Boonville, Missouri
August 16, 1882

Dear Ma:

The Financial Agent of Westminster College (I cannot remember his name) called to see me, and I subscribed $5 to the College. I paid him $3, which leaves $2 still due. Enclosed I send you $7. Please pay him the $2, and keep $5 for yourself. I often lament that I cannot do more for you, but I am compelled to support a large family on a meager salary and often am unable to keep myself decently clothed.

36. Letitia "Miss Tish" Henderson, sister of Theodore "The" Henderson. See April 22, 1866. Laura Rickenbaugh and her twin sister, Sarah, were good friends of Sue Scott.

37. Isabella Hook, widow of Zadok Hook and sister-in-law of Mary Ann Christian, was a milliner.

Mrs. Shelton has been on a visit to Liberty, and on her way back stopped yesterday to see Lizzie.... Lizzie has been without any help for some two weeks or more, and has nearly worked herself down [during] this terrible hot weather. Etta is sick this morning, and we think probably she is taking whooping cough, as it is in the neighborhood. Lizzie's help has returned. Had been sick....

Dear Edgar

I am so sorry the boys did not kill a bird yesterday so you might have one for your breakfast, but they will hunt for one today, and you shall have the first one that is brought home, and Clive shall have the second. We all hope you are better this morning.
Your friend
Mrs. E. Quisenberry

From Emily Quisenberry[38] to Edgar Machette Scott

Edgar Machette Scott.
born July 5th Sunday 1874
died Monday night October 23rd 1882

From the small scrapbook of Susan Machette Scott

October 25th 1882

I assume the high privilege of writing a brief tribute to the memory of dear little Edgar Scott, whose precious remains I saw a few hours ago laid away in the Fulton Cemetery. He was the son of Mrs. Susan and Professor Scott.

The Angels came last Monday night at 10 o'clock and sweetly bore him away to *his* home and theirs; and though the fond parents wanted him oh so much here with them in their earthly home, it has never before been my lot to witness such perfect resignation to the divine will. Edgar was a child of rare endowment. In the providence of God I have dealt much in training the young mind and can truly say it never was my charge to direct a higher intellect than belonged to Edgar Scott. Though only [a] little over 8 years of age, his general information, comprehensive mind and matured thought placed him far above the ordinary of twice his age. A great mathematical mind was his by inheritance. Once when I was telling my little pupil that a knowledge of arithmetic was not only of great benefit to us in our everyday life, but enabled men to measure the distance of the stars from us and from each other, bright little Edgar eagerly exclaimed, "That's what I'm going to be when I am a man — an astronomer."

Tribute by a teacher of Edgar Machette Scott in the death and consolation scrapbook of Susan Machette Scott

38. In 1886, Emily Quisenberry and her teenage sons, Oliver and John, burned to death when their home caught fire after they had attended a revival at the Presbyterian church. A widow, Emily had moved to Fulton so that her sons could attend Westminster College. The *Fulton Gazette* (March 5, 1886) reported that the mother died trying to save her sons.

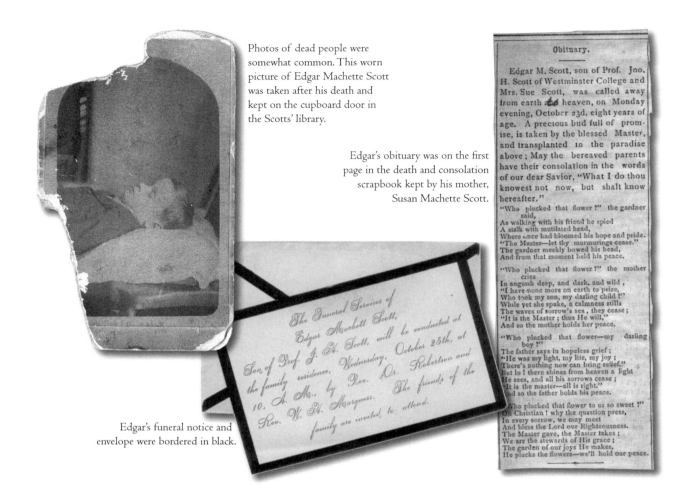

Photos of dead people were somewhat common. This worn picture of Edgar Machette Scott was taken after his death and kept on the cupboard door in the Scotts' library.

Edgar's obituary was on the first page in the death and consolation scrapbook kept by his mother, Susan Machette Scott.

Edgar's funeral notice and envelope were bordered in black.

Obituary.

Edgar M. Scott, son of Prof. Jno. H. Scott of Westminster College and Mrs. Sue Scott, was called away from earth to heaven, on Monday evening, October 23d, eight years of age. A precious bud full of promise, is taken by the blessed Master, and transplanted in the paradise above; May the bereaved parents have their consolation in the words of our dear Savior, "What I do thou knowest not now, but shalt know hereafter."

"Who plucked that flower ?" the gardner said,
As walking with his friend he spied
A stalk with mutilated head,
Where once had bloomed his hope and pride.
"The Master—let thy murmurings cease."
The gardner meekly bowed his head,
And from that moment held his peace.

"Who plucked that flower ?" the mother cries
In anguish deep, and dark, and wild ,
"I have none more on earth to prize,
Who took my son, my darling child ?"
While yet she spake, a calmness stills
The waves of sorrow's sea , they cease ;
"It is the Master ; thus He will,"
And so the mother holds her peace.

"Who plucked that flower—my darling boy ?"
The father says in hopeless grief ;
"He was my light, my life, my joy ;
There's nothing now can bring relief."
But lo ! there shines from heaven a light
He sees, and all his sorrows cease ;
"It is the master—all is right."
And so the father holds his peace.

"Who plucked that flower to us so sweet ?"
Oh Christian ! why the question press,
In every sorrow, we may meet
And bless the Lord our Righteousness.
The Master gave, the Master takes ;
We are the stewards of His grace ;
The garden of our joys He makes,
He plucks the flowers—we'll hold our peace.

The Funeral Services of Edgar Machett Scott, Son of Prof. J. H. Scott, will be conducted at the family residence, Wednesday, October 25th, at 10. A. M., by Rev. Dr. Robertson and Rev. W. H. Marquess. The friends of the family are invited to attend.

And the dear Lord soon raised the precious child far above his brightest anticipations — for who of us knows now but what Edgar measures the distance of the stars by his own winged, glorified flight from one to another. Who of us can form any estimate of the privilege, or employment of the redeemed? But with all this high aspiration for knowledge, Edgar did not impress you as a prodigy, and though possessed with a good deal of manly independence, he was a very child in all its childlike simplicity and earnestness. None at school loved better their marbles, balls and tops, and none more frankly acknowledged that he loved play better than hard study. His parents had early instilled into him a love of truth and I never knew him in the least degree to depart from it.

But sorrowing parents, your Edgar is now where there is no need of study, but knowledge flows in as a glorious fountain of light and love and is an endless stream of delight. So though you miss darling Edgar in your home, we miss him in the school room, and the loving relatives miss him in their social gatherings, we must not be selfish — but think of him in that blissful home above. I know that he is infinitely happier than when with us — it is best as it is, for God is love.

Edgar died Monday October 23, 1882 at 10:15 p.m.
Buried Wednesday a.m.

lot in cemetery	$ 30.00
casket[39]	65.00
dig grave	7.00
vault	32.00
hearse &c.	17.00
shoes & stockings	2.50
photograph	3.00
remove rubbish	1.50
funeral notices	5.00
fence around grave, tombstone	58.00
doctor	12.00

From the notebook of John Harvey Scott

A lamb is carved into the tombstone of Edgar Machette Scott located in Hillcrest Cemetery in Fulton (photo by Margaret Baker Graham).

Letter from Annie Street Reed, a friend, in the death and consolation scrapbook of Susan Machette Scott

Fulton, Missouri

Dear Mrs. Scott.

In a late copy of our New York *Advocate* I found the enclosed extract from the Reverend T.L. Cuyler's sermon....[40]

Edgar was a lovely child and one in whom I felt an interest even after I met him at the hotel where we all boarded. When death invaded your home and claimed your boy, it was indeed a dark hour to you; but He who promises a blessing to the eyes that weep no doubt gave you grace to accept the cup, with the thankful resignation that all was well with Edgar.

Another link of that golden chain in your family circle has only crossed the river, to add new interest there. Another one is waiting on the other side for you.

Two months ago an aunt and her daughter in *our family* were lain in *one grave*, both unexpectedly called away from us. These events come upon us all in *some way*, and when we know *they* are among the redeemed, it does sweeten the cup and help us to say, "*Thy will be done*."

Very truly your friend
Mrs. J.H. Reed[41]

39. "Casket," which originally had meant a case for valuables, was used instead of "coffin" in the latter part of the nineteenth century. Green, *Light of the Home*, 168, 179.

40. The New York *Advocate*, probably the *Christian Advocate*, a religious newspaper published in New York. The Reverend Theodore L. Cuyler, a religious columnist, wrote *The Empty Crib: A Memorial of Little Georgie* (New York: Baker & Taylor, 1868) on the death of his own son.

41. In 1873, Annie Street married J.H. Reed, colonel in the Third Missouri Volunteers during the Civil War.

"On classic cups and vases we have sometimes seen devices carved by the cunning hand of the sculptor.

"So around the cup of *sorrow* which God commands to the lips of *suffering, tried Christians* are wreathed *many comforting* assurances. Here is one of them — '*All things* work together *for good to them* which *love God.*' Here is another like unto it, 'As thy days, so shall thy strength be.'

"Afflicted friend, turn thy cup of sorrow around and thou will see engraved upon it these precious words, 'As one whom his mother comforteth, so will I comfort you.'

"Turn it again and read: 'My grace is sufficient for thee.' The whole cup is encircled with words of love; but it requires Faith to read them. They are invisible to selfishness or blind unbelief.

"And God sometimes washes the eyes of His children with tears in order that they may read aright His providence and His commandment."[42]

T.L. Cuyler, D.D.

Written on a piece of paper by Susan Machette Scott

December 22, 1882

Clive was standing before the fire as I tried on his coat — which was rather tight for him. He blew his breath hard and said, "Ethel, that's *the* way I blow the *hot* out."

He was running around, calling, "Tittle mouse Little mouse." I said, "Who is that?" "Why," said he, "he lives in a little house." He meant the kitty who had the night quarters in a hen coup.

Tuesday, March 27, 1883. Clive is too funny — he sat before the fire with a long face and said, "I've got the headache, Mama — sometimes I have such curious spells come over me." He could scarcely keep from laughing as he said so.

He said to me a while ago, "Mama, you are so sweet tempered." I said, "You sweet thing, what makes you talk so sweet?" "I just have the habit," said he.

May 22, 1883. [We] were in the garden looking at the vegetables turned dark with frost. Clive stooped down by a weed and said, "just see, this has turned deliberately black!"

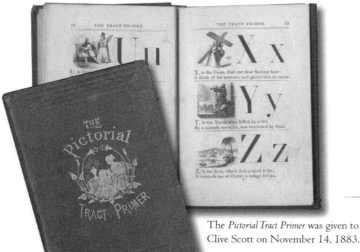

The *Pictorial Tract Primer* was given to Clive Scott on November 14, 1883.

---

42. Biblical passages from Cuyler's statement are taken from Romans 8:28, Deuteronomy 33:25, Isaiah 66:13, and 2 Corinthians 12:9.

October 28th, 1883

I have so seldom a chance to write I will seize this hour, when Papa and Clive are at church, for a few lines —

Dear little Edgar on Sabbath morning, October 15, 1882, got ready and went to church with us — I remember he wore light pants and vest and dark blue coat — all made at home, and at church I felt just like looking at him to see how pretty he looked — such a perfect form and lovely head and he behaved so nicely — how little did I think it was the last time! When we returned home I prepared dinner. Maggie Hersman came in and sat down with us. When she went away [she] asked us to "come up" to her house. I did not feel very well but when I had heard Edgar's catechism, the 16 questions and answers he learned that afternoon — he always recited from the first[43] — when he was through, [we] went up to see Grand Ma. I got Clive and Edgar ready, and he proposed that they should start on. I consented and when I got out of the gate they were walking fast, half way there. Edgar would place his hand on Clive's shoulder to urge him on. When I got to Ma's room they were there and Edgar was seated looking over some books.

That night when he left the supper table, he said, "Papa, can I go to church with you?" But I told him he had better stay with Clive and I. He laid down on my bed while I got Clive to sleep which took some time, and

From the death and consolation scrapbook of Susan Machette Scott

This clipping on a cure for diphtheria, the disease that killed Edgar, was in Susan's death and consolation scrapbook.[44]

TAR SMOKE FOR DIPHTHERIA.

DR. DELTHIL'S CURE TRIED WITH SUCCESS UPON A NEW YORK PATIENT.

Ruth Lockwood, the nine-year-old child of Thomas Lockwood, a compositor in the *Times* office, became violently ill with diphtheria on Tuesday night (May 6). She was so weak that it was deemed dangerous to try tracheotomy, or cutting open the windpipe. On Thursday Dr. Nichols of 117 West Washington place, who was attending her, received a copy of the Paris *Figaro*, which contained a report made to the French Academy of Medicine by Dr. Delthil. Dr. Delthil said that the vapors of liquid tar and turpentine would dissolve the fibrinous exudations which choke up the throat in croup and diphtheria.

Dr. Delthil's process was described. He pours equal parts of turpentine and liquid tar into a tin pan or cup and sets fire to the mixture. A dense resinous smoke arises, which obscures the air of the room.

"The patient," Dr. Delthil says, "immediately seems to experience relief; the choking and rattle stop; the patient falls into a slumber and seems to inhale the smoke with pleasure. The fibrinous membrane soon becomes detached, and the patient coughs up microbicides. These, when caught in a glass, may be seen to dissolve in the smoke. In the course of three days afterwards the patient entirely recovers."

Dr. Nichols tried this treatment yesterday with little Ruth Lockwood. She was lying gasping for breath when he visited her. First pouring about two tablespoonfuls of liquefied tar on an iron pan, he poured as much turpentine over it and set it on fire. The rich resinous smoke which rose to the ceiling was by no means unpleasant. As it filled the room the child's breathing became natural, and as the smoke grew dense she fell asleep.—*N. Y. Sun.*

The Scotts had this portrait painted of Edgar after he died. Sue Scott wrote the instructions for the portrait, right (photo of portrait by Margaret Baker Graham).

43. See the introduction to this chapter on the catechism, p. 156.

44. The article first appeared in the *New York Sun* (May 11, 1884) and was possibly reprinted in the *St. Louis Presbyterian*. (Issues of the *Presbyterian* for May and June 1884 are not extant.) Because diphtheria can obstruct breathing, a tracheotomy may be performed. A serum to treat diphtheria was developed in 1890, but widespread immunization was not available until after the First World War. *The Cambridge World History of Human Disease*, ed. Kenneth F. Kiple (Cambridge: Cambridge University Press, 1993), 680–683.

when I put Clive down I took my low chair to the table to read. Edgar got up and came and sat on the other side of the table. I asked him if I should read to him — he usually preferred reading to himself — he said yes. I read to him the 14th chapter of Mark and the lesson in the *Observer* on it.[45] In explaining the Passover I turned back in the Bible and read about the plagues of Egypt to him.

When we came to the last plague — where the first born of the Egyptians were slain, he showed his understanding of it by saying — "That's like Finley and I should die." Dear precious pretty serious little face — The Lord who loved the little ones must have loved him. He said presently that he felt chilly and would put on his coat — he did so, and then in a few minutes he said he felt chilly and would go to bed. He undressed himself and went and laid down by Clive and was asleep when Papa came home. How strange it does seem that [I] was not uneasy about his feeling cold — I never once thought of his being sick. And 'way in the night I felt restless and wanted to put him in my place and found that he had a raging fever: which continued all the next day — just to think we did nothing for him till [the] next night. I gave him a pill and when I put him to bed I saw something so strange about his eyes. I just told his Papa he had to go for the Doctor. He came and gave him medicine, but I think it was too late. I believe the disease developed in that fever. Nothing seemed to act on his bowels.

From George W. Cole[46] to his mother-in-law, Margaret Bruin Machette

Denver, Colorado
March 15, 1884

Dear Ma

Your token of affection was received in due time, and I assure you it was duly appreciated. It is convenient for silver and gold for I am always carrying it loose in my pocket.[47] We are having good weather. We have commenced to put the crops in — expect to put in about two hundred acres of wheat. There has been quite a loss of cattle and sheep in our state by the cold winter. I sold all my stock but 34 cows and 500 sheep [and] 10 horses, and I fed them hay all through the bad part of the winter. I have thought of buying Eastern cattle but don't think I will buy but a few if any.

Forest had his teeth filled this morning, and we let him have his picture taken, and I will send you one. He wants you to see how he has grown. He thinks he is quite a man.

We all join in love to all. Write soon.

---

45. Sue Scott clipped the lesson from the *New York Observer* for her scrapbook on death and consolation.

46. George Cole and Nealie Flood married in November 1881, five months after his wife, Sarah, died.

47. The one-dollar gold piece was in circulation at this time.

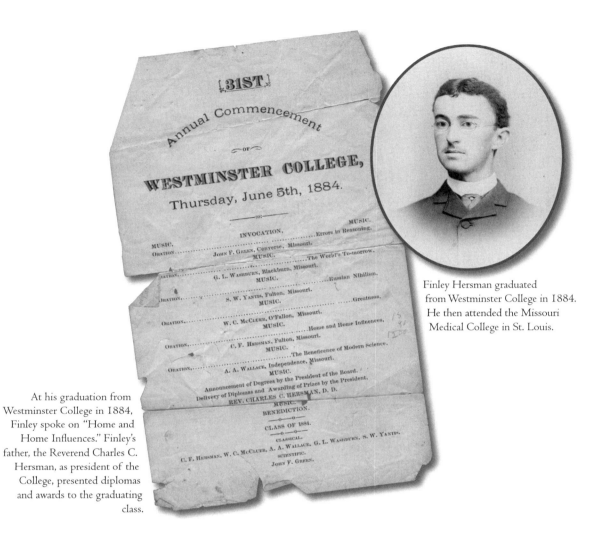

Finley Hersman graduated
from Westminster College in 1884.
He then attended the Missouri
Medical College in St. Louis.

At his graduation from
Westminster College in 1884,
Finley spoke on "Home and
Home Influences." Finley's
father, the Reverend Charles C.
Hersman, as president of the
College, presented diplomas
and awards to the graduating
class.

May 12	planted flowers at Edgar's grave
June 12th	began digging foundation for house
19th	foundation done, began on house
July 3rd	got slate on roof
Edgar's birthday on 5th	went [to] his grave
7th	lathing the house
22nd	2nd coat of plastering
Aug. 4	last coat of plastering
16	carpenters came to finish work
22	took Clive to Fair
2nd Sept.	Painters at work
Oct. 24th	got carpets down

*From the journal of Susan
Machette Scott for 1884*

The Scott home in Fulton (photo taken in the early 1900s)

From the small scrapbook of
Susan Machette Scott

Tomato Catsup — Cut the tomatoes, heat thoroughly and strain; to one gallon of juice put four small tablespoonfuls of salt, four of ground black pepper, three of ground mustard, one half tablespoonful of cloves, one-half teaspoonful of red pepper, one pint of vinegar. Boil slowly four hours, then bottle and seal.

To Keep Off Mosquitoes — Take a small quantity of a two per cent carbolic acid solution and sprinkle sheets, coverlets, pillow and bolster on both sides, the edges of bed curtains, and the wall next the bed. The face and neck may also be slightly wetted with the solution. Not a single gnat or mosquito, it is said, will come near.

Felon On The Finger[48] — The following simple remedy is recommended as a cure for felon on the finger. Take common rock salt, such as is used for salting down beef or pork; dry it in an oven; then pound it fine, and mix it with spirits of turpentine, in equal parts; put it in a rag, and wrap it around the parts affected, and, as it gets dry, put on more, and in twenty-four hours you are cured.

Potato Cakes — Take one dozen large potatoes, fresh boiled and mashed very fine, ¼ lb. of butter, three eggs beaten, and ½ lb. of flour, mix all together with a fork (do not handle it), roll into thin cakes, and bake quickly in a hot oven.

Cream Crackers

I quart flour	I teaspoon baking power
pinch salt	4 tablespoon butter
2 tablespoons sugar	3 eggs

Mix in firm smooth dough — roll thin. Cut with biscuit cutter and drop in pot of boiling water for a minute. Skim out and lay in cold water. Then place on grated tins and bake in hot oven.

Bluing for Washing Clothes

[P]our ½ gallon boiling water on 2 ounces Prussian Blue [and] 2 ounces oxalic acid. When coloring rags, put them on the fire with enough water to simmer and put the above to them.

For the Hair

I part Bay rum
3 part olive oil
I part good brandy

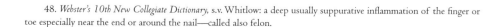

48. *Webster's 10th New Collegiate Dictionary*, s.v. Whitlow: a deep usually suppurative inflammation of the finger or toe especially near the end or around the nail—called also felon.

Mr. Noel's Pills

40 grams of Calomel
40 grams Aloes
40 grams of Rhubarb
80 grams Carbonate of Soda
40 grams of Ipecacuanha
40 drops [of] oil of Cloves

Makes 80 pills. 2 doses every other night for 9 times.

Medicine for Children

1 tablespoonful Rhubarb   1 tablespoonful Cloves
1 tablespoonful Soda   2 tablespoonfuls Sugar

Pour over this 1 ½ pints [of] boiling water.

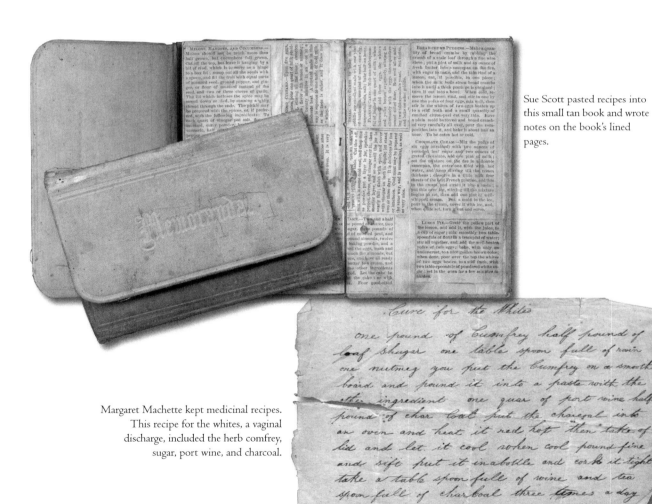

Sue Scott pasted recipes into this small tan book and wrote notes on the book's lined pages.

Margaret Machette kept medicinal recipes. This recipe for the whites, a vaginal discharge, included the herb comfrey, sugar, port wine, and charcoal.

From Forest Flood to his grandmother, Margaret Bruin Machette

Denver, Colorado
December 2, 1884

Dear Grandma:

I have been expecting to write for a long time and have been very long about it. I am a little bit sick. Papa is reading some History. I am expecting [for] Christmas some candy, nuts, and apples. I am writing by candle light, and it's making my eyes smart. I am doing well at school. I have a few marbles. My chum is expecting to go to his Grandpa's ranch — Write soon.

aff. Forest

From George W. Cole to his mother-in-law, Margaret Bruin Machette

Denver, Colorado
February 15, 1885

Dear Ma

… Nealie is a little better this morning. The doctor thinks she will get up in a short time. She has been quite sick since we got home. Her stomach was congested, had a good deal of fever with it. Forest is feeling first rate. I was very sorry to hear that Professor Scott had to have his eye taken out.[49] No one knows the loss of [such] except one that has had a similar experience.

We have had delightful weather until yesterday. It snowed a little but enough to make it [more] disagreeable than has been. Some grain [has been] sown this month. Some farmers were just starting into their spring work. Ma, I like the folks that I met in Missouri very much, especially the home folks as I shall call them and hope to be remembered. Love to all.

Story told to Susan Machette Scott by her mother, Margaret Bruin Machette, on February 23, 1886.

"Sister Dutton came down with her cotton and wool to have it ginned and carded, and Mother and Father and Sister and brother Dutton got in the wagon [the] next morning and went to St. Charles about 12 miles on the Boonslick road and left me and Sister's Ellen and Jimmy at home."[50]

"How old were [you] then, Ma?"

"Well, I couldn't have been more than seven and Ellen was three years younger and Jim was two. I don't remember that we were afraid. Mother told us when it was 12 o'clock — she showed us on the door where the sun would be — we were to eat our dinner and go over to Mrs. Wolfe's, a neighbor [who] lived about a half mile off. I remember that was the prettiest road

---

49. George and Nealie Cole had recently visited Fulton. One of Harvey's eyes was removed after getting a cinder in it; after that, he wore a glass eye. A receipt for 1891 shows that he bought one dozen artificial eyes for $90.

50. On the manuscript, Sue Scott identified 1824 as the year her mother was describing. Mary "Sister" and her husband, John H. Dutton, lived in Montgomery County then. See October 12, 1865, on Ellen's death. The Booneslick road or Boone's Lick Trail extended from St. Charles, through Callaway County, and to the salt lick in Howard County. Around 1806, Daniel Morgan and Nathan, sons of Daniel Boone, manufactured salt from the salt lick. John K. Hulston, "Daniel Boone's Sons in Missouri," *Missouri Historical Review* (July 1947): 365–366.

— we went down the hill and crossed a small branch and up the side of the next hill and past a beautiful oak grove and after that it was a level strip of pasture till we reached Mrs. Wolfe's. It seemed to us a long distance and we felt relieved to get there.

"Mrs. Wolfe was a good old German woman and the kindest soul. She made us welcome — but when she took a good look at Jimmy she burst out laughing and said, 'Why, Jim! Them gals have put your pants on hind part before. Come here and let me fix you.' So she righted his garment. I remember during the afternoon she went to the spring house — got us the nicest of sweet milk and gave us bread and butter — and the bread had some red ants on it. The dear old woman could not see them, they were so small. We were too polite to tell her. So we brushed them off. They were great big biscuits, shaped by hand, but sweet and light.

"Grandpa moved to St. Charles City in 1827 — he moved from Black Jack neighborhood — from the kind of oak that grew there.[51] The land was not much prized by the early settlers, but the Dutch developed the soil and have grown rich there."

Church & Co. of New York packaged a colorful card in each box of their Arm & Hammer Brand Soda & Saleratus (baking soda) as an early brand name promotion. Each of the sixty cards in the set explained that a housekeeper "should buy package soda in preference to... unknown and inferior... bulk soda... of anybody's manufacture and generally of a poor quality."

On ironing days I often take my work and sit by the table where Aunt Lucy is ironing with the excuse of enjoying her good fire, but really to draw her in to talks of good old times she remembers, both here in Missouri and back in Virginia. Although she is very appreciative of freedom, yet she looks back on the flesh pots[53] of the past with relish — nor does she conceal her contempt of empty smoke houses and [the] hand-to-mouth way of living of town people.

Story told by Aunt Lucy and written down by Susan Machette Scott[52]

51. Margaret Machette and Mary Dutton's father was Timothy Bruin, a constable in St. Charles. He and his wife, Margaret Galbraith Bruin, died in 1847, the same year Jimmy Dutton died.

52. Aunt Lucy, apparently a slave of Charles Chambers Machette in St. Charles, Missouri. After his first wife, Abigail Rice "Old Miss," died in 1833, Charles married Margaret Bruin "Miss" in 1834. When Charles wrote his sister, Mary Hessinville Machette, of his intention to marry less than eight months after his wife's death to a woman twenty years younger than himself, Mary wrote back: "Shall I tell you, my dear brother, when I came to that part of your letter, where you introduced this subject, a blush like crimson covered my face?... It was the last thing your poor wife thought of, that you whom she loved and cherished so tenderly, that you in a few short months could so far forget her as to be looking for another. I don't think your choice exactly suitable. You say she is but little past seventeen. So far as I can judge of your age, you can't be short of forty. Now permit me to ask you what do you think she will marry you for? Do you think it is love? I hope so but I fear not. Can she bring you a fortune equal to yours? If she can I may think she professes a regard for you. When I see one so young consent to marry a man who is old enough to be their Father, there is interest in the case."

53. See Exodus 16:3, "And the children of Israel said unto them, Would to God we had died by the hand of the LORD in the land of Egypt, when we sat by the flesh pots, and when we did eat bread to the full; for ye have brought us forth into this wilderness, to kill this whole assembly with hunger." This verse and the story surrounding it would have been well known to both Aunt Lucy and Susan Machette Scott.

"How many hogs did you kill then?"

"Laws! bless your soul, in my old Missus' time we'd kill 35 hogs in the fall, makes my mouth water just to think of them bacon sides as wide as this table and as thick as that one (measuring in her hand). Work? I tell you, there's no kind of work on the farm that I haven't done. I could plough from morning to night. I'd get up before light and go out and hitch up them hosses. If you could jest [see] them hosses, the fat one of 'em would shake, jest shake! as they'd trot off — I tell you the corn crib was full from one year's end to the other. When they'd go to put away corn in the fall, they'd have to take out the old corn to make room for it. Mebbe I'd go and plough before breakfast till the horn blew. Then I['d] take and feed 'em and rest a bit after breakfast. Then I'd plough the enduring morning till the horn blew for dinner and so on till night. Yes, ma'am, I've done it day in and day out. Old Miss would get the meals and take care of the children. That was in the old man's time. He was mighty tight I tell you, but things changed round mightily.

"Miss was heap younger than him and when he died here flocked the old widdowers and old bachelors — Miss wasn't more than 30 — purty and plump as a partridge.[54] 'Tweren't three weeks after her husband died when here came old Judge Tucker — he had eight children — just one an' another acourting — them was fun times. Heaw! heaw! I tell you, nothing to do but cook pies and sweetcakes and kill chickens and fry ham Sundays! Them was the big days — here would ride up the Judge in his Sundays to ride to meetin' with her and when meetin' was over here would come three or four more — and one day that was the worst day for Missy old man W— came a-ridin' by her side. I felt like when Miss come in she had give herself away, she looked all rosy and flustered like. And so it turned out he never come but once more and then he come to get her and all of us. He used to send letters and poetry. It almost looked like one of them little birds charmed with a serpent."

From the journal of Susan Machette Scott for 1886		
	5th April	making waist of black dress
	May 1st	Clive went to picnic
	2nd	Maggie, Ethel & Finley took tea with Clive
	27	peas for dinner
	June 5 Sat.	spent day at Abbie's
	16	began on dining room
	28 Mon.	plastering kitchen &c.

54. Margaret Machette was actually thirty-three years old when her husband died in 1851.

Boonville, Missouri
August 8, 1886

*From Alexander Machette to his
mother, Margaret Bruin Machette*

Dear Ma:

... Went out to Chateau Springs, some ten miles west of this. Took Lizzie and the two younger children with me, and stayed till Thursday evening. Had the use of a tent, but did not find it very pleasant, especially at night. Etta got stung by a yellow jacket, and then she was so nervous over every hornet or yellow jacket she saw sailing round that she was quite miserable, till we got started home. I feel as if I had taken in a good share of malaria, and have been having headaches ever since Wednesday. There are a goodly number attending the springs everyday, and on some Sundays they say there have been more than a *thousand* people there. Some who ought to be at church at home prefer to ride out to the Springs on Sunday.

Our people here are very much taken up just now with politics. Yesterday was the day for the Democratic *primary* election, and a goodly number of candidates have drawn blanks, and I suppose feel blank over the result. Then, next week, comes the excitement of determining who will be candidate for Congress. I see our Dr. Yeaman is aspiring to that honor, and (they say) with good prospect of getting there.[55]

... We hear every few days from Lilian. She was to go with her sister-in-law, Mrs. Frey, up into the mountains to spend a week or two, so that we shall not be likely to hear from her for awhile. She seems happy, except that Mr. Hall has to be away from home a good deal of the time. Mrs. Frey is spending the summer out there for her health and is pleasant company for Lilian.[56] We expect them in along toward Christmas.

Anna is visiting down at Clinton and attending the Teacher's Institute at that place. We do not know just when to look for her home — not for a week or two, I suppose.

I enjoyed preaching this morning very much (from John 13:1 seq) on the love of Christ toward His own.[57] The people gave very good attention. To night we are to have a union meeting or rather the Annual Meeting of the Bible Society of Cooper County....

Alexander Machette

Aimee and Anna, daughters of
Alexander and Lizzie Machette

---

55. W. Pope Yeaman, a Baptist minister, was defeated in his run for Congress.

56. Earlier that year, Lilian Machette had married Christopher Columbus "Lum" Hall and moved to Albuquerque, New Mexico. Lum Hall's sister was married to J.J. Frey, general manager of the Atchison, Topeka, and Santa Fe Railroad.

57. John 13 describes Jesus washing the feet of his disciples.

Written on a scrap of paper by Susan Machette Scott

Born Sunday, July 31, 1887, at 3 hours, 3 minutes, a.m. Harold Hersman Scott

> Present: Dr. E. T. Scott, Grandma, and self, and nurse Marriah Bass (colored), and Clive upstairs.

Harold Hersman Scott, son of John Harvey and Susan Machette Scott

From Cornelia Machette Flood Cole to her sister, Susan Machette Scott

Denver, Colorado
September 7, 1887

My dear Susie:

I wish I had you face to face this after noon to talk a while. Abbie and I have been corresponding about how we all could concur in the best form to make Ma's last days her best — so far as is in our power. You know I have always said any way the rest thought best that was my pleasure. Abbie stated her plan to pay Ma's board — all giving their part to same. That is all right if the rest want same. I have no pet plan — but merely lay this before you — as I have already to Abbie and she seemed to take to same with enthusiasm. It is this: Our dear, precious Mother's days, at best, are nigh close, and as she has no pleasure out side of her God and her children, why not let her vibrate between the 3 Sisters — just leaving Alex out — the Lord will deal with him — and when Ma has remained with you until May, all 3 club together and next year Ma's expenses [go] to me and let her remain until October with me. And all club together then and let Ma winter with Abbie and then club again and spend the summer with you and then come to me again.

In this way Ma would have the needed change — it does any one good, and Ma loves to travel, and now we are so scattered it is needless to all hope to be together again — if so it would be a special Providence, so far we are able to judge, and not at all among the probabilities.

Do you catch what I am trying to express? Pen and ink are such a poor medium. If this, or Abbie's first suggestion, or some plan of yours, meets all the requirements, why you and Abbie let me know and my share will be on hand. I thought by Ma's remaining 6 months with each, and us 3 Sisters furnishing the traveling expenses, we each would share equally this blessed duty and pleasure of providing for our precious Mother and have the comfort of her presence with us and the change would keep dear Ma fresh in mind and body — and the blessing would rest up on us. I love to write or talk to you freely for I believe you never in your life impugned my motives. My desire has always been to obey the command of our blessed Lord. Bear ye one another's burdens — for I know it is a precious burden or a gracious care to act toward our Mother as God would have us, and hold us *all* to a strict account.[58]

This leaves us as usual — Forest has just entered school. Do trust his health will be such he can continue.... How is the College progressing? I have forgotten who you have in Brother Charley's place.[59] Do hope Brother Harvey will find who ever it is pleasant to work with. Do write soon. Dearest love to all — kiss to the Baby—

The obituary of Lilian Machette Hall, who died after childbirth, published in the December 28, 1887, *Albuquerque Morning Democrat* and kept in Sue Scott's death and consolation scrapbook.

Passed Away.

Gently as though borne upon angles' wings the spirit of Lillian Hall has flitted to the better land. Weeping parents, loving brothers and sisters, and a heart broken husband may mourn her as dead, but such lives never die, and while her christian example will continue in endless eddies of influence upon those who are left behind, her pure soul hovers about the throne where her christian faith taught her she would kneel at the feet of Jesus.

Mrs. Lillian Hall, wife of C. C. Hall, died on Christmas evening at 7 o'clock. She came to Albuquerque only a year ago last June, a beautiful bride, a loving and lovable women. Her babe was born and died two weeks ago. Her mother, Mrs. Machette, came from Fulton, Mo., in time to see her daughter before death claimed its shining mark.

At 11 o'clock yesterday morning a large concourse of sorrowing friends followed the remains to the grave in Fairview cemetery. Rev. J. S. Jewell, assisted by Rev. J. A. Menaul, performed the last sad rites of religion, and the pure white coffin, covering the loved remains, clad in the wedding garments of only eighteen months ago, were gently and tearfully consigned to their last resting place.

Booming San Pedro.

March 19, 1888	Clive took whooping cough
29th	Harold took whooping cough
	Harold cut upper front teeth
May 10th	Harold put on short clothes

From the small scrapbook of Susan Machette Scott

My Boy
　　　by Mary W. Plummer[60]

Brown heads and gold around my knee,
　　Dispute in eager play.
Sweet childish voices in my ear
　　Are sounding all the day,
Yet sometimes in a sudden hush,
　　I seem to hear a tone,
Such as my little boy's had been,
　　If he had lived—my own.

And when ofttimes they come to me,
　　As evening hours grow long,

Clipping from the death and consolation scrapbook of Susan Machette Scott

---

58. "Bear ye one another's burdens, and so fulfill the law of Christ" (Galatians 6:2).

59. Charley Hersman, who had been president of Westminster College since 1877, left Missouri to teach at Presbyterian Theological Seminary in Columbia, South Carolina. William Marquess followed Charley as president of Westminster.

60. Mary Wright Plummer (1856–1916).

And beg me winningly, to give
　　A story, or a song,
I see a pair of star bright eyes,
　　Among the others shine,
The eyes of *him who does not hear,*
　　Story or song of mine.

At night I go my rounds and pause
　　Each white-draped cot beside
And note how flushed is this one's cheek,
　　How that one's curls lie wide,
And to a corner tenantless,
　　My swift thoughts fly apace,
That would have been, if *he* had lived,
　　My other darling's place.

The years go fast; my children soon,
　　Within the world of men,
Will find their work, and venture forth,
　　Not to return again,
But there *is one* who cannot go,
　　I shall not be alone,
My little boy who *did not live,*
　　Will always be my own.

From the journal of Susan
Machette Scott for 1888

June 3rd	Harold cut his 5th & 6th teeth
13–14th	papered Ma's & my rooms....
June 25 Mon.	Harold's picture taken
July 23	making Papa's shirts....
Aug. 6th	Papa and Clive went to Tenn. to visit Hersmans — went on boat
Aug. 9th	got there at night....
Nov.	Harold began to walk
19th	put up stove in sitting room

From Abigail Machette Hersman
to her sister, Susan Machette Scott

Clarksville, Tennessee[61]
December 16, 1888

My dearest Sister:
　　Your good letter was received in due time and was appreciated by the whole family.
Ethel is always so glad, as well as Margaret, when a letter comes from Aunt Sue. Ethel

---

61. After teaching for a year at Presbyterian Theological Seminary in Columbia, South Carolina, Charley Hersman became chancellor of Southwestern Presbyterian University in Clarksville, Tennessee.

said only a few moments ago, "I would give just anything if Aunt Sue could bring her baby and make us a nice visit." This would be, indeed, a great pleasure to us all....

No doubt you have seen Matsie since her return. We miss the girls very much as of course any one would! Both the girls made themselves so agreeable — they were no trouble, but a pleasure, all the time they were here. We received a nice long letter from Mr. Will Dobyns yesterday — he said Mary enjoyed her visit to Clarksville splendidly. I will tell you a secret, but don't mention it out of the family. Mary told me she will be married in June and invited us all to her wedding. Mary has made such a lovely woman — has grown fleshy, just enough to be very becoming.[62]

I received a letter from Finley a few days since.[63] I wanted him to try for a position in an Asylum at Hopkinsville, Kentucky, which will be vacant shortly. I thought it might be well for him to get a place of this kind for a few years, until he had at least made a little money. You know, so far, he has not been in a position to make one cent. Mary says he is building up quite a reputation in St. Louis; she says the older physicians think so highly of him. He told me he had asked Mudd what he thought of his taking a position in an Asylum and he replied, "Do nothing of the kind. You have sense enough to get along by yourself and ought not to tie yourself to any institution."[64] Mudd has *money* and of course feels *independent*; perhaps in ten or fifteen years hence Finley can afford to feel so too.

... Charley [Hersman] likes his work here very much. How much I wish the chair of Mathematics was vacant. Charley would get Brother here mighty fast I can tell you. Give my love to Ma, Brother, children. Write as often as you can.

Kansas City, Missouri
December 31, 1888

From Samuel Machette to his stepmother, Margaret Bruin Machette

Dear Mother

Yours of December 26th to hand in reply to your questions regarding Charlie's [Machette] sickness — [I] will say from the time he was first taken [ill] about eighteen months ago he was able

Charles Machette, son of Samuel and Susan Jarboe Machette, died in 1888.

to be about and attend to business to about the latter part of January last, at which time he was taken down and confined to his bed and room for about five weeks. He then recovered sufficient to be about, though feeble and not able to do anything, until about six weeks ago when he was taken down in his last sickness which ended in death at twenty minutes to ten on the night of December 24.

The first two weeks of his last sickness we had him at home as he needed constant attention both day and night, and not being able to get trained nurses that could be relied on, I took him to the Episcopal Hospital where he had the best of nursing both day and night and everything was done for him that could be done until death

---

62. Matsie and Mary, friends of Margaret Hersman. Martha "Matsie" Curd, daughter of Edwin and Harriet Webster Curd. Mary Buckland, sister of Thomas Buckland, who was mentioned on September 11, 1876. In June 1889, Mary married William Dobyns, a minister and probably a nephew of Edward Dobyns. See love letter 18 and August 1, 1876, on the Curds.

63. Finley lived in St. Louis where he was a physician.

64. Henry H. or Harvey G. Mudd, brothers who practiced medicine in St. Louis.

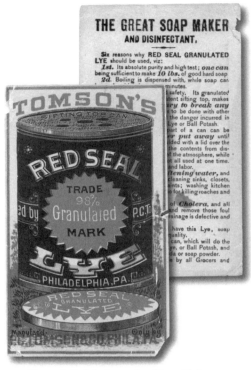

Tomson's Red Seal granulated lye with its new patented sift top suggested convenience, speed, and safety in making soap, and it promised to "destroy the germs of Cholera, and all other contagious disease." Cholera killed several members of the Machette family in the first half of the nineteenth century.

ended his sufferings. While he was at the Hospital, some one of the family was with him every day, I myself being with him the most of the time in the last ten days of his sickness.

I don't think he thought about dying until about one week before his death. Going into his room one evening as he was not allowed to talk but little on account of the extreme distress his throat gave him when he attempted to talk, he wrote me on a scrap of paper, "The Catholic Priest has been to see me — What shall I do?" After thinking a moment, I said to him, "Your Mother was a Catholic and had you baptized in the Catholic faith. If you want that faith, I have no objection." He wrote again in reply to what I had said, "Say yes or no." I replied to him, "I say yes and I say so because your Mother was a Catholic and I know if she was alive and with you she would want you to die in the Catholic faith."[65]

From that [time] on, the priest was with him, and he died in the faith that his Mother died in and was buried along side his Mother in the Catholic Cemetery. Now you well know, Ma, that I am no Catholic and probably will wonder that I consented for Charlie to embrace that faith. My reasons for doing so were first I wanted him buried along side his Mother. The only way to have this done was for him to embrace the faith of his Mother. In the second place I felt it my duty to let him go to his Mother in the faith she believed in.

Eddie, Charlie's brother, left here some six weeks ago. Where he went and where he is, none of us know. Before leaving he was up to see Charlie — did not say he was going away. The first we knew he was gone, and no one knows whither he went. He is like my brother Charles — he seems destined to be a wanderer on the face of the Earth,[66] doing no good for himself or any one else.[67]

I wish you would drop me a line and give me Nealie's husband's name and address. Anna, the children, and myself all send you, Mr. Scott, and Susie our best love. Will send you Charlie's picture.

From the small scrapbook of
Susan Machette Scott for 1889

Sat. 16 of Feb	Had Clive & Harold vaccinated.[68]
March 25th	Ma left for visit
29th	running down lye — made soap

---

65. See December 16, 1864, on the death of Charlie's mother and Sam's first wife.

66. See Genesis 4:13–14, "Cain said unto the LORD . . . 'Behold, thou hast driven me out this day from the face of the earth; and from thy face shall I be hid; and I shall be a fugitive and a vagabond in the earth. . . .'"

67. Sam's younger brother Charles, who was thought to have gone to the California gold rush, was never heard from again.

68. Probably a smallpox vaccination, which was developed in the late eighteenth century.

Friends Matsie Curd, Mary Buckland, and Margaret Hersman,
daughter of Charles C. and Abigail Machette Hersman

The Reverend William Dobyns,
who married Mary Buckland in 1889

Clarksville, Tennessee
March 29, 1889

From Margaret Bruin Machette
to Susan Machette and John
Harvey Scott

Dear children

Ethel wrote to let you know that I got here safe without much fatigue. On Tuesday
evening, she and Mr. Hersman met me at Guthrie. Mrs. Dobyns was at the depot waiting when I got to Mexico. Ben Charles went over on the cars as I did. He was very kind
to me. We waited till after one at Mexico. The trip to St. Louis was pleasant. Finley
and Joe Dobyns met us at the Union depot. We took a hack to Mary Buckland's,
found supper waiting us. I was nicely entertained by Mary, Sadie and Tom....[69]

Finley stayed all night with Tom [and] took breakfast and went with me to the
depot — went on the street cars.[70] He put me in the parlor coach, paid a dollar for a
chair. There was not more than seven in at one time. It was very quiet and comfortable,
the porter very attentive. I objected to taking the parlor coach, but Finley would have
it so. On the trip to St. Louis we were much annoyed by negro men with their loud
talk and laughing so I escaped all that on Tuesday.

69. Benjamin Charles, attorney and friend of Finley Hersman and Clive Scott. His father, the Reverend Benjamin Charles, was president of Fulton Synodical Female College, 1877–1888. Joseph Dobyns, son of Edward and
Elizabeth Dobyns and a St. Louis attorney; half-brother of Mollie Dobyns. Mary, Sadie, and Tom Buckland, siblings,
lived in St. Louis.

70. In St. Louis, horse- or mule-drawn streetcar service began in 1859 and cable streetcar service in 1886. The
first electric streetcar line in Missouri opened in St. Joseph in 1887 and quickly spread to other major cities in the
state. "Transportation: Railways on City Streets," *Missouri Historical Review* (October 1968): 133–134.

The country is beautiful. The plum trees was in bloom in southern Illinois, the peach in Indiana and Kentucky and Tennessee. The wheat in Illinois and Kentucky looks better than any on the trip. The dry weather was against it in Indiana. There was but little dust through Missouri and Illinois, but Indiana and on to Clarksville it was very disagreeable.

I like the appearance of Clarksville. The people are very social. I had seven ladies call on me yesterday.... Every thing looks springlike. Mr. Hersman has hot bed plants large enough to put out, has cabbage plants out. The white butterflies are here ready for mischief. We had turnip greens for dinner yesterday, sent in by a neighbor.

... Margaret is making her mother a sateen dress all by herself. She has made one for herself. It is nicely made. If you have the *Delineator,* you can see the dress — 24594 dress skirt, 2628 waist. Margaret's is just [like] the waist of your new calico. Hers is pleated in the back as in the front. If yours was sheered down the back like a yoke, it would be prettier....

Saturday. I feel better this morning. The peach bloom looks beautiful. It rained last night. The woods are full of wild flowers. These little flowers are the same shrub you have in the yard. Kiss the children for me.

From the journal of Susan Machette Scott for 1889

April 6th   weaned Harold

From Margaret Bruin Machette to her daughter, Susan Machette Scott

Clarksville, Tennessee
April 11, 1889

Dear Susie

... My health is the same as at home — spend much of the time grunting and lame. Abbie and I went out to return some of my calls on Monday. Professor and Clive can tell you how much speed I would be likely to make over the rough stony street about the part of town near Abbie. I cannot tell what the different places looked like as I had to be looking where I put my feet to keep from falling down.... The professors' wives that called me — they are all very pleasant people. On last Sunday I went with the family to church. As at home I could hear but little that the preacher said. The singing was good. They have a pipe organ. I could hear that very well.

About the walk to church: If you will go out to the old place and go over west to Robnetts' fence then retrace your steps down the hill, then up the hill to the house, through the yard to the styles, then down hill to Brooks' fence, then up hill to the Georges' pasture, and down through the meadow to the creek, then up to the college, and on to the steps in front of the college, then stop to think of your walk you have had, you can judge of the walk to the Presbyterian church pretty correctly. It's pretty much the same in every direction if I judge by the appearance of every thing as I look out from the house — except on the north — there is quite a pretty level country in that direction for some distance.

Susan Machette Scott

There is much more dust here than at home. A rain does not lay the dust for any time. Every thing in the rooms is covered with dust. Mr. Hersman has been wishing for rain on his garden. He thinks the place is over caves, that after a rain the lower part of his garden is like a pond but in a few hours it has all disappeared....

You ask about Kitty Graves. Abbie says she can wash right well but is very mean. You would have to watch her close. Abbie's washing is [as] badly done as yours but can't get it done any better.... Susie, please give Mrs. Garvin the book of sermons she loaned me and look in a box at the head of my bed and get my netting needle and send [it] in your next letter.[71] Margaret wants me to make her a net to wear as a night cap. That gray flannel skirt I left hanging at the head of my bed — you had better make some use of [it] or the moths will eat it up. You will see they have already almost done so. We heard from Nelia since I wrote to you last. They were all well....

I am more than satisfied that Missouri is the best place I have seen. There is but little energy here — nothing but sloth excepting gossip — that is lively....

Margaret is remodeling her summer dresses she got in Fulton to wear this spring. Abbie is making Ethel skirts and drawers. I am knitting on my cotton you got me. Finley told me he thought he would go to Fulton with his Father but in his letter to his mother says he can't go but will be home in July on a visit.

Give dearest love to Prof. and the little boys. I am going to write to Clive soon....

Clarksville, Tennessee
April 14, 1889

From Margaret Bruin Machette
to her grandson, Clive Scott

My Dear Clive

Grand Ma wants to see her precious boys very much. How are you both this Sabbath day? This morning you are getting ready for Sabbath school. I know dear little brother is playing about the room, and Papa and Mama thinking what dear boys they have the care of. I want you to help them take care of your brother. Be very sure there is no windows up when he is up stairs. I am so much afraid he may fall out. How does your Puppy come on? Does Harold play with him, or does the Puppy bite him too much for that?

Clive, I wish you could have seen the little yoke of calves and little cart that passed on the street the other day. The calves or oxen were about like year old calves, nice and fat. The cart wheels were small, the little box body just large enough for a man and boy to sit on. I could not see what they had in the cart. Another time I saw the prettiest little pony. It must have been a shetland pony of very dark color with long flowing tail. The under part of tail black, the top part just beautiful white. The white was the whole length of the tail. It looked very strange. A man on horse back was leading the pony.

Clive Douglas Scott,
son of John Harvey and Susan Machette Scott

71. Elizabeth Boyd Garvin, wife of Alexander Garvin.

Uncle Charley has a hen with ten little black chickens, has one other hen setting, has his peas stuck. The potatoes are up about two inches high and full of potato bugs. He is sorry he planted potatoes. Every thing looks nice this morning. It rained last night and is raining now. Before this rain the dust was horrid. They say a rain don't lay the dust long at a time. The well does not hold water very good. They are always likely to be short of water.

There is very beautiful wild flowers here. Some of the young men go walking in the woods and bring large bunches to Margaret every few days. I have not been out much. Ethel and I went down in the garden last evening. You know how steep it is from the house to the middle of the garden. It would be fine coasting if you had such a hill near you in winter. You would not enjoy such a hill in your yard in summer. Dear little Harold would have many a tumble down the hill. Clive, your Aunt Abbie thought the knife rest you sent her ever so nice. She wishes me to thank you for it.

… Now, my dear Clive, give my dearest love to your Father and Mother and a kiss to Harold. Tell him he must not forget Grand Ma, and accept a heart full of love for your self from

Grand Ma.

From Margaret Bruin Machette to her daughter, Susan Machette Scott

Clarksville, Tennessee
April 22, 1889

Dear Susie

… The garden looks nice. Abbie had lettuce and radishes for dinner yesterday. I have never told you how she has the house furnished. They got their furniture to suit their house in Columbia, and it is better than any I have seen here as I have not been any where but at the houses of the Professors and they can't afford any thing more than if they were in Fulton in Westminster College. The parlor outfit cost one hundred and twenty-five dollars, that in the bedrooms seventy-five each. Two of the bedrooms has matting instead of carpet on the floor — so has the dining room [and] on the parlor floor the same carpet they had in Fulton. The one Mr. Hersman had on the study floor Abbie has in her room. He got a new one for his study in Columbia. It is all too costly for the meager salary they get here.

I told you that I had not heard anything about matrimony since [I have been] here so I can say this morning, but if the number of letters sent from here to New Orleans and received from New Orleans are any indication, Marquess was not far wrong in his saying there was an engagement.[72] I have not heard from Alex since I left home and but once from Nelia.

Mr. Hersman got home since I commenced writing. He is quite sick, has taken cold and rheumatism in his hips — is in bed. He had a pleasant time at Presbytery [in McMinneyville, Tennessee]. The three young men that went with him stood a fine examination. Every one was much pleased. He preached once in McMinneyville and twice in Murfreesboro while he was gone.

72. William Marquess, the Fulton Presbyterian Church's minister since 1878 and a minister at the funeral of Edgar Machette, became president of Westminster in 1887. His brother Edgar taught at Westminster, 1882–1917. In 1888, their sister Anne married the Reverend Addison Alexander Wallace, whose baptism was mentioned on April 30, 1864 and who graduated from Westminster with Finley Hersman, see the commencement program p. 169.

The people here are very kind. I returned my calls…, and now if I keep it up [I] must begin over again as every one has been returned. It is the university people and two or three others living near. The Clarksville people seem to take but little interest in the institution.

I begin to think people are much alike in one respect — that is, a few in every church want to rule. The parsonage here is a poor thing, and they have the money to build a new one, but they can't agree as to a lot. One party wants it here, another there, and will not come to any agreement unless they can have their wish as to location. I mean the Presbyterians — other churches I don't know any thing about.…

Calling cards from members of the Machette family

Clarksville, Tennessee
April 28, 1889

From Margaret Bruin Machette to her daughter, Susan Machette Scott

Dear Susie

Mr. Hersman is still in bed, has not been up since last Monday when he first got home. The Doctor thinks he may be up to morrow if his hip does not get bad again. He has no fever now. This spell will prevent his going to Fulton which is a disappointment to him. Abbie did not hear from Finley last week. She hopes to send Ethel to Monticello this fall.[73] She is anxious to go and finish her school days. She is doing very well with her vocal lessons and practices a great deal, says she may teach some day. She is afraid her voice is not strong enough to sing well — wants to know if you think it will improve with practice. Her mother says she is very easily discouraged, so timid and backward. If only she had some of Margaret's go ahead disposition, it might be better for her.

Monday. Mr. Hersman is up this morning but not much better, has head ache. Abbie had a letter from Finley this morning. He has been sick for several days, not able to attend to his duties. I wish you would send me my old dictionary. I don't know how to spell any thing correct without one. My hearing is worse than it was at home. There has been no rain here since I wrote last. The garden is very dry for three nights.…

Perhaps the dictionary Margaret Machette wanted in the letter above was the one she bought for $2.25 in 1857.

73. See January 1, 1866, and February 23, 1866, on Ethel's Aunt Nealie attending Monticello Seminary in Illinois.

Thursday is dear Clive's birthday. Margaret went down to the store and got him a necktie from me for him, a pocket handkerchief from herself for him, and Ethel sends ten cents to get him some lemons to make lemonade as she knows his mother has cake for him. All send much love and good wishes for him. This leaves all well except Mr. Hersman. I heard from Alex and Nelia last week. They were all well....

From Margaret Bruin Machette to her daughter, Susan Machette Scott

Clarksville, Tennessee
May 5, 1889

Dear Susie

... I went to church this morning, the second time since I have been in Clarksville. I can't hear enough to go often over such walks as are here. Mr. Hersman was out this morning. The walk was too long for him. His hip hurts him this evening.

The water in the well is getting very scarce already. The well leaks, will always give trouble. There is very little here that is attractive. The trees are beautiful, and if there is any beauty in up hill and down hill there is plenty of that here, but it would take a great while for me to fall in love with Clarksville. I have seen nothing here that compares with Missouri. The garden does not do very well. It is so dry the tomatoes are in bloom and young peas on the vines. There was frost one night last week that bit the potatoes slightly....

From Margaret Bruin Machette to her daughter, Susan Machette Scott

Clarksville, Tennessee
May 16, 1889

Dear Susie

Yours received yesterday morning. It got to Clarksville Tuesday evening, but the mail is not brought out till next morning at ten o'clock. The negro man that takes care of the University, as John does Westminster, takes the mail in and brings it out to the Professors after the second bell rings. The teaching goes on from Chapel service till half past two when it closes for the day, from Monday till Saturday. They teach every day except Sunday....

This is Finley's twenty-fifth birth day....

You spoke of the geraniums — did not you give Mrs. Garvin some last fall? I expect she hung them in her cellar and has divided with you. The ladies here are just putting theirs out in their yards now. They do not stand the cold very well. I hope you will have an abundance of peaches. I am anxious to hear what kind of peach the white bloom has. The early pears are all killed by frost here. What are your prospects for pears in Missouri?

Abbie's cook took a notion about a week ago. She must have a rest so Abbie got an old woman with a young child to come. She was the dirtiest creature I ever ate after in my life. One week killed all appetite for her cooking. Abbie sent for the one that had gone to take a rest, and she sent one to stay a week when she will come back herself to stay until she gets tired again. The one that is here now is very neat and a good cook. The one that is coming is just splendid in every respect.

... Give my dearest love to Professor and the dear little boys. I want to see you all very much.... All send love to all. I received the dictionary and monthly you sent.

Clarksville, Tennessee
May 21, 1889

From Margaret Bruin Machette to her daughter, Susan Machette Scott

Dear Susie

At breakfast this morning Mr. Hersman said, "I do not like the South," and I am of the same mind. I do not like the South. Perhaps I have not seen enough of it, but I do not wish to see more of it. I think if he could get a position [in the] north, he would accept it.... I believe Mr. Hersman thinks the Synod [of Missouri] would do better to go north. This people have no sympathy with Missouri. They will never do any thing for her College. One of the businessmen and a member of the Presbyterian Church said if the Synod wants to go north let them — those that do not wish to go can come down here.[74] They are very selfish, and I think they are in need of emancipation as much as the north thought the negroes were. I think when people are afraid to take hold and attend to their own affairs for fear of losing caste, [they] must be slaves to public opinion.

At this moment the ice is lying out in the yard melting. No one must touch it. The negro woman has not come yet, and ice must wait until she comes and brings it in. It is much more difficult to get help here than at home. The tobacco factories employ so many and give better wages than any other industry here [that] Abbie has great difficulty in keeping a cook. She is hunting one now. The one she has is going to leave to work in the factory at fifty cents a day. She has to pay $1.25 a week for the washing and ironing....

Tell [Clive] that he must not forget me, but write to me when he has time. And that dear little baby, I am almost sick to see him. Indeed I want to see you all more than you can imagine. Do hope you may all keep well.

May 24. Received letters from Alex and Nelia today. They were all well, no news. I expect you are very busy as commencement is so near, and I am very glad the college work is so near done for this term so Professor Scott will have time to rest. The University closes on the 12 of June. Nelia wants Mr. Hersman to make them a visit, but he will not for the want of money. I don't think he was ever in a more straightened fix than now.

Sabbath morning 26. After a two days' rain this is a bright day. Would like to go to church but the walk is long and my hearing so bad I will stay at home.... Margaret

The Scotts subscribed to the popular periodical *The Youth's Companion*, in which "The Pledge of Allegiance" was first published in 1892.

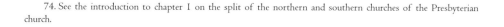

74. See the introduction to chapter 1 on the split of the northern and southern churches of the Presbyterian church.

had a letter from Finley last week. He will not be here to commencement, probably will not come this summer. It will take all his wages to clothe him and get some books as he gets only 25 dollars a month, and he can't expect any thing from his Father. It is much more expensive living here than in Fulton, so Mr. Hersman says. They want to send Ethel to Monticello to school next fall if possible. I think Ethel has a great notion to teach. She said last night, "I think it would be so nice to teach." I had heard her say once before, "I may teach music some day." She is doing nicely with her vocal lessons. Her teacher is going to have her play and sing at the close of the school in June....

From Margaret Bruin Machette to her daughter, Susan Machette Scott

Clarksville, Tennessee
June 9, 1889

Dear Susie

... Mr. Marquess came yesterday morning, does not look as though his work hurt him much.[75] I believe Mr. Hersman looks worse than I ever saw him. If Mr. Marquess stays a few days and is going back to St. Louis, Abbie wants to send Ethel with him to St. Louis to have her eyes examined. She is troubled with one, her right eye, and has head aches so much they want to see what is wrong if they can.

11th. Mr. Marquess left this evening immediately after supper. He is not going to St. Louis. I did not learn where but [he] expects to be home by Sunday. Ethel will go by her self. The exercises are passing off very satisfactory to all concerned, more visitors than ever before, so the Professors say.

12th.... Commencement over. One young man captured all the medals, three in number. Stagg and Elwang are here attending the commencement. The last name is the one that so many letters are written to by Margaret.[76] Abbie or any one of the family have never mentioned a word about it to me. I presume they are afraid I might tell some one. The young lady that has been stopping here leaves for home to morrow. Most of the boys leave today. This leaves me in usual health. Hope it may find you all well....

From Margaret Bruin Machette to her daughter, Susan Machette Scott

Clarksville, Tennessee
July 9, 1889

Dear Susie

... Abbie is expecting Finley the last of this week. He left St. Louis Monday morning, is going to see Anne Bates two or three days, then comes home for ten days.[77] I shall go home with him as far as St. Louis. He will see me on the train for Fulton. Don't let Harold have any fruit. Please don't. He may have flux.

75. This comment might be an allusion to a concern among Fulton Presbyterians that Marquess was overburdened as both college president and local pastor; see Parrish, *Westminster College*, 68–69.

76. The Reverend John Weldon Stagg attended Westminster College, 1885–1886. The Reverend William Elwang of New Orleans was Margaret "Maggie" Hersman's fiancé.

77. Anne, daughter of Richard and Ellen Woodson Bates and granddaughter of Edward Bates, attorney general under Abraham Lincoln. See the footnote to the January 26, 1866, letter.

Wednesday morning. 6 o'clock just striking. I am up at five every morning. The family do not rise till seven, and this the only cool part of the day. They enjoy being up until ten or eleven at night. I retire early, glad to get under the bars out of the mosquitoes. They are much worse than they used to be in St. Charles. They bite all day. I am just worn out at night fighting them. Abbie says they don't hurt her. They are very hard on Margaret.

I had a postal from Alex last week. He is going to leave Boonville. I don't know where he is going. I think he had written, and I have not received his letter as he said on the postal. Alex visited the church at Sedalia on last Sabbath and had a very pleasant visit — will likely enter on the work in August but will not move before fall....

Oct. 16   finished Papa's overcoat

From the journal of Susan
Machette Scott for 1889

A home not made with hands

1890–1902

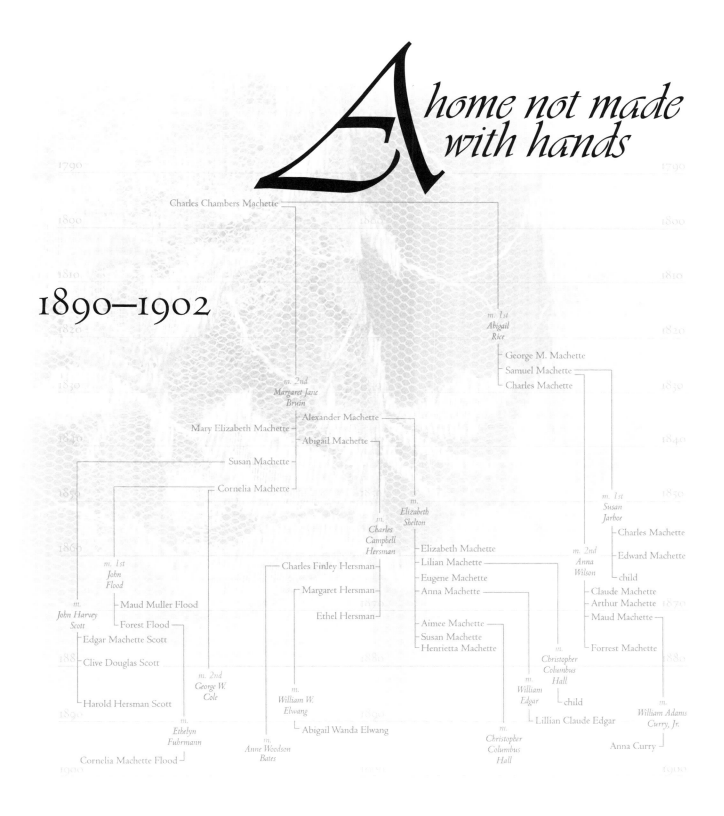

Chapter 4

Machette Family
January 1, 1890

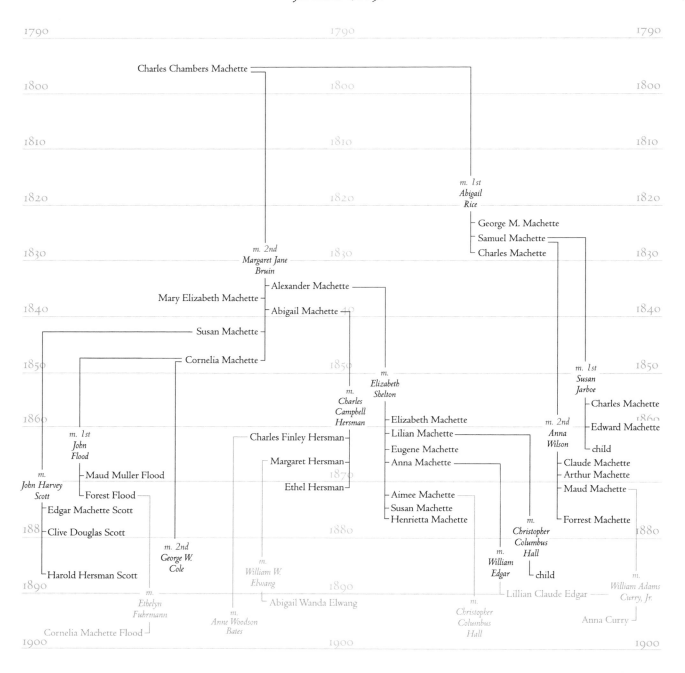

In 1879, the *Missouri Republican* reported Thomas Edison's prediction that electricity would transform the future, and by the 1890s, that future was now. On May 2, 1893, the paper proclaimed that President Cleveland ushered in "the electric age" by pressing a button that turned on the fountains and revolving wheels at the World's Fair in Chicago.[1] On the same day, Alexander Machette wrote about his family's plans to attend the fair. With other visitors, he and his family might have enjoyed circus shows, the first Ferris wheel, and balloon rides. The highest excitement, however, was reserved for the electric marvels.[2]

Other marvels were also changing society. The longest telephone line—from Chicago to New York—was tried out in 1892. In 1902, wireless messages were sent from New York to England; in the same year, Thomas Edison proclaimed that one of his inventions, the storage battery, would mean "the passing of the horse" as a primary mode of transportation. As the *St. Louis Republic* exclaimed at the end of 1902, "The Dreams of Yesterday Are the Realities of To-day."[3]

At the same time that science seemed capable of producing limitless technological advancements, social injustice and unrest were part of the fabric of the United States. "The Negro question," for example, was of concern at the national and state level. On December 25, 1898, the *St. Louis Republic* reported that President McKinley was "fully convinced of the necessity of white supremacy." At a speech at Tuskegee Institute, founded for blacks in 1881 by Booker T. Washington, President McKinley spoke in favor of education for blacks but did not discuss the need for a "a free ballot and a fair count." The newspaper reporter took this omission to mean that the President would not pursue a federal bill ensuring the black man's right to vote. When Theodore Roosevelt became President after McKinley's

1890–1902

1. *Missouri Republican* (December 22, 1879). *St. Louis Republic* (May 2, 1893).

2. Schlereth, *Victorian America: Transformations*, 171–172. Frank A. Cassell, "Missouri and the Columbian Exposition of 1893," *Missouri Historical Review* (Summer 1968): 369–394.

3. *St. Louis Republic* (October 19, 1892, May 31, 1902, December 22, 1902). A more gruesome application of electricity was the electric chair. On August 6, 1890, the *Republic* reported that a murderer was to be electrocuted as part of "a legal experiment." The next day the *Republic* reported that the experiment was "a miserable failure." After a 17–second jolt, the condemned man was still alive and had to be electrocuted a second time. The electric chair was fully operational by 1901 when President McKinley's assassin was executed by such means.

assassination, he was severely criticized for inviting Booker T. Washington to dinner at the White House.[4]

One of the most striking stories of black-white relationships in Missouri was covered for several days in the *Republic*. In 1897, Kate Neal, the daughter of a white physician in Missouri, eloped to Kansas City with her father's coachman, identified as "a mulatto" named Joe Johnson. Her father hired Pinkerton detectives, who found them in Denver. Johnson managed to escape, but Kate Neal was detained. Escorted back to Kansas City by the Pinkerton detectives, she tried to kill herself by taking morphine and strychnine. In the paper's last report of the story, Kate Neal confessed that she had been unable to resist Johnson's "powerful influence." Declared "to be of unsound mind," she was committed to an insane asylum.[5]

Women's suffrage was also an issue throughout the country. In 1869, women received the right to vote in Wyoming and the following year in Utah, but after the matter of women's suffrage was referred to the states, it suffered defeat in state after state.[6] Between 1870 and 1910, only two states—Colorado and Idaho—gave women the right to vote in state and local elections. Many states granted women only partial suffrage, and women in nineteen states could vote in school elections by 1890.[7] In Missouri, women did not fare even that well. The *Republic* reported that one February day in 1895, women—many of them wearing "the yellow ribbons of the Equal Suffrage Society"—crowded into the capitol at Jefferson City to watch the debate for suffrage. The Missouri House defeated not only women's right to vote in statewide elections but a more conservative amendment allowing women to vote in city and school elections.[8]

In 1896, hundreds of people in St. Louis and East St. Louis were killed by a tornado, and in early 1900, three blocks of businesses were burned in downtown St. Louis.[9] Clive Scott, who was attending medical school at Washington University in St. Louis, witnessed the fire and wrote about it in his February 6, 1900, letter.[10] In the summer of 1900, streetcar workers were shot and killed during a transit strike in St. Louis.[11] The turn of the century held promise as well for St. Louis. St. Louis citizens in 1893 marveled at the new fast mail train, which could travel sixty miles an hour.[12] In 1901, Andrew Carnegie offered the city one million dollars to build a public library, and in 1902, Mark Twain, Missouri's beloved author, visited St. Louis.[13] Most exciting of all, preparations for the 1904 World's Fair in St. Louis had begun.[14]

---

4. *St. Louis Republic* (October 18, 1901).

5. *St. Louis Republic* (December 3–9, 1897).

6. Women in Utah won the vote in 1870, but the United States Congress revoked the right in 1887; the right was regained in 1896. Eleanor Flexner and Ellen Fitzpatrick, *Century of Struggle: The Woman's Rights Movement in the United States* (Cambridge: Belknap Press of Harvard University Press, 1975), 154–156.

7. Flexner and Fitzpatrick, *Century of Struggle*, 167–168, 213–214. Christine Bolt, *The Women's Movements in the United States and Britain from the 1790s to the 1920s* (Amherst: University of Massachusetts Press, 1993), 152.

8. *St. Louis Republic* (February 26, 1895). Missouri women had also campaigned for the vote in 1867 and during the 1875 Constitutional Convention; see Christensen and Kremer, *History of Missouri*, 4:25–26.

9. *St. Louis Republic* (May 28, 1896, February 5, 1900).

10. In 1899, the Missouri Medical College, which Finley Hersman attended, and the St. Louis Medical College merged to form the Washington University Medical School.

11. The *St. Louis Republic* (June 11, 1900) provides a summary of the violence in the streetcar strike.

12. *St. Louis Republic* (June 19, 1893).

13. *St. Louis Republic* (March 16, 1901, May 30, 1902).

14. *St. Louis Republic* (November 24, 1901).

By the 1890s, most of Margaret Bruin Machette's surviving grandchildren were grown. Finley Hersman was a physician in St. Louis; both he and his sister Margaret married in the 1890s. Clive Scott, following in his cousin Finley's footsteps, began attending medical school at Washington University. Alex's daughter Anna married in 1889, and in 1895 his daughter Aimee married the widower of her sister Lilian. The most unusual occupation of Margaret Bruin Machette's grandchildren was that of Forest Flood, who became a stage actor.

Benjamin McArthur in his history on the American theater observes, "Through most of history, until the late nineteenth century, players existed outside the boundaries of respectable society. Between the years 1880 and 1920 actors became significant figures in the American social landscape...."[15] Forest thus embarked on his career just as acting was gaining some respectability in the United States. McArthur credits the rise of theater during this time period not only to urbanization but also to new religious beliefs. Many Christians, especially young, urban Christians, did not accept the traditional indictment against theater, and even some leaders of the church believed that the theater had the potential to offer its audience intellectual and even spiritual growth.[16]

Theater around the turn of the century included melodrama, minstrel shows, vaudeville, ethnic comedies, Shakespearean drama, and the beginnings of modern drama.[17] Lewis Saum credits journalist Eugene Field with popularizing theater across Missouri in the 1870s.[18] St. Louis was a center of theater in the Midwest by the 1870s, and on November 12, 1899, Clive Scott wrote home about seeing Richard Mansfield perform in St. Louis. Noted for playing the heroic leading man, Mansfield performed not only in Shakespearean drama but also brought the drama of George Bernard Shaw to the United States.[19] Famous actresses of the time included Lillian Russell, Lillie Langtry, Sarah Bernhardt, and Maude Adams.

Forest Flood was a member of repertory companies that performed in various cities, including New York City (see Nealie's letter for November 17, 1895). The company he belonged to in 1895 was headed by the actress Olga Nethersole at a time when it was highly unusual for an actress to manage her own company. Noted for playing the fallen woman, Olga Nethersole was arrested in 1900 in New York City on a charge of public indecency for her role in "Sappho." She was later acquitted, and both before and after her arrest, audiences flocked to the play.[20]

When Forest appeared in a melodrama at the Opera House in Fulton, the *Fulton Sun* for November 30, 1900, reported that he "was given an ovation on his appearance in the act and while his part was that of a most consummate villain in the play his interpretation of the part was excellent and often made the audience shudder with his make-believe infamy." The reporter made a point of noting that Forest's wife, who performed in the play, was "a lady of the highest breeding and intellectuality...."

15. Benjamin McArthur, *Actors and American Culture, 1880–1920* (Philadelphia: Temple University Press, 1984), ix.

16. McArthur, *Actors and American Culture*, 130–131.

17. Felicia Hardison Londré and Daniel J. Watermeier, *American Theater, The United States, Canada, and Mexico: From Pre-Columbian Times to the Present* (New York: Continuum, 1999), 200–201, 215–222.

18. Lewis O. Saum, "Eugene Field and Theater: The Missouri Years," *Missouri Historical Review* (January 2001): 159–181.

19. Londré and Watermeier, *American Theater*, 200–201.

20. William Young, *Famous Actors and Actresses of the American Stage* (New York: R.R. Bowker, 1875): 864–872; *St. Louis Republic* (February 22, 1900).

Although Nealie was delighted with her son's career, other members of the family were probably less sanguine. See, for example, Alexander's comment on theater on January 9, 1893.

Melodrama, a staple of American theater in the late nineteenth century, was part of the sentimental tradition of the era. The customs and beliefs relating to death were another aspect of the sentimental tradition, and it is this aspect of Victorian America that is particularly evident in the collection. Eliza Major Flood's June 18, 1871, letter on the death of Maud Flood represents fully Victorian sentimentalism, which often focused on the death of children: "Wherever you look you see something to remind you of her, the little chair and cup, her bonnet and shoes, the cradle and buggy, the little dog, and a thousand little instances will remind you of her. You will find your selves listening for her, looking for her—a little while and you will be with her." Another example of sentimentalism is the obituary of Lilian Machette Hall on December 28, 1887, which described how "the loved remains, clad in the wedding garments of only eighteen months ago, were gently and tearfully consigned to their last resting piece." The most sustained example is Sue Machette Scott's scrapbook on death and consolation. This dark green book, with "Scrap Book" inscribed in black on the cover, was a brand of books known as "Mark Twain's Scrap Book." Sue evidently began the scrapbook after her son Edgar died and kept it for several years, adding to it obituaries of other family members. Many of the clippings in the scrapbook were poems on the death of children, the kind of poetry that was so popular in the nineteenth century. Sue also included the speech given at Edgar's funeral, letters of condolence, her remembrance of Edgar's last day before he became ill, and even the clipping of the lesson from the *New York Observer*, which they had been reading just before he became ill. Her scrapbook was very much like *The Empty Crib*, a book published in 1868 by the Reverend Theodore L. Cuyler, who was quoted in a letter of condolence on the death of Edgar (see Mrs. J.H. Reed's letter in chapter 3). In his book, Cuyler described the short life of his son George and his death from scarlet fever at the age of four, quoted from his son's obituary and letters of condolence, and included sentimental poetry. Whether or not Sue Scott had read *The Empty Crib*, she was practicing a genre common to her time.

The funeral and burial of Edgar also followed customs of the time period. Sue and Harvey sent out a mourning card edged in black to invite family and friends to the funeral. They had a picture taken of Edgar after his death and dressed in a suit, looking very much asleep. For decades, the picture was kept on the inside door of a cupboard in the Scotts' library so that every time the door was opened his picture was seen. Edgar was undoubtedly buried in the suit. It is unclear if Edgar was embalmed although it is possible that Harvey's note, $17 for "hearse &c.," included embalming. The Scotts did purchase a vault to enclose the casket and help preserve the body (see Harvey's list of costs incurred after Edgar's death in chapter 3). Preserving the body was a relatively new custom in the United States and, according to oral family history, Harvey's brother Joe criticized him for not letting Edgar's body return to dust.[21]

As her journal indicates, Sue visited Edgar's grave; this too was common among nineteenth-century Protestants. Edgar was buried in the New Cemetery, later known

21. Lawrence Taylor, "Symbolic Death: An Anthropological View of Mourning Ritual in the Nineteenth Century," *A Time to Mourn: Expressions of Grief in Nineteenth Century America*, ed. Martha V. Pike and Janice Gray Armstrong (Stony Brook, N.Y.: The Museums at Stony Brook, 1980), 39–48. See also Farrell, *Inventing the American Way of Death*, 157.

as Hillcrest Cemetery. East of town, it was originally platted in 1867 by the Tuttle family (Warren Woodson Tuttle is mentioned in the 1860 letters) and was deeded to the city in 1915. A large expanse of lanes, grass, trees, and shrubbery, it stands as an example of the kind of cemetery that emerged in the middle years of the nineteenth century. Replacing family and church graveyards, the new cemetery evoked Romantic sensibility. As James J. Farrell explains in his book *Inventing the American Way of Death*, at this new kind of cemetery "the individual could expect to commune with God, with nature, and with deceased family and friends."[22]

Again following the custom of the time, Sue and Harvey later had a portrait made of Edgar.[23] Sue sent a photograph of Edgar, a swatch of material from a suit she undoubtedly made, and the following undated instructions to the painter: "This Boy is 9 years old, complex[ion] light, not very much color but a healthy color.[24] I will enclose a piece of his coat. [I] want his pants & coat made like the piece enclosed. Fix the collar and tie. Now I want you to be very careful and make this good for the clothes to represent the piece sent."

The outward manifestations of sentimentalism of nineteenth-century Americans reflected changing religious beliefs. As mentioned earlier, American Protestants of the middle class embraced a new view of death and immortality, a view markedly different from that of the Puritans. Farrell explains, "Sentimental Americans domesticated death, thus trying to overcome their terror of it, by developing socially acceptable channels for Romantic expressionism." He further states that Americans in the last decades of the nineteenth century "brashly believed in their ability to understand and order death."[25] Efforts to preserve the body as it was before death—dressed in a suit, photographed in a natural pose, embalmed, and buried in a vault—were all ways of imposing order, of "domesticating" death.

Before Victorian Americans began to reconceive the end of life, death had been seen as punishment for sin and depravity. Farrell explains that Protestants and in particular Presbyterians "believed that God intervened directly with death to chastise his sinful children and to remind survivors of their own mortality."[26] This belief can be seen in the words of Mary Hessinville Machette, who was the sister-in-law of Margaret Machette.[27] In 1841, when she learned that her husband, also a cousin, had died while on a business trip, she wrote to her brother Charles that God determined that her husband would die. In fact, God determined that her husband had died in order to teach her and others a lesson: "He has seen that I have needed this sad bereavement in order to draw me closer to him. He has seen how tardy have been my movements in making preparations for that Kingdom that never shall end. May this sad and mournful afflic-tion excite each one of us to greater activity in making our calling and election sure."

Strict Calvinists could accept the death of children as a manifestation of humanity's innate depravity. However, Christians in Victorian America were more likely to see Jesus' regard toward children as indicative of their special grace. For example, an article

22. Farrell, *Inventing the American Way of Death*, 105. See also David E. Stannard, "Where All Our Steps Are Tend-ing," in *A Time to Mourn*, ed. Pike and Armstrong, 19–29.

23. Margaret Bruin Machette similarly commissioned an oil painting of her oldest daughter, Mary Elizabeth, after she died at school in 1854. The receipt shows that she paid $36 in 1859 for the portrait and frame.

24. Edgar was eight years old when he died; apparently when his mother commissioned the painting, he would have been nine. Her use of present tense, "This Boy *is* [emphasis added] 9 years old," is striking.

25. Farrell, *Inventing the American Way of Death*, 34, 217.

26. Farrell, *Inventing the American Way of Death*, 36.

27. Mary Hessinville Machette is also quoted in a footnote to the narrative told by Aunt Lucy, p. 173, n. 52.

in the April 15, 1875, *New York Observer* stated, "On young believers He confers His own sweetest name, as if they were His pet lambs; and He thus teaches older Christians to love the young and to take great care of them, and to remember that they are very dear to Jesus." Faced with the difficulty of explaining why children, precious in the sight of Jesus, died, some saw such death as God's way of punishing the family. This is the view of death that Sallie Flood referred to in her August 26, 1870, letter when she described the painful death of her little niece, Mamie. "Every one," Sallie wrote, "says that she was taken from us because we made her our idol."

The idea of death as God's will continued throughout the nineteenth century and into the twentieth century; however, there was also a move to see death as a natural part of life.[28] As science was better able to explain the nature of disease, people were less likely to attribute death to divine intervention, or at least to divine intervention alone. Although Sue Scott must have wondered about Edgar's dying shortly after he read about the plagues of Egypt and said, "That's like Finley and I should die," she did not in her narrative of October 28, 1883, attribute divine intervention to his death. Moreover, even though she apparently blamed herself in part for his death when she wrote, "How strange it does seem that [I] was not uneasy about his feeling cold— I never once thought of his being sick," she did not attribute his death to her own sinful nature. Both her statement, "I believe the disease developed in that fever. Nothing seemed to act on his bowels," and the clipping on a cure for diphtheria suggest that she looked to medical science to explain and prevent the disease that killed her son.

Sue Scott might turn to science to explain her son's death, but she turned to religion to find consolation for her loss. Her nineteenth-century society afforded her more consolation than Puritans would have found. While the Puritans tended to emphasize the horrors of hell that awaited people unless they were saved by God's grace, by the mid-nineteenth century people embraced a less terrifying notion of death. Fear of hell gave way to the promise of salvation as Protestants embraced the notion of a God of love rather than a God of vengeance.

A key figure who modified Calvinism by employing Romantic concepts of optimism, individuality, and an inherent relationship between nature, God, and humanity was Henry Ward Beecher, the minister mentioned with admiration by John Flood in his September 6, 1878, letter. Influenced by the brand of Romanticism known as Transcendentalism, Beecher preached a God of love and contrasted the Calvinist and Romantic concepts of religion: "The terrors of the Lord may dissuade men from evil; but it is the warm shining of the heart of God that brings men toward His goodness and toward Him."[29] In an article on the front page of the January 26, 1883, *Fulton Telegraph*, Beecher is quoted rejecting the notion of original sin: "The idea that succeeding generations were to be stained through—because their ancestors ate an apple— because of crime they never committed and never thought of—Mr. Beecher ridiculed."[30] Believing in a loving and forgiving God, Beecher saw death not as something to be feared. Rather, he stated, "The door of death is the door of hope; the grave is that lens through which we see immortality."[31] In the Romantic tradition, Beecher

---

28. Farrell, *Inventing the American Way of Death*, 55.

29. Henry Ward Beecher, *The Crown of Life*, ed. Mary Storr Haynes (Boston: D. Lothrop, 1890), 53.

30. The Reverend Theodore Cuyler, praising the older school of ministers like Lyman Beecher who "emphasize[d] the heinousness and the desert of sin as a great argument for repentance and acceptance of Jesus Christ," wrote of Henry Ward Beecher: "Henry Ward Beecher hardly exaggerated when he once said to me, 'Put all of his children together and we do not equal my father at his best'"; Cuyler, *Recollections of a Long Life*, 75–76.

31. Beecher, *Crown of Life*, 94.

often drew a relationship between nature and the promise of immortality. Flowers, which Beecher referred to as "the sweetest things that God ever made, and forgot to put a soul into," represented the promise of immortality: "And when friends have gone out from us joyously, I think we should go with them to the grave, not singing mournful psalms, but scattering flowers."[32] Lizzie Shelton Machette, who loved her flowers passionately and who made a garland of heliotrope and geranium for a child's coffin, seemed to share Beecher's regard for and use of flowers (see February 19, 1877). Following the optimistic beliefs of people like Beecher, the letter writers in the last chapter of this volume wrote confidently of promised salvation for their loved ones.

As the nineteenth century progressed, society became increasingly interested in imagining what heaven might be like. A popular conception of heaven in Victorian America was the reunion of loved ones. Beecher himself spoke confidently of reunion with his children: "I shall find them; they will find me; and they will be more to me there than they ever were here."[33] The letters on death written in the last decades of the nineteenth century and the early years of the twentieth similarly offered the promise of reunion after death, and dying relatives in the Machette family spoke of communing with relatives already dead (see, for example, January 3, 1897).

While Beecher in the quotation above did not speculate on how his children would appear to him in heaven, others of the nineteenth century did. One of the most popular portraits of heaven was that of Elizabeth Stuart Phelps. The daughter of Austin Phelps, who wrote the book about prayer referred to in the October 13, 1860, letter, Elizabeth Stuart Phelps published *The Gates Ajar* in 1869. In this popular novel, the protagonist learns to reject Calvinist notions of death and immortality for more Romantic ones. Phelps's concept of heaven was more fully imagined in a subsequent novel, *Beyond the Gates*, published in 1883. In this novel, a young woman is escorted by her deceased father to heaven where she enjoys seas, birds, flowers, and forests, and comes to a perfect city where she lives with her family and communes with artists, scientists, and poets.

Phelps's view of heaven seems to have influenced Sue Scott. Besides clipping poetry for her scrapbook, she also clipped religious essays on immortality. In one of these essays, the writer imagined a heaven much like the heaven in *The Gates Ajar* and *Beyond the Gates*, where people will "meet with the great ones of whom we have read and heard; the prophets, the kings; the sages; the potentates of earth!" The writer went on to assure the reader that a baby who died fifty years ago will not appear to his mother as a man but as the baby she lost: "You, sorrowing mothers, shall meet your sweet babes in glory in all the sweetness and beauty of their babyhood." The writer of another clipped essay in Sue's scrapbook took exception to such certain views of heaven: "I do not believe that to Miss Phelps, or anybody else on this side of the river, the gates are ajar.... While we are in the body, a purely spiritual life must be a mystery and an enigma to us." The writer ended by stating that the bereaved should find comfort in simply knowing that those who believed in Christ would find immortality. All in all, the scrapbook suggests that Sue Scott was attracted to the sentimentalism of her age and wanted to believe in a physical immortality but could not fully reconcile herself to such a belief.

---

32. Henry Ward Beecher, *Life Thoughts: Gathered from the Extemporaneous Discourses* (Boston: Phillips, Sampson, 1858), 189, 234.

33. Beecher, *Crown of Life*, 120.

Phelps's view of heaven was extreme and not generally accepted by Protestant theologians. Charley Hersman, for example, who was a minister as well as a professor of Greek, wrote on February 19, 1900, to his mother-in-law about "a home not made with hands," which she would soon find in heaven, but he explicitly based his description on the Bible and identified the heavenly home as spiritual, not physical.

During Margaret Bruin Machette's lifetime, Missouri was transformed from a wilderness territory to a well-populated state of farms, towns, and cities. When she died, the home she lived in had neither city water, electric lights, nor a telephone although the technologies that would make all of them possible were coming to the middle-class home. In 1882, twenty-six businesses and residents signed up for the first telephone exchange in Fulton.[34] By the turn of century, Fulton had also had an electric light plant and a waterworks system. With a population of almost five thousand people in 1900, Fulton had three colleges, three public school buildings ("one for the education of colored children"), three banks, four newspapers, a tobacco factory, a flour mill, a steam laundry, and two brick plants.[35] The State Insane Asylum No. 1 continued as did the Asylum for the Education of the Deaf and Dumb, although the latter became known as the Missouri School for the Deaf in 1897.[36] Fulton boasted ten churches, and a 1904 census conducted by Westminster students found that half of Fultonians belonged to a church.[37] Pratt's Theatre, known as the Fulton Opera House, was built by 1896 and then rebuilt in 1904 after it was destroyed by a fire.[38] Not quite ready to turn its back on the old ways, Fulton also had harness makers, blacksmiths, and horseshoers. In 1900, Fultonians could travel by wagon, by railcar, and even by automobile.

If one of the great projects of Victorian America was domesticity—domesticating the wilderness, society, religion, and even death—then that project was largely completed in the heartland by the first years of the twentieth century.

34. *Fulton Telegraph* (December 10, 1882). Subscribers included the Edwin Curd family and the Joseph Rickey family. The Scotts would not have a telephone until 1907.

35. *Thirteenth Census of the United States Taken in the Year 1910*, vol. 2. (Washington, D.C.: Government Printing Office, 1913), table 1. *Missouri State Gazetteer and Business Directory, 1898–1899* (St. Louis: R.L. Polk, 1898), 374–379.

36. Reed, *Historic MSD*, 21.

37. *Fulton Gazette* (March 18, 1904). According to this survey, the Presbyterian church had more members than any other denomination in Fulton.

38. *Fulton Gazette* (January 9, 1903, and March 18, 1904).

Clive and Harold
Scott, sons of
Harvey and Susan
Machette Scott

Harvey and
Susan Machette Scott

13th Feb.	cut out Clive's pants	*From the journal of Susan*
Feb. 24th	set 4 hens	*Machette Scott for 1890*
5th March	made pique skirt	
	cold weather 1st week in March — put up ice....	
20	young chickens 1 doz....	
Apr. 21st	set hens & took up dining room carpet....	
May 11	cleaned house — put sitting room carpet down	
13th	papered dining room — took parlor carpet up....	
July 31	Harold's 3rd birthday	
18th Aug.	Harold quit sucking his finger	
Sept. 1st	Clive went to school	

Sedalia, Missouri
January 18, 1891

Telegram from Alexander
Machette to his mother, Margaret
Bruin Machette

    Lizzie is with the Lord. Funeral Wednesday morning.

        Alex

Clarksville, Tennessee
June 3, 1891

From Margaret Hersman to her
aunt, Susan Machette Scott

Dear Aunt Sue,
    ... I am so sorry that Uncle Harvey is having such a trial with his ankle. Tell him I wish I could walk in and read to him as I used to do when I was a little girl....
    I urged Matsie in my last letter to come down and of course had to ask Mary. I am anxious to know if they will come. I really want Matsie to come very much. Dear

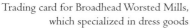

Harold Scott collected cigarette cards from Duke's Cigarettes.

Trading card for Broadhead Worsted Mills, which specialized in dress goods

Aunt, why couldn't you come with her? It seems too bad that none of you can come. I would like so much for you to see my things. I would give any thing if we all could live near together. I have always missed you so much. I wish you would make up your mind to come with Matsie. Before I forget it, Finley's address is 2604 Lucas Avenue.[39]

I am having one of my dresses made now — the batiste with the blue and black stripes. I am going to use lace and blue silk to trim the waist in, instead of the black velvet. My dress maker thought the velvet too heavy. I am going to have my other dresses made week after next. My batiste — the shirt — is slightly looped and has a ruffle that is *very* wide at the sides and narrower at the front.

Our commencement begins with Sunday. Some of the Board came in to-night. This meeting will be very important as they have a professor and a chancellor to elect.[40]

I almost forgot to tell you about my underclothes. I made a few pieces my self, but got most of them at Altman's, New York, and they have come and are entirely satisfactory.[41] I have a half dozen of each article....

From Margaret Hersman to her grandmother, Margaret Bruin Machette

Clarksville, Tennessee
June 26, 1891

My dear Grandmother,

The very idea of you saying that the quilt is not pretty! Matsie and Mary helped unpack the box, and we all think it is so pretty, but best of all is the thought that it was all made by my dear grandmother's fingers. I could not take any thing in the world for it. I do hope you have not made your self sick finishing it. Matsie and Mary are both here and send love to you all....

39. Matsie Curd and Mary Buckland Dobyns; see December 16, 1888. Finley Hersman, a physician, lived in St. Louis.

40. Southwestern Presbyterian University was looking for a chancellor; Charley Hersman had accepted a position at Union Theological Seminary in Richmond, Virginia.

41. B. Altman's, a fine department store in New York City.

July 1st   Margaret Hersman was married in Tennessee[42]

From the journal of Susan Machette Scott for 1891

Sedalia, Missouri
July 7, 1891

From Margaret Bruin Machette to her daughter, Susan Machette Scott

My Dear Susie

I got to Sedalia safe, found Alex sick. He got out of bed to meet me at the train. He has been in bed ever since. I hope [he] is better this morning. He has had bowel trouble and indigestion and torpid liver — did not have a doctor. Took very little medicine, just ate very little. Yesterday he commenced taking Hall's liver medicine and I hope it is doing him good. The girls have not got home yet. He expects them today. He has a girl to do the work for the last week. She has lived with them for several years but is very poor help except for the washing and ironing. When the girls went to visit in Liberty, this girl went to her sister's on a visit until Alex was expecting me. He sent for her to come home. You can't think how much Alex has broken since you saw him. He is looking very badly. Mrs. Kemper and her two daughters came as far as Mexico with me. The first person I saw when I got off the car was Mrs. Willis coming to meet me. She stayed with me until I left Mexico. She got my ticket, had my trunk checked, and helped me on the car. Please don't forget her kindness to me. Mrs. Dobyns came to the depot to see me, was very kind to me. Mrs. Patton traveled as far as Boonville with me, was very kind. In the hurry of getting on we got into different cars, but Mrs. Patton sent the conductor for me, and we sat together until she got off at Boonville.[43]

7th. Aimee and Etta got home last evening. They are nice girls. Alex is better this morning, hope he will soon be well. Be sure to direct my letters to Alex's care. Yours and Abbie's letters received, glad to hear from you and the dear ones. Precious little Harold Hersman Scott, I miss him so much, and Clive, dear boy, tell him I see a number of boys, but none to compare to my Clive. It is lonely without the two boys — the two girls are very nice, play beautifully and are good house keepers. Alex is very proud of them and ought to be....

July 16th	tore down Stable
17th	made back fence....
Sept. 7th	Nealie and Forest came
Oct.	made my black silk
Nov. 9th	I went to St. Louis — Ethel & Finley were there. I got spectacles from Dr. Wolfner — first pair[44]

From the journal of Susan Machette Scott for 1891

42. Margaret Hersman married William Elwang, a Presbyterian minister. See June 9, 1889.

43. Frederick Thomas Kemper, husband of Susan Kemper, died in 1881. See June 24, 1874, for his grand reunion. Mrs. Willis, Martha Patton Willis; see August 31, 1873, on her marriage to the Reverend Henry Willis. Mrs. Patton, probably Laura Myers Patton, wife of Charles Patton and sister-in-law to Martha Willis.

44. Henry Lincoln Wolfner, doctor of ophthalmology in St. Louis. The Wolfner Library for the Blind and Physically Handicapped in Jefferson City is named in his honor.

*From J. B. Garrett, secretary of
the faculty of Hanover College,
to John Harvey Scott*

Hanover, Indiana
June 20, 1892

Dear Sir:

It gives me pleasure to inform you that the Faculty of Hanover College, with the approbation of the Board of Trustees, conferred upon you at their last meeting the degree of Dr. of Philosophy. We hope it will be pleasant to you to receive this degree from our College, as it has given us great pleasure to confer it.

*From Charles Campbell
Hersman to his brother-in-law
and cousin, John Harvey Scott*

Richmond, Virginia[45]
July 1, 1892

My dear *Dr:*

I am so glad that Hanover College has honored herself in giving you the well deserved title. In this age of shams and hollow pretensions, it does one good to see *real genuine merit* rewarded. Were all honors as well deserved and as judiciously bestowed as this, there would be less reason to decry the whole business....

I look back with so much pleasure on my visit to you all. It is one bright spot in my life, and the memory of it will ever be cherished. You, Susie, Ma, and the children were so kind and made me so happy while visiting you. I wish I had remained longer. I wish you and Susie could come to see us.... I returned through Cincinnati and up the Ohio. The scenery was fine and the accommodations superb. I wish I had come on a boat to Cincinnati and thence by sail through the Blue Ridge.

... Give my love to Ma, Susie and the boys.

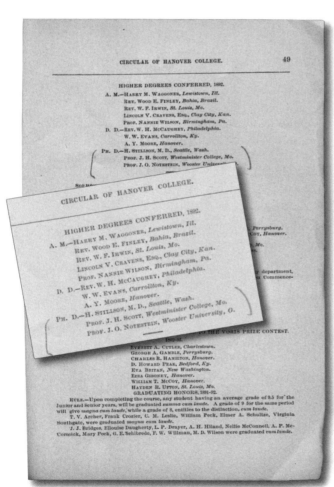

Hanover College, a Presbyterian school in Indiana, offered a doctorate in philosophy to "teachers of known attainments." Harvey Scott received his degree from Hanover in 1892.

45. The Hersmans moved to Richmond where Charley was a professor at Union Theological Seminary.

Denver, Colorado
August 6, 1892

From Susan Machette Scott to
Margaret Bruin Machette and
Clive Scott

Dear Ma,

… We went to the train on Thursday night to try to get our sleeper, but they pretended there had been some misunderstanding and there was not even standing room to be had. Next morning Harvey got them to promise him two upper berths. We were so lucky to get one lower one for Harold and me with the upper one for Harvey. We had a much better time in this part of our trip as water was plentiful for drinking and washing.… We got in this morning about ten. As we did not telegraph to them we did not expect them to meet us, so Harvey went out to look up some one to take us to Nealie's. They wanted to charge $4.00, but he found some one that brought us in an express wagon for a dollar. Brother George says people are going to be awfully gouged for everything and that rogues of every sort are pouring in. Brother and Nealie and Forest are looking very well. I don't think Nealie has recovered her strength.… Nealie's house is so pretty and comfortable.…

Dear Clive,

… We are very well and enjoying ourselves so much. Last Saturday night we went to see an Indian show — although we were so tired. Harold was delighted. Brother George thought it was tame but it was new to us. Saw ponies bucking [and a] ghost dance. Four of the Indians started in to perform and when they got right in the middle of the ground they looked around and saw 2 Texas steers rushing in from the opposite gate. It was so funny to see them run for the fence and scramble up. The ghost (this was just one dressed in white) tumbled down and could hardly scramble up. They lassoed a steer and a drunken Negro tried to ride him and the steer threw him off and kicked him in the head. I will tell you the rest when we get back.

Uncle took me to the cemetery Sunday afternoon. I got out at Brother John's grave — it looked lovely.…

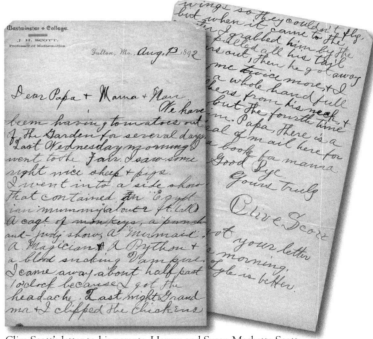

Clive Scott's letter to his parents, Harvey and Susan Machette Scott
(transcribed below).

Fulton, Missouri
August 13, 1892

From Clive Scott to his family

Dear Papa and Mama and Man

We have been having tomatoes out of the Garden for several days. Last Wednesday morning I went to the Fair. I saw some right nice sheep and pigs. I went into a side show that contained an "Egyptian mummy" (about 2 feet tall), a cage of monkeys, a "punch-and-judy" show, a "Mermaid," a Magician, and a Python and a blood sucking Vampire. I came away about half past 1 o'clock because I got the head-ache. Last night Grandma and I clipped the chickens wings so they couldn't fly, but when it came to the rooster I grabbed him by the tail and pulled all his tail feathers out, then he got away from me twice more, and I pulled a whole hand full of feathers from his neck and wings, but the fourth time I got him. Papa, there is a good deal of mail here for you, and a book for mama. Good Bye.

yours truly
Clive Scott

... Write *soon.*

From Alexander Machette to his
mother, Margaret Bruin Machette

Charleston, Missouri
September 5, 1892

Dear Ma,

I arrived in Charleston Saturday afternoon at 4 o'clock. On my way down, I passed through some broken, swampy, poorly cultivated country; but a pleasant surprise awaited me as I neared Charleston. The town was founded in 1837, is situated in the midst of a rich district, level as a floor. It is bottom land, sandy soil, but under a good state of cultivation. Some farmers raised wheat 40 bushels to the acre — 30 bushels was not considered extra. 2,600 carloads of watermelons have been shipped from two or three stations near here — and yet they say it has not been "a good year" for melons. Corn fields look well. Some trees strange to me are used for shade trees, brought from the south. The lower altitude and being farther south gives a milder climate. Magnolia trees, twenty feet high, adorn the yards.

The people are mostly the better class of southerners. The Methodist and Baptist churches are in the lead. Our church is made up of the best people in the community. They have an excellent church building. On the whole, I am favorably impressed. Pray for me that I may be guided aright in making a location.

From Alexander Machette to his
mother, Margaret Bruin Machette

Charleston, Missouri
October 8, 1892

Dear Ma,

... I think I shall like my field here. Only it seems a long ways off from my friends and is of course a little lonely sometimes. I am rooming in the home of an old lady — sister Bridges. She is visiting her daughter in St. Louis just now, so that I have the house all to myself — am taking my meals with Mrs. Frank just next door.

I heard from the children in Cincinnati the other day. I went up and met them in St. Louis and put them aboard of their train for Cincinnati last Thursday [a] week ago. They made a nice visit to Liberty and then a trip with Mrs. Frey down into Texas, where they met Lum. He came back with them as far as Sedalia. I hope they will keep well and make good progress in their music and other studies this year, as it will be in all probability their last year in school....

Had a letter from Anna not long ago. [46] They were well. The children went over from Sedalia, just before leaving, to see Anna and to tell her "Good-bye." They said Anna was looking better than she had done for a long time.

Charleston, Missouri
November 5, 1892

From Alexander Machette to his mother, Margaret Bruin Machette

Dear Ma:

... I suppose you are settled down for the winter — am glad you enjoyed a pleasant visit in Montgomery — I would love very much to see them all myself....

How time flies. It is hard to realize that we are so near Thanksgiving-day. [47] It seems to me I never knew time to fly faster. One reason, no doubt, is that I have had my hands full. There is a great work to do here, if the Lord will only enable me to do it. The standard here is rather low. The saloon flourishes and of course there is much drunkenness. [48] Church members think or say it is "no harm to dance." The men are run mad over politics and think most of money making. Of course, that means a low spirituality, poorly attended prayer meetings, &c. But we have some good earnest Christians, and we must work to raise the standard. The children were well when I heard from them last. Aimee and Etta want to come home to see me Christmas. I doubt the propriety of it, but it is hard to refuse them. My love to all the family and a double portion
for yourself.

On the back of this picture of Aimee Machette is written "December 1892" and "With much love to Grandma."

Charleston, Missouri
January 9, 1893

From Alexander Machette to his mother, Margaret Bruin Machette

Dear Ma,

I have been putting off writing, waiting for my church to let me have some money so that I could send you something. I let the children have what I could spare about Christmas. The church here is very much like they are in most places, a little slow in meeting their obligations to the pastor. They were very kind in making me some nice presents for Christmas. I received a nice umbrella (silk), a half dozen nice linen handkerchiefs, a suit of clothes (coat, pants, and vest), &c. Enclosed I send you a postal order — am sorry it could not be more.

We had a very good day yesterday in our church work. I do not think, though, that the standard among church members is near so high as it is up in the central parts of the state. There is a good deal of liquor used, and it affects even the churches more or less. I am doing my best to elevate the standard among my people. They do not seem

46. Alex and Lizzie Machette's daughter Anna married William Edgar in 1889.

47. In 1863, President Lincoln established the last Thursday in November as Thanksgiving Day. In 1939 President Franklin Roosevelt moved it to the third Thursday in November; later Congress ruled that starting in 1942 it would again be observed on the fourth thursday of November.

48. David Thelen, *Paths of Resistance,*154, notes, "By 1890 there was a church for every 438 Missourians and a saloon for every 318."

to think it out of place for church members to go to the theater and dance and such like. Still, we have some very earnest, devoted people who regret those things and cooperate with their pastors.

I can't help thinking that wickedness everywhere is on the increase. Romanism is getting more bold, and I fear that many who have refused to accept the truth will be swallowed up by it.

... Just had a letter from Aimee. She gives me an outline of the pastor's sermon every week.... If it is possible, I would like so much to take the girls to see you. I do not know whether I shall go to housekeeping next summer or not. We have a very nice parsonage and Etta wants to keep house....

A note written by Margaret Bruin Machette and attached to dried flowers

February 12, 1893

These flowers were sent from Denver to me by my precious daughter Nelia as a birthday present on my 76th birthday.

From Alexander Machette to his mother, Margaret Bruin Machette

Charleston, Missouri
February 19, 1893

Lillian Claude Edgar, daughter of William and Anna Machette Edgar and granddaughter of Alexander and Lizzie Machette

Dear Ma:

... I have had a very good day of it — preached morning and evening as usual. My subject this morning was the "Feast of Pentecost." To-night I used the familiar text in Revelation 22:17 and enjoyed preaching very much.[49] There is, however, a wonderful amount of indifference here by men generally toward the Gospel. I think I never saw a worse condition, in that respect, any where. I sometimes wonder if the people are not being given over to unbelief and a sort of religious indifference.

I had a letter from Anna the other day. They are well. Anna expects to go to housekeeping by summer time. You know they have been boarding heretofore at old Mr. Edgar's.[50] I think Anna will enjoy keeping house to herself. As to my housekeeping, Aimee rather discourages it, as she expects to leave us in September, and Etta may want to go to school another year.

This is rather a peculiar country down here. It would remind you a little of the country below St. Charles — the Point prairie — flat, some portions easily overflowed when the rivers are up. It seems real gloomy when the weather is bad, and for some time past we have had little else except gloomy, rainy weather. One thing I see here occasionally that has long since passed away in your part of the state — that is, *ox teams* from one to four yoke, drawing great loads after them. I had to stop and stare awhile at the first one I saw — it looked so odd. This seems to be a great country for game. It is nothing unusual to see boys or men from the country bringing in [a] great bunch of coonskins for sale and other pelts. The

49. Revelation 22:17: "And the Spirit and the bride say, Come. And let him that heareth say, Come. And let him that is athirst come."

50. H.R. Edgar, father-in-law of Alex's daughter Anna Machette Edgar.

country abounds in lakes and sloughs, and we often see wagon loads of fine fish on the streets.

I think I told you once before that the standard of morals is rather low, even among the church members. There are few young men here that I would allow to wait on a daughter of mine. I almost dread the thought of bringing the girls here at all. This, however, is the dark side of the matter — there are some excellent people here who moan over the low state of religion and morals and long for better conditions....

Charleston, Missouri
May 2, 1893

From Alexander Machette to his mother, Margaret Bruin Machette

Dear Ma

... There is a great deal of complaint from the farmers on account of high water, low lands overflowed already, and a prospect for worse still. I suppose you have been reading newspaper accounts of storms, cyclones, &c.[51] It does look as if "the whole creation" were "groaning and travailing in pain" till now.[52] The astronomers and weather prophets do not give us any reason to hope for any improvement in this respect for some time to come.

I had a letter from Mr. Hall a week or so ago. He wants the girls to visit the "Columbian Exposition" at Chicago when school is out (May 25th) and wants me to go with them.[53] So far as I am concerned personally, I do not care to go — am getting too old to enjoy being in a crowd and jam. For the sake of the girls I may conclude to go. Would much prefer for myself to use the money in making a visit to our relations. I have been so anxious to take Aimee and Etta and visit some when their school is out. Lu Semple has been writing to them to come to see her.[54] It would be nice if we go to Chicago, to meet friends there. Are Susie, Nealie, Abbie, or any of their families going and if so at what time? Perhaps we could arrange to meet then. Please let me know.

Columbian Exhibition — World's Fair — ticket for May 1–31, 1893

July 19th Wed.   We got Buggy

From the journal of Susan Machette Scott for 1893

51. In April, cyclones hit Cisco, Texas, and Norman, Oklahoma, razing buildings and killing people. *St. Louis Republic* (April 27 and 30, 1893).

52. Romans 8:22: "For we know that the whole creation groaneth and travaileth in pain together until now."

53. The 1893 World's Fair, the Columbian Exposition, celebrated the four hundredth anniversary of Columbus's arrival in the New World. See the introduction to this chapter.

54. In 1870, Lucy "Lu" Shelton, mentioned frequently in the 1860 letters as Lizzie Machette's sister, married Robert Semple, a professor. The Semples lived in Liberty, Missouri.

From Alexander Machette to his mother, Margaret Bruin Machette

Charleston, Missouri
July 21, 1893

Dear Ma:

... It will soon be a year since I came into southeast Missouri. I hope I won't have to spend another year here. I never was more sick of any place in my life. True religion is very nearly dead — there is very little to encourage anyone to labor in such a field.

The Fulton Presbyterian Church at the turn of the century. Built in 1884, the church was dedicated in 1885.

I had a letter from Aimee this morning — they went with their Uncle Jake to Troy last Saturday. They went by the old Shelton farm and visited little Susie's grave. They met their Uncle Nat Shelton and his family at Peachey's. Lum Hall also met them there. So they have been having a fine time and are enjoying their visit very much indeed. Aimee does not expect to be married until some time in November.[55]

Monday. As I did not finish this as I intended, I will add a line or two. We had a terrible hot day yesterday and it was hard work. Our people do not know anything about *letting up* on a preacher in hot weather, though many of them are visiting watering places and feel the need of a rest for themselves.

I have just been requested to attend and conduct services at a funeral this afternoon — an old lady, 84 years old. The family ignores preachers and churches almost altogether; but, like many others, when in trouble expect preachers and churches to move at their bidding — such is human nature! I see so much of the mean side of humanity that I fear I will become a cynic, but must try to avoid that spirit. After all, there are very many good people in the world, and we are permitted to enjoy many blessings for which we should be thankful....

Written on piece of paper by Margaret Bruin Machette

Mr. Cole was here on the 20th of October 1893. My Dear Alex came to see me on October 30th, stayed all night and until the afternoon of the 31st.

From Finley Hersman to his grandmother, Margaret Bruin Machette

St. Louis, Missouri
January 16, 1894

Dear Grandma:

I hope you will not take it amiss that I wrote you on the type writer; for it is a great deal easier for me to do than writing, and I think it will be much easier for you to

---

55. Susie, Alex and Lizzie Machette's daughter, who probably died in infancy. After the death of his parents, Peachy Shelton was raised by his uncle and aunt, Meacon and Anna Shelton. In 1853, he married his first cousin and one of Lizzie Machette's sisters, Susanna. Alex's daughter Aimee was engaged to marry Christopher Columbus "Lum" Hall, widower of her sister Lilian.

read.[56] I was glad to hear that you are getting better. You must not expect to get back your strength in too much of a hurry....

I think often of the very pleasant time I spent with you. Aunt Susie and Uncle Harvey are certainly the very kindest of persons. If Clive should ever really wish to study Medicine, I should be more than glad to help him in any way. I should discourage any one who wanted Medicine for a business. It is the very worst business of all I believe; but if one wants a life work which will absorb all his energies and a good deal more besides, with an opportunity of doing good in the most certain way, that is to men's bodies, I should say by all means go into Medicine....

Finley Hersman played with Francis Hardaway, the son of Dr. William Hardaway, a dermatologist. Francis would serve as a battalion commander during the First World War.

Feb.	Clive joined the church
Feb. 27th	sold 9 ½ lb. butter[57]
March 16th	made garden
18th	pie plant up
April 1st	Harold started to Sunday School
2nd Mon.	Harold started to Miss Fannie....[58]
9th	Clive took mumps
28 Mon.	Harold took mumps

From the journal of Susan Machette Scott for 1894

St. Louis, Missouri
June 29, 1894

From Finley Hersman to his grandmother, Margaret Bruin Machette

Dear Grandma:

... I have been quite busy lately with some writing I have been doing for several new medical works which are soon to come out. I am fond of writing even if it only medical work. Some day when I get time I am going to write something of more general interest. I suppose it is a very common quality in one who is fond of books to wish to see books which he has helped to make. In a small way I now have this pleasure as I have an article in a *System of Dermatology* which has just been published by Appleton.[59]

56. The typewriter was first marketed in 1874 and exhibited at the Centennial Exposition in 1876.

57. In her small scrapbook, Sue Scott also noted that she made money giving piano lessons in the late 1870s and early 1880s.

58. Miss Fannie Harper ran a private school that the Scott boys attended.

59. Finley's work appeared in *A System of Genito-Urinary Diseases, Syphilology and Dermatology* (1893), edited by Prince Albert Morrow.

Finley Hersman, a physician in St. Louis, was engaged to Anne Bates.

I am not doing so well from a business point of view. In the first place I despise business methods. In the second place I have very serious doubts if a keen business man can be a very honest man. In the third place I don't think I could be a business man if I wanted to ever so much. So I have already made up my mind to be a poor man all my days. Not that I am above loving money and the things that money brings. On the contrary, I am very fond of refined and beautiful things, and one can not have them without some money. I was thinking of getting married this month but it has been deferred for a time. As a matter of fact, I am the very last man that ought to think of getting married. I have very little business and no very good prospect of having much, and then my life will not be a very long one and I dare say not a very merry one.[60] Besides all this, what is worse, I am afraid I am a crank. I really am lost in admiration at the daring of a woman who would marry me.

I suppose it is not cool with you just now, but I am sure it can be no warmer than it is here. The idea of staying here all summer is not at all attractive, but I think I shall have to stay. When you have enough money to go away you are so busy you can't and when you are not busy you have not the money.

Give my love to Aunt Susie, to Uncle Harvey and to the boys and accept much for yourself.

From Finley Hersman to his grandmother, Margaret Bruin Machette

St. Louis, Missouri
August 4, 1894

Dear Grandma:

I saw Miss Garvin today, and she told me that you had told her that you did not know anything of my intended marriage.[61] You must have forgotten for I wrote you in the spring that I intended to get married in the summer. I did not do that, but I have now determined to marry next month. You see I have been waiting for my prospects to

---

60. Finley had Bright's disease or nephritis, a kidney disease marked by high blood pressure and albumin in the urine.

61. Gertrude or Lela Garvin, daughters of Alexander and Elizabeth Boyd Garvin. See April 11, 1889.

improve, but as they seem to be getting worse rather than better I have determined to take the plunge in spite of fate.

Really from a financial point of view my marriage is a piece of folly entirely worthy of my unbusinesslike mind. I have no money and no settled income. Some months I make a little money and some I don't. But you see I have only a little time to live and as the young lady says that she had rather run the risk of starving than be separated from me, I think her devotion should be rewarded — if you could call marrying one who may die any day a reward. Well, I hope that as the ravens are fed so shall I be — certainly I have a ravening appetite at times.[62] I don't just know what the day will be, but you will hear as soon as I know it myself. Of course you know the lady is Miss Anne Bates. You would like her if you knew her and so would aunt Susie.

I am going out into the country to a watering place near here tomorrow to spend the day. I ate lunch today on the Roof Garden, two hundred and fifty feet in the air. This is very high eating but the *eating* was not very high....

Kansas City, Missouri
October 6, 1894

From Maud Machette Curry to her stepgrandmother, Margaret Bruin Machette

My Dear Grandmother:

I trust that you will excuse me for not writing sooner, but I was so busy before my wedding and now that I am back from my wedding trip, I take the earliest opportunity of writing to you. I am well and happy and hope that you are the same.

Accept my warmest and kindest thanks for your present. It was very kind of you to think of me in that way. With it I purchased a silver berry spoon, the bowl of which is gold. I bought something, dear grandmother, that I could always keep and remember you by. It is a beautiful thing and I wish you could see it; every one admires it very much. I received many handsome presents, among which was a beautiful glass and silver berry bowl that will go so nicely with the spoon.

Anna's husband (Mr. Edgar) was up to see us the other day and brought us two pictures of his little girl. She is such a sweet pretty little thing. All of us send our love and best wishes to you all.

Maud Machette Curry, daughter of Samuel and Anna Wilson Machette

Maud's wedding invitation

---

62. In Luke 12:24, Jesus spoke to his disciples, "Consider the ravens: for they neither sow nor reap; which neither have storehouse nor barn; and God feedeth them: how much more are ye better than the fowls?"

*From the journal of Susan
Machette Scott for 1894*

Nov.   I have lovely chrysanthemums

---

*From Alexander Machette to his
mother, Margaret Bruin Machette*

Boonville, Missouri
April 25, 1895

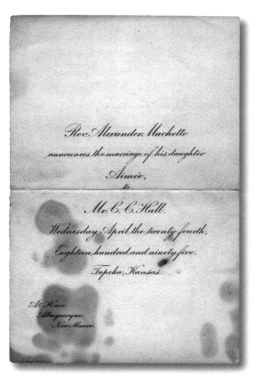

Marriage announcement for Aimee
Machette to her sister Lilian's widower,
Christopher Columbus "Lum" Hall. They
married seven years and four months after
Lilian's death, when Aimee was 21 and
Lum was 38 years old.

My dear Ma:

Mr. Hall, Aimee, and I left here last Monday for Topeka. I went by Liberty for Mrs. Semple. She and her little daughter (Virginia) went with me on Tuesday (23rd) to Topeka (about 60 miles from Kansas City). The road lies right along up the south bank of the Kansas River — a beautiful stream and a lovely country at this season of the year. Topeka is the loveliest place I have ever seen. It is Broadway, Sedalia, multiplied by about ten — such beautiful streets, stores, residences, &c. &c. It is the capital of the State and the public buildings are fine indeed — those Yankees have wonderful push and energy.

But you want to hear about the wedding. It is enough to say that Mr. and Mrs. Frey never do things by halves. Mr. and Mrs. Galbraith of Dennison, Texas, Mrs. Small, Mr. Logan Hall and wife and son of Sherman, Texas, Mr. Robinson (President of the A.T. & Santa Fe Railroad) and wife, daughter and two sons from Chicago, and several others besides old Mr. Hall and family from Springfield, Missouri, made as happy a crowd as you ever saw. The ceremony over, we had an elegant repast and then several hacks took us down to the train which was to leave at 3:45 p.m. Then came the fun — Mr. Frey had supplied everyone with a handful of *rice*, and the Bride and Groom were *well pelted* as they passed out to the train. All enjoyed the fun very much. Aimee and Lum seemed very happy....

I have not settled the question as to where I will locate as yet, but have several possibilities before me. Will let you know when events have developed.

---

*From Arthur Machette, son of
Samuel and Anna Wilson
Machette, to his stepgrandmother,
Margaret Bruin Machette*

Kansas City, Missouri
August 27, 1895

My Dear Grand-Ma—

My father's letter from you was received in due time but was not opened until he came home on the 20th, and as he had to go out on the road the following day, he thought he would answer your letter while on the road. I have mailed you a paper containing an account of an accident he had and this is why I am answering your letter in his stead as he is still in bed. Now, don't be uneasy as he is doing as nicely as we could wish and he will be up in a week or ten days. Sister Maud has a little daughter — born today, and herself and baby are doing well. Father says he will be down to see you about the last of October.

July 31st Wed.   began the new room

From the journal of Susan Machette Scott for 1895

St. Louis, Missouri
October 11, 1895

Finley has passed away.[63]

Telegram from Charles Campbell Hersman to his brother-in-law, John Harvey Scott

---

Albuquerque, New Mexico
October 23, 1895

From Aimee Machette Hall to her grandmother, Margaret Bruin Machette

My Darling Grandma:—

   Words are poor and inadequate, at best; and I feel utterly incapable of giving utterance to the shock and grief we felt, on learning, from your letter, the sad news of cousin Finley's death. While I knew he must be very ill, I had no idea the end was so near. He was very dear to us as little as we had opportunity of knowing him. And, Grandma, I wish you would convey our sympathy and inexpressible sadness to Aunt Abbie and Uncle Charley, in their bereavement. Of course our sense of loss cannot parallel theirs even in degree; but if it is the slightest comfort, to know other hearts are bowed, with theirs, to the painful stroke, beg them receive that

A tribute to the memory of Finley Hersman was held in St. Louis, where he was Professor of Clinical Medicine at the Missouri Medical College. Contributors included Drs. H.C. Dalton, W.A. Hardaway, and E.S. Smith, Jr., with remarks by Drs. Homan and Moore.

Mrs. M. A. Machette.

...A...
Tribute to the Memory
...of...
Dr.
Chas. Finley
Hersman

---

63. Abbie and Charley Hersman were visiting St. Louis when their son, Finley, died.

assurance. Also to cousin Finley's wife — I know that there are no words of sympathy that can ease her sorrow, in this affliction.[64] It is so great that only time [will help] and a determination to submit to the mandates of fate and following closely His steps, until admitted to that blessed company, where all such shall hold eternal fellowship with the blest ones who have preceded us.

Arthur Machette, left, son of Samuel and Anna Wilson Machette, sent this telegram notifying Margaret Machette of her stepson Samuel's death. Samuel was eight years old when his father Charles Machette married Margaret, his stepmother.

Written by Margaret Bruin Machette on a scrap of paper

Samuel Machette, son of Abigail and C.C. Machette, departed this life November 5, 1895, aged 69 years, 8 months, and 25 days.

From Arthur Machette to his stepgrandmother, Margaret Bruin Machette

Kansas City, Missouri
November 12, 1895

My Dear Grand-Ma:—

... Poor old Father, he is in his last resting place now. We all hated it terribly to see him go, as he was a good father to us all. It seems so strange and sudden. He came home the Friday before he died and on Tuesday morning he was taken from us. I do not think he had a very severe attack of Pneumonia, but the accident he met with weakened him so he could not stand his last illness.[65] My mother begged and pleaded

64. After Finley's death, his widow, Anne Bates Hersman, went to law school and became one of the first female attorneys in St. Louis. Admitted to the Missouri bar in 1919 and an expert in criminality, she wrote an article for the April 25, 1921, *St. Louis Globe-Democrat* in which she argued that white society was partly to blame for criminality, specifically "by our conquest and treatment of the Indians, by our slave-holding, by our fear and contempt of the freed negro, by our ignorance, prejudice and superciliousness to the foreigner." See Lucile Wiley Ring's chapter on Anne Bates Hersman in *Breaking the Barriers: The St. Louis Legacy of Women in Law, 1869–1969* (Manchester, Mo.: Independent Publishing, 1996), 82–87.

65. See August 27, 1895, for a reference to Sam's accident.

with him not to go out this last time; she wanted him to spend the winter in Texas. But he was such an ambitious man he hated to give up his work.

We were all with him his last night and it was a heart-rendering sight — Poor old Father, it was awful hard to see him suffer so. He intended coming to see you last month but I expect he didn't have the time to spare. He told us all he was going to see you and he used to speak of you so much....

Denver, Colorado
November 17, 1895

From Cornelia Machette Flood
Cole to Susan Machette Scott and
Margaret Bruin Machette

Dear Sue and Ma: —

Your much enjoyed letters were received and dear Finley's picture, which I think is so good and many thanks for it. I was so sorry to learn, Ma, of Sam's death. Yes, indeed, I know it is hard on you, dear Ma. What a treasure Harold must be indeed to you. God bless the little boy for his help to his dear Grandma by his nice, refreshing ways. You both speak of us visiting, but unless there is serious illness, Ma, of yourself or Forest dear I do not think we can come. I am not strong and at home generally — have reasonable good health so think it wisest to let it remain that way. Any way the winter is a poor time for visiting unless necessary, but if you were very sick, dear Ma, I would do all in my power to come to you.

... You asked, Sue, if Mother Flood left any property — yes, she left about $8000 worth, real estate and everything counted. It will be divided among the children, after all that they got from the estate has been deducted. [66]

Forest dear is well and doing nicely — he has played in the following places — Concord, and New Haven, Connecticut, Syracuse, Rochester, Buffalo, New York, Baltimore, Maryland, Washington, D.C., and commencing tomorrow night the next two weeks at Boston, Massachusetts. Then following five weeks of December [he will be] in New York at the "Empire."[67] After that I do not know his "Route." He has had a nice chance to travel through these states at a lovely time of the year. He was at Washington all last week. I see from the papers where Mrs. Cleveland entertained "Miss Nethersole" (in whose "company" Forest is).[68] I will copy the little article as I want it myself —

Forest Flood, son of Cornelia and John Flood,
became a stage actor.

Called on Mrs. Cleveland

Washington. Nov. 12 — Miss Nethersole, the distinguished English actress, who is playing in this city, visited Mrs. Cleveland at Woodley

66. John Flood's mother, Eliza, died earlier that year.

67. Performing at the Empire Theater in New York was considered a crowning achievement (Londré and Watermeier, *American Theatre*, 182).

68. See p. 195 on Forest Flood's acting career. In 1886, Frances Folsom married President Cleveland while he was in the White House. In 1900, Olga Nethersole, an English actress popular on the American stage and noted for playing the role of the fallen woman, was arrested for starring in "Sappho," a play based on Alphonse Daudet's 1884 novel.

today by special invitation and spent the afternoon with her. Mrs. Cleveland had met Miss Nethersole on a former occasion and had been charmed with her personality.

Forest has been inexpressively busy, as Miss Nethersole's repertory contains various plays. This week they were in Baltimore. They rehearsed until 6 o'clock in the morning, and then Forest would sleep until 2 or 3 in the afternoon, then go to studying his "part" in other "plays" they were putting on, until time for the night performance. He scarcely had time for his meals.

One of my "Aldermen" from this ward visited Forest while he was in New York — said when he called Forest was hard at his studies, and that he studied all day and most of the night. This was the Saturday before the "Company" started on "tour" Monday morning — that was about the 19th of October. He said Forest was handsome, splendid looking and looked well. It was then 4 o'clock in the afternoon and he hadn't thought to even take a bit to eat. Forest is the youngest Actor in the Company and has to cope with old experienced Actors. I will close for this time. Love to all — write soon —

From the journal of Susan Machette Scott for 1896

January 9th Thurs.	Ladies to tea
16th	Ladies to tea....
April 9th	planted mushroom bed

From Anna Wilson Machette, wife of Samuel Machette, to Margaret Bruin Machette and Susan Machette Scott

Kansas City, Missouri
April 19, 1896

My dear Mother and Sister

I have several times longed to write you, but from some uncontrollable emotion I have failed, although my heart has often been with you. There has been times I had not control of my self. I dare not speak of my grief-stricken heart for it has been too full for utterance. Why this affliction [was] sent upon me without meaning I cannot understand. My dear husband came home on the 23 of last August with his left arm broken. [He had] dreamed that he was in a wreck, and jumped through an open window of a passenger car that he was in. He reached home the next day. For two months and a half he was confined to his room. With the best care and nursing I could give him he gained and was soon out again. I begged of him to give up traveling. He said he would when his year was up which would have been last December; he started out on another trip for a few days the last week in October. On Friday, November 1, [he] came home quite sick. On Monday the fourth day he commenced to sink and grow worse. I had Dr. Cloud, Arthur, Forrest and myself all day Monday and Monday night....[69] Cloud and Arthur had raised him a little to give him some beef tea. He had a coughing spell and strangled and passed away....

The dear departed one is buried in a beautiful lot where my Father [and] Mother lie. I have had a two hundred dollar monument erected. Edward Machette was with us

69. Arthur and Forrest Machette, sons of Samuel and Anna Wilson Machette.

ten or more days. I talked and reasoned with him to promise me that he would reform.[70] I have settled with him his share of his Father's estate which was a house and lot [and] five hundred in cash; it grieves me much to say that he is getting rid of it as fast as he can. How I would love to see *you* all and have a talk. Perhaps you could say one word of comfort to me. I am keeping house for my children. Maud and her husband and babe are here. We live within ourselves and our home is dear to us. God has made one vacant chair....

Think of me kindly for I will often cast a thought and live within the past of your own devoted daughter,

Anna Machette.

Edward Machette,
son of Samuel and Susan Jarboe Machette

June 16th   Clive, Harold & I went camping on the Auxvasse with [the] Watsons and Curds

29th   Got Pug dog

*From the journal of Susan
Machette Scott for 1896*

Another camping trip. Harvey Scott is standing in front of the outdoor fireplace with his son Harold in front of him and the camp cook standing immediately to his right. Sue Scott is to their right with a fan in front of her face (see inset).

70. Edward, the stepson of Anna Wilson Machette, apparently led a dissolute life. See December 31, 1888.

*From Alexander Machette to his
mother, Margaret Bruin Machette*

Fredericktown, Missouri
July 10, 1896

Dear Ma:

    Yours of the 7th came to hand this noon, also the two pairs of socks which you
were kind enough to knit and send me. I appreciate them more than I can tell you....

*From the journal of Susan
Machette Scott for 1896*

July   Harold made ice cream. Aunt Abbie sent him a lovely
            sailor suit [for his birthday]. He had books & a gun
            also.

*Clipping from the death and
consolation scrapbook of Susan
Machette Scott*

Will You Be There?

Beyond this life of hopes and fears,
Beyond this world of grief and tears,
    There is a region fair;
It knows no change and no decay—
No night but one unending day:
    Oh say, will you be there?

Its glorious gates are closed to sin,
Naught that defiles can enter in,
    To mar its beauty are;
Upon that bright, eternal shore,
Earth's bitter curse is known no more:
    Oh say, will you be there?

No drooping form, no tearful eye,
No hoary head, no weary sigh,
    No pain, no grief, no care;
But joys which mortals may not know,
Like a calm river ever flow:
    Oh say, will you be there?

Our Savior, once as mortal child—
As mortal man, by man reviled,
    There many crowns doth wear;
While thousand thousands swell the strain,
Of glory to the Lamb once slain:
    Oh say, will you be there?

Who shall be there? The lowly here,
All those who serve the Lord with fear,
    The world's proud mockery dare;
Who by the Holy Spirit led,

Rejoice the narrow way to tread—
    These, these shall all be there.

Those who have learned at Jesus' cross,
All earthly gain to count but loss,
    So that his love they share;
Who, gazing on the Crucified,
By faith can say, "for me he died"—
    These, these shall be there.

Will you be there? You shall, you must,
If, hating sin in Christ you trust;
    Who did that place prepare;
Still doth his voice sound sweetly, "Come,
I am the way, I'll lead you home:
    With me you shall be there."

A sentimental poem about death from Sue Scott's well-worn scrapbook on death and consolation, above right.

For the New York Observer.

ASLEEP.

Canst thou tell us, little sleeper,
  Whiter than the snow,
Of the glory that surrounds thee?
  We would know.

Tell us of the heavenly city,
  With its streets of gold,
Where His lambs the Shepherd gathers
  In the fold.

For the gate seems widely open,
  Where thou dwellest now,
And we see the pure light shining
  On thy brow.

Fare thee well, dear little sleeper,
  Hear our last good-night;
Thou hast conquered in the battle:
  We must fight.

May we live that when the summons
  Come for us to die,
We may meet thee in the cloudland
  By and by.

Richmond, Virginia
November 26, 1896

From Abigail Machette Hersman to her mother, Margaret Bruin Machette

My dear Mother:

… You can't think what a surprise we received yesterday in a letter from Mr. Colin McPheeters from Columbia, South Carolina.[71] He says he will spend the winter there and attend the seminary. He has had catarrhs for years — says his physician tells him that is all that is the matter with his eyes. He speaks of having his wife with him. Do you know who he married and did she have money? If she hadn't I expect the Judge would a little rather Colin hadn't married. Do they like her?

In the same mail we received another surprise: a letter from Mr. Dobyns stating that he had sent us two (2) barrels of apples. Don't you think it was nice of Mr. Dobyns to do this?[72] We shall certainly enjoy them as apples are very scarce and high.

71. Colin, son of Judge Robert McPheeters, the man who courted Abbie before her engagement to Charles Hersman. See January 14, 1861. Colin McPheeters, president of Fulton Female Synodical College from 1906 to 1909, married Laura Robinson in 1895.

72. The Reverend William Dobyns, husband of Mary Buckland Dobyns. See December 16, 1888.

Will Elwang and his daughter, Abbie Wanda. Abigail Wanda Elwang was named after her grandmother, Abigail Machette Hersman.

There is really very little really fine fruit in this part of Virginia.

I received a letter from Anne or rather the letter was addressed to Charley, not a great while since, in which she says that she is not willing to have Finley's body moved (in case we so wished) to *any* place but up to the family burying place on the Woodson farm.[73] And that she is unwilling to have his grave marked by a tombstone. I wrote to her that if Finley had left her a large fortune we would have thought it right, but when it came to his resting place or a monument over his grave, I wanted her to understand that his father and mother had something to say in the matter. She gave me to understand that *her* wishes alone were to be consulted. She is certainly a very queer woman.

You know, Ma, Finley's dear body was laid away in Dr. and Mrs. Hardaway's lot — such a beautiful spot.[74] I am going to write or have Charley to write to Dr. Hardaway not to allow any one to disturb this grave. We would not on any account allow his body to be moved to the Woodson farm. Finley felt no interest whatever in the Bates or Woodson families beyond Anne and Charlie.[75] I think he always had a very high regard for Charles Bates, but Ethel said that beyond that he did *not* admire or like the rest. He told her so when she visited him. They are queer people, with very queer ideas....

I have heard from Margaret a few days since. They were all well. Margaret is enjoying the new manse so much. She speaks of it being so nicely finished both inside and outside. Building is done very cheaply. I think she said this house cost about $2500, and she speaks of its having a really elegant appearance. I am so glad they are so nicely fixed. Mr. Elwang had every thing ready when Margaret and little Abbie Wanda got back.[76] He had several little surprises for her. He is certainly one of the kindest husbands I have ever known....

From George W. Cole to his mother-in-law, Margaret Bruin Machette

Denver, Colorado
December 1, 1896

My Dear Mother
... You said in your letter that it was hard for you to hear well. I have sent you a little trumpet. I think you can hear all right with [it]. Put the little tube in your ear and

---

73. Anne Bates Hersman's mother, Ellen, was a Woodson before her marriage.

74. Finley had been in practice with William Hardaway, a dermatologist in St. Louis.

75. Charles Bates, a St. Louis attorney. His sister, Anne Bates Hersman, joined his practice.

76. Margaret and Will Elwang's only child, Abigail Wanda, was born in 1892. The Elwangs settled in Columbia, Missouri, where Will Elwang was a Presbyterian minister.

hold your hand over it and leave the bottom holes so as the sound will catch. You can take your handkerchief and hold it in your hand [with] the trumpet inside, and nobody will suspect you have it. Keep trying with it until you get used to it and you will like it. Perhaps you can make it do all right at first.

Nealie is looking better than I ever saw her. I think if she keeps on she will be as fleshy as yourself. I have such a cold I cannot see the paper clearly. Send love to all.

Fredericktown, Missouri
December 5, 1896

From Alexander Machette to his mother, Margaret Bruin Machette[77]

Dear Ma,

Your last was received day before yesterday, and both very highly appreciated. I have a very good supply of socks now.[78] Aimee also remembered my birthday and sent me a supply of handkerchiefs, so that I am quite well off in that respect also.

We are now in the midst of a good meeting — commenced last Sunday. Brother James of Holden is assisting us. There were about a dozen [who] rose for prayer last night. We are expecting a good meeting and we very much need it. We have been very much favored in having good weather the past week. Our meeting will continue probably some two weeks yet.

Well, Etta and I have had another move. We are back at brother Graham's — some things don't suit us here altogether, but it is much better than being at the hotel we think. People boarding can't, of course, have everything to suit their convenience and ought not to expect it, I reckon.

I would love to see you all Christmas and Anna's family too, but I do not expect to be able to go anywhere this winter. I shall be very busy till my meeting closes. Remember me to all the family and accept much love for yourself.

Alex

December 7th   Jane Brooks — negro — came to cook
10th   made corduroy vest for Clive

From the journal of Susan Machette Scott for 1896

Fredericktown, Missouri
December 27, 1896

Papa died this morning at four o'clock and ten minutes.

Etta

Telegram from Henrietta Machette, daughter of Alexander Machette, to her uncle, John Harvey Scott

---

77. Margaret Machette had wrapped a note around this letter: "my precious Alex's last letter to me."
78. See Alex's letter of July 10, 1896.

From Aimee Machette Hall to her grandmother, Margaret Bruin Machette

Boonville, Missouri
January 3, 1897

My Precious Grandma:

Your letters to sisters Anna and Henrietta have both been received. And I feel ashamed when I think of how many days we have allowed to pass without writing you. But when I tell you — Henrietta is *very* ill and sister Anna and I have both hardly been able to be *up* — I am sure you will forgive this seeming neglect.

Photo of Alexander Machette, son of C.C. and Margaret Bruin Machette

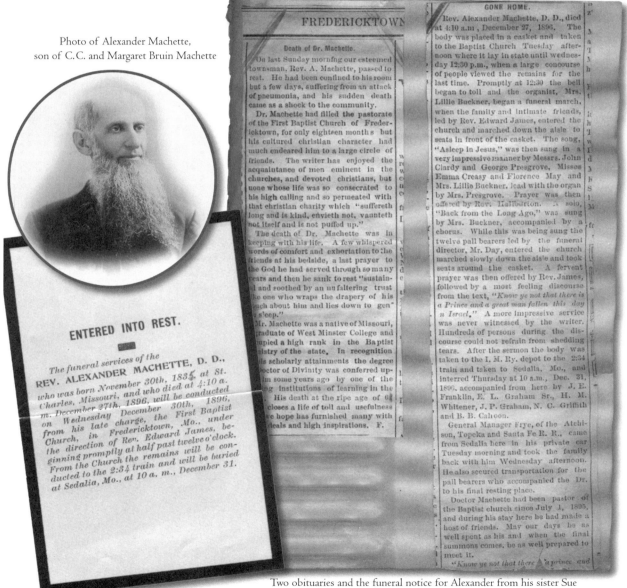

Two obituaries and the funeral notice for Alexander from his sister Sue Scott's scrapbook on death and consolation. Probably Alexander's sister or mother corrected his birth date to 1835 rather than 1834 on his funeral notice, above left.

Henrietta would be in Fredericktown today, had it not been for *Mr. Frey*. He went down with his special car and brought her (Henrietta) up here, where she is having the attention of a *good doctor*, who we hope will soon have her case under control. She has catarrh fever, a dreadful cough with other complications. She says [to] tell you she will write you as soon as she is able to hold a pen. And [she] wants to go to *see* you when she is up. She has not been able to *talk* much — so there is but little I can tell you of dear Papa's last days. He was conscious most of the time and knew from the *first* he was soon to depart. But seeing it hurt and frightened "Etta," I think he refrained from talking of it as much as he would have liked.

You know he was only ill one week. And though I started to him the very day I heard he was not well, I had hardly reached Colorado, before I received the sad tidings of his death. That was one *long* week ago this a.m. I felt from the first he would not recover — but did have the *hope* of seeing him *once more*. And when that was taken from me, I felt it was *more* than I could endure. Mr. and Mrs. Frey met me in Kansas City and took me the rest of the trip, or I am sure I do not know what would have become of me. Mr. Hall started from New Mexico the night following. Sister Anna and her husband also arrived in Fredericktown a little *too late*.

Papa passed away just as he had always wanted — with sword in hand. He and Rev. Edward James were in the midst of a good meeting. There had been great interest and about thirty-five conversions up to the day of Papa's illness. In his last moments, he saw Mama and our loved ones there and talked with them. And he was *so happy* and *rejoiced to go*. The friends who were with him told me. He knew I had *started* to him — and he told them he would love to live till I could come. But they could not save him, even that long. They say he left no messages for any of us, except "Etta" — but called all of our names. The *services* in Fredericktown were beautiful, also in Sedalia....

I will be here till Etta is better. And if the weather does not get too bad, and nothing else prevents, I will try and *see you*, if only for one day before I go back to New Mexico.

Little [Lillian] Claude and all the rest join me in *much* love for our dear Grandma.[79]

Boonville, Missouri
January 13, 1897

From Aimee Machette Hall to her grandmother, Margaret Bruin Machette

My Precious Grandma:

... I am glad to report Henrietta [is] improving, though her trouble — catarrh of the bowels — is one that we cannot expect sudden changes for the better, as it is something very hard to conquer. She passes quantities of blood and mucus, and her nourishment consists *only* of boiled milk, so you can imagine she is kept very weak. Her fever is all gone, and she is not nearly so nervous. She has allowed this bowel trouble to run on since last September which seems very strange for a girl of her age and understanding. But the doctors in Fredericktown did not impress her as being particularly up-to-date, and besides she disliked to have Papa worried about her condition, so she kept it to herself....

Yes, Grandma, *most* of our family has passed over to the other side. How much nearer and dearer it makes heaven to us who remain. I wish dear uncle Jacob [Shelton] could have been with us in Sedalia. Papa was very fond of him. And he was such a

79. Lillian Claude Edgar, daughter of Anna Machette Edgar.

comfort to Papa at the time of Mama's death. You know he was in Sedalia at that time and remained a few days with Papa.... Love to aunt Susie and family *and* dear Grandma in which *all join* me —

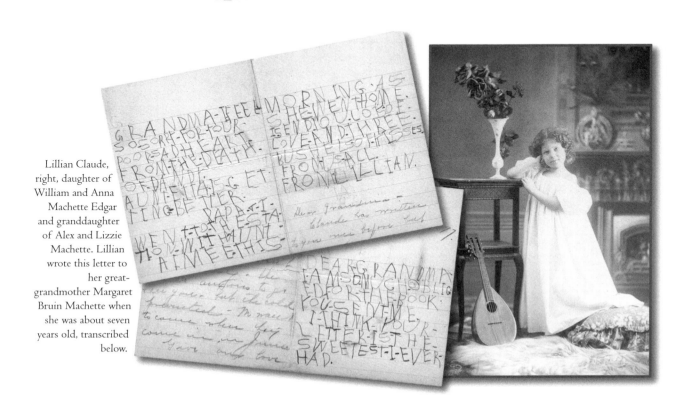

Lillian Claude, right, daughter of William and Anna Machette Edgar and granddaughter of Alex and Lizzie Machette. Lillian wrote this letter to her great-grandmother Margaret Bruin Machette when she was about seven years old, transcribed below.

From Lillian Claude Edgar, granddaughter of Alexander Machette, to Margaret Bruin Machette

Concordia, Missouri
January 28, 1897

Dear Grandma

I am so much obliged for the book you sent me. I think your letter is the sweetest I ever had.

Grandma I feel so sorry for your poor sad heart from the death of Dandy.

Aunt Etta is getting better.

Papa and I went to the station with aunt aimee this morning as she went home. I send you lots of love and three bushels of kisses from all.

From Cornelia Machette Flood Cole to her mother, Margaret Bruin Machette

Denver, Colorado
February 21, 1897

My dear Mother: —

This is Sunday and I drop you a few lines to tell you of dear Forest's marriage. He married the 11th of this month in New York City — she, his wife, is said to be a

226

charming, sensible girl of 19 years of age, and she and Forest love each other to distraction. She is of German ancestry — the great-grandfather was a German baron. Forest dear is doing splendid. The "Press" of all the cities speak of him in the most complimentary terms. I received a letter from a friend in New York and he said that Forest was the finest looking man on the "stage," that when he entered he looked like he had just stepped down from a picture.

His wife's name was "Ethelyn Fuhrmann" and may God bless them always. This leaves us nicely. Some snow but not cold. I sent you $5.00 on your birthday which I hope you received. Don't be uneasy about your having your own little money — as long as I have any, you have part of it....

Forest and Ethelyn Fuhrmann Flood. Ethelyn sometimes acted on the stage with her husband.

March	A negro — Jane — and Pearle worked for us — no account	*From the journal of Susan Machette Scott for 1897*
30th Tues.	Harold sprained ankle	

April 3rd 1897. I got this book out of Edgar's satchel where it had been ever since he put it there, Oct. 1882.[80]

Written by Susan Machette Scott in Edgar Scott's textbook

1897 July 26. My dear Nealia left Fulton this morning for her home in Denver, Colorado.

Written by Susan Machette Scott on a scrap of paper

Oct.	Chrysanthemums in bloom	*From the journal of Susan Machette Scott for 1897*
Nov. 13th	had "afternoon" — 18 friends came	

80. Sue covered the book in paisley fabric as she did four other textbooks belonging to Edgar, and she kept them all in his woven satchel. She also made a paisley bag for Edgar's marbles. (See illustration on next page.)

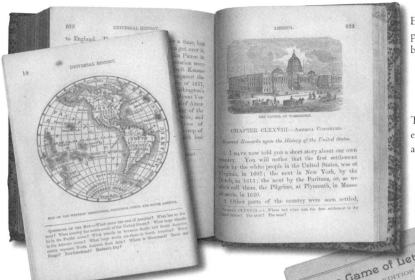

Edgar Scott's *Peter Parley's Universal History*, published in 1873, was found undisturbed by his mother fifteen years after his death.

The Scott children played this Salem edition of "The Game of Letters," below, an early game by Parker Brothers.

From Cornelia Machette Flood Cole to her mother, Margaret Bruin Machette

Denver, Colorado
December 2, 1897

My dear Mother: —

Well, I write to tell you that I am a grand ma — and I feel about 10 years younger. The dispatch was as follows — "Dear Grandma and Grandpa, I weigh 8 pounds, arrived at three this morning, feel very sleepy, Mama is doing well, Papa walks around like a prince and won't let me sleep. Cornelia Machette Flood."

This leaves us nicely. Our weather is bitter cold with snow. O isn't it nice for you to live to be a great-grandmother to my darling boy's child? God bless the dear children and their lovely babe. How sweet to name it after me, wasn't it? I only drop these lines to let you know of our dear baby's arrival. Dearest love to each and all.

Written by Margaret Bruin Machette on a piece of paper[81]

Henrietta Machette came to Fulton the 31st of January 98 to make me a visit. Remained two days and returned to Montgomery City.

81. This appears on the reverse side of the note Margaret wrote about receiving Alex's last letter. See the footnote for December 5, 1896.

March 8th   made garden. Sweet peas, lettuce & radish
  15th   Harold takes vocal lessons
  31st   Flower show will meet here

*From the journal of Susan
Machette Scott for 1898*

Denver, Colorado
April 11, 1898

*From Cornelia Machette Flood
Cole to Margaret Bruin Machette
and Harold Hersman Scott*

Dear Ma and Harold

Your sweet letters received in due time and I was so glad to get them. I think your letter, Harold, delightful and that both you and your teacher deserve great praise. Forest saw it and said I must be sure and write to you. I wish you all could see the baby. She is too pretty, cute and good for any thing — her little form is perfect. She has your flesh, short neck, and hands. Ma, she is a very fat baby — weighs 15 ½ pounds, is 2 feet tall.

Forest dear is in the mountains recuperating — has some mining interests he is looking after, more for his health than any thing else.[82] He came home Sunday too sunburnt for any thing but looking much better but very tired. Ethelyn sends much love and told the baby to do so too. It is raining hard here to night — our weather has tried itself since Forest and family came.

We do so love to have them with us. They are such a lovely family. You would love Ethelyn and her babe I know. Mr. Cole is terribly pleased with them. He nurses the babe and she likes him too. She is so smart and amiable, sleeps so much — we never hear of her after she goes to sleep early in the evening until next morning at breakfast. Ethelyn is so very neat with her too.

Forest was talking the other day of what a fine fellow Clive was.[83] Well, I will close for to night, dearest, but love from us all to each of you. The children appreciated you wishing to see their dear Ma. Tell your teacher, Harold, to make you write often to your Auntie. Write soon —

Affectionately Nealie

Here is $5 for you, Ma.

Cornelia Machette Flood, daughter of Forest and Ethelyn Fuhrmann Flood, granddaughter of John (deceased) and Cornelia Machette Flood Cole, and stepgranddaughter of George Cole. This photo was sent to Margaret Machette. On the back of the photo, grandmother Nealie wrote, "To my dear Great grandmother, With much love, Cornelia Machette Flood. April 18th 1898."

82. Forest Flood contracted tuberculosis, the same disease that killed his father. He would die in 1906.

83. Clive Scott was a student at Westminster College; Forest Flood briefly attended Westminster.

*From Cornelia Machette Flood
Cole to Margaret Bruin Machette
and Susan Machette Scott*

Denver, Colorado
May 16, 1898

Dear Ma and Sue: —

... Our dear Cornelia has two lovely little teeth, lower ones. She looks too cute for any thing. She is so very fat and white and lovely — fat like you said Clive was when he was a baby, I guess. Ethelyn says she intends writing soon. Forest dear is at Idaho Springs, was down Sabbath, is feeling better of the grippe.[84] There is considerable grippe around now.

There is much excitement here over the "war."[85] A good many of the town boys left today for the front. Poor fellows, much experience they will have before they ever return. I hate the "war" — had plenty of it during the Civil War. No wonder it makes you nervous, Ma.

Our garden is coming on nicely. There was a good deal of hail near here today but we escaped. The lilacs will soon be in bloom and later the snow balls....

Wednesday morning.... It was a thousand men Denver sent yesterday to the "war." They went to San Francisco to go to the Philippine Islands. Forest says if he was a single man he would go, and Mr. Cole says if he had his good hands he would too....

*From the journal of Susan
Machette Scott for 1898*

November 18   Henrietta died 3:30 a.m. Alex's youngest daughter.
New Mexico.

*From Abigail Machette Hersman
to her mother, Margaret Bruin
Machette*

Richmond, Virginia
February 12, 1899

My dear Mother:

I believe this is your birthday — is it not? How much I should love to see you and give my dear Mother a hearty kiss and assure you of my deep affection for the dearest Mother in this world.

... I think Mr. Elwang and Margaret are quite pleased with Columbia. I am sure when they get their furniture and go to housekeeping they will be much more comfortable. Margaret said she was invited to dine with the Hockadays Thursday, in honor of Mr. and Mrs. Sneed from St. Louis.[86] Mr. Elwang and Mr. Sneed will exchange pulpits next Sabbath.

I want so much to come and see all the dear ones once more, and will certainly try to do so when Margaret gets to housekeeping. Margaret said Abbie Wanda was not at school the day she wrote. The weather was so cold. I do hope she will be careful with

84. Grippe or influenza.

85. In 1898, the Spanish-American War broke out when the United States battleship USS *Maine* was blown up, killing and injuring several hundred Marines. As a result of the war, Spain granted independence to Cuba and ceded the Philippines, Guam, and Puerto Rico to the United States.

86. Frank Sneed, minister of the Washington and Compton Avenue Presbyterian Church in St. Louis, was married to Eulalie Hockaday, niece of John A. Hockaday. Eulalie's parents, Irvine and Laura Hockaday, were prominent citizens in Columbia where the Elwangs lived.

the little thing. Ma, I know you thought Abbie Wanda a remarkable child — she has such a sweet disposition. Did you notice what sweet table manners she has? However hungry she is, she is always willing to have every body helped first....

I hope you received the money I sent you last week. Take good care of your dear self. Much love to all the dear ones and accept a large share for your own dear self. Charley and Ethel send love.

March	Ma took sick on 24th
27	We got new sewing machine
June 1st	Clive graduated [from Westminster College]
	Canterbury bells & sweet peas bloom
July 13th	Ma had a fall
17th	Abbie came & left 24th

From the journal of Susan Machette Scott for 1899

Harold Hersman Scott wrote this letter to his mother while visiting his father's family in Monroe County Missouri, transcribed below.

Harold Scott on the left with one of his friends

Milton, Missouri
August 8, 1899

From Harold Scott to his mother, Susan Machette Scott

Dear mama —

Papa and I had a nice ride on the Chicago and Alton. We had to wate about an hour and a half at Mexico where we ate our dinner. We then got on the wabash a little before we got to Moberly we got to hot and papa almost got the headache when we got to the depot and got off the train we looked around two are three minutes before we found Joe.[87] papa wanted to go to the post office and Joe took me around to a drug store and gave me an ice cream soda. We then went to the wagon which was a good way off. We had a nice ride out to Joes. I have got a sty coming on my eye. I am now going out to Milton to mail this letter.

Good-bye Mamma

Harold H Scott

From the journal of Susan
Machette Scott for 1899

Aug. 10–12	Cousin Jake Shelton and Jane came....
Sept. 4th	sold the cow....
16th	Margaret came
26th	Clive went to St. Louis[88]
Oct. 12	Margaret left
Nov.	we were paying Becky $5.00 a month

From Clive Scott to his mother,
Susan Machette Scott

St. Louis, Missouri
November 12, 1899

My Dear Mother, —

Well, Sunday night has rolled around again, and I believe I will tell you of the week's doing, though they have not been many or exciting.... Since beginning human dissection, we have had a few hours added onto our course (making it now 30 per week) and three days in the week find me "at it" until 6 p.m....

Tonight I attended the Second Baptist. There was a man there who was setting forth the virtues of a southern school for Negroes, and in furtherance of his object he brought with him a Negro quartet. They sang some of the sweetest negro melodies that I ever heard — "Swing Low, Sweet Chariot" and others. They were all so quaint and sung by negroes of the old school with that subtle touch and sympathy that only a negro can put into a song. I think it was as sweet music as I ever listened to....

I did not go to the Grand Opera, but I could not resist hearing Mansfield in "Cyrano."[89] It cost me .50 (gallery), but to hear an actor like Mansfield one might spend a great deal more and then not be the loser. Never before have I seen such acting. His is a wonderful genius truly. The last act of "Cyrano" as Mansfield renders it is a thing that once seen will not be soon forgotten....

I suppose the recent visit of Miss Gould to Fulton has set the people to speculating quite a good deal in regard to future possibilities.[90] Well, whatever may be the outcome,

---

87. After Joe Scott, Harvey's brother, graduated from Westminster, he returned to Monroe County where he was a farmer and attorney. He served in the Missouri legislature from 1890 to 1894.

88. Clive was a medical student at Washington University in St. Louis.

89. Richard Mansfield, acclaimed actor, noted for playing Cyrano de Bergerac, Beau Brummell, and Dr. Jekyll and Mr. Hyde. Edmond Rostand wrote *Cyrano de Bergerac* (1897).

90. Helen Gould, philanthropist and daughter of Jay Gould, the American financier who was the basis for F. Scott Fitzgerald's Gatsby; Helen was in Fulton visiting John MacCracken, the new president of Westminster College. Gould bought up many of the railroads in the United States, including railroads in Missouri. V. V. Masterson, *The Katy Railroad and the Last Frontier* (Norman: University of Oklahoma Press, 1952), 214–217.

the fact that she visited Westminster seems a token, if not of good, at least not of evil.... Am very sorry to hear that Grand Ma is progressing so slowly.

———

St. Louis, Missouri
February 6, 1900

From Clive Scott to his mother,
Susan Machette Scott

My dear Mother —

I suppose that you have read in the papers of the big fire we had here Sunday p.m.... The first I heard of it was at dinner. When dinner was over, five or six of us from the house went down to see it. We took the Washington Avenue car and long before we reached Jefferson we saw the smoke enveloping that whole quarter of the city. When we reached 8th Street, we struck the first of the fire engines. A general alarm had been turned in and between 25 and 30 engines were on the scene. At every corner we found puffing and panting engines, spitting fire and smoke. The streets for blocks and blocks were packed with people.

We gained access to the roof of a 7-story building and had an excellent view. While there we saw a large wholesale seed store in the next block burn. You could see the flames shooting away up through the collapsed roof. The firemen were on the roofs of neighboring houses with their hoses, and reaching high up into the air was an enormous hose supported on a framework pouring water into the fifth story. It was a foggy day and the smoke came down so that one could see only when a gust of wind came and blew it away a little. We watched it for about 3 hours and came home dirty with soot and smoke and shoes soaked with the water which ran through the streets.

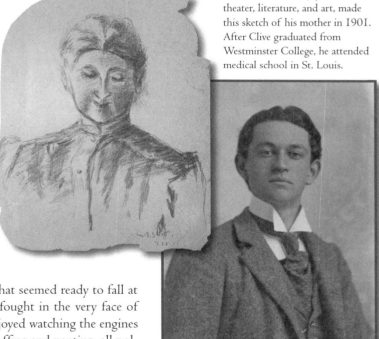

Clive Scott, who enjoyed music, theater, literature, and art, made this sketch of his mother in 1901. After Clive graduated from Westminster College, he attended medical school in St. Louis.

I never before realized how much courage a city fireman needs. I saw a cluster of men standing on a roof at the foot of a wall that seemed ready to fall at any moment. Yet they held their ground and fought in the very face of death until ordered down by their chief.[91] I enjoyed watching the engines very much — to see them at the water plug, puffing and panting, all polished and shining in brass and nickel. Every now and then a fresh fire would break out, and away some of them would go down the street in search of it, clattering over the cobbles with clanging bells, at full gallop....

Have made good progress in my studies. At one exam in anatomy this a.m. I scored 100 so far as I can judge.... Money came O.K.

———

91. The *St. Louis Republic* for February 5, 1900, reported that one firefighter was killed and eleven were injured.

From Charles Campbell Hersman to his mother-in-law, Margaret Bruin Machette

Richmond, Virginia
February 19, 1900

My dear Mother:

I am sorry to hear that you are confined to your bed. I have thought much of you since we left Fulton, and much of you lately. I would like to see you today in your room.

I remember how you have denied yourself for the sake of your children, and surely you were ever a kind and careful mother to your children, and it must afford you great pleasure and satisfaction to look back on a life that has been so unselfish as yours has been. I remember how kind you were always to my children when they were little tots, and especially your devotion to dear Finley, who has crossed over on the other shore and now waits to welcome us. I have only to regret that I was not more kind and thoughtful of your comfort.

I am glad to learn that you are so cheerful: this is right. You are soon to end your race here and enter into the joys of the kingdom on high. You have nothing to regret and nothing to fear, united to the Saviour, as you have been these many years. There is a home not made with hands, eternal in the heavens for those who love the Lord and who wait for His appearing.[92] You remember what Christ says in the 14th chapter of John: "In my Father's house are many mansions; if it were not so, I would have told you; for I go to prepare a place for you. And if I go and prepare a place for you, I will come again, and receive you unto myself; that where I am, there ye may be also." Paul, in 2 Corinthians, Chapter 5: "For we know if the earthly house of our tabernacle be dissolved, we have a building of God, a house not made with hands, eternal in the heavens."[93] Neither you nor I have had a home for many years here on earth, but we hope to have one forever in glory....

Now, Ma, if you want any thing at any time be sure to let me know. Do not trouble yourself about any thing, but cast all your cares on Him who careth for His own. May God bless, keep you, and comfort you with the sense of His presence and His unfailing love....

Charles Hersman,
husband of Abigail Machette

From the small scrapbook of Susan Machette Scott and dated March 1, 1900

Recipe for 1 gallon wash for cloth

Boil 3 oz. Castile soap in 1 quart of water till dissolved, then add

3 qts. of soft water	3 oz. Alcohol
3 oz. Ammonia	2 oz. Glycerin
3 oz. Ether	

Shake & it is ready for use.

Sallie Tureman gave me this recipe — it came from California.[94]

---

92. "Who love the Lord and wait for His appearing," a Christian article of faith in the Second Coming; based on 2 Timothy 4:8: "Henceforth there is laid up for me a crown of righteousness, which the Lord, the righteous judge, shall give me at that day: and not to me only, but unto all them also that love his appearing."

93. When Charlie first referred to 2 Corinthians, he used the word *home* rather than *house* used in the King James Version.

94. Sallie Flood Tureman, Nealie's sister-in-law, died in 1890. See August 26, 1870, and August 31, 1873.

March 26th Mon.   made garden
April 5 & 6   cleaned Ma's room, dining [room] & bed room
16   Asparagus up....
Aug. 1st   Harold had company to dinner
6th   began lace collar — finished 20th

From the journal of Susan
Machette Scott for 1900

Denver, Colorado
October 8, 1900

From Cornelia Machette Flood
Cole to Margaret Bruin Machette
and Susan Machette Scott

Dear Ma and Sue: —

... Last week Forest and Ethelyn played at one of the theaters here and Forest was just grand. But he took cold, the "grippe." Every one has it and came near pneumonia. I guess Clive is at St. Louis by now. Hope he will keep well.

Politics is running high here as every where, I suppose, when "Roosevelt" campaigned [in] the state. He met with a warm reception at Victor — people seemed to regret it out here the way he was treated up there.[95] I care nothing about politics any way. One party seems so like [the] other when they get the power. Well, good bye for now. Love to all. Write soon.

Fordyce P. Cleaves and Forest Flood founded
the Cleaves-Flood School of Expression and
Dramatic Arts in Denver.

Denver, Colorado
October 31, 1900

From Cornelia Machette Flood
Cole to Margaret Bruin Machette
and Susan Machette Scott

Dear Ma and Sue: —

... Forest and Ethelyn are out on the "road" now, in a play entitled *A Man of Mystery*. Forest is the leading man and fine. I don't know how long they expect to be gone. May be back at just any time. Did Brother receive a catalogue of a dramatic school here? It is where Forest is one of the "faculty" and has a good picture of him in it with a little sketch of his life — he is considered a very fine teacher.... Last night was Halloween night — but such a stormy, snowy night the frolickers could not do much mischief. We usually have our gate run off with but last night put it away our selves....

95. The Spanish-American War catapulted Theodore Roosevelt, the leader of the Rough Riders, to national prominence. He became governor of New York in 1899, and in 1900 he ran as the vice presidential candidate on President McKinley's ticket. While on the campaign trail, he was attacked by ruffians in Colorado. The *St. Louis Republic* for September 27, 1900, reported on his escape from injury: "Rough Riders Surround Him and He Safely Regains His Train." The following year when McKinley was assassinated, Roosevelt became President.

From Abigail Machette Hersman to her mother, Margaret Bruin Machette

Richmond, Virginia
November 16, 1900

My dear Mother:

... I was sorry to know you were not feeling so well. I hope as time passes you may even get able to get about again. But let us try to be reconciled to God's will, whatever it may be. He knows what is for our best interests, both for this world and that which is to come. I feel so thankful you do not have to suffer much pain.

In Margaret's last letter she said she had received a letter from Mary Dobyns. She gave Margaret some account of poor Mrs. Dobyns's condition. Poor woman! she grows worse all the time. Mary says she doesn't know any one and can scarcely say any thing. When one thinks of what a bright woman she once was, her condition seems indeed pitiable. Mary said Will had gone down to see Joe about what it would be best to do. I think Joe Dobyns is about too mean to live.[96]

... Ethel sends much love to dear Grand *Ma*! She is not very well today, only a little head ache. Do you often hear from Jane [Shelton] now? I should love dearly to see her. It has been many years since I saw her and yet I remember her so well. Jake and Jane must feel very lonely at times now that their children are all pretty much settled down in houses of their own. Have they any single daughters now?...

From the journal of Susan Machette Scott for 1901

Jan. 2	Clive went to St. Louis
March 22nd	planted potatoes
April 26th	Clive came home
May 2	Clive's shirts cut out
June 11th	Clive went camping. Came back 18th
25	Becky took sick, died July 14[97]
July	Martha washed 3rd and 17th
22 Mon.	Betty came[98]

A picture taken in the early 1900s of Betty, who worked for the Scotts

96. Elizabeth Dobyns, the widow of Major Edward Dobyns (d. 1885), lived with Will and Mary Buckland Dobyns. Joe, her son, was an attorney in St. Louis. Her March 29, 1901, obituary in the *Fulton Telegraph* stated, "She had been failing for months, not being able to take solid food and for weeks she had been suffering with symptoms of grip...."

97. Becky, a woman who worked for Sue; see Sue's journal entry for November 1899 (p. 232).

98. After Becky died, Sue Scott hired Betty, who would work for the Scotts for years. Betty was probably Betty Miller. Census records indicate that Betty Miller was single and could neither read nor write. Born in Missouri in 1849, she could have been a slave before the Civil War.

Denver, Colorado
July 1901

From Cornelia Machette Flood Cole to Margaret Bruin Machette and Susan Machette Scott

Dear Ma and Sue:

... This leaves us as usual and enjoying (?) the warmest weather they say Colorado has known for over 40 years, certainly the hottest since ever I came west — and still keeping it up.[99] Forest has been playing out at "Elitch Gardens," the swell resort here, now for 6 weeks. He is thin and very tired, but not withstanding his health is some better than for some time — still far from well. Forest has signed for work with "Blanche Walsh" for next season and has been playing with her at the "Gardens" and is still. He goes to New York City the 11th of August to begin rehearsing with her company in *Joan of the Sword Hand*, her new play for next season. Miss Walsh saw Forest in *The Little Minister* at the Gardens when she first came and she was dead struck with his work and engaged him at once for her play the coming season. Miss Walsh is America's finest "tragedienne" and to be judged favorably by her is great....[100]

St. Louis, Missouri
November 24, 1901

From Clive Scott to his father, John Harvey Scott

My dear Father —

... You remember I said that Dr. Hardaway invited me to assist him; well I went to see him a few days afterward, and after explaining the work and the electrical apparatus, he incidentally mentioned that "the compensation would be from $1.50 to $2.00 per forty-five minutes"![101] You may imagine my surprise at learning that he was going to pay me for the work that I would be only too glad to do gratis, for the experience. The idea of money had not occurred to me. I explained this to him, and he said that he would not think of taking my work without paying me. This is my first chance to earn money for myself, and you may imagine the gratification it gives me....

I have been practicing every day with the "electric needle" and am getting quite proficient in its use, I think. You see, if I do not get more than one work week, I will be making eight or nine dollars a month.... Furthermore, the Doctor has decided to let me do his chemical analysis (urinalysis) for him. This, he says, will take a great load off him, besides giving me invaluable practice. He is going to arrange to give me access to the laboratory of the "Polio clinic."[102]

Dr. William Hardaway, a leading dermatologist, invited Clive Scott to work with him.

99. States in the West and as far east as Missouri were suffering a drought. June 1901 was the hottest June in Missouri in thirty years. Rain broke the drought in late July. *St. Louis Republic* (July 2 and 28, 1901).

100. Blanche Walsh performed such roles as Queen Elizabeth and Cleopatra. *Joan of the Sword Hand* (1900), by Samuel Rutherford Crockett; *The Little Minister* (1891), by James Matthew Barrie, the author of the Peter Pan stories.

101. Finley Hersman had been in practice with William Hardaway. See November 26, 1896. In a letter not included in the collection, Clive used the term "electrolysis" to describe this medical work. Dr. Charles Michel of St. Louis invented electrolysis to remove unwanted hair, and he first reported on its use in 1875 in a journal edited by William Hardaway. Dr. Hardaway was one of the first users of the instrument and wrote about it himself. Dr. Michel worked until 1907, so Clive likely knew him. Gordon Blackwell, "The 100th Year of Electrolysis and the Triumph of Dr. Michel (1833–1913)," *Electrolysis Digest* (April 1975): 23–42.

102. The first large polio epidemic in the United States occurred in Vermont in 1894; the virus that caused poliomyelitis was not discovered until 1908. Tony Gould, *A Summer Plague: Polio and Its Survivors* (New Haven: Yale University Press, 1995), 13; John R. Paul, *A History of Poliomyelitis* (New Haven: Yale University Press, 1971), 79.

This is an excellently appointed lab with all necessary instruments and will be fine experience....

We had a written exam in medicine two weeks ago and I am glad to say that I am one of the two or three that obtained the grade of 9. (Dr. Baumgarten, by the way, never gives higher than 9, as he says no one is quite ever perfect.) The exam was on Pneumonia, and there was not a blue mark on my paper....

From the journal of Susan Machette Scott for 1901 and 1902

Dec.	Clive came home the 21st
January 6th	finished rags for rug
20th Mon.	sent Clive [his] pants

From Abigail Machette Hersman to Margaret Bruin Machette and Susan Machette Scott

Ethel, the daughter of Charley and Abbie Hersman

Richmond, Virginia
January 19, 1902

My dear Mother and Sister:

... I asked Ethel this evening if she didn't wish we had plenty of money and did not have to consider expense and could get ready to go to Missouri to visit the dear ones there? She thought of course it would be ever so nice....

Susie, I wish you would ask Brother Harvey to find out what Mrs. Little would ask for the old home. I sometimes think I would like to come back to old Missouri when we make a change. I have no doubt the old Lady would ask a big price unless the old house should burn down. If Charley should be taken from me, I do not think I should like to remain in Virginia. I should love to come to the old house; Charley and I often talk it over, and he feels just as I do about it.[103] Tell Brother Harvey if he ever hears of a nice little piece of property selling *cheap* to let us know about it. I often think if I had my own living to make and had a nice little house of my own I could do better at taking boarders than any thing else....

From Abigail Machette Hersman to Margaret Bruin Machette and Susan Machette Scott

Richmond, Virginia
February 16, 1902

My dear Mother and Sister:

I wrote to you a few days ago and sent Ma a bundle. Please do not fail to write me at your earliest convenience and tell me if the bundle arrived. In the bundle was a

---

103. The Hersmans would never move back to Fulton. Fannie Little owned the house the Hersmans built in the summer of 1876. In 1913, after Fannie Little had died, Sue Scott wrote her son Clive, "I wish you could be here, right now — looking out of the front window and you would see Uncle Charley's old house — the front half in the street. They are taking it down near the creek for the negroes. They sawed it across the dining room and second north room. Wasn't it odd they should have left it in front of us Saturday evening — to stay till Monday — like it was telling us good-bye. How many sweet memories it awakens, of dear ones gone and distant. Just facing me is the dining room — it used to be Grandma's room and I can see where her bed used to be and her bureau &c., and the wardrobe built in the wall of the girls' room. Then a door is open letting me see into the study, &c."

dressing sacque and a cake of fine toilet (violet) soap for Ma. I believe I addressed the bundle to Brother Harvey.

I do hope Ma will find the sacque comfortable. I thought when she sat up in bed, it might prove a comfort. Bless my dear old Mother. I thought of you on your "birth day" and how much you always did for the comfort of others when they were sick and needed to be cared for.

… Sue, write to me soon and let me know how you all are getting on by this time. I love to have you tell me about dear Clive: how it reminds me of my own dear Finley. Several years have gone now since we laid him away — *his dear body I mean*. Thanks be to our dear Lord — his blessed spirit I trust is now one of that happy throng who are ever singing praises around the great white throne.

Dear Mother, I sometimes think that you may be the first to greet those dear ones on that radiant shore. Alex, Finley, and dear precious Edgar! *all loved you so much* — I cannot but think that the recognition of the loved ones who have gone before will be *one of the joys* of Heaven.…

March 6th Thurs.	Cousin Jane Shelton died	*From the journal of Susan Machette Scott for 1902*
10th Mon.	made garden	
April 3rd Thurs.	sent Clive's shirts	
25th	cleaned Ma's room	
26th Sat.	spring holiday	
May 22	put down carpet in Library	
23rd Fri.	wash curtains	
August 5th Tues.	Harold taken sick, appendicitis	
6th Wed.	Dr. Baker performed operation[104]	
September 8th Mon.	Harold out of bed [for the] first time	

Denver, Colorado
October 28, 1902

Dear Ma and Sue: —

… I am so sorry, dear Ma, you have been so sick — how I trust you are better now. The Lord's dear restful arms are underneath you always — that is our comfort whether in sickness or health, isn't it, dear Mother? I hope Harold is well now — youth pulls back quickly. Forest has started on the road again — went out from New York Thursday. Mr. Cole sends love, dear Ma. He brought some such nice cabbage from the ranch the last time he visited his nephew. Well, I will close — wish dearest love to all and especially to my mother dear. Write soon.

From Cornelia Machette Flood Cole to Margaret Bruin Machette and Susan Machette Scott

104. Noah Baker, a local physician who had served in the Confederate army.

From the journal of Susan
Machette Scott for October
1902

25th Saturday   Ma was taken sick
29th Wednesday   Ma died 15 minutes to 7:00. 6:45
        30th   Ma was buried. Clive came

From Aimee Machette Hall to her
aunt, Susan Machette Scott

Albuquerque, New Mexico
October 30, 1902

My Dear Aunt Sue:

Uncle Scott's message, telling us of dear Grandma's death, has been received. It was good of him to wire us. Notwithstanding Grandma's age and poor health, the announcement came as a shock to us. Thoughts of her had been running through my mind for days — and I had begun a letter to her — when the news came.

You, Aunt Sue, who have had the care of her, will miss her most. And you have the love and sympathy of one who knows a little of how empty your hands and heart now seem. *I* cannot think of Grandma as dead. Those who know her soul, in its passage through nature into eternity, know that its *life* has just begun. She had long been ready for the change. And the knowledge of her happiness complete should reconcile us.

Please thank Uncle Scott for the telegram. I hope you are very well, and would be so glad to hear from you and family.

Margaret Bruin Machette
with the black, gold, and
silver mourning card used
at her death

From Abigail Machette Hersman
to her sister, Susan Machette Scott

Richmond, Virginia
October 31, 1902

My dear Sister:

How sad I am today over our dear Mother's departure. You, my dear Sister, from your own experience can well imagine — *dear old Mother*: God grant that when the time comes for our departure from earthly things, we may be as well prepared as I fully realize that she must have been. Dear Mother! in imagination I fancy you now, among that great throng before our Father's great white throne singing praise to His most Holy name. *Dear, dear* Mother! it is there I hope next to meet you.

I have so often thought of her as she looked when I last parted with her. I bade her "good by" as she lay there, and when I reached the door I took another look at her, and she looked at me with such a longing, tender look that I went back to her again and kissed her and then left her, never to look upon her face again in my life. My heart is wrung with anguish when I think of the many things I might have done for her happiness, which I sadly neglected to do. She was a good and noble Mother: unselfish in every thing she ever did; thinking not of herself, but always of others. God grant her a happy reunion with the dear ones who have so long since gone to their Heavenly Home.

Susie, while I think of it, please look in the left end of Ma's trunk and there you will find Ma's pocket-book with thirty dollars in it. She told me about it and made me go and get it out and count it. She said Alex had given it to her at different times, and as [she had] the money we sent her (and others), she had always had enough to get things she wanted, and she saved this to help defray expenses when she was buried. I did not ask her if she had told any one else. She seemed to want to tell me all about her things. She made me get out her clothes, too — the ones she wished to be buried in. I hope to hear from you soon. I can't write more now.

Affectionately

Abbie

Excuse my short letter — I am feeling quite unwell and hope to write again soon.

Clive, left, and his younger brother Harold, below, at age fourteen, sons of John Harvey and Susan Machette Scott

November 4th	Clive returned to St. Louis
16th Sun.	no church — fixing organ & furnace
30th	Harold joined the church
Dec. 20th	Clive came home

From the journal of Susan Machette Scott for 1902

Descendants

1860–1902

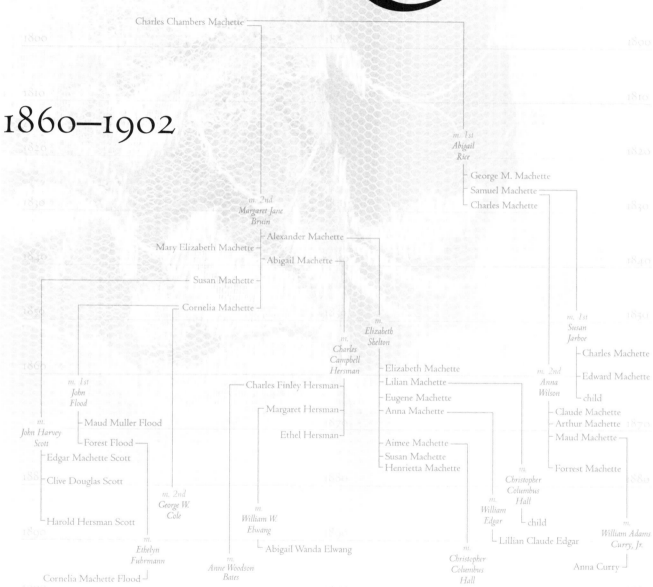

Charles Chambers Machette

m. 1st
Abigail
Rice

- George M. Machette
- Samuel Machette
- Charles Machette

m. 2nd
Margaret Jane
Bruin

- Alexander Machette

Mary Elizabeth Machette

- Abigail Machette

- Susan Machette

- Cornelia Machette

m.
Elizabeth
Shelton

m.
Charles
Campbell
Hersman

- Elizabeth Machette
- Lilian Machette
- Eugene Machette
- Anna Machette

Charles Finley Hersman

Margaret Hersman

Ethel Hersman

- Aimee Machette
- Susan Machette
- Henrietta Machette

m. 1st
John
Flood

- Maud Muller Flood
- Forest Flood

m.
John Harvey
Scott

- Edgar Machette Scott
- Clive Douglas Scott

- Harold Hersman Scott

m. 2nd
George W.
Cole

m.
William W.
Elwang

- Abigail Wanda Elwang

m.
Ethelyn
Fuhrmann

Cornelia Machette Flood

m.
Anne Woodson
Bates

m.
William
Edgar

m.
Christopher
Columbus
Hall

m.
Christopher
Columbus
Hall

- Lillian Claude Edgar

m. 1st
Susan
Jarboe

- Charles Machette

m. 2nd
Anna
Wilson

- Edward Machette

- child

- Claude Machette
- Arthur Machette
- Maud Machette

- Forrest Machette

m.
William Adams
Curry, Jr.

Anna Curry

Charles Chambers Machette Descendants
as of December 31, 1902

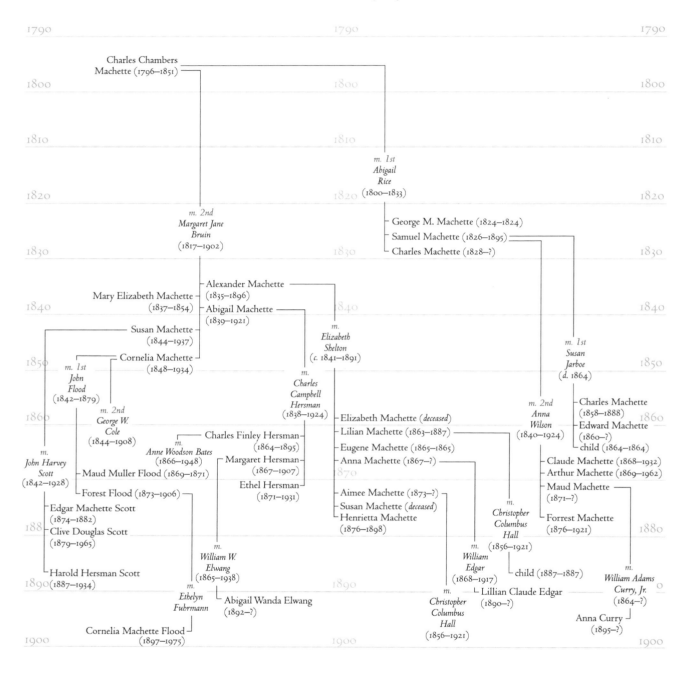

Charles Chambers Machette (1796–1851), son of James Bell & Mary Tucker Machette

m. 1st   *Abigail Rice (1800–1833), daughter of Simeon & Anne Rice*

George M. Machette (1824–1824)

Samuel Machette (1826–1895)

m. 1st   *Susan Jarboe (d. 1864)*

Charles Machette (1858–1888)

Edward Machette (1860–?)

child (1864–1864)

m. 2nd   *Anna Wilson (1840-1924), daughter of Thomas & Deborah Wilson*

Claude Machette (1868–1932)

Arthur Machette (1869–1962)

Maud Machette (1871–?)

m.   *William Adams Curry, Jr. (1864–?)*

Anna Curry (1895–?)

Forrest Machette (1876–1921)

Charles Machette (1828–?)

Descendants of Charles Chambers and Abigail Rice Machette

m. 2nd   *Margaret Jane Bruin (1817–1902), daughter of Timothy & Margaret Galbraith Bruin*

Alexander Machette (1835–1896)

m.   *Elizabeth "Lizzie" Shelton (c. 1841–1891), daughter of Meacon & Anna Berger Shelton*

Elizabeth "Lizzie" Machette (died in infancy or childhood)

Lilian Machette (1863–1887)

m.   *Christopher Columbus "Lum" Hall (1856–1921)*

child (1887–1887)

Eugene Machette (1865–1865)

Anna Machette (1867–?)

m.   *William Edgar (1868–1917), son of H.R. & Lavinia Edgar*

Lillian Claude "Claude" Edgar (1890–?)

Aimee Machette (1873–?)

m.   *Christopher Columbus "Lum" Hall, widower of Lilian Machette*

Susan Machette (died in infancy or childhood)

Henrietta "Etta" Machette (1876–1898)

Mary Elizabeth Machette (1837–1854)

Abigail Machette (1839–1921)

m.   *Charles Campbell Hersman (1838–1924), son of Joseph & Margaret Scott Hersman*

Charles Finley "Finley" Hersman (1864–1895)

m.   *Anne Woodson Bates (1866–1948), daughter of Richard & Ellen Woodson Bates*

Margaret "Maggie" Hersman (1867–1907)

m.   *William W. Elwang (1865–1938)*

Abigail Wanda Elwang (1892–?)

Ethel Hersman (1871–1931)

Descendants of Charles Chambers and Margaret J. Bruin Machette

Susan Machette (1844–1937)

> m.   *John Harvey "Harvey" Scott (1842–1928), son of William & Jane Scott Scott*
>> Edgar Machette Scott (1874–1882)
>> Clive Douglas Scott (1879–1965)
>> Harold Hersman Scott (1887–1934)

Cornelia "Nealie" Machette (1848–1934)

> *m. 1st*   *John Flood (1842–1879), son of Joseph & Eliza Major Flood*
>> Maud Muller Flood (1869–1871)
>> Forest Flood (1873–1906)
>>> *m.   Ethelyn Fuhrmann*
>>>> Cornelia Machette Flood (1897–1975)

> *m. 2nd George W. Cole (1844–1908)*

References
& Selected Bibliography

American Osteopathic Association
Daughters of the American Revolution
Denver, Col., Public Library
First Presbyterian Church, Fulton, Mo.
Kearney, Mo., Public Library
Montgomery County (Mo.) Historical Society
Presbyterian Historical Society, Montreat, N.C.
Southern Baptist Historical Commission
St. Charles County (Mo.) Historical Society
St. Louis County Public Library
State Historical Society of Missouri, Columbia and St. Louis
Washington and Lee University
Washington University School of Medicine Archives, Becker Medical Library
Westminster College

Archives

Boone County
Callaway County
Clay County
Jackson County
Kansas City
Liberty County
Linn County
Montgomery County
Ray County
Saline County
St. Charles City and County
St. Louis City and County

Cemetery Records in Missouri

Callaway County, Mo., marriage records
Fulton, Mo., city records
Jefferson City, Mo., directories
Lincoln County, Mo., marriage records
Missouri Census
Missouri Department of Health, death certificates
Montgomery County, Mo., marriage records
Montgomery County, Tenn., marriage records
Saline County, Kan., marriage records
St. Charles, Mo., city directories
St. Louis, Mo., city directories
State of Missouri, 1865 and 1875 Constitutions

City and Government Records

Newspapers and Periodicals

Albuquerque Journal
Albuquerque Morning Democrat
Columbia Daily Tribune
The Columbia Statesman
Daily Intelligencer (Mexico, Mo.)
The Democrat-News (Fredericktown, Mo.)
Denver Post
Fulton Gazette
Fulton Sun
Fulton Sun-Gazette
Fulton Weekly Telegraph
Good Housekeeping, 1885–1900
Harper's Monthly
Jefferson City Tribune
Kansas City Globe
Kansas City Journal
Kansas City Star
Kansas City Times
Liberty Tribune
The Living Age
Louisiana (Mo.) *Press-Journal*
Louisville Christian Observer
Missouri Republican (St. Louis)
The Missouri Richmond
Missouri Telegraph (Fulton)
New York Observer
The New York Times
Rocky Mountain News
San Francisco Call
Santa Monica Evening Outlook
The Saturday Evening Post
Scribner's
St. Louis Globe-Democrat
St. Louis Observer
St. Louis Post-Dispatch
St. Louis Presbyterian
St. Louis Republic
The Twice-a-Week Times (Louisiana, Mo.)

Books and Articles

Addresses Delivered at the Centennial Celebration of the Founding of the First Presbyterian Church, Columbia, Missouri, October 17, 1928. Columbia, 1928.

Allibone, Samuel Austin. *A Critical Dictionary of English Literature and British and American Authors. . . .* Philadelphia: Lippincott, 1872.

American Medical Directory. Chicago: American Medical Association, 1906.

Atherton, Lewis. *Main Street on the Middle Border.* Chicago: Quadrangle, 1954.

Avrich, Paul. *The Haymarket Tragedy.* Princeton: Princeton University Press, 1984.

Barrett, James T. "Cholera in Missouri." *Missouri Historical Review* (July 1961): 344–54.

Beecher, Catharine E., and Harriet Beecher Stowe. *The American Woman's Home, or Principles of Domestic Science.* New York: J.B. Ford, 1869.

Beecher, Henry Ward. *The Crown of Life.* Ed. Mary Storrs Haynes. Boston: D. Lothrop, 1890.

————. *Life Thoughts: Gathered from the Extemporaneous Discourses.* Boston: Phillips, Sampson, 1858.

Bell, Ovid H. *Political Conditions in Callaway Before the Civil War Began.* Fulton, Mo.: Ovid Bell Press, 1952.

————. *The Story of the Kingdom of Callaway.* Fulton, Mo.: Ovid Bell Press, 1952.

————. *This Large Crowd of Witnesses: A Sesquicentennial History of the First Presbyterian Church, Fulton, Missouri.* Fulton, Mo.: Ovid Bell Press, 1985.

Bellamann, Henry. *Kings Row.* New York: Simon and Schuster, 1940.

Berlin, Ira, ed. *Freedom: A Documentary History of Emancipation 1861–1867.* Series 2, *The Black Military Experience.* Cambridge: Cambridge University Press, 1982.

Biographical Directory of the United States Congress, 1774–1989.... Washington, D.C.: Government Printing Office, 1989.

Blackwell, Gordon. "The 100th Year of Electroylsis and the Triumph of Dr. Michel (1833–1913)." *Electrolysis Digest* 22 (April 1975): 23–42.

Bolt, Christine. *The Women's Movements in the United States and Britain from the 1790s to the 1920.* Amherst: University of Massachusetts Press, 1993,

Boyd, Lois A., and R. Douglas Brackenridge. *Presbyterian Women in America: Two Centuries of a Quest for Status.* Westport, Conn: Greenwood Press, 1983.

Brownlee, Richard S. *Gray Ghosts of the Confederacy: Guerilla Warfare in the West, 1861–1865.* Baton Rough: Louisiana State University Press, 1958.

Bryan, William S., and Robert Rose. *A History of the Pioneer Families of Missouri....* St. Louis: Bryan, Brand, & Co., 1876; 1935 edition was prepared by William W. Elwang.

Bryant, Keith L., Jr., ed. *Railroads in the Age of Regulation, 1900–1980.* New York: Bruccoli Clark Layman, 1988.

Burns, Robert. *The Poetical Works,* ed. J. Logie Robertson. London: Oxford University Press, 1910.

Cassell, Frank A. "Missouri and the Columbian Exposition of 1893," *Missouri Historical Review* (Summer 1968): 369–394.

Christensen, Lawrence O., and Gary R. Kremer, *A History of Missouri.* Vol. 4: *1875 to 1919.* Columbia: University of Missouri Press, 1997.

Coker, William S. "The Bruins and the Formulation of Spanish Immigration Policy in the Old Southwest, 1787–88." In *The Spanish in the Mississippi Valley 1762–1804.* Ed. John Francis McDermott. Urbana: University of Illinois Press, 1974.

————. "Peter Bryan Bruin: Soldier, Judge and Frontiersman." *West Virginia History* (July 1969): 579–85.

Conard, Howard Louis, ed. *Encyclopedia of the History of Missouri.* New York: Southern History Co., 1901.

Conot, Robert. *A Streak of Luck.* New York: Seaview Books, 1979.

Conway, Jill K. *The Female Experience in Eighteenth- and Nineteenth-Century America: A Guide to the History of American Women.* New York: Garland, 1982.

Crighton, John C. *A History of Columbia and Boone County.* Columbia: Computer Color Graphics, 1987.

Cunningham, C. Willett, and Phillis Cunnington. *The History of Underclothes.* London: Faber & Faber, 1981.

Current Biography Yearbook. New York: H. W. Wilson, 1940–54.

Cuyler, Theodore L. *The Empty Crib: A Memorial of Little Georgie.* New York: Baker & Taylor, 1868.

—————. *Recollections of a Long Life.* New York: Baker & Taylor, 1902.

Dains, Mary K., ed. *Show Me Missouri Women: Selected Biographies.* Kirksville, Mo.: Thomas Jefferson University Press, 1989.

Dakin, A. *Calvinism.* Port Washington, N.Y.: Kennikat, 1972.

Davison, Kenneth E. *The Presidency of Rutherford B. Hayes.* Westport, Conn: Greenwood Press, 1972.

Dawson, Jill. *Kisses on Paper.* Boston: Faber & Faber, 1994.

Dictionary of American Biography. New York: Charles Scribner's Sons, 1928–58.

Dormandy, Thomas. *The White Death: A History of Tuberculosis.* New York: New York University Press, 2000.

Douglas, Ann. *The Feminization of American Culture.* New York: Alfred A. Knopf, 1977.

Duncan, Robert Samuel. *A History of the Baptists in Missouri.* St. Louis: Scammell, 1882.

Eakin, Joanne Chiles, and Donald R. Hale. *A List of Bushwhackers, Guerrillas, Partisan Rangers, Confederates and Southern Sympathizes for Missouri during the War Years.* Independence, Mo.: Print America, 1994.

Edwards, Richard, and Merna Hopewell. *Edward's Great West and Her Commercial Metropolis.* St. Louis: Edward's Monthly, 1860.

Encyclopedia of Southern Baptists. Nashville: Broadman Press, 1958.

Farrell, James J. *Inventing the American Way of Death, 1830–1920.* Philadelphia: Temple University Press, 1980.

Fisher, M.M. Continued by John J. Rice. *History of Westminster College, 1851–1903.* Columbia, Mo.: E. W. Stephens, 1903.

Flexner, Eleanor, and Ellen Fitzpatrick. *Century of Struggle: The Woman's Rights Movement in the United States.* Cambridge: Belknap Press of Harvard University Press, 1975.

Franklin, John Hope. *Reconstruction after the Civil War,* 2nd ed. Chicago: University of Chicago Press, 1994.

Fox, Richard Wightman. *Trials of Intimacy: Love and Loss in the Beecher-Tilton Scandal.* Chicago: University of Chicago Press, 1999.

Frey, Robert L., ed. *Railroads in the Nineteenth Century.* New York: Bruccoli Clark Layman, 1988.

General Catalogue of the McCormick Theological Seminary. Chicago: Rogerson Press, 1912.

Goldstein, Max A., ed. *One Hundred Years of Medicine and Surgery in Missouri.* St. Louis: St. Louis Star, 1900.

Gould, Tony. *A Summer Plague: Polio and Its Survivors.* New Haven: Yale University Press, 1995.

Graham, Stephen R. *Cosmos in the Chaos: Philip Schaff's Interpretation of Nineteenth-Century American Religion.* Grand Rapids: William B. Eerdmans, 1995.

Green, Harvey. *The Light of the Home: An Intimate View of the Lives of Women in Victorian America.* New York: Pantheon, 1983.

Greene, Lorenzo, Gary R. Kremer, and Antonio F. Holland. *Missouri's Black Heritage.* Rev. ed. Columbia: University of Missouri Press, 1980.

Hall, Thomas B., Jr., and Thomas B. Hall, III. *Dr. John Sappington of Saline County, Missouri 1776–1856.* 2nd ed. Arrow Rock, Mo.: Friends of Arrow Rock, Inc., 1986.

Hamlin, Griffin A. *In Faith and History: The Story of William Woods College.* St. Louis: Bethany Press, 1965.

Hart, D. G. ed., *Dictionary of the Presbyterian and Reformed Tradition in America.* Downers Grove, Ill.: InterVarsity Press, 1999.

Hazen, Craig James. *The Village Enlightenment in America: Popular Religion and Science in the Nineteenth Century.* Urbana: University of Illinois Press, 2000.

Hickok, Ralph. *The Encyclopedia of North American Sports History.* New York: Facts on File, 1991.

History of Boone County, Missouri. St. Louis: Western Historical Co., 1882.

A History of Callaway County, Missouri. Fulton, Mo.: Kingdom of Callaway Historical Society, 1984.

History of Callaway County, Missouri. St. Louis: National Historical Co., 1884.

History of Clay and Platte Counties, Missouri. St. Louis: National Historical Company, 1885.

History of Lafayette County, Missouri. St. Louis: Missouri Historical Co., 1881.

History of Lewis, Clark, Knox and Scotland Counties, Missouri. St. Louis: Goodspeed, 1887.

History of Lincoln County, Missouri from the Earliest Time to the Present. Chicago: Goodspeed, 1888.

The History of Pike County, Missouri. Des Moines: Mills, 1883.

History of St. Charles, Montgomery, and Warren Counties, Missouri. St. Louis: National Historical Company, 1885.

Hulston, John K. "Daniel Boone's Sons in Missouri," *Missouri Historical Review* (July 1947): 361–372.

Hyde, William, and Howard Louis Conard, eds. *Encyclopedia of the History of St. Louis.* New York: Southern History Co., 1899.

James, Edward T. *Notable American Women 1607–1950.* Cambridge: Harvard University Press, 1971.

Kaempffert, Waldemar, ed. *A Popular History of American Invention.* Vol. I. New York: Charles Scribner's Sons, 1924.

Kingsley, J. Gordon. *Frontiers: The Story of the Missouri Baptist Convention.* Jefferson City: Missouri Baptist Historical Commission, 1983.

Kiple, Kenneth F., ed. *The Cambridge History of Human Disease.* Cambridge: Cambridge University Press, 1993.

Lasher, George W. *The Ministerial Directory of the Baptist Churches in the United States of America.* Oxford, Ohio: Ministerial Directory Co., 1899.

Lingle, Walter L., and John W. Kuykendall. *Presbyterians: Their History and Beliefs.* Atlanta: John Knox Press, 1978.

Locke, Kenneth R., and J. Joseph Trower. *Like Prairie Wildfire...Presbyterianism Spreads Westward.* Locke, 1997.

Loetscher, Lefferts A., and George Laird Hunt. *A Brief History of the Presbyterians,* 4th ed. Philadelphia: Westminster Press, 1983.

Londré, Felicia Hardison, and Daniel J. Watermeier. *American Theater, The United States, Canada, and Mexico: From Pre-Columbian Times to the Present.* New York: Continuum, 1999.

Lystra, Karen. *Searching the Heart: Women, Men, and Romantic Love in Nineteenth-Century America.* New York: Oxford University Press, 1989.

Manring, Maurice M. "The President and the Emperor: How Samuel Spahr Laws Found an Elephant and Lost His Job," *Missouri Historical Review* (October 1999): 59–79.

Maple, J.C., and R.P. Rider. *Missouri Baptist Biography.* Kansas City: Western Baptist Publishing Co., 1914.

Marsden, George M. *Fundamentalism and American Culture: The Shaping of Twentieth-Century Evangelicalism, 1870–1925.* New York: Oxford University Press, 1980.

Marsh, Margaret. *Suburban Lives.* New Brunswick, N.J.: Rutgers University Press, 1990.

Masterson, V.V. *The Katy Railroad and the Last Frontier.* Norman: University of Oklahoma Press, 1952.

McArthur, Benjamin. *Actors and American Culture, 1880–1920.* Philadelphia: Temple University Press, 1984.

McCandless, Perry. *A History of Missouri.* Vol. 2: *1820 to 1860.* Columbia: University of Missouri Press, 1972.

McDannell, Colleen. *The Christian Home in Victorian America 1840–1900.* Bloomington: Indiana University Press, 1986.

McLaurin, Melton A. *Celia, A Slave.* Athens: University of Georgia Press, 1991.

McLoughlin, William G. *The Meaning of Henry Ward Beecher: An Essay on the Shifting Values of Mid-Victorian America, 1840–1870.* New York: Alfred A. Knopf, 1970.

Meyer, Duane G. *The Heritage of Missouri.* 3rd ed. St. Louis: River City Publishers, 1982.

The Ministerial Directory of the Ministers in the Presbyterian Church in the United States (Southern) and in the Presbyterian Church in the United States of America (Northern).... Oxford, Ohio: Ministerial Directory Co., 1898.

Minutes of the Synod of Virginia. 9–12 September 1924. Richmond: Richmond Press.

Missouri State Gazetteer and Business Directory. St. Louis: Sutherland & McEvoy, 1860.

————, *1879–1880.* St. Louis: R.L. Polk & A.C. Danser, 1879.

————, *1893–1894.* St. Louis: R.L. Polk, 1893.

————, *1898–1899.* St. Louis: R.L. Polk, 1898.

Nagel, Paul C. *Missouri: A Bicentennial History.* New York: W.W. Norton, 1977.

Napton, William Barclay. *Past and Present of Saline County, Missouri.* Indianapolis: B.F. Bowen, 1910.

The National Cyclopaedia of American Biography. New York: James T. White, 1900.

The New York Times Theater Reviews, 1895–1902.

Niepman, Ann Davis. "General Orders No. 11 and Border Warfare during the Civil War," *Missouri Historical Review* (January 1972): 185–210.

Parrish, William E. *A History of Missouri.* Vol. 3: *1860 to 1875.* Columbia: University of Missouri Press, 1973.

————. *Missouri under Radical Rule: 1865–1870.* Columbia: University of Missouri Press, 1964.

————. *Westminster College: An Informal History 1851–1999.* 2nd. ed. Fulton: Westminster College, 2000.

Paul, John R. *A History of Poliomyelitis.* New Haven: Yale University Press, 1971.

Phelps, Elizabeth Stuart. *Beyond the Gates.* Boston: Houghton Mifflin, 1883.

————. *The Gates Ajar.* Ed. Helen Sootin Smith. Cambridge: Belknap Press of Harvard University Press, 1964. First published in 1869.

Phillips, Claude A. *A History of Education in Missouri.* Jefferson City: Hugh Stephens, 1911.

Pike, Martha V., and Janice Gray Armstrong. *A Time to Mourn: Expressions of Grief in Nineteenth Century America.* Stony Brook, N.Y.: Museums at Stony Brook, 1980.

Poor's Directory of Railway Officials and Railway Directors. New York, 1886.

Popular American Composers from Revolutionary Times to the Present. New York: H.W. Wilson, 1962.

Population Schedules of the Eighth Census of the United States, 1860. Missouri Slave Schedules. Washington, D.C.: National Archives, 1967.

Population of the United States in 1860…the Eighth Census. Washington, D.C.: Government Printing Office, 1864.

Portrait and Biographical Record of Clay, Ray, Carroll, Chariton, and Linn Counties, Missouri. Chicago: Chapman, 1893.

Portrait and Biographical Record of St. Charles, Lincoln and Warren Counties, Missouri. Chicago: Chapman, 1895.

Powell, William H., ed. *Officers of the Army and Navy Who Served in the Civil War.* Philadelphia: L.R. Hamensly, 1893.

Quarles, James Addison. *The Life of Prof. F.T. Kemper, A.M., The Christian Educator.* New York: Burr, 1884.

Reed, Richard D. *Historic MSD: The Story of the Missouri School for the Deaf.* Fulton, Mo.: Richard D. Reed, 2000.

Ring, Lucile Wiley. "Anne Bates Hersman: Born to the Aristocracy of Talent." In *Breaking the Barriers: The St. Louis Legacy of Women in Law, 1869–1969.* Manchester, Mo.: Independent Publishing, 1996.

Roster and Record of Iowa Soldiers in the War of the Rebellion. Vol. I. Des Moines: Emory H. English, 1908.

Rothman, Sheila M., *Living in the Shadow of Death: Tuberculosis and the Social Experience of Illness in American History.* New York: Basic Books, 1994.

Ruether, Rosemary Radford, and Rosemary Skinner Keller. *Women and Religion in America.* Vol. I: *The Nineteenth Century.* San Francisco: Harper & Row, 1981.

Ryan, Halford R. *Henry Ward Beecher: Peripatetic Preacher.* New York: Greenwood Press, 1990.

Sanders, Robert S. *Sketches of Ministers in the Presbyteries of Transylvania (Presbyterian Church in the U.S.A.) 1786–1968.* N.p., n.d.

Saum, Lewis O. "Eugene Field and Theater: The Missouri Years," *Missouri Historical Review* (January 2001): 159–81.

Scharf, J. Thomas. *History of St. Louis City and County.* Philadelphia: Louis H. Everts & Co., 1883.

Schlereth, Thomas J. *Victorian America: Transformations in Everyday Life, 1876–1915.* New York: HarperPerennial, 1991.

Schnell, Christopher. "Chicago Versus St. Louis: A Reassessment of the Great Rivalry," *Missouri Historical Society* (April 1977): 245–65.

Schwarz, Julius Caesar, ed. *Who's Who in the Clergy, 1935–36.* New York, 1936.

Scott, Eugene Crampton. *Ministerial Directory of the Presbyterian Church, U.S., 1861–1941;* revised 1942–1950. Atlanta: Hubbard Printing, 1950.

Scott, Janet Weir. *A Genealogical Study of Machet/Machett/Machette Families.* N.p., 1995.

Selby, Paul Owen. *Missouri College Presidents Past and Present.* Kirksville: Northeast Missouri State University, 1971.

Settle, William A., Jr. *Jesse James Was His Name.* Columbia: University of Missouri Press, 1966.

Shoemaker, Floyd C. *Missouri, Day by Day.* Columbia: State Historical Society of Missouri, 1942–43.

Smylie, James H. *A Brief History of the Presbyterians.* Louisville: Geneva Press, 1996.

Statistics of the Population of the United States . . . from the Original Returns of the Ninth Census, June 1, 1870. Washington, D.C.: Government Printing Office, 1872.

Stevens, Walter B. *Centennial History of Missouri.* St. Louis: S. J. Clarke, 1921.

————. *Missouri the Center State, 1821–1915.* St. Louis: S. J. Clarke, 1915.

Strasser, Susan. *Never Done: A History of American Housework.* New York: Pantheon, 1982.

Strawn, Phyllis J. *"Kings Row" Revisited: One Hundred Years of Fulton Architecture.* Jefferson City: Missouri Heritage Trust, 1980.

Thelen, David. *Paths of Resistance: Tradition and Dignity in Industrializing Missouri.* New York: Oxford University Press, 1986.

Thirteenth Census of the United States Taken in the Year 1910. Vol. 2. Washington, D.C.: Government Printing Office, 1913.

Thomas, Emory M. *Robert E. Lee.* New York: W. W. Norton, 1995.

Todd, Janet M., ed. *British Women Writers: A Critical Reference Guide.* New York: Continuum Publishing Company, 1989.

"Transportation: Railways on City Streets." *Missouri Historical Review* (October 1968): 133–34.

Union Cemetery. 6 vols. Kansas City: Union Cemetery Historical Society 1988–1990.

U.S. Bureau of the Census. *Twelfth Census of the United States Taken in the Year 1900. Population,* part 1. Washington, D.C., 1901.

Volunteer Forces of the United States Army for the Years 1861, '62, '63, '64, '65. Part 7. Washington, D.C.: Adjutant General's Office, 1865.

Wallace, William Hockaday. *Speeches and Writings with Autobiography.* Kansas City: Western Baptist Publishing, 1914.

Waller, Alexander H. *History of Randolph County, Missouri.* Topeka: Historical Publishing Co., 1920.

Waller, Altina L. *Reverend Beecher and Mrs. Tilton: Sex and Class in Victorian America.* Amherst: University of Massachusetts Press, 1982.

The War of the Rebellion: A Compilation of the Official Records of the Union and Confederate Armies. Washington, D.C.: Government Printing Office, 1893–1900.

Weant, Kenneth E. *Callaway County, Missouri* [an index of obituaries from the *Missouri Telegraph, Fulton Gazette,* and *Fulton Sun*]. 1996–1999.

Webster's Biographical Dictionary. 1976.

The Westminster Shorter Catechism. Richmond, Va.: Presbyterian Church of the United States, 1861.

The Westminster Shorter Catechism Explained, by Way of Question and Answer. Part 1. Philadelphia: Presbyterian Board of Publications, 1845.

Who Was Who in America. Chicago: Marquis Who's Who, 1973.

Who Was Who in the Theatre, 1912–1976. Detroit: Gale Research, 1978.

Williams, Walter, ed. *A History of Northeast Missouri.* Chicago: Lewis Publishing, 1915.

Williams, Walter, and Floyd Calvin Shoemaker. *Missouri, Mother of the West.* Chicago: American Historical Society, 1930.

Williamson, Hugh P. "The Argonauts of '98," *Missouri Historical Society* (January 1961). 142–54.

Woodson, William H. *History of Clay County, Missouri.* Topeka: Historical Publishing Co., 1920.

Young, William C. *Famous Actors and Actresses on the American Stage.* New York: R. R. Bowker, 1975.

Index

Page numbers in *italics* refer to captions and illustrations.
"MM" refers to Margaret Machette.

C

G